First published 2010
Reprinted 2010,
Revised editions 2011, 2012, 2013, 2014, 2015, 2016
This Seventh Edition published 2017 by Crécy Publishing

ISBN 978 0 7110 3856 1

Printed in Bulgaria by Multiprint

Crécy Publishing Ltd
1a Ringway Trading Estate
Shadowmoss Road
Manchester
M22 5LH
Tel +44 (0) 161 499 0024

www.crecy.co.uk

Front cover top: *The new age of rail travel in the UK, the Hitachi-built IEP stock. Painted in full Great Western Railway green livery, five-car set set No. 800004, a, is seen at London Paddington on 30 June 2016.* **Antony Christie**

Front cover bottom: *Franchise changes in April 2016 saw a new TransPennine Express livery unveiled on Class 185 No. 185108; the set is seen passing Church Fenton on 22 April 2016.* **Antony Christie**

Back cover top: *Built by Stadler, the new Beacon Rail-owned, DRS-operated dual-power Class 88s are entering traffic in 2017. Based on the bodyshell of the Class 68, No. 88003 is illustrated before delivery to the UK in Berlin in September 2016.* **CJM**

Back cover bottom: *Dublin Area Rapid Transit (DART) 8100 class, led by driving trailer No. 8315, is seen at Howth on 22 April 2016. These two-car sets were introduced in 1983 and built by GEC/Linke-Hofmann-Busch.* **CJM**

Right: *Testing on both the Great Western and East Coast main lines of new Class 800 and 801 IEP stock is now well under way, with several sets commissioned for testing by the end of 2016. Here, Virgin East Coast-liveried set No. 800101 passes Dawlish on 6 October 2016 with a test run from Bristol Stoke Gifford depot to Plymouth.* **CJM**

Acknowledgement – The Author would like to record his thanks to the many railway staff who have provided invaluable information for the production of this book. Also to the many photographers, especially Antony Christie, Nathan Williamson and John Binch, for providing many of the images. I would also like to express my thanks to Keith Ewins and Antony Christie for reading the updated manuscript. **CJM**

Introduction

The year of 2017 looks set to see more major changes to the UK railway scene, with new classes entering service and many new designed types under construction. So, on that thought, I welcome readers to the Crécy *abc Rail Guide 2017*, the only product which continues to provide listings of locomotives, multiple units and stock in operator order.

Over the past year we have seen the final Class 66s delivered to the UK for operator GBRf, and more Class 68s enter traffic, while deliveries continue, although slow, of the IEP Class 800/801 stock, set to replace the 40-year-old HSTs from the end of 2017 over a rolling several year project.

Huge financial challenges to the Great Western electrification project saw an announcement that sections between Bath and Bristol, Bristol Temple Meads and Bristol Parkway, Didcot and Oxford and some of the Thames Valley branches would be 'deferred' until further notice. This sees a major 'knock-on' effect of the cascade plan of rolling stock, and plans to move Class 158s to the West Country have now been shelved. A number of Class 165s will move to the Bristol area, after Class 387s are introduced, but the time scale will now be revised. This has led to the demise of the West Country Class 143s being put back until around 2019.

Ordering of new rolling stock has continued, with Abellio Anglia announcing a total replacement of its fleet with Bombardier and Stadler-built multiple units, many of which will be of the bi-mode type, allowing operation from the overhead power system as well as on-board diesels. Hull Trains has announced replacement of its Class 180s with Hitachi AT300 five-car sets, while First TransPennine, Transport for London and Northern are set to see large numbers of new trains.

In 2017 we should see a number of new designs emerge and enter service, with the eagerly awaited Bombardier Class 345s for CrossRail delivered and the first of the new CAF sleeper stock for Serco Caledonian Sleepers arriving from Spain.

At the end of 2016, 10 state-of-the-art Stadler/Vossloh Class 88 electro-diesel locos arrived in the UK from Spain. Owned by Beacon Rail and operated by DRS, these should commence service on long-distance freight duties in the spring.

The year of 2017 should see the remaining Siemens Class 374 sets for Eurostar delivered and commissioned; this will see a drastic reduction in the number of Class 373 sets, with withdrawn units being broken up rather than offered for sale.

The UK's main freight operator, DB-Cargo, is going through challenging times with huge re-organisation following the loss of many freight flows and contracts; this has seen a drastic reduction in the number of trains, staff numbers and terminals and it is likely to reflect in the number of locos retained operational. Inroads have already been made into the Class 67 fleet and many of the DB-C Class 92s are now based in Mainland Europe.

Freight operator Colas Rail Freight seems to buck the trend and has seen extra locos taken into stock and new flows won.

The converted ex-London Transport 'D' Stock, owned by Vivarail, should have been entering service in early 2017 on the Coventry-Nuneaton line but due to a fire this has been postponed.

In the London area Class 700 'Desiro City' sets have now been introduced on GTR services and in 2017 South West Trains will be introducing its Class 707 five-car 'Desiro City' stock.

The Editor and Publishers hope you will continue to enjoy watching and following our ever-interesting and changing world of railways in 2017.

Colin J. Marsden
Dawlish, January 2017
Information in Rail Guide 2017 is correct to 14 January 2017

Train Operators, The Rail Operations Group, and Network Rail welcome rail enthusiasts and photographers, but in today's safety-led railway and with the continued concerns about possible transport terrorism, guidelines are very important and we encourage all to follow these published guidelines as much as possible. They are available to view and download from the National Rail and ROG websites, but are reproduced in full below to assist you with this information. ■

The Official Railway Enthusiasts Guidelines

■ Network Rail welcomes rail enthusiasts to our stations.

■ The following guidelines are designed to help you to have a safe and enjoyable experience. Please keep them with you when you are at Network Rail-managed stations.

■ You may also wish to take a copy of the Railway by-laws which are available from the Office of Public Sector Information website.

Before you enter the platform

■ When you arrive at a station, please let the staff at the Network Rail Reception Desk know that you are on the station. This will help keep station staff informed so that they can go about their duties without concern as to your reasons for being there.

■ You may require a platform ticket to allow access to platforms.

While you are on the platform

■ You need to act safely and sensibly at all times.
  ● Stay clear of the platform edge and stay behind the yellow lines where they are provided.
  ● Be aware of your surroundings.

Please DO NOT:
  ● Trespass on to the tracks or any other part of the railway that is not available to passengers.
  ● Use flash photography because it can distract train drivers and train despatch staff and so is potentially very dangerous.
  ● Climb on any structure or interfere with platform equipment.
  ● Obstruct any signalling equipment or signs which are vital to the safe running of the railway.
  ● Wear anything which is similar in colour to safety clothing, such as high-visibility jackets, as this could cause confusion to drivers and other railway employees.
  ● Gather together in groups at busy areas of the platform (e.g. customer information points, departure screens, waiting areas, seating etc.) or where this may interfere with the duties of station staff.

■ If possible, please try to avoid peak hours which are Monday – Friday 6:00am (06.00) – 10:30am (10.30) and 3:30pm (15.30) – 7:30pm (19.30).

Extra eyes and ears

■ If you see anything suspicious or notice any unusual behaviour or activities, please tell a member of staff immediately.

■ For emergencies and serious incidents, either call:
  The British Transport Police on 0800 40 50 40.
  The Police on 999, or 101

■ Your presence at a station can be very helpful to us as extra 'eyes and ears' and can have a positive security benefit.

Photography

■ You can take photographs at stations provided you do not sell them. However, you are not allowed to take photographs of security-related equipment, such as CCTV cameras.

■ Flash photography on platforms is not allowed at any time. It can distract train drivers and train despatch staff and so is potentially very dangerous.

■ Tripod legs must be kept away from platform edges and behind the yellow lines. On busy stations, you may not be allowed to use a tripod because it could be a dangerous obstruction to passengers.

Railway by-laws

For safety and ease of travel on the railway system (which includes passengers, staff, property and equipment), the by-laws must be observed by everyone. A copy of the by-laws can be obtained at stations or downloaded from the Office of Public Sector Information website.

General

Train operators must put the safety of their passengers and staff first. You may very occasionally be asked by station staff to move to another part of the station or to leave the station altogether. Station staff should be happy to explain why this is necessary. If you are travelling by train, they may ask you to remain in the normal waiting areas with other passengers. If this occurs, please follow their instructions with goodwill as staff have many things to consider, including the safety and security of all passengers, and are authorised to use judgement in this regard.

Below: *The Bombardier 'Electrostar' product range extends to a large number of classes and sub-classes operating for many UK operators. The Class 387/1 fleet operated by Govia Thameslink Railway (GTR) is found operating both north and south of the Thames on Thameslink services as well as on West Anglia routes. On 30 August 2016, set No. 387102 leads the 13.10 Bedford to Brighton into East Croydon station.* **CJM**

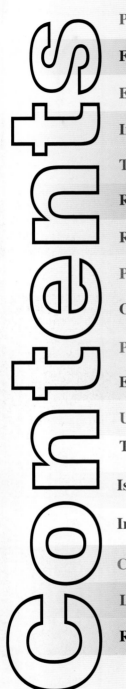

Contents

Arriva Trains Wales
Trenau Arriva Cymru

Address: ✉ St Mary's House, 47 Penarth Road, Cardiff, CF10 5DJ
🖎 customer.relations@arrivatrainswales.co.uk
✆ 0845 6061 660
ⓘ www.arrivatrainswales.co.uk

Managing Director: Ian Bullock
Franchise Dates: 7 December 2003 - October 2018
Principal Routes: Cardiff to Swansea and West Wales
Cardiff Valleys
Cardiff - Hereford - Shrewsbury - Crewe - Manchester Piccadilly
Cardiff - Hereford - Shrewsbury - Chester - Bangor - Holyhead
Manchester - Crewe - Bangor - Holyhead
Shrewsbury - Pwllheli / Aberystwyth
Swansea - Shrewsbury
Depots: Cardiff Canton (CF), Chester (CH), Holyhead* (HD)
Machynlleth (MN), Shrewsbury* (SX) * Stabling point
Parent Company: Deutsche Bahn AG (DB Regio)

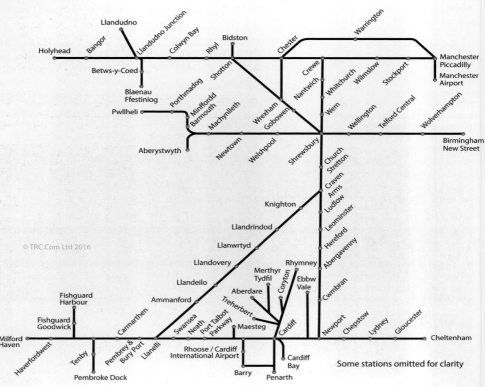

Some stations omitted for clarity

Passenger Train Operating Companies – Arriva Trains Wales

Class 67

		Vehicle Length: 64ft 7in (19.68m)	Engine: EMD 12N-710G3B-EC
		Height: 12ft 9in (3.88m)	Horsepower: 2,980hp (2,223kW)
		Width: 8ft 9in (2.66m)	Electrical Equipment: EMD

Number	Depot	Pool	Livery	Owner	Operator
67001	CE	WAWC	ATW	DBS	DBS/ATW
67002	CE	WAWC	ATW	DBS	DBS/ATW
67003	CE	WAAC	ATW	DBS	DBS/ATW

Right: *Arriva Trains Wales operates Class 67-powered loco-hauled services on both the Cardiff-Holyhead and North Wales routes. The locos are sub-leased from DB-Cargo and three of the fleet are painted in Arriva Trains turquoise livery. No branding is carried by the locos and frequently other members of the fleet are used. When in use on the ATW services maintenance is carried out at Cardiff Canton, with major repairs undertaken by DB-C at Crewe depot. No. 67003 is seen stabled in the bay platform at York on 18 June 2016.*
Ron Cover

Class 142
Pacer

		Vehicle Length: 51ft 0½in (15.55m)	Engine: 1 x Cummins LTA10-R per vehicle
		Height: 12ft 8in (3.86m)	Horsepower: 460hp (343kW)
		Width: 9ft 2¼in (2.80m)	Seats (total/car): 90S, 46S/44S

Number	Formation DMS+DMSL	Depot	Livery	Owner	Operator
142002	55543+55593	CV	ATW	ANG	ATW
142006	55547+55597	CV	ATW	ANG	ATW
142010	55551+55601	CV	ATW	ANG	ATW
142069	55719+55765	CV	ATW	ANG	ATW
142072	55722+55768	CV	ATW	ANG	ATW
142073	55723+55769	CV	ATW	ANG	ATW
142074	55724+55770	CV	ATW	ANG	ATW
142075	55725+55771	CV	ATW	ANG	ATW
142076	55726+55772	CV	ATW	ANG	ATW
142077	55727+55773	CV	ATW	ANG	ATW
142080	55730+55776	CV	ATW	ANG	ATW
142081	55731+55777	CV	ATW	ANG	ATW
142082	55732+55778	CV	ATW	ANG	ATW
142083	55733+55779	CV	ATW	ANG	ATW
142085	55735+55781	CV	ATW	ANG	ATW

Name applied
142072 *Myfanwy*

Below: *South Wales local services are operated by a fleet of Class 142 and 143 sets operated as a single pool, as well as Class 150 and 153 stock. In 2017 a fleet of 15 Class 142s was in traffic owned by Angel Trains. On 15 August 2016, set No. 142083 is seen arriving at Cardiff General. All ATW '142s' carry the earlier ATW turquoise and cream livery.* **Nathan Williamson**

Passenger Train Operating Companies - Arriva Trains Wales

Arriva Trains Wales

Class 143
Pacer

Vehicle Length: 51ft 0½in (15.55m)
Height: 12ft 2¼in (3.73m)
Width: 8ft 10½in (2.70m)

Engine: 1 x Cummins LTA10-R per vehicle
Horsepower: 460hp (343kW)
Seats (total/car): 92S, 48S/44S

Number	Formation DMS+DMSL	Depot	Livery	Owner	Operator
143601	55642+55667	CV	ATT	BCC	ATW
143602	55651+55668	CV	ATT	PTR	ATW
143604	55645+55670	CV	ATT	PTR	ATW
143605	55646+55671	CV	ATT	PTR	ATW
143606	55647+55672	CV	ATT	PTR	ATW
143607	55648+55673	CV	ATT	PTR	ATW
143608	55649+55674	CV	ATT	PTR	ATW
143609	55650+55675	CV	ATW	CCC	ATW
143610	55643+55676	CV	ATW	BCC	ATW
143614	55655+55680	CV	ATW	BCC	ATW
143616	55657+55682	CV	ATT	PTR	ATW
143622	55663+55688	CV	ATT	PTR	ATW
143623	55664+55689	CV	ATT	PTR	ATW
143624	55665+55690	CV	ATT	PTR	ATW
143625	55666+55691	CV	ATT	PTR	ATW

Name applied
143609 *Sir Tom Jones*

Below: *Canton depot has an allocation of 15 Class 143s, which operate with the Class 142 and 150/2 fleets to provide local services, frequently running as mixed-formation pairs. Showing the revised two-tone turquoise livery, set No. 143605 is seen at Cardiff General on 29 January 2016.* **Antony Christie**

Class 150/2
Sprinter

Vehicle Length: 64ft 9¾in (19.74m)
Height: 12ft 4½in (3.77m)
Width: 9ft 3⅛in (2.82m)

Engine: 1 x NT855R5 of 285hp per vehicle
Horsepower: 570hp (425kW)
Seats (total/car): 128S, 60S/68S

Number	Formation DMSL+DMS	Depot	Livery	Owner	Operator
150208	52208+57208	CV	ATW	PTR	ATW
150213	52213+57213	CV	ATT	PTR	ATW
150217	52217+57217	CV	ATT	PTR	ATW
150227	52227+57227	CV	ATT	PTR	ATW
150229	52227+57227	CV	ATT	PTR	ATW
150230	52230+57230	CV	ATT	PTR	ATW
150231	52231+57231	CV	ATT	PTR	ATW
150235	52235+57235	CV	ATT	PTR	ATW
150236	52236+57236	CV	ATT	PTR	ATW
150237	52237+57237	CV	ATT	PTR	ATW
150240	52240+57240	CV	ATT	PTR	ATW
150241	52241+57241	CV	ATT	PTR	ATW
150242	52242+57242	CV	ATT	PTR	ATW
150245	52245+57245	CV	ATW	PTR	ATW
150250	52250+57250	CV	ATT	PTR	ATW
150251	52251+57251	CV	ATT	PTR	ATW
150252	52252+57252	CV	ATT	PTR	ATW
150253	52253+57253	CV	ATT	PTR	ATW
150254	52254+57254	CV	ATT	PTR	ATW
150255	52213+57255	CV	ATT	PTR	ATW
150256	52256+57256	CV	ATW	PTR	ATW
150257	52257+57257	CV	ATT	PTR	ATW
150258	52258+57258	CV	ATW	PTR	ATW
150259	52259+57259	CV	ATW	PTR	ATW
150260	52260+57260	CV	ATW	PTR	ATW
150262	52262+57262	CV	ATT	PTR	ATW
150264	52264+57264	CV	ATW	PTR	ATW
150267	52267+57267	CV	ATT	PTR	ATW

150278	52278+57278 CV	ATT	PTR	ATW		150282	52282+57282 CV	ATT	PTR	ATW
150279	52270+57279 CV	ATT	PTR	ATW		150283	52283+57283 CV	ATW	PTR	ATW
150280	52280+57280 CV	ATT	PTR	ATW		150284	52284+57284 CV	ATT	PTR	ATW
150281	52281+57281 CV	ATW	PTR	ATW		150285	52285+57280 CV	ATW	PTR	ATW

Right: *The largest fleet of suburban units operating in the Cardiff area are 36 Class 150/2 sets. These have all been internally upgraded with 2+2 seating and sets are currently being repainted into the latest ATW two-tone turquoise livery. Set No. 150213 is seen in the latest colours at Pontypridd on 19 June 2014.* **CJM**

Class 153

Vehicle Length: 76ft 5in (23.29m)	Engine: 1 x NT855R5 of 285hp
Height: 12ft 3⅛in (3.75m)	Horsepower: 285hp (213kW)
Width: 8ft 10in (2.70m)	Seats (total/car): 72S

Number	Formation DMSL	Depot	Livery	Owner	Operator		153323	52323	CV	ATT	PTR	ATW
153303	52303	CV	ATT	ANG	ATW		153327	52327	CV	ATT	ANG	ATW
153312	52312	CV	ATT	ANG	ATW		153353	57353	CV	ATT	ANG	ATW
153320	52320	CV	ATW	PTR	ATW		153362	57362	CV	ATT	ANG	ATW
							153367	57367	CV	ATW	PTR	ATW

Right: *The rural branch lines and short-haul passenger services operated by ATW use a fleet of eight Cardiff Canton-allocated Class 153s; these carry a mix of older and the latest Arriva Trains Wales liveries and are owned by Angel and Porterbrook leasing companies. Viewed from its small driving cab end, No. 153367 is seen at Cheltenham.* **Antony Christie**

Class 158

Vehicle Length: 76ft 1¾in (23.21m)	Engine: 1 x Perkins 2006-TWH of 350hp per vehicle
Height: 12ft 6in (3.81m)	Horsepower: 700hp (522kW)
Width: 9ft 3¼in (2.82m)	Seats (total/car): 134S, 66S/68S

Number	Formation DMSL+DMSL	Depot	Livery	Owner	Operator		158829	52829+57829	MN	ATT	ANG	ATW
							158830	52830+57830	MN	ATT	ANG	ATW
158818	52818+57818	MN	ATT	ANG	ATW		158831	52831+57831	MN	ATT	ANG	ATW
158819	52819+57819	MN	ATT	ANG	ATW		158832	52832+57832	MN	ATT	ANG	ATW
158820	52820+57820	MN	ATT	ANG	ATW		158833	52833+57833	MN	ATT	ANG	ATW
158821	52821+57821	MN	ATT	ANG	ATW		158834	52834+57834	MN	ATT	ANG	ATW
158822	52822+57822	MN	ATT	ANG	ATW		158835	52835+57835	MN	ATT	ANG	ATW
158823	52823+57823	MN	ATT	ANG	ATW		158836	52836+57836	MN	ATT	ANG	ATW
158824	52824+57824	MN	ATT	ANG	ATW		158837	52837+57837	CV	ATT	ANG	ATW
158825	52825+57825	MN	ATT	ANG	ATW		158838	52838+57838	CV	ATT	ANG	ATW
158826	52826+57826	MN	ATT	ANG	ATW		158839	52839+57839	CV	ATT	ANG	ATW
158827	52827+57827	MN	ATT	ANG	ATW		158840	52840+57840	CV	ATT	ANG	ATW
158828	52828+57828	MN	ATT	ANG	ATW		158841	52841+57841	CV	ATT	ANG	ATW

Arriva Trains Wales

Left: *Arriva Trains Wales longer-distance services are operated by a fleet of 24 two-car Class 158s based at both Cardiff Canton and Machynlleth depots. All these sets have been fitted with European Rail Traffic Management System (ERTMS) for operation over the trial-fitted Cambrian routes. All sets sport the latest two-tone turquoise livery. Set No. 158837 is seen near Cheltenham on 26 November 2015.* **CJM**

Class 175/0
Coradia 1000

Vehicle Length: 75ft 7in (23.06m)	Engine: 1 x Cummins N14 of 450hp per vehicle
Height: 12ft 4in (3.75m)	Horsepower: 900hp (671kW)
Width: 9ft 2in (2.80m)	Seats (total/car): 118S, 54S/64S

Number	Formation DMSL+DMSL	Depot	Livery	Owner	Operator
175001	50701+79701	CH	ATW	ANG	ATW
175002	50702+79702	CH	ATW	ANG	ATW
175003	50703+79703	CH	ATW	ANG	ATW
175004	50704+79704	CH	ATW	ANG	ATW
175005	50705+79705	CH	ATW	ANG	ATW
175006	50706+79706	CH	ATW	ANG	ATW
175007	50707+79707	CH	ATW	ANG	ATW
175008	50708+79708	CH	ATW	ANG	ATW
175009	50709+79709	CH	ATW	ANG	ATW
175010	50710+79710	CH	ATW	ANG	ATW
175011	50711+79711	CH	ATW	ANG	ATW

Class 175/1
Coradia 1000

Vehicle Length: 75ft 7in (23.06m)	Engine: 1 x Cummins N14 of 450hp per vehicle
Height: 12ft 4in (3.75m)	Horsepower: 1,350hp (1,007kW)
Width: 9ft 2in (2.80m)	Seats (total/car): 186S, 54S/68S/64S

Number	Formation DMSL+MSL+DMSL	Depot	Livery	Owner	Op'r
175101	50751+56751+79751	CH	ATW	ANG	ATW
175102	50752+56752+79752	CH	ATW	ANG	ATW
175103	50753+56753+79753	CH	ATW	ANG	ATW
175104	50754+56754+79754	CH	ATW	ANG	ATW
175105	50755+56755+79755	CH	ATW	ANG	ATW
175106	50756+56756+79756	CH	ATW	ANG	ATW
175107	50757+56757+79757	CH	ATW	ANG	ATW
175108	50758+56758+79758	CH	ATW	ANG	ATW
175109	50759+56759+79759	CH	ATW	ANG	ATW
175110	50760+56760+79760	CH	ATW	ANG	ATW
175111	50761+56761+79761	CH	ATW	ANG	ATW
175112	50762+56762+79762	CH	ATW	ANG	ATW
175113	50763+56763+79763	CH	ATW	ANG	ATW
175114	50764+56764+79764	CH	ATW	ANG	ATW
175115	50765+56765+79765	CH	ATW	ANG	ATW
175116	50766+56766+79766	CH	ATW	ANG	ATW

Left: *Eleven two-car and 16 three-car Class 175s operate for Arriva Trains Wales, based at Chester depot and operating the long-distance main-line services on the North-South Wales corridor and the North Wales to Manchester routes. Built as part of the Alstom 'Coradia' family, the sets were built concurrent with the Class 180s with which they share a number of components. At present the sets carry the older-style ATW livery. The pioneer of the fleet, two-car set No. 175001, is seen at Newport on 19 June 2015.* **CJM**

Class AJ1G / RFM

Vehicle Length: 75ft 0in (22.86m)
Height: 12ft 9in (3.88m)
Width: 8ft 11in (2.71m)
Bogie Type: BT10
Seats: 23F

Number	Type	Depot	Livery	Owner	Operator
10249 (10012)	RFM	CV	ATT	DBR	ATW
10259 (10025)	RFM	CV	ATT	ATW	ATW

Below: *Sponsored by the Welsh Assembly Government, the ATW loco-hauled services on the North-South Wales and North Wales to Manchester corridor use a fleet of refurbished Mk3 stock, based at Cardiff Canton. Catering facilities are provided by a fleet of two RFM vehicles. Car No. 10259 is illustrated from the first class seating end at Newport.* **Nathan Williamson**

Class AD1H / TSO

Vehicle Length: 75ft 0in (22.86m)
Height: 12ft 9in (3.88m)
Width: 8ft 11in (2.71m)
Bogie Type: BT10

Number	Type	Depot	Livery	Owner	Operator
12176 (11064)	TSO	CV	ATT	ATW	ATW
12177 (11065)	TSO	CV	ATT	ATW	ATW
12178 (11071)	TSO	CV	ATT	ATW	ATW
12179 (11083)	TSO	CV	ATT	ATW	ATW
12180 (11084)	TSO	CV	ATT	ATW	ATW
12181 (11086)	TSO	CV	ATT	ATW	ATW
12182 (11013)	TSO	CV	ATT	ATW	ATW
12183 (11027)	TSO	CV	ATT	ATW	ATW
12184 (11044)	TSO	CV	ATT	ATW	ATW
12185 (11089)	TSO	CV	ATT	ATW	ATW

Right: *Ten refurbished Mk3b TSO vehicles provide the standard class seating for ATW loco-hauled duties. Each coach seats 70 in the low-density 2+2 style. Vehicle No. 12181 is illustrated.* **CJM**

Mk3 Hauled Stock (NPCCS)

Length: 75ft 0in (22.86m)
Height: 12ft 9in (3.88m)
Width: 8ft 11in (2.71m)
Bogie Type: BT7

NZAG - DVT

Number	Depot	Livery	Owner	Operator
82306 (82144)	CV	ATT	ATW	ATW
82307 (82131)	CV	ATT	ATW	ATW
82308 (82108)	CV	ATT	DBR	ATW

Right: *A fleet of three refurbished Mk3 Driving Van Trailers (DVTs) provides the remote driving controls for ATW loco-powered services. These vehicles still sport a large luggage van from their previous West Coast Main Line use, which is not required on this route. These vehicles have not been modified with a generator like similar conversions for Chiltern Railways. Vehicle 82307 is illustrated.* **Nathan Williamson**

Passenger Train Operating Companies - c2c

c2c - Essex/East Thameside

Address: ✉ 10th Floor, 207 Old Street, London, EC1V 9NR
✎ c2c.customerrelations@nationalexpress.com
☏ 0845 6014873
ⓘ www.c2c-online.co.uk

Managing Director: Julian Drury
Franchise Dates: 26 May 1996 - 2029
Principal Routes: London Fenchurch Street - Shoeburyness
Barking - Pitsea via Purfleet
Ockendon branch
London Liverpool Street - Barking (limited service)
Depots: East Ham (EM), Shoeburyness*
* Stabling point
Parent Company: Trenitalia

Note: Under the terms of the new East Thameside franchise, a commitment has been made to introduce 68 new vehicles (17 four-car sets) by 2019. These are likely to be an 'Electrostar'-based product to keep uniformity with the existing fleet.

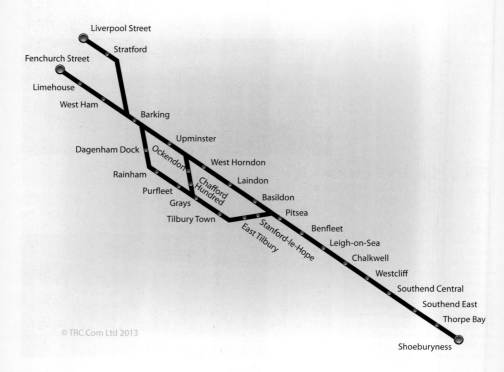

© TRC.Com Ltd 2013

Class 357/0
Electrostar

	Vehicle Length: (Driving) 68ft 1in (20.75m)	Width: 9ft 2½in (2.80m)
	(Inter) 65ft 11½in (20.10m)	Horsepower: 2,011hp (1,500kW)
	Height: 12ft 4½in (3.78m)	Seats (total/car): 282S, 71S/78S/62S/71S

Number	Formation DMSO(A)+MSO+PTSO+DMSO(B)	Depot	Livery	Owner	Op'r	Name
357001	67651+74151+74051+67751	EM	C2C	PTR	c2c	*Barry Flaxman*
357002	67652+74152+74052+67752	EM	C2C	PTR	c2c	*Arthur Lewis Stride 1841-1922*
357003	67653+74153+74053+67753	EM	C2C	PTR	c2c	*Southend City on Sea*
357004	67654+74154+74054+67754	EM	C2C	PTR	c2c	*Tony Amos*
357005	67655+74155+74055+67755	EM	C2C	PTR	c2c	*Southend : 2017 Alternative City of Culture*
357006	67656+74156+74056+67756	EM	C2C	PTR	c2c	*Diamond Jubilee 1952 - 2012*
357007	67657+74157+74057+67757	EM	C2C	PTR	c2c	*Sir Andrew Foster*
357008	67658+74158+74058+67758	EM	C2C	PTR	c2c	
357009	67659+74159+74059+67759	EM	C2C	PTR	c2c	
357010	67660+74160+74060+67760	EM	C2C	PTR	c2c	
357011	67661+74161+74061+67761	EM	C2C	PTR	c2c	*John Lowing*
357012	67662+74162+74062+67762	EM	C2C	PTR	c2c	
357013	67663+74163+74063+67763	EM	C2C	PTR	c2c	
357014	67664+74164+74064+67764	EM	C2C	PTR	c2c	
357015	67665+74165+74065+67765	EM	C2C	PTR	c2c	
357016	67666+74166+74066+67766	EM	C2C	PTR	c2c	
357017	67667+74167+74067+67767	EM	C2C	PTR	c2c	
357018	67668+74168+74068+67768	EM	C2C	PTR	c2c	
357019	67669+74169+74069+67769	EM	C2C	PTR	c2c	
357020	67670+74170+74070+67770	EM	C2C	PTR	c2c	
357021	67621+74171+74071+67771	EM	C2C	PTR	c2c	
357022	67672+74172+74072+67772	EM	C2C	PTR	c2c	
357023	67673+74173+74073+67773	EM	C2C	PTR	c2c	
357024	67674+74174+74074+67774	EM	C2C	PTR	c2c	
357025	67675+74175+74075+67775	EM	C2C	PTR	c2c	
357026	67676+74176+74076+67776	EM	C2C	PTR	c2c	
357027	67677+74177+74077+67777	EM	C2C	PTR	c2c	
357028	67678+74178+74078+67778	EM	C2C	PTR	c2c	*London, Tilbury & Southend Railway 1854-2004*
357029	67679+74179+74079+67779	EM	C2C	PTR	c2c	*Thomas Whitelegg 1840-1922*
357030	67680+74180+74080+67780	EM	C2C	PTR	c2c	*Robert Harben Whitelegg 1871-1957*
357031	67681+74181+74081+67781	EM	C2C	PTR	c2c	
357032	67682+74182+74082+67782	EM	C2C	PTR	c2c	
357033	67683+74183+74083+67783	EM	C2C	PTR	c2c	
357034	67684+74184+74084+67784	EM	C2C	PTR	c2c	
357035	67685+74185+74085+67785	EM	C2C	PTR	c2c	
357036	67686+74186+74086+67786	EM	C2C	PTR	c2c	
357037	67687+74187+74087+67787	EM	C2C	PTR	c2c	
357038	67688+74188+74088+67788	EM	C2C	PTR	c2c	
357039	67689+74189+74089+67789	EM	C2C	PTR	c2c	
357040	67690+74190+74090+67790	EM	C2C	PTR	c2c	
357041	67691+74191+74091+67791	EM	C2C	PTR	c2c	
357042	67692+74192+74092+67792	EM	C2C	PTR	c2c	
357043	67693+74193+74093+67793	EM	C2C	PTR	c2c	
357044	67694+74194+74094+67794	EM	C2C	PTR	c2c	
357045	67695+74195+74095+67795	EM	C2C	PTR	c2c	
357046	67696+74196+74096+67796	EM	C2C	PTR	c2c	

Right: *A fleet of 74 early-design 'Electrostar' sets is operated by c2c; classified as '357' these non-corridor units fall into three sub-classes. The 46 Class 357/0 sets are owned by Porterbrook and operate in a common pool with the 11 members of Class 357/2. Sets are finished in National Express white with blue contrasting passenger doors. Unit No. 357009 is seen at Upminster. Sets are likely to receive Trenitalia branding in the near future.* **Antony Christie**

c2c

Class 357/2 & 357/3
Electrostar

Vehicle Length: (Driving) 68ft 1in (20.75m) Width: 9ft 2½in (2.80m)
(Inter) 65ft 11½in (20.10m) Horsepower: 2,011hp (1,500kW)
Height: 12ft 4½in (3.78m) Seats (total/car): 282S, 71S/78S/62S/71S
Class 357/3 sets are fitted with revised interiors using 2+2 low-density layout with total seating for 223S passengers

Number	Formation DMSO(A)+MSO+PTSO+DMSO(B)	Depot	Livery	Owner	Operator	Name
357201	68601+74701+74601+68701	EM	C2C	ANG	c2c	*Ken Bird*
357202	68602+74702+74602+68702	EM	C2C	ANG	c2c	*Kenny Mitchell*
357203	68603+74703+74603+68703	EM	C2C	ANG	c2c	*Henry Pumfrett*
357204	68604+74704+74604+68704	EM	C2C	ANG	c2c	*Derek Flowers*
357205	68605+74705+74605+68705	EM	C2C	ANG	c2c	*John D'Silva*
357206	68606+74706+74606+68706	EM	C2C	ANG	c2c	*Martin Aungier*
357207	68607+74707+74607+68707	EM	C2C	ANG	c2c	*John Page*
357208	68608+74708+74608+68708	EM	C2C	ANG	c2c	*Dave Davis*
357209	68609+74709+74609+68709	EM	C2C	ANG	c2c	*James Snelling*
357210	68610+74710+74610+68710	EM	C2C	ANG	c2c	
357211	68611+74711+74611+68711	EM	C2C	ANG	c2c	
357312 (357212)	68612+74712+74612+68712	EM	C2C	ANG	c2c	
357313 (357213)	68613+74713+74613+68713	EM	C2C	ANG	c2c	*Upminster IECC*
357314 (357214)	68614+74714+74614+68714	EM	C2C	ANG	c2c	
357315 (357215)	68615+74715+74615+68715	EM	C2C	ANG	c2c	
357316 (357216)	68616+74716+74616+68716	EM	C2C	ANG	c2c	
357317 (357217)	68617+74717+74617+68717	EM	C2C	ANG	c2c	*Allan Burnell*
357318 (357218)	68618+74218+74618+68718	EM	C2C	ANG	c2c	
357319 (357219)	68619+74719+74619+68719	EM	C2C	ANG	c2c	
357320 (357220)	68620+74720+74620+68720	EM	C2C	ANG	c2c	
357321 (357221)	68621+74721+74621+68721	EM	C2C	ANG	c2c	
357322 (357222)	68622+74722+74622+68722	EM	C2C	ANG	c2c	
357323 (357223)	68623+74723+74623+68723	EM	C2C	ANG	c2c	
357324 (357224)	68624+74724+74624+68724	EM	C2C	ANG	c2c	
357325 (357225)	68625+74725+74625+68725	EM	C2C	ANG	c2c	
357326 (357226)	68626+74726+74626+68726	EM	C2C	ANG	c2c	
357327 (357227)	68627+74727+74627+68727	EM	C2C	ANG	c2c	*Southend United*
357328 (357228)	68628+74728+74628+68728	EM	C2C	ANG	c2c	

Class 387
Electrostar

Vehicle Length: (Driving) 66ft 9in (20.3m) Width: 9ft 2in (2.79m)
(Inter) 65ft 6in (19.96m) Horsepower: 2,012hp (1,500kW)
Height: 12ft 4in (3.75m) Seats (total/car): 223S. 56S/62S/45S/60S

Number	Formation DMSO(A)+MSO+TSO+DMSO(B)	Depot	Livery	Owner	Operator
387301	421301+422301+423301+424301	EM	C2C	PTR	c2c
387302	421302+422302+423302+424302	EM	C2C	PTR	c2c
387303	421303+422303+423303+424303	EM	C2C	PTR	c2c
387304	421304+422304+423304+424304	EM	C2C	PTR	c2c
387305	421305+422305+423305+424305	EM	C2C	PTR	c2c
387306	421306+422306+423306+424306	EM	C2C	PTR	c2c

Left: *In late 2016, six four-car Bombardier 'Electrostar' sets of Class 387/3 entered service with c2c. These sets will usually operate in pairs and have been obtained from lease-owner Porterbrook to assist in route overcrowding. The interiors are largely based on the Southern style. Externally sets are finished in base white, with c2c branding and mauve passenger doors. Sets are allocated to East Ham depot. Sets Nos. 387301 and 387302 are illustrated near Chalkwell.*
Antony Christie

Chiltern Railways

Address: ✉ 2nd floor, Western House, Rickfords Hill, Aylesbury, Buckinghamshire, HP20 2RX

🖰 Via website (www.chilternrailways.co.uk)

✆ 08456 005165   ⓘ www.chilternrailways.co.uk

Managing Director: Rob Brighouse

Franchise Dates: 21 July 1996 - 21 December 2021

Principal Routes: London Marylebone - Birmingham Snow Hill

London Marylebone - Aylesbury

London Marylebone - Stratford-upon-Avon

Depots: Aylesbury (AL), Wembley*   * Stabling point

Parent Company: Deutsche Bahn AG (DB Regio)

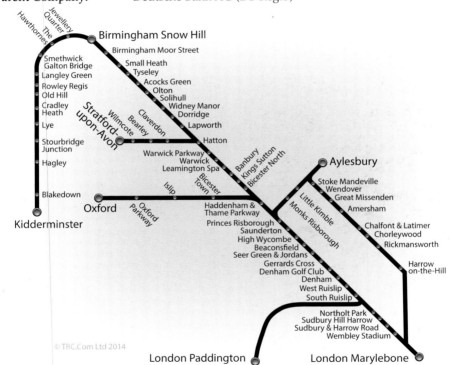

© TRC.Com Ltd 2014

Class 121

Length: 64ft 6in (19.66m)		Engine: 2 x Leyland 150hp	
Height: 12ft 8½in (3.87m)		Horsepower: 300hp (224kW)	
Width: 9ft 3in (2.81m)		Seats (total/car): 65S	

Number	Formation DMBS	Depot	Livery	Owner	Operator
121020	55020	AY	BLU	CRW	CRW
121034	55034	AY	GRN	CRW	CRW

Chiltern Railways

Left: *The last two remaining Network Rail heritage 'Bubble cars' are on the books of Chiltern, allocated to Aylesbury for use on the Princes Risborough branch. One is painted in blue livery and the other 1960s BR green. Carrying set number 121034 and vehicle No. 55034, the green-liveried vehicle is seen at Princes Risborough. To meet modern safety requirements for slam-door stock, both Class 121s now have central locking.* **Antony Christie**

Class 165/0 (2-car)
Networker Turbo

Vehicle Length: (Driving) 75ft 2½in (22.91m), (Inter) 74ft 6½in (22.72m)
Height: 12ft 5¼in (3.79m)   Engine: 1 x Perkins 2006 TWH of 350hp per vehicle
Width: 9ft 2½in (2.81m)   Horsepower: 700hp (522kW)
Seats (total/car): 183S, 89S/94S

Number	Formation DMSL+DMS	Depot	Livery	Owner	Operator
165001	58801+58834	AL	CRW	ANG	CRW
165002	58802+58835	AL	CRW	ANG	CRW
165003	58803+58836	AL	CRW	ANG	CRW
165004	58804+58837	AL	CRW	ANG	CRW
165005	58805+58838	AL	CRW	ANG	CRW
165006	58806+58839	AL	CRW	ANG	CRW
165007	58807+58840	AL	CRW	ANG	CRW
165008	58808+58841	AL	CRW	ANG	CRW
165009	58809+58842	AL	CRW	ANG	CRW
165010	58810+58843	AL	CRW	ANG	CRW
165011	58811+58844	AL	CRW	ANG	CRW
165012	58812+58845	AL	CRW	ANG	CRW
165013	58813+58846	AL	CRW	ANG	CRW
165014	58814+58847	AL	CRW	ANG	CRW
165015	58815+58848	AL	CRW	ANG	CRW
165016	58816+58849	AL	CRW	ANG	CRW
165017	58817+58850	AL	CRW	ANG	CRW
165018	58818+58851	AL	CRW	ANG	CRW
165019	58819+58852	AL	CRW	ANG	CRW
165020	58820+58853	AL	CRW	ANG	CRW
165021	58821+58854	AL	CRW	ANG	CRW
165022	58822+58855	AL	CRW	ANG	CRW
165023	58873+58867	AL	CRW	ANG	CRW
165024	58874+58868	AL	CRW	ANG	CRW
165025	58874+58869	AL	CRW	ANG	CRW
165026	58876+58870	AL	CRW	ANG	CRW
165027	58877+58871	AL	CRW	ANG	CRW
165028	58878+58872	AL	CRW	ANG	CRW

Class 165/0 (3-car)
Networker Turbo

Vehicle Length: (driving) 75ft 2½in (22.91m), (Inter) 74ft 6½in (22.72m)
Height: 12ft 5¼in (3.79m)   Engine: 1 x Perkins 2006 TWH of 350hp per vehicle
Width: 9ft 2½in (2.81m)   Horsepower: 1,050hp (783kW)
Seats (total/car): 289S, 89S/106S/94S

Number	Formation DMSL+MS+DMS	Depot	Livery	Owner	Operator
165029	58823+55404+58856	AL	CRW	ANG	CRW
165030	58824+55405+58857	AL	CRW	ANG	CRW
165031	58825+55406+58858	AL	CRW	ANG	CRW
165032	58826+55407+58859	AL	CRW	ANG	CRW
165033	58827+55408+58860	AL	CRW	ANG	CRW
165034	58828+55409+58861	AL	CRW	ANG	CRW
165035	58829+55410+58862	AL	CRW	ANG	CRW
165036	58830+55411+58863	AL	CRW	ANG	CRW
165037	58831+55412+58864	AL	CRW	ANG	CRW
165038	58832+55413+58865	AL	CRW	ANG	CRW
165039	58833+55414+58866	AL	CRW	ANG	CRW

Left: *Chiltern Railways suburban services are operated by a fleet of Class 165 'Networker Turbo' sets, allocated to Aylesbury. The fleet consists of 28 two-car and 11 three-car sets. The sets have been slightly modified from when first introduced and now have all standard class seating and sport a revised front end when viewed alongside a Great Western Railway set of the same class. A pair of two-car sets led by No. 165024 is seen passing the London Underground depot at Neasden Junction.* **Antony Christie**

Class 168/0
Turbostar

Vehicle Length: 77ft 6in (23.62m)
Height: 12ft 4½in (3.77m)
Width: 8ft 10in (2.69m)

Engine: 1 x MTU 6R 183TD13H pf 422hp per vehicle
Horsepower: 1,688hp (1,259kW)
Seats (total/car): 278S, 60S/73S/77S/68S

Number	Formation	Depot	Livery	Owner	Operator
	DMSL(A)+MSL+MS+DMSL(B)				
168001	58151+58651+58451+58251	AL	CRG	PTR	CRW
168002	58152+58652+58452+58252	AL	CRG	PTR	CRW
168003	58153+58653+58453+58253	AL	CRG	PTR	CRW
168004	58154+58654+58454+58254	AL	CRG	PTR	CRW
168005	58155+58655+58455+58255	AL	CRG	PTR	CRW

Right: *Chiltern Railways also operates a fleet of main-line Class 168 DMUs of the 'Turbostar' design, with several different builds in operation. Chiltern was the first TOC to receive 'Turbostar' stock and its first five sets are of a different body profile from all the remainder of the 'Turbostar' product range. Today, the original Class 168/0s are all formed of four cars, providing seats for 278 standard class passengers. Set No. 168004 is seen at South Ruislip.* **Antony Christie**

Class 168/1
Turbostar

Vehicle Length: 77ft 6in (23.62m)
Height: 12ft 4½in (3.77m)
Width: 8ft 10in (2.69m)

Engine: 1 x MTU 6R 183TD13H of 422hp per vehicle
Horsepower: 3/4-car 1,266hp (944kW)/1,688hp (1,259kW)
Seats (total/car): 3-car - 208S, 59S/73S/76S, 4-car - 284S, 59S/73S/76S/76S

Number	Formation	Depot	Livery	Owner	Operator	Notes
	DMSL(A)+MS+MS+DMSL(B)					
168106	58156+58756§+58456+58256	AL	CRG	PTR	CRW	§ is a MSL vehicle
168107	58157+58457+58757§+58257	AL	CRG	PTR	CRW	§ is a MSL vehicle
168108	58158+58458+58258	AL	CRG	PTR	CRW	
168109	58159+58459+58259	AL	CRG	PTR	CRW	
168110	58160+58460+58260	AL	CRG	PTR	CRW	
168111	58161+58461+58261	AL	CRG	EVL	CRW	58461 was originally 58661
168112	58162+58462+58262	AL	CRG	EVL	CRW	58462 was originally 58662
168113	58163+58463+58263	AL	CRG	EVL	CRW	58463 was originally 58663

Right: *The follow-on orders for Class 168s were built to the standard 'Turbostar' design as used for Class 168, 170 and 171 fleets. The Class 168/1 sub-class is a mix of four- and three-car units, with five sets owned by Porterbrook and three by Eversholt Leasing. All sets carry the new Chiltern white and silver livery and are allocated to Aylesbury depot. On 4 May 2016 sets Nos. 168108 and 168112, with a Class 172 coupled on the rear, pass Kings Sutton.* **Antony Christie**

Class 168/2
Turbostar

Vehicle Length: 77ft 6in (23.62m)
Height: 12ft 4½in (3.77m)
Width: 8ft 10in (2.69m)

Engine: 1 x MTU 6R 183TD13H of 422hp per vehicle
Horsepower: 3/4-car 1,266hp (944kW)/1,688hp (1,259kW)
Seats (total/car): 3-car - 204S, 59S/76S/69S, 4-car - 277S, 59S/73S/76S/69S

Number	Formation	Depot	Livery	Owner	Operator
	DMSL(A)+MS+MS+DMSL(B)				
168214	58164+58464+58264	AL	CRG	PTR	CRW
168215	58165+58465+58365+58265	AL	CRG	PTR	CRW

Passenger Train Operating Companies - Chiltern Railways

Chiltern Railways

168216	58166+58466+58366+58266	AL	CRG	PTR	CRW
168217	58167+58467+58367+58267	AL	CRG	PTR	CRW
168218	58168+58468+58268	AL	CRG	PTR	CRW
168219	58169+58469+58269	AL	CRG	PTR	CRW

Class 168/3
Turbostar

Vehicle Length: 77ft 6in (23.62m)	Engine: 1 x MTU 6R 183TD13H of 422hp per vehicle
Height: 12ft 4½in (3.77m)	Horsepower: 844hp (629kW)
Width: 8ft 10in (2.69m)	Seats (total/car): 8F/108S 8F-43S/65S

Number	Formation DMCL+DMS	Depot	Livery	Owner	Operator
168321	50301+79301	AL	CRG	PTR	CRW
168322	50302+79302	AL	CRG	PTR	CRW
168323	50303+79303	AL	CRG	PTR	CRW
168324	50304+79304	AL	CRG	PTR	CRW
168325	50305+79305	AL	CRG	PTR	CRW
168326	50306+79306	AL	CRG	PTR	CRW
168327	50307+79307	AL	CRG	PTR	CRW
168328	50308+79308	AL	CRG	PTR	CRW
168329	50399+79399	AL	CRG	PTR	CRW

Previously numbered 170301 - 170309 and operated by South West Trains and First TransPennine

Left: *In 2015-16 nine two-car Class 170/3s were transferred to Chiltern from FTPE and modified to Class 168 standards and repainted in standard Chiltern colours. Set No. 168321, the former 170301, is illustrated.* **Antony Christie**

Class 172/1

Vehicle Length: 73ft 4in (22.37m)	Engine: MTU 6H1800 of 360kW
Height: 12ft 4½in (3.77m)	Horsepower: 965hp (720kW)
Width: 8ft 8in (2.69m)	Seats (total/car): 121S, 53S/68S

Number	Formation DMS+DMS	Depot	Livery	Owner	Operator
172101	59111+59211	AL	CRW	ANG	CRW
172102	59112+59212	AL	CRW	ANG	CRW
172103	59113+59213	AL	CRW	ANG	CRW
172104	59114+59214	AL	CRW	ANG	CRW

Left: *With Chiltern Railways seeking extra rolling stock, the company obtained four two-car Class 172 sets in 2009-10. These sets are fitted with a diesel-mechanical transmission rather than diesel-hydraulic, and have a slightly higher output MTU power unit on each vehicle. Painted in Chiltern blue and white suburban colours, set No. 172104 is seen at Gerrards Cross.* **Antony Christie**

Class 68 'UK Light'

Vehicle Length: 67ft 3in (20.5m)	Engine: Caterpillar C175-16
Height: 12ft 6½in (3.82m)	Horsepower: 3,750hp (2,800kW)
Speed: 100mph (161km/h)	Electrical Equipment: ABB

Left: *The huge success of the Chiltern Railways loco-hauled London Marylebone to Birmingham main-line service has seen it increase and now uses a dedicated fleet of modified Class 68s, leased from DRS to power rakes of refurbished Mk3 stock. The dedicated locos, Nos. 68010-68015, are finished in unbranded Chiltern main-line grey livery. No. 68014 is seen heading north at Kings Sutton in summer 2016.* **Antony Christie**

Number	Depot	Pool	Livery	Owner	Operator
68010	CG	XHVE	CRG	BEA	DRS/CRW
68011	CG	XHVE	CRG	BEA	DRS/CRW
68012	CG	XHVE	CRG	BEA	DRS/CRW
68013	CG	XHVE	CRG	BEA	DRS/CRW
68014	CG	XHVE	CRG	BEA	DRS/CRW
68015	CG	XHVE	CRG	BEA	DRS/CRW

Names applied - **68010** *Oxford Flyer*

Mk3 Hauled Stock (Passenger)

Vehicle Length: 75ft 0in (22.86m)
Height: 12ft 9in (3.88m)   Width: 8ft 11in (2.71m)
Bogie Type: BT10

AJ1F - GFW *Seating 30F*

Number		Depot	Livery	Owner
10271	(10236/10018)	AL	CRG	DBR
10272	(10208/40517)	AL	CRG	DBR
10273	(10230/10021)	AL	CRG	DBR
10274	(10255/11010)	AL	CRG	DBR

AC2G - TSO/TSOL* *Seating 72S*

Number		Depot	Livery	Owner
11029		AL	CRG	DBR
11031		AL	CRG	DBR
12602	(12072)	AL	CRG	DBR
12603*	(12053)	AL	CRG	DBR
12604	(12131)	AL	CRG	DBR
12605*	(11040)	AL	CRG	DBR
12606	(12048)	AL	CRG	DBR
12607*	(12038)	AL	CRG	DBR
12608	(12069)	AL	CRG	DBR
12609*	(12014)	AL	CRG	DBR
12612	(12117)	AL	CRG	DBR
12613*	(12173/11042)	AL	CRG	DBR
12614	(12145)	AL	CRG	DBR
12615*	(12059)	AL	CRG	DBR
12616	(12127)	AL	CRG	DBR
12617*	(12174/11050)	AL	CRG	DBR
12618	(12169)	AL	CRG	DBR
12619*	(12175/11052)	AL	CRG	DBR
12620	(12124)	AL	CRG	DBR
12621	(11046)	AL	CRG	DBR
12623	(11019)	AL	CRG	DBR
12625	(11030)	AL	CRG	DBR
12627	(11054)	AL	CRG	DBR
12017		AL	CRG	DBR
12036		AL	CRG	DBR
12043		AL	CRG	DBR
12094		AL	CRG	DBR
12119		AL	CRG	DBR

Right: *A sizeable fleet of mainly refurbished Mk3s, fitted with power-operated passenger doors, works the Chiltern main-line services between London and Birmingham. In late 2016 a fleet of 31 vehicles was on the Chiltern books and this number looks set to rise. Painted in Chiltern Railways main-line grey livery, TSO No. 12602 is seen at Marylebone.*
Antony Christie

Mk3 Hauled Stock (NPCCS)

Vehicle Length: 75ft 0in (22.86m)
Height: 12ft 9in (3.88m)
Width: 8ft 11in (2.71m)
Bogie Type: BT7

NZAG - DVT

Number	Depot	Livery	Owner				
82301 (82117)	AL	CRG	DBR	82304 (82130)	AL	CRG	DBR
82302 (82151)	AL	CRG	DBR	82305 (82134)	AL	CRG	DBR
82303 (82135)	AL	CRG	DBR	82309 (82104)	AL	CRG	DBR

Class 960 – Service Units

Length: 64ft 6in (19.66m)
Height: 12ft 8½in (3.87m)
Width: 9ft 3in (2.81m)

Engine: 2 x Leyland 150hp
Horsepower: 300hp (224kW)
Seats (total/car): None

Number	Formation	Depot	Livery	Owner	Operator	Notes
960014	977873	AL	BLG	CRW	CRW	Ex-Class 121 55022, Route Learning/Sandite

Class 01.5 (0-6-0)

Number		Depot	Pool	Livery	Owner	Operator	Name
01509 (433)	RH468043	AL	MBDL	BLU	CRW	CRW	*Lesley*

CrossCountry Trains

Address: ✉ Cannon House, 18 The Priory, Queensway, Birmingham, B4 6BS
🖰 info@crosscountrytrains.co.uk
✆ 0870 0100084
ⓘ www.crosscountrytrains.co.uk

Managing Director: Andy Cooper
Franchise Dates: 11 November 2007 - October 2019
Principal Routes: Penzance / Paignton -
Manchester / Edinburgh / Aberdeen
Bournemouth - Manchester /
Edinburgh / Aberdeen
Birmingham - Stansted
Nottingham - Cardiff
Depots: Central Rivers (CZ),
Tyseley (TS),
Craigentinny (EC)
Parent Company: Deutsche Bahn AG
(DB Regio) / Arriva

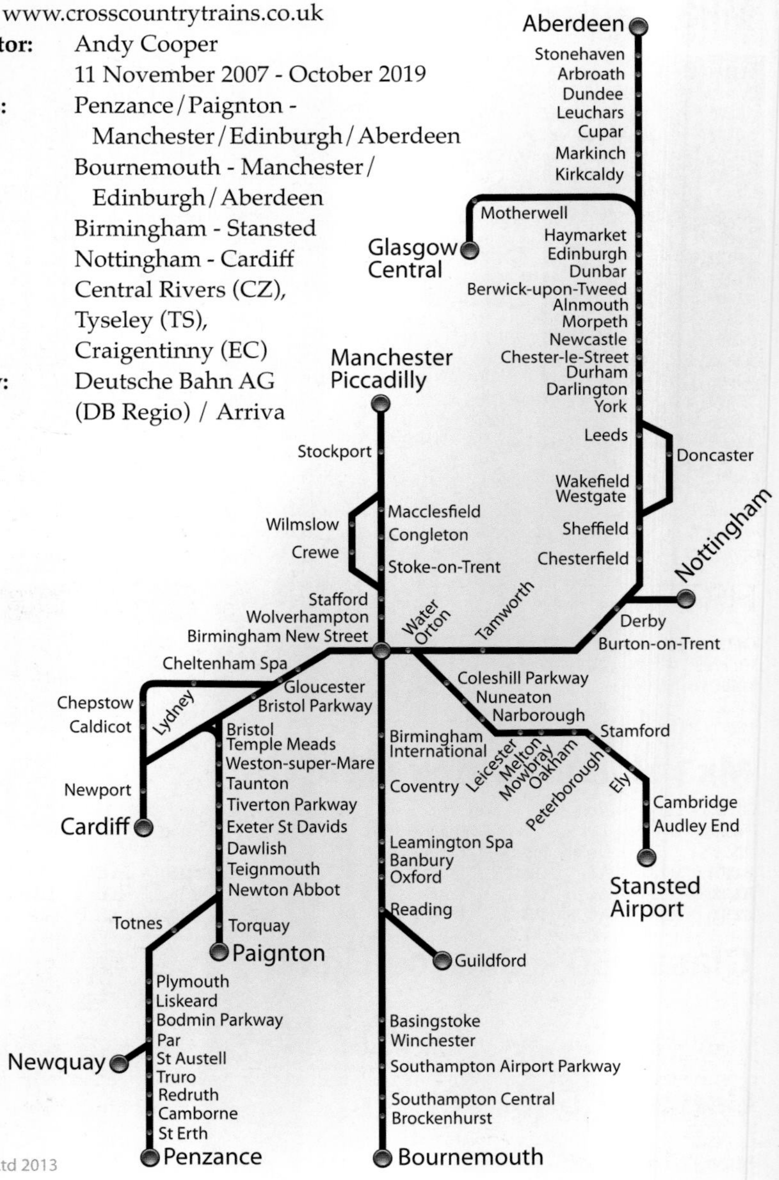

Aberdeen
Stonehaven
Arbroath
Dundee
Leuchars
Cupar
Markinch
Kirkcaldy
Motherwell
Glasgow Central
Haymarket
Edinburgh
Dunbar
Berwick-upon-Tweed
Alnmouth
Morpeth
Newcastle
Chester-le-Street
Durham
Darlington
York
Manchester Piccadilly
Leeds
Doncaster
Stockport
Wakefield Westgate
Sheffield
Chesterfield
Nottingham
Wilmslow
Crewe
Macclesfield
Congleton
Stoke-on-Trent
Stafford
Wolverhampton
Birmingham New Street
Water Orton
Tamworth
Derby
Burton-on-Trent
Cheltenham Spa
Coleshill Parkway
Nuneaton
Narborough
Chepstow
Caldicot
Lydney
Gloucester
Bristol Parkway
Birmingham International
Stamford
Bristol Temple Meads
Weston-super-Mare
Taunton
Tiverton Parkway
Exeter St Davids
Dawlish
Teignmouth
Newton Abbot
Leicester
Melton Mowbray
Oakham
Peterborough
Ely
Newport
Coventry
Cambridge
Audley End
Cardiff
Leamington Spa
Banbury
Oxford
Stansted Airport
Totnes
Torquay
Reading
Paignton
Guildford
Plymouth
Liskeard
Bodmin Parkway
Par
St Austell
Truro
Redruth
Camborne
St Erth
Basingstoke
Winchester
Southampton Airport Parkway
Southampton Central
Brockenhurst
Newquay
Penzance
Bournemouth

© TRC.Com Ltd 2013

Class 43 – HST

Vehicle Length: 58ft 5in (18.80m)
Height: 12ft 10in (3.90m)
Width: 8ft 11in (2.73m)

Engine: MTU 16V4000 R41R
Horsepower: 2,250hp (1,680kW)
Electrical Equipment: Brush

Number	Depot	Pool	Livery	Owner	Operator						
43207 (43007)	EC	EHPC	AXC	ANG	AXC	43321 (43121)	EC	EHPC	AXC	PTR	AXC
43285 (43085)	EC	EHPC	AXC	PTR	AXC	43357 (43157)	EC	EHPC	AXC	PTR	AXC
43301 (43101)	EC	EHPC	AXC	PTR	AXC	43366 (43166)	EC	EHPC	AXC	ANG	AXC
43303 (43103)	EC	EHPC	AXC	PTR	AXC	43378 (43178)	EC	EHPC	AXC	ANG	AXC
43304 (43104)	EC	EHPC	AXC	ANG	AXC	43384 (43184)	EC	EHPC	AXC	ANG	AXC

Above: *Ten Class 43 HST power cars are in operation with CrossCountry Trains, based at Edinburgh Craigentinny and used on up to four daily HST formations used on the long-distance XC routes to the South West. On 22 January 2016 No. 43285 approaches Shaldon Bridge, Teignmouth, with the 06.06 Edinburgh Waverley to Plymouth service.* **CJM**

HST passenger fleet

Vehicle Length: 75ft 0in (22.86m)
Height: 12ft 9in (3.88m)
Width: 8ft 11in (2.71m)
Bogie Type: BT10

GH1G - TF Seating 40F

Number	Depot	Livery	Owner	
41026	EC	AXC	ANG	
41035	EC	AXC	ANG	
41193 (11060)	EC	AXC	PTR	
41194 (11016)	EC	AXC	PTR	
41195¤ (11020)	EC	AXC	PTR	¤ = TFD

GH2G - TS Seating 82S

Number	Depot	Livery	Owner
42036§	EC	AXC	ANG
42037	EC	AXC	ANG
42038	EC	AXC	ANG
42051	EC	AXC	ANG
42052	EC	AXC	ANG
42053	EC	AXC	ANG
42097	EC	AXC	ANG
42234	EC	AXC	PTR
42290	EC	AXC	PTR
42342 (44082)	EC	AXC	ANG
42366 (12007)	EC	AXC	PTR
42367 (12025)	EC	AXC	PTR
42368 (12028)	EC	AXC	PTR
42369 (12050)	EC	AXC	PTR
42370 (12086)§	EC	AXC	PTR
42371 (12052)	EC	AXC	PTR

Number	Depot	Livery	Owner	
42372 (12055)	EC	AXC	PTR	
42373 (12071)	EC	AXC	PTR	
42374 (12075)	EC	AXC	PTR	
42375 (12113)	EC	AXC	PTR	
42376 (12085)	EC	AXC	PTR	
42377 (12102)	EC	AXC	PTR	
42378 (12123)	EC	AXC	PTR	
42379* (41036)	EC	AXC	ANG	*=TSD
42380* (41025)	EC	AXC	ANG	*=TSD

§ Being fitted with plug doors

GJ2G - TGS Seating 67S

Number	Depot	Livery	Owner
44012	EC	AXC	ANG
44017	EC	AXC	ANG
44021	EC	AXC	ANG
44052	EC	AXC	PTR
44072	EC	AXC	PTR

GH3G - TCC Seating 30F/10S

Number	Depot	Livery	Owner
45001 (12004)	EC	AXC	PTR
45002 (12106)	EC	AXC	PTR
45003 (12076)	EC	AXC	PTR
45004 (12077)	EC	AXC	PTR
45005 (12080)	EC	AXC	PTR

CrossCountry Trains

Passenger Train Operating Companies – CrossCountry Trains

Left: *A fleet of 40 Mk3 vehicles is operated by CrossCountry, again allocated to Edinburgh Craigentinny depot. These are a mix of rebuilt loco-hauled Mk3s brought up to HST standards and rebuilt original HST stock. Vehicles are all painted in XC silver/grey and black with pink contrasting passenger doors. Sufficient vehicles are available to form five passenger rakes if needed. Trailer Standard No. 42053 is illustrated.* **CJM**

Class 170/1
Turbostar

Vehicle Length: 77ft 6in (23.62m)
Height: 12ft 4½in (3.77m)
Width: 8ft 10in (2.69m)

Engine: 1 x MTU 6R 183TD13H of 422hp per vehicle
Horsepower: 1,266hp (944kW)
Seats (total/car): 9F/191S 52S/80S/9F-59S

Number	Formation DMS+MS+DMCL	Depot	Livery	Owner	Operator
170101	50101+55101+79101	TS	AXC	PTR	AXC
170102	50102+55102+79102	TS	AXC	PTR	AXC
170103	50103+55103+79103	TS	AXC	PTR	AXC
170104	50104+55104+79104	TS	AXC	PTR	AXC
170105	50105+55105+79105	TS	AXC	PTR	AXC
170106	50106+55106+79106	TS	AXC	PTR	AXC
170107	50107+55107+79107	TS	AXC	PTR	AXC
170108*	50108+55108+79108	TS	AXC	PTR	AXC
170109*	50109+55109+79109	TS	AXC	PTR	AXC
170110	50110+55110+79110	TS	AXC	PTR	AXC

Left: *Several different batches of Class 170 'Turbostar' stock are operated by CrossCountry, all have been refurbished to the same standard and now internally look the same. Of the original Class 170/1 fleet, used when built on the Midland Main Line, 10 three-car and seven two-car sets are in traffic. Three-car set No. 170109 painted in standard XC livery with bodyside company advertising is seen approaching Cheltenham on a Cardiff to Nottingham service.* **CJM**

Vehicle Length: 77ft 6in (23.62m)
Height: 12ft 4½in (3.77m)
Width: 8ft 10in (2.69m)

Engine: 1 x MTU 6R 183TD13H of 422hp per vehicle
Horsepower: 844hp (629kW)
Seats (total/car): 9F-111S 59S/9F-52S

Number	Formation DMS+DMCL	Depot	Livery	Owner	Operator
170111*	50111+79111	TS	AXC	PTR	AXC
170112	50112+79112	TS	AXC	PTR	AXC
170113	50113+79113	TS	AXC	PTR	AXC
170114	50114+79114	TS	AXC	PTR	AXC
170115	50115+79115	TS	AXC	PTR	AXC
170116	50116+79116	TS	AXC	PTR	AXC
170117	50117+79117	TS	AXC	PTR	AXC

* Fitted with passenger counters

Right: *Due to the length of the routes on which the XC Class 170s are deployed and the customer base, first class accommodation is retained, provided by the area directly behind the driving cab on DMCL vehicles with seating for nine passengers. Two-car set No. 170116 with its DMCL vehicle nearest the camera is seen at Derby.*
Antony Christie

Class 170/3
Turbostar

Vehicle Length: 77ft 6in (23.62m)				Engine: 1 x MTU 6R 183TD13H of 422hp per vehicle			
Height: 12ft 4½in (3.77m)				Horsepower: 1,266hp (944kW)			
Width: 8ft 10in (2.69m)				Seats (total/car): 9F-191S 59S/80S/9F-52S			

Number	Formation DMSL+MS+DMCL	Depot	Livery	Owner	Operator
170397	50397+56397+79397	TS	AXC	PTR	AXC
170398	50398+56398+79398	TS	AXC	PTR	AXC

Class 170/5
Turbostar

Vehicle Length: 77ft 6in (23.62m)				Engine: 1 x MTU 6R 183TD13H of 422hp per vehicle			
Height: 12ft 4½in (3.77m)				Horsepower: 844hp (629kW)			
Width: 8ft 10in (2.69m)				Seats (total/car): 9F-111S 59S/9F-52S			

Number	Formation DMSL+DMCL	Depot	Livery	Owner	Operator
170518	50518+79518	TS	AXC	PTR	AXC
170519	50519+79519	TS	AXC	PTR	AXC
170520	50520+79520	TS	AXC	PTR	AXC
170521	50521+79521	TS	AXC	PTR	AXC
170522	50522+79522	TS	AXC	PTR	AXC
170523	50523+79523	TS	AXC	PTR	AXC

Right: *Six two-car Class 170s of the Class 170/5 classification are in traffic, and generally all Class 170s are operated as a common pool for either two-car or three-car sets. Recorded at Sawley near Long Eaton, set No. 170518 is shown from its DMS vehicle.*
Antony Christie

Class 170/6
Turbostar

Vehicle Length: 77ft 6in (23.62m)				Engine: 1 x MTU 6R 183TD13H of 422hp per vehicle			
Height: 12ft 4½in (3.77m)				Horsepower: 1,266hp (944kW)			
Width: 8ft 10in (2.69m)				Seats (total/car): 9F-191S 59S/80S/9F-52S			

Number	Formation DMSL+MS+DMCL	Depot	Livery	Owner	Operator
170636	50636+56636+79636	TS	AXC	PTR	AXC
170637	50637+56637+79637	TS	AXC	PTR	AXC
170638	50638+56638+79638	TS	AXC	PTR	AXC
170639	50639+56639+79639	TS	AXC	PTR	AXC

CrossCountry Trains

Passenger Train Operating Companies - CrossCountry Trains

Class 220
Voyager

Vehicle Length: 77ft 6in (23.62m)	Engine: 1 x Cummins of 750hp per vehicle
Height: 12ft 4in (3.75m)	Horsepower: 3,000hp (2,237kW)
Width: 8ft 11in (2.73m)	Seats (total/car): 26F/174S 42S/66S/66S/26F

Number	Formation DMS+MS+MS+DMF	Depot	Livery	Owner	Operator
220001	60301+60701+60201+60401	CZ	AXC	HBS	AXC
220002	60302+60702+60202+60402	CZ	AXC	HBS	AXC
220003	60303+60703+60203+60403	CZ	AXC	HBS	AXC
220004	60304+60704+60204+60404	CZ	AXC	HBS	AXC
220005	60305+60705+60205+60405	CZ	AXC	HBS	AXC
220006	60306+60706+60206+60406	CZ	AXC	HBS	AXC
220007	60307+60707+60207+60407	CZ	AXC	HBS	AXC
220008	60308+60708+60208+60408	CZ	AXC	HBS	AXC
220009	60309+60709+60209+60409	CZ	AXC	HBS	AXC
220010	60310+60710+60210+60410	CZ	AXC	HBS	AXC
220011	60311+60711+60211+60411	CZ	AXC	HBS	AXC
220012	60312+60712+60212+60412	CZ	AXC	HBS	AXC
220013	60313+60713+60213+60413	CZ	AXC	HBS	AXC
220014	60314+60714+60214+60414	CZ	AXC	HBS	AXC
220015	60315+60715+60215+60415	CZ	AXC	HBS	AXC
220016	60316+60716+60216+60416	CZ	AXC	HBS	AXC
220017	60317+60717+60217+60417	CZ	AXC	HBS	AXC
220018	60318+60718+60218+60418	CZ	AXC	HBS	AXC
220019	60319+60719+60219+60419	CZ	AXC	HBS	AXC
220020	60320+60720+60220+60420	CZ	AXC	HBS	AXC
220021	60321+60721+60221+60421	CZ	AXC	HBS	AXC
220022	60322+60722+60222+60422	CZ	AXC	HBS	AXC
220023	60323+60723+60223+60423	CZ	AXC	HBS	AXC
220024	60324+60724+60224+60424	CZ	AXC	HBS	AXC
220025	60325+60725+60225+60425	CZ	AXC	HBS ·	AXC
220026	60326+60726+60226+60426	CZ	AXC	HBS	AXC
220027	60327+60727+60227+60427	CZ	AXC	HBS	AXC
220028	60328+60728+60228+60428	CZ	AXC	HBS	AXC
220029	60329+60729+60229+60429	CZ	AXC	HBS	AXC
220030	60330+60730+60230+60430	CZ	AXC	HBS	AXC
220031	60331+60731+60231+60431	CZ	AXC	HBS	AXC
220032	60332+60732+60232+60432	CZ	AXC	HBS	AXC
220033	60333+60733+60233+60433	CZ	AXC	HBS	AXC
220034	60334+60734+60234+60434	CZ	AXC	HBS	AXC

Below: *CrossCountry Trains' core operating fleet for long-distance operations is the 'Voyager' fleet, inherited from the previous franchise operator Virgin Trains. Thirty-four Class 220 four-car sets are in operation, based at Central Rivers depot near Burton and operating throughout the main XC network. Sets normally operate as just one unit, but can operate in multiple if required. Led by its Driving Motor First (DMF) vehicle, set No. 220005 departs from Doncaster on 16 January 2016 with the 09.05 Darlington to Reading.* **CJM**

Class 221
Super Voyager

Vehicle Length: 77ft 6in (23.62m)	Engine: 1 x Cummins of 750hp per vehicle
Height: 12ft 4in (3.75m)	Horsepower: 3,750hp (2,796kW)
Width: 8ft 11in (2.73m)	Seats (total/car): 26F/236S 42S/66S/66S/62S/26F

Originally fitted with tilt system to allow higher speeds over curves. Equipment now isolated.

Number	Formation DMS+MS+MS+MS+DMF	Depot	Livery	Owner	Operator	
221119	60369+60769+60969+60869+60469	CZ	AXC	HBS	AXC	
221120	60370+60770+60970+60870+60470	CZ	AXC	HBS	AXC	
221121	60371+60771+60971+60871+60471	CZ	AXC	HBS	AXC	
221122	60372+60772+60972+60872+60472	CZ	AXC	HBS	AXC	
221123	60373+60773+60973+60873+60473	CZ	AXC	HBS	AXC	
221124	60374+60774+60974+60874+60474	CZ	AXC	HBS	AXC	
221125	60375+60775+60975+60875+60475	CZ	AXC	HBS	AXC	
221126	60376+60776+60976+60876+60476	CZ	AXC	HBS	AXC	
221127	60377+60777+60977+60877+60477	CZ	AXC	HBS	AXC	
221128	60378+60778+60978+60878+60478	CZ	AXC	HBS	AXC	
221129	60379+60779+60979+60879+60479	CZ	AXC	HBS	AXC	
221130	60380+60780+60980+60880+60480	CZ	AXC	HBS	AXC	
221131	60381+60781+60981+60881+60481	CZ	AXC	HBS	AXC	
221132	60382+60782+60982+60882+60482	CZ	AXC	HBS	AXC	
221133	60383+60783+60983+60883+60483	CZ	AXC	HBS	AXC	
221134	60384+60784+60984+60884+60484	CZ	AXC	HBS	AXC	
221135	60385+60785+60985+60885+60485	CZ	AXC	HBS	AXC	
221136	60386+60786+60986+60886+60486	CZ	AXC	HBS	AXC	
221137	60387+60787+60987+60887+60487	CZ	AXC	HBS	AXC	
221138	60388+60788+60988+60888+60488	CZ	AXC	HBS	AXC	
221139	60389+60789+60989+60889+60489	CZ	AXC	HBS	AXC	
221140	60390+60790+60990+60890+60490	CZ	AXC	HBS	AXC	
221141	60391+60791+60991+-+60491	CZ	AXC	HBS	AXC	*(four-car set)*
221144§	60394+-+-+-+60494	CZ	-	HBS	To be formed	

Below: *Twenty-three of the original 'Super Voyager' sets fitted with a tilt system were inherited by XC, but the tilt equipment has now been isolated. All but one of the Class 221s are five-car sets and when possible these are rostered for the more heavily used services. Sets now sport a revised front end valance. With its standard class driving coach nearest the camera, set No. 221136 passes Dawlish on 8 August 2008 forming train 1S41, the 07.25 Plymouth to Edinburgh Waverley. Set No. 221141 is a four-car set and in the future another three four-car sets are likely to be formed by the reintroduction of off-lease driving cars of set No. 221144.* **CJM**

CrossRail

Passenger Train Operating Companies - CrossRail

Address:	✉ 6th Floor, St Mary Axe, London, EC3A 8NH
	✆ helpdesk@crossrail.co.uk
	✆ 03432 2211234
	① http://www.crossrail.co.uk
Managing Director:	Steve Murphy
Principal Routes:	Present - Liverpool Street - Shenfield
	Future - Reading to Shenfield / Abbey Wood, Heathrow spur
Depots:	Present - Ilford (IL)
	Future - Old Oak Common
Parent Company:	MTR Corporation (Crossrail) Limited (MTR)
	Transport for London

London
Liverpool Street   Shenfield

Stratford · Maryland · Forest Gate · Manor Park · Ilford · Seven Kings · Goodmayes · Chadwell Heath · Romford · Gidea Park · Harold Wood · Brentwood

Existing network, soon to be extended from Reading and Heathrow
in the west to Shenfield and Abbey Wood in the east.

© TRC.Com Ltd 2015

Class 315

Vehicle Length: (Driving) 64ft 11½in (19.80m)	Width: 9ft 3in (2.82m)
(Inter) 65ft 4½in (19.92m)	Horsepower: 880hp (656kW)
Height: 11ft 6½in (3.58m)	Seats (total/car): 318S, 74S/86S/84S/74S

Number	Formation DMSO(A)+TSO+PTSO+DMSO(B)	Depot	Livery	Owner	Operator	Name
315818	64495+71298+71406+64496	IL	CRO	EVL	CRO	
315819	64497+71299+71407+64498	IL	CRO	EVL	CRO	
315820	64499+71300+71408+64500	IL	CRO	EVL	CRO	
315821	64501+71301+71409+64502	IL	CRO	EVL	CRO	
315822	64503+71302+71410+64504	IL	CRO	EVL	CRO	
315823	64505+71303+71411+64506	IL	CRO	EVL	CRO	
315824	64507+71304+71412+64508	IL	CRO	EVL	CRO	
315825	64509+71305+71413+64510	IL	CRO	EVL	CRO	
315826	64511+71306+71414+64512	IL	CRO	EVL	CRO	
315827	64513+71307+71415+64514	IL	CRO	EVL	CRO	
315828	64515+71308+71416+64516	IL	CRO	EVL	CRO	
315829	64517+71309+71417+64518	IL	CRO	EVL	CRO	*London Borough of Havering Celebrating 40 Years*
315830	64519+71310+71418+64520	IL	CRO	EVL	CRO	
315831	64521+71311+71419+64522	IL	CRO	EVL	CRO	
315832	64523+71312+71420+64524	IL	CRO	EVL	CRO	
315833	64525+71313+71421+64526	IL	CRO	EVL	CRO	
315834	64527+71314+71422+64528	IL	CRO	EVL	CRO	
315835	64529+71315+71423+64530	IL	CRO	EVL	CRO	
315836	64531+71316+71424+64532	IL	CRO	EVL	CRO	
315837	64533+71317+71425+64534	IL	CRO	EVL	CRO	
315838	64535+71318+71426+64536	IL	CRO	EVL	CRO	
315839	64537+71319+71427+64538	IL	CRO	EVL	CRO	
315840	64539+71320+71428+64540	IL	CRO	EVL	CRO	
315841	64541+71321+71429+64542	IL	CRO	EVL	CRO	
315842	64543+71322+71430+64544	IL	CRO	EVL	CRO	

315843	64545+71323+71431+64546	IL	CRO	EVL	CRO	
315844	64547+71324+71432+64548	IL	CRO	EVL	CRO	
315845	64549+71325+71433+64550	IL	CRO	EVL	CRO	
315846	64551+71326+71434+64552	IL	CRO	EVL	CRO	*Herbie Woodward*
315847	64553+71327+71435+64554	IL	CRO	EVL	CRO	
315848	64555+71328+71436+64556	IL	CRO	EVL	CRO	
315849	64557+71329+71437+64558	IL	CRO	EVL	CRO	
315850	64559+71330+71438+64560	IL	CRO	EVL	CRO	
315851	64561+71331+71439+64562	IL	CRO	EVL	CRO	
315852	64563+71332+71440+64564	IL	CRO	EVL	CRO	
315853	64565+71333+71441+64566	IL	CRO	EVL	CRO	
315854	64567+71334+71442+64568	IL	CRO	EVL	CRO	
315855	64569+71335+71443+64570	IL	CRO	EVL	CRO	
315856	64571+71336+71444+64572	IL	CRO	EVL	CRO	
315857	64573+71337+71445+64574	IL	CRO	EVL	CRO	
315858	64575+71338+71446+64576	IL	CRO	EVL	CRO	
315859	64577+71339+71447+64578	IL	CRO	EVL	CRO	
315860	64579+71340+71448+64580	IL	CRO	EVL	CRO	
315861	64581+71341+71449+64582	IL	CRO	EVL	CRO	

Right: *A fleet of 44 Class 315s is currently the operational fleet of Crossrail, based at Ilford and used on the London Liverpool Street to Shenfield route. These sets are scheduled to be withdrawn and replaced by Class 345s in 2018. Painted in Crossrail/TfL livery, Class 315 No. 315849 is illustrated.*
Nathan Williamson

Class 345

Vehicle Length: (Driving) - awaited	Width: - awaited
(Inter) - awaited	Horsepower:
Height: - awaited	Seats (total/car): 450S

A fleet of 66 nine-car Bombardier 'Aventra' EMUs, Nos. 345001-345066, is under construction to operate on the new CrossRail route from Reading/Heathrow in the west to Shenfield and Abbey Wood in the east via Central London - a route to be known as the Elizabeth Line. The first 15 sets to be delivered will be formed as seven-car units to allow operation into Liverpool Street until platform extensions are complete by 2019. Sets will then be reformed to their full length.

Number	Formation	Depot	Livery	Owner	Operator
	DMSO(A)+PMSO(A)+MSO+MSO+TSO+MSO+MSO+PMSO+DMSO(B)				
345001	340101+340201+340301+340401+340501+340601+340701+340801+340901	OC	CRO	TFL	CRO
345002	340102+340202+340302+340402+340502+340602+340702+340802+340902	OC	CRO	TFL	CRO
345003	340103+340203+340303+340403+340503+340603+340703+340803+340903	OC	CRO	TFL	CRO
345004	340104+340204+340304+340404+340504+340604+340704+340804+340904	OC	CRO	TFL	CRO
345005	340105+340205+340305+340405+340505+340605+340705+340805+340905	OC	CRO	TFL	CRO
345006	340106+340206+340306+340406+340506+340606+340706+340806+340906	OC	CRO	TFL	CRO
345007	340107+340207+340307+340407+340507+340607+340707+340807+340907	OC	CRO	TFL	CRO
345008	340108+340208+340308+340408+340508+340608+340708+340808+340908	OC	CRO	TFL	CRO
345009	340109+340209+340309+340409+340509+340609+340709+340809+340909	OC	CRO	TFL	CRO
345010	340110+340210+340310+340410+340510+340610+340710+340810+340910	OC	CRO	TFL	CRO
345011	340111+340211+340311+340411+340511+340611+340711+340811+340911	OC	CRO	TFL	CRO
345012	340112+340212+340312+340412+340512+340612+340712+340812+340912	OC	CRO	TFL	CRO
345013	340113+340213+340313+340413+340513+340613+340713+340813+340913	OC	CRO	TFL	CRO
345014	340114+340214+340314+340414+340514+340614+340714+340814+340914	OC	CRO	TFL	CRO
345015	340115+340215+340315+340415+340515+340615+340715+340815+340915	OC	CRO	TFL	CRO
345016	340116+340216+340316+340416+340516+340616+340716+340816+340916	OC	CRO	TFL	CRO
345017	340117+340217+340317+340417+340517+340617+340717+340817+340917	OC	CRO	TFL	CRO
345018	340118+340218+340318+340418+340518+340618+340718+340818+340918	OC	CRO	TFL	CRO
345019	340119+340219+340319+340419+340519+340619+340719+340819+340919	OC	CRO	TFL	CRO

Cross Rail

345020	340120+340220+340320+340420+340520+340620+340720+340820+340920	OC	CRO	TFL	CRO
345021	340121+340221+340321+340421+340521+340621+340721+340821+340921	OC	CRO	TFL	CRO
345022	340122+340222+340322+340422+340522+340622+340722+340822+340922	OC	CRO	TFL	CRO
345023	340123+340223+340323+340423+340523+340623+340723+340823+340923	OC	CRO	TFL	CRO
345024	340124+340224+340324+340424+340524+340624+340724+340824+340924	OC	CRO	TFL	CRO
345025	340125+340225+340325+340425+340525+340625+340725+340825+340925	OC	CRO	TFL	CRO
345026	340126+340226+340326+340426+340526+340626+340726+340826+340926	OC	CRO	TFL	CRO
345027	340127+340227+340327+340427+340527+340627+340727+340827+340927	OC	CRO	TFL	CRO
345028	340128+340228+340328+340428+340528+340628+340728+340828+340928	OC	CRO	TFL	CRO
345029	340129+340229+340329+340429+340529+340629+340729+340829+340929	OC	CRO	TFL	CRO
345030	340130+340230+340330+340430+340530+340630+340730+340830+340930	OC	CRO	TFL	CRO
345031	340131+340231+340331+340431+340531+340631+340731+340831+340931	OC	CRO	TFL	CRO
345032	340132+340232+340332+340432+340532+340632+340732+340832+340932	OC	CRO	TFL	CRO
345033	340133+340233+340333+340433+340533+340633+340733+340833+340933	OC	CRO	TFL	CRO
345034	340134+340234+340334+340434+340534+340634+340734+340834+340934	OC	CRO	TFL	CRO
345035	340135+340235+340335+340435+340535+340635+340735+340835+340935	OC	CRO	TFL	CRO
345036	340136+340236+340336+340436+340536+340636+340736+340836+340936	OC	CRO	TFL	CRO
345037	340137+340237+340337+340437+340537+340637+340737+340837+340937	OC	CRO	TFL	CRO
345038	340138+340238+340338+340438+340538+340638+340738+340838+340938	OC	CRO	TFL	CRO
345039	340139+340239+340339+340439+340539+340639+340739+340839+340939	OC	CRO	TFL	CRO
345040	340140+340240+340340+340440+340540+340640+340740+340840+340940	OC	CRO	TFL	CRO
345041	340141+340241+340341+340441+340541+340641+340741+340841+340941	OC	CRO	TFL	CRO
345042	340142+340242+340342+340442+340542+340642+340742+340842+340942	OC	CRO	TFL	CRO
345043	340143+340243+340343+340443+340543+340643+340743+340843+340943	OC	CRO	TFL	CRO
345044	340144+340244+340344+340444+340544+340644+340744+340844+340944	OC	CRO	TFL	CRO
345045	340145+340245+340345+340445+340545+340645+340745+340845+340945	OC	CRO	TFL	CRO
345046	340146+340246+340346+340446+340546+340646+340746+340846+340946	OC	CRO	TFL	CRO
345047	340147+340247+340347+340447+340547+340647+340747+340847+340947	OC	CRO	TFL	CRO
345048	340148+340248+340348+340448+340548+340648+340748+340848+340948	OC	CRO	TFL	CRO
345049	340149+340249+340349+340449+340549+340649+340749+340849+340949	OC	CRO	TFL	CRO
345050	340150+340250+340350+340450+340550+340650+340750+340850+340950	OC	CRO	TFL	CRO

345051	340151+340251+340351+340451+340551+340651+340751+340851+340951	OC	CRO	TFL	CRO
345052	340152+340252+340352+340452+340552+340652+340752+340852+340952	OC	CRO	TFL	CRO
345053	340153+340253+340353+340453+340553+340653+340753+340853+340953	OC	CRO	TFL	CRO
345054	340154+340254+340354+340454+340554+340654+340754+340854+340954	OC	CRO	TFL	CRO
345055	340155+340255+340355+340455+340555+340655+340755+340855+340955	OC	CRO	TFL	CRO
345056	340156+340256+340356+340456+340556+340656+340756+340856+340956	OC	CRO	TFL	CRO
345057	340157+340257+340357+340457+340557+340657+340757+340857+340957	OC	CRO	TFL	CRO
345058	340158+340258+340358+340458+340558+340658+340758+340858+340958	OC	CRO	TFL	CRO
345059	340159+340259+340359+340459+340559+340659+340759+340859+340959	OC	CRO	TFL	CRO
345060	340160+340260+340360+340460+340560+340660+340760+340860+340960	OC	CRO	TFL	CRO
345061	340161+340261+340361+340461+340561+340661+340761+340861+340961	OC	CRO	TFL	CRO
345062	340162+340262+340362+340462+340562+340662+340762+340862+340962	OC	CRO	TFL	CRO
345063	340163+340263+340363+340463+340563+340663+340763+340863+340963	OC	CRO	TFL	CRO
345064	340164+340264+340364+340464+340564+340664+340764+340864+340964	OC	CRO	TFL	CRO
345065	340165+340265+340365+340465+340565+340665+340765+340865+340965	OC	CRO	TFL	CRO
345066	340166+340266+340366+340466+340566+340666+340766+340866+340966	OC	CRO	TFL	CRO

Left: *The 66-strong nine-car Class 345 fleet, comprising 594 vehicles, is being built at Bombardier Derby Litchurch Lane Works, with production now well under way. The first set, No. 345001, illustrated on the Derby Works test track, was delivered to the vehicle testing facility at Old Dalby in mid-2016. These are the first trains to take advantage of new legislation that does not require a yellow front end on new rolling stock.* **CJM**

Right ppper: *The front end of the Class 345 is very different from what we have seen before, with very European styling using a single large front window. Two light clusters are positioned either side of a central horn grille, while the coupling is of the Dellner type.* **Richard Tuplin**

Right lower: *Passenger accommodation is a mix of groups and longitudinal, very much like London Underground longer-distance stock. Three pairs of bi-parting sliding doors are on each side of each vehicle. A full nine-car set has seating for 450 with standing room for well over 1,000.* **Richard Tuplin**

East Midlands Trains

Address: ✉ 1 Prospect Place, Millennium Way, Pride Park, Derby, DE24 8HG
✍ getintouch@eastmidlandstrains.co.uk
✆ 08457 125678
ⓘ www.eastmidlandstrains.co.uk

Managing Director: Jake Kelly
Franchise Dates: 11 November 2007 - October 2017
Principal Routes: St Pancras - Sheffield/York/Leeds/Nottingham
Norwich/Skegness/Cleethorpes - Nottingham/Crewe/
Liverpool and Matlock
Depots: Derby (DY), Nottingham (NM), Neville Hill (NL)
Parent Company: Stagecoach Group

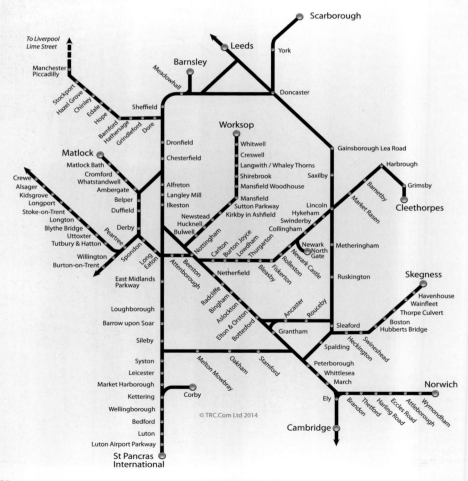

Class 08

Vehicle Length: 29ft 3in (8.91m)			Engine: English Electric 6K			
Height: 12ft 8⅜in (3.87m)			Horsepower: 400hp (298kW)			
Width: 8ft 6in (2.59m)			Electrical Equipment: English Electric			

Number	Depot	Pool	Livery	Owner	Operator	Name
08525	NL	EMSL	EMT	EMT	EMT	Duncan Bedford
08690	NL	EMSL	EMT	EMT	EMT	David Thirkill
08899	DY	EMSL	MAR	EMT	EMT	Midland Counties Railway 175 1839-2014
08908	DY	EMSL	EMT	EMT	EMT	Ivan Stephenson
08950	NL	EMSL	EMT	EMT	EMT	David Lightfoot

Right: *East Midlands Trains requires pilot locos for its depots at Leeds Neville Hill and Derby Etches Park, and for this a fleet of five Class 08s is maintained and can be found at either depot. Four of the fleet are painted in EMT colours, while No. 08899 is painted in Midland Counties maroon and named* Midland Counties Railway 175 1839-2014. *The loco is illustrated from its cab end at Derby.* **Antony Christie**

Class 43 – HST

Vehicle Length: 58ft 5in (18.80m)		Engine: Paxman VP185	
Height: 12ft 10in (3.90m)		Horsepower: 2,100hp (1,565kW)	
Width: 8ft 11in (2.73m)		Electrical Equipment: Brush	

Number	Depot	Pool	Livery	Owner	Operator
43043	NL	EMPC	SCE	PTR	EMT
43044	NL	EMPC	SCE	PTR	EMT
43045	NL	EMPC	SCE	PTR	EMT
43046	NL	EMPC	SCE	PTR	EMT
43047	NL	EMPC	SCE	PTR	EMT
43048	NL	EMPC	SCE	PTR	EMT
43049	NL	EMPC	SCE	PTR	EMT
43050	NL	EMPC	SCE	PTR	EMT
43052	NL	EMPC	SCE	PTR	EMT
43054	NL	EMPC	SCE	PTR	EMT
43055	NL	EMPC	SCE	PTR	EMT
43058	NL	EMPC	SCE	PTR	EMT
43059	NL	EMPC	SCE	PTR	EMT
43060	NL	EMPC	SCE	PTR	EMT
43061	NL	EMPC	SCE	PTR	EMT
43064	NL	EMPC	SCE	PTR	EMT
43066	NL	EMPC	SCE	PTR	EMT
43073	NL	EMPC	SCE	PTR	EMT
43075	NL	EMPC	SCE	PTR	EMT
43076	NL	EMPC	SCE	PTR	EMT
43081	NL	EMPC	SCE	PTR	EMT
43082	NL	EMPC	SCE	PTR	EMT
43083	NL	EMPC	SCE	PTR	EMT
43089	NL	EMPC	SCE	PTR	EMT

Names applied

43045	EMT Customer Service Week #TrainWatch
43048	T. C. B Miller MBE
43049	Neville Hill
43055	The Sheffield Star 125 Years
43061	The Fearless Foxes
43076	In Support of Help for Heroes
43082	Railway Children The Voice for Street Children Worldwide

Right: *A fleet of 24 Class 43 power cars is allocated to Leeds Neville Hill depot and operates prime main-line services on the London St Pancras International to Nottingham and Sheffield route. These power cars still have their Paxman VP185 prime movers and were not part of the Brush refurbishment project to install MTU engines. All are painted in Stagecoach/ EMT blue livery. No. 43046 is seen leading a northbound service near Wellingborough.* **Antony Christie**

East Midlands Trains

Class 153

Vehicle Length: 76ft 5in (23.29m)	Engine: 1 x NT855R5 of 285hp
Height: 12ft 3⅛in (3.75m)	Horsepower: 285hp (213kW)
Width: 8ft 10in (2.70m)	Seats (total/car): 66S

Number	Formation DMSL	Depot	Livery	Owner	Operator
153302	52302	NM	EMT	ANG	EMT
153308	52308	NM	EMT	ANG	EMT
153310	52310	NM	EMT	PTR	EMT
153311	52311	NM	EMT	PTR	EMT
153313	52313	NM	EMT	PTR	EMT
153319	52319	NM	EMT	ANG	EMT
153321	52321	NM	EMT	PTR	EMT
153326	52326	NM	EMT	PTR	EMT
153355	57355	NM	EMT	ANG	EMT
153357	57357	NM	EMT	ANG	EMT
153374	57374	NM	EMT	ANG	EMT
153376	57376	NM	EMT	PTR	EMT
153379	57379	NM	EMT	PTR	EMT
153381	57381	NM	EMT	PTR	EMT
153383	57383	NM	EMT	PTR	EMT
153384	57384	NM	EMT	PTR	EMT
153385	57385	NM	EMT	PTR	EMT

Name applied
153376   X-24 Expeditious

Left: A fleet of 17 single-car Class 153s is on the books of EMT and used on rural and branch lines. The vehicles carry Stagecoach outer-suburban blue livery with red/orange swirls at vehicle ends. Passenger doors are finished in yellow. No. 153376 is seen at Doncaster from its original 'large' cab end. **CJM**

Class 156

Vehicle Length: 75ft 6in (23.03m)	Engine: 1 x Cummins NT855R5 of 285hp
Height: 12ft 6in (3.81m)	Horsepower: 570hp (425kW)
Width: 8ft 11in (2.73m)	Seats (total/car): 148S, 72S/76S

Number	Formation DMSL+DMS	Depot	Livery	Owner	Operator
156401	52401+57401	NM	EMT	PTR	EMT
156403	52403+57403	NM	EMT	PTR	EMT
156404	52404+57404	NM	EMT	PTR	EMT
156405	52405+57405	NM	EMT	PTR	EMT
156406	52406+57406	NM	EMT	PTR	EMT
156408	52408+57408	NM	EMT	PTR	EMT
156410	52410+57410	NM	EMT	PTR	EMT
156411	52411+57411	NM	EMT	PTR	EMT
156413	52413+57413	NM	EMT	PTR	EMT
156414	52414+57414	NM	EMT	PTR	EMT
156415	52415+57415	NM	EMT	PTR	EMT
156470	52470+57470	NM	EMT	PTR	EMT
156473	52473+57473	NM	EMT	PTR	EMT
156497	52497+57497	NM	EMT	PTR	EMT
156498	52498+57498	NM	EMT	PTR	EMT

Below: *Medium- to long-distance East Midlands Trains services are formed of Class 156 stock, with a fleet of 15 units based at Nottingham Eastcroft. These sets have low-density 2+2 seating with accommodation for 148 standard class passengers. Set No. 156413 is shown at Nottingham.* **CJM**

Name applied
156404   EMT Customer Service Week #TrainWatch

Class 158

Vehicle Length: 76ft 1¾in (23.21m)	Engine: 158770-813 - 1 x Cummins NT855R5 of 350hp
Height: 12ft 6in (3.81m)	Horsepower: 700hp (522kW)
Width: 9ft 3¼in (2.82m)	Engine: 158846-862 - 1 x Perkins 2006TWH of 350hp
	Horsepower: 700hp (522kW)
	Engine: 158863-866 - 1 x Cummins NT855R5 of 400hp
	Horsepower: 800hp (597kW)
	Seats (total/car): 146S - 74S, 72S

Number	Formation DMSL+DMSL	Depot	Livery	Owner	Operator	Number		Depot	Livery	Owner	Operator
						158813	52813+57813	NM	SCE	PTR	EMT
158770	52770+57770	NM	SCE	PTR	EMT	158846	52846+57846	NM	SCE	ANG	EMT
158773	52773+57773	NM	SCE	PTR	EMT	158847	52847+57847	NM	SCE	ANG	EMT
158774	52774+57774	NM	SCE	PTR	EMT	158852	52852+57852	NM	SCE	ANG	EMT
158777	52777+57777	NM	SCE	PTR	EMT	158854	52854+57854	NM	SCE	ANG	EMT
158780	52780+57780	NM	SCE	ANG	EMT	158856	52856+57856	NM	SCE	ANG	EMT
158783	52783+57783	NM	SCE	ANG	EMT	158857	52857+57857	NM	SCE	ANG	EMT
158785	52785+57785	NM	SCE	ANG	EMT	158858	52858+57858	NM	SCE	ANG	EMT
158788	52788+57788	NM	SCE	ANG	EMT	158862	52862+57862	NM	SCE	ANG	EMT
158799	52799+57799	NM	SCE	PTR	EMT	158863	52863+57863	NM	SCE	ANG	EMT
158806	52806+57806	NM	SCE	PTR	EMT	158864	52864+57864	NM	SCE	ANG	EMT
158810	52810+57810	NM	SCE	PTR	EMT	158865	52865+57865	NM	SCE	ANG	EMT
158812	52812+57812	NM	SCE	PTR	EMT	158866	52866+57866	NM	SCE	ANG	EMT
						158889	52808+57808	NM	SCE	PTR	EMT

Names applied
178773   **Eastcroft Depot**
158847   **Lincoln Castle Explorer**

Below: *A fleet of 26 two-car Class 158s operates from Nottingham Eastcroft on EMT long-distance domestic services. These sets are painted in Stagecoach mainline white livery. Set No. 158773 Eastcroft Depot is shown.* **CJM**

Class 222

Vehicle Length: 77ft 6in (23.62m)	Horsepower: 5,250hp (3,914kW)
Height: 12ft 4in (3.75m)	Seats (total/car): 106F/236S
Width: 8ft 11in (2.73m)	38S/68S/68S/62S/42F/42F/22F
Engine: 1 x Cummins QSK9R of 750hp per vehicle	

Number	Formation DMS+MS+MS+MSRMB+MF+MF+DMRFO	Depot	Livery	Owner	Op'r	Name
222001	60161+60551+60561+60621+60341+60445+60241	DY	SCE	EVL	EMT	*The Entrepreneur Express*
222002	60162+60544+60562+60622+60342+60346+60242	DY	SCE	EVL	EMT	*The Cutlers' Company*
222003	60163+60553+60563+60623+60343+60446+60243	DY	SCE	EVL	EMT	*Tornado*
222004	60164+60554+60564+60624+60344+60345+60244	DY	SCE	EVL	EMT	*Childrens Hospital Sheffield*
222005	60165+60555+60565+60625+60443+60347+60245	DY	SCE	EVL	EMT	
222006	60166+60556+60566+60626+60441+60447+60246	DY	SCE	EVL	EMT	*The Carbon Cutter*

Vehicle Length: 77ft 6in (23.62m)	Horsepower: 3,750hp (2,796kW)
Height: 12ft 4in (3.75m)	Seats (total/car): 50F/190S
Width: 8ft 11in (2.73m)	38S/68S/62S/28F-22S/22F
Engine: 1 x Cummins QSK9R of 750hp per vehicle	

Number	Formation DMS+MS+MSRMB+MC+DMRFO	Depot	Livery	Owner	Operator	Name
222007	60167+60567+60627+60442+60247	DY	SCE	EVL	EMT	
222008	60168+60545+60628+60918+60248	DY	SCE	EVL	EMT	*Derby Etches Park*
222009	60169+60557+60629+60919+60249	DY	SCE	EVL	EMT	
222010	60170+60546+60630+60920+60250	DY	SCE	EVL	EMT	
222011	60171+60531+60631+60921+60251	DY	SCE	EVL	EMT	*Sheffield City Battalion 1914 - 1918*
222012	60172+60532+60632+60922+60252	DY	SCE	EVL	EMT	

Passenger Train Operating Companies - East Midlands Trains

East Midlands Trains

222013	60173+60536+60633+60923+60253	DY	SCE	EVL	EMT
222014	60174+60534+60634+60924+60254	DY	SCE	EVL	EMT
222015	60175+60535+60635+60925+60255	DY	SCE	EVL	EMT
222016	60176+60533+60636+60926+60256	DY	SCE	EVL	EMT
222017	60177+60537+60637+60927+60257	DY	SCE	EVL	EMT
222018	60178+60444+60638+60928+60258	DY	SCE	EVL	EMT
222019	60179+60547+60639+60929+60259	DY	SCE	EVL	EMT
222020	60180+60543+60640+60930+60260	DY	SCE	EVL	EMT
222021	60181+60552+60641+60931+60261	DY	SCE	EVL	EMT
222022	60182+60542+60642+60932+60262	DY	SCE	EVL	EMT
222023	60183+60541+60643+60933+60263	DY	SCE	EVL	EMT

175 Years of Derby's Railways 1839-2014

Invest in Nottingham

Left: *Operating alongside the EMT HST fleet are 23 Class 222/0 sets formed of either seven or five vehicles. These Bombardier-built sets, based on the Virgin Voyager design, are painted in Stagecoach/EMT main-line white livery with traditional swirl driving car ends. Five-car set No. 222019 is illustrated.* **Antony Christie**

Class 222/1

Vehicle Length: 77ft 6in (23.62m)	Horsepower: 3,000hp (2,237kW)
Height: 12ft 4in (3.75m)	Seats (total/car): 33F/148S
Width: 8ft 11in (2.73m)	22F/11F-46S/62S/40S
Engine: 1 x Cummins OSK9R of 750hp per vehicle	

Number	Formation DMF+MC+MSRMB+DMS	Depot	Livery	Owner	Operator
222101	60271+60571+60681+60191	DY	SCE	EVL	EMT
222102	60272+60572+60682+60192	DY	SCE	EVL	EMT
222103	60273+60573+60683+60193	DY	SCE	EVL	EMT
222104	60274+60574+60684+60194	DY	SCE	EVL	EMT

Below: *Originally used by Hull Trains, the four Class 222/1 four-car sets now operate on EMT. They have been refurbished to Class 22/0 style and operate as a core fleet. No. 222103 is illustrated at Derby.* **Antony Christie**

Class 374 (e320)

Vehicle Length: Car 1 - 26.075m, Car 2-8 - 24.775m. Train length (8-car) 199.46m
Height: Details awaited   Width: Details awaited
Horsepower: 25kV ac operation - 21,000hp (16,000kW) 3,000V dc, 1,500V dc tba
Seats (total/car): 107F/336S, 40F/36F/31F/76S/76S/76S/76S/32S (half train)
Electrical Equipment: Siemens

Set Number	Formation eight vehicles [half-set] DM, T, M, T, T, M, T, M	Depot	Livery	Owner	Operator
374001	93-70-3740-011 GB-EIL – 93-70-3740-018 GB-EIL	TI	EUN	EUS	EUS
374002	93-70-3740-021 GB-EIL – 93-70-3740-028 GB-EIL	TI	EUN	EUS	EUS
374003	93-70-3740-031 GB-EIL – 93-70-3740-038 GB-EIL	TI	EUN	EUS	EUS
374004	93-70-3740-041 GB-EIL – 93-70-3740-048 GB-EIL	TI	EUN	EUS	EUS
374005	93-70-3740-051 GB-EIL – 93-70-3740-058 GB-EIL	TI	EUN	EUS	EUS
374006	93-70-3740-061 GB-EIL – 93-70-3740-068 GB-EIL	TI	EUN	EUS	EUS
374007	93-70-3740-071 GB-EIL – 93-70-3740-078 GB-EIL	TI	EUN	EUS	EUS
374008	93-70-3740-081 GB-EIL – 93-70-3740-088 GB-EIL	TI	EUN	EUS	EUS

Eurostar

374009	93-70-3740-091 GB-EIL – 93-70-3740-098 GB-EIL	TI	EUN	EUS	EUS
374010	93-70-3740-101 GB-EIL – 93-70-3740-108 GB-EIL	TI	EUN	EUS	EUS
374011	93-70-3740-111 GB-EIL – 93-70-3740-118 GB-EIL	TI	EUN	EUS	EUS
374012	93-70-3740-121 GB-EIL – 93-70-3740-128 GB-EIL	TI	EUN	EUS	EUS
374013	93-70-3740-131 GB-EIL – 93-70-3740-138 GB-EIL	TI	EUN	EUS	EUS
374014	93-70-3740-141 GB-EIL – 93-70-3740-148 GB-EIL	TI	EUN	EUS	EUS
374015	93-70-3740-151 GB-EIL – 93-70-3740-158 GB-EIL	TI	EUN	EUS	EUS
374016	93-70-3740-161 GB-EIL – 93-70-3740-168 GB-EIL	TI	EUN	EUS	EUS
374017	93-70-3740-171 GB-EIL – 93-70-3740-178 GB-EIL	TI	EUN	EUS	EUS
374018	93-70-3740-181 GB-EIL – 93-70-3740-188 GB-EIL	TI	EUN	EUS	EUS
374019	93-70-3740-191 GB-EIL – 93-70-3740-198 GB-EIL	TI	EUN	EUS	EUS
374020	93-70-3740-201 GB-EIL – 93-70-3740-208 GB-EIL	TI	EUN	EUS	EUS
374021	93-70-3740-211 GB-EIL – 93-70-3740-218 GB-EIL	TI	EUN	EUS	EUS
374022	93-70-3740-221 GB-EIL – 93-70-3740-228 GB-EIL	TI	EUN	EUS	EUS
374023	93-70-3740-231 GB-EIL – 93-70-3740-238 GB-EIL	TI	EUN	EUS	EUS
374024	93-70-3740-241 GB-EIL – 93-70-3740-248 GB-EIL	TI	EUN	EUS	EUS
374025	93-70-3740-251 GB-EIL – 93-70-3740-258 GB-EIL	TI	EUN	EUS	EUS
374026	93-70-3740-261 GB-EIL – 93-70-3740-268 GB-EIL	TI	EUN	EUS	EUS
374027	93-70-3740-271 GB-EIL – 93-70-3740-278 GB-EIL *(under commissioning)*	TI	EUN	EUS	EUS
374028	93-70-3740-281 GB-EIL – 93-70-3740-288 GB-EIL *(under commissioning)*	TI	EUN	EUS	EUS
374029	93-70-3740-291 GB-EIL – 93-70-3740-298 GB-EIL *(under commissioning)*	TI	EUN	EUS	EUS
374030	93-70-3740-301 GB-EIL – 93-70-3740-308 GB-EIL *(under commissioning)*	TI	EUN	EUS	EUS
374031	93-70-3740-311 GB-EIL – 93-70-3740-318 GB-EIL *(under commissioning)*	TI	EUN	EUS	EUS
374032	93-70-3740-321 GB-EIL – 93-70-3740-328 GB-EIL *(under commissioning)*	TI	EUN	EUS	EUS
374033	93-70-3740-331 GB-EIL – 93-70-3740-338 GB-EIL *(under commissioning)*	TI	EUN	EUS	EUS
374034	93-70-3740-341 GB-EIL – 93-70-3740-348 GB-EIL *(under commissioning)*	TI	EUN	EUS	EUS

Above: *The new Siemens 'Velaro' Class 374 Eurostar sets are 16-coach formations, capable of carrying some 900 passengers. The sets, still on delivery, are based at Temple Mills and will eventually take over all Eurostar services. Led by half-set No. 4011 with set No. 4012 on the rear, a Eurostar train is seen on HS1 in Kent.* **Jamie Squibbs**

Class 08

Vehicle Length: 29ft 3in (8.91m)	*Engine: English Electric 6K*
Height: 12ft 8⅝in (3.87m)	*Horsepower: 400hp (298kW)*
Width: 8ft 6in (2.59m)	*Electrical Equipment: English Electric*

Number	Depot	Pool	Livery	Owner	Operator
08948	TI	GPSS	TTG	EUS	EUS

Great Western Railway

Address:	✉ Milford House, 1 Milford Street, Swindon, SN1 1HL
	✍ gwrfeedback@gwr.com
	☎ 08457 000125 ⓘ www.gwr.com
Managing Director:	Mark Hopwood
Franchise Dates:	1 April 2006 - Extension to April 2019
Principal Routes:	Paddington - Penzance/Paignton, Bristol, Swansea
	Thames Valley local lines, to Worcester, Hereford and Gloucester
	Local lines in Bristol, Exeter, Plymouth and Cornwall
	Bristol - Weymouth, Portsmouth/Brighton/Great Malvern
Depots:	Exeter (EX), Old Oak Common (OO), Laira (LA), Landore (LE),
	St Philip's Marsh (PM), Penzance (PZ), Reading (RG)
Parent Company:	First Group PLC

Class 08

Vehicle Length: 29ft 3in (8.91m)	Engine: English Electric 6K
Height: 12ft 8⅜in (3.87m)	Horsepower: 400hp (298kW)
Width: 8ft 6in (2.59m)	Electrical Equipment: English Electric

Number	Depot	Pool	Livery	Owner	Operator
08410	LA	EFSH	GRN	FGP	GWR
08483	OO	EFSH	BLK	FGP	GWR
08641	PZ	EFSH	BLU	FGP	GWR
08644	PZ	EFSH	BLU	FGP	GWR
08645	LA	EFSH	GRY	FGP	GWR
08663	PM	EFSH	BLU	FGP	GWR
08795	LE	EFSH	BLK	FGP	GWR
08822	LE	EFSH	ICS	FGP	GWR
08836	OC	EFSH	GWG	FGP	GWR

Names applied

08483	*Neil Morgan 1964-2014 Team Leader OOC*
08644	*Laira Diesel Depot 50 years 1962-2012*
08645	*Mike Baggott*
08663	*St Silas*
08822	*Dave Mills*

Below: *With sizeable depots at Penzance, Plymouth (Laira), Bristol (St Philip's Marsh), Landore (Swansea) and Old Oak Common (London), Great Western has a need for several Class 08 pilot locos. In 2017 nine locos are on the company books and are painted in a number of different heritage or current GWR liveries and many carry cast names. No. 08663* St Silas *carried 1970s BR rail blue with wasp ends and is seen in mid-2016 at Bristol St Philip's Marsh depot.* **Antony Christie**

Passenger Train Operating Companies - Great Western Railway

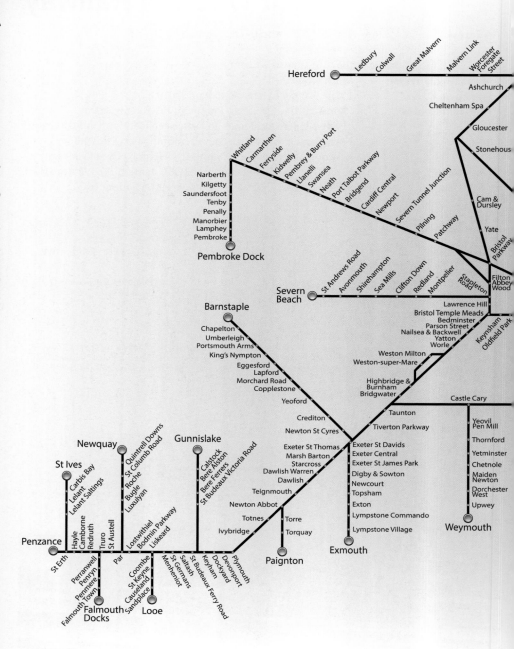

Passenger Train Operating Companies - Great Western Railway

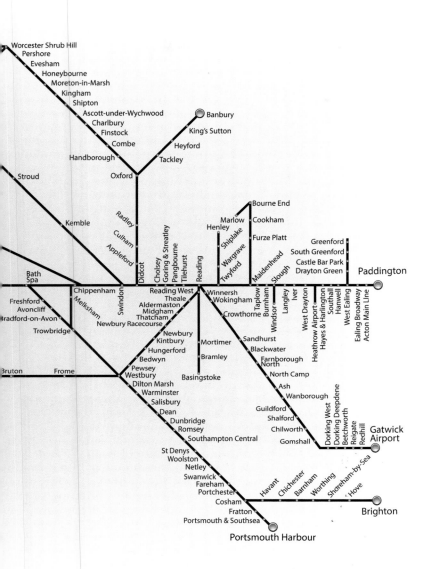

Worcester Shrub Hill
Pershore
Evesham
Honeybourne
Moreton-in-Marsh
Kingham
Shipton
Ascott-under-Wychwood
Charlbury
Finstock
Combe
Handborough
Oxford
Stroud
Kemble
Radley
Culham
Appleford
Bath Spa
Chippenham
Melksham
Swindon
Didcot
Cholsey
Goring & Streatley
Pangbourne
Tilehurst
Reading
Freshford
Avoncliff
Bradford-on-Avon
Trowbridge
Newbury
Kintbury
Hungerford
Bedwyn
Pewsey
Westbury
Dilton Marsh
Warminster
Salisbury
Dean
Dunbridge
Romsey
Southampton Central
Bruton
Frome
Basingstoke
Banbury
King's Sutton
Heyford
Tackley
Bourne End
Marlow
Henley
Shiplake
Wargrave
Twyford
Cookham
Furze Platt
Maidenhead
Slough
Greenford
South Greenford
Castle Bar Park
Drayton Green
Paddington
Reading West
Theale
Aldermaston
Midgham
Thatcham
Newbury Racecourse
Winnersh
Wokingham
Crowthorne
Taplow
Burnham
Windsor
Langley
Iver
West Drayton
Heathrow Airport
Hayes & Harlington
Southall
Hanwell
West Ealing
Ealing Broadway
Acton Main Line
Mortimer
Bramley
Sandhurst
Blackwater
Farnborough North
North Camp
Ash
Wanborough
Guildford
Shalford
Chilworth
Gomshall
Dorking West
Dorking Deepdene
Betchworth
Reigate
Redhill
Gatwick Airport
St Denys
Woolston
Netley
Swanwick
Fareham
Portchester
Cosham
Fratton
Portsmouth & Southsea
Havant
Chichester
Barnham
Worthing
Shoreham-by-Sea
Hove
Brighton
Portsmouth Harbour

Great Western Railway

Class 43 – HST

Vehicle Length: 58ft 5in (18.80m)		Engine: MTU 16V4000 R41R
Height: 12ft 10in (3.90m)		Horsepower: 2,250hp (1,680kW)
Width: 8ft 11in (2.73m)		Electrical Equipment: Brush

Number	Depot	Pool	Livery	Owner	Operator	Number	Depot	Pool	Livery	Owner	Operator
43002	LA	EFPC	SPL	ANG	GWR	43042	LE	EFPC	FGB	ANG	GWR
43003	LA	EFPC	FGB	ANG	GWR	43053	LE	EFPC	FGB	PTR	GWR
43004	LA	EFPC	FGB	ANG	GWR	43056	LE	EFPC	FGB	PTR	GWR
43005	LA	EFPC	GWG	ANG	GWR	43063	LE	EFPC	FGB	PTR	GWR
43009	LA	EFPC	FGB	ANG	GWR	43069	LE	EFPC	FGB	PTR	GWR
43010	LA	EFPC	FGB	ANG	GWR	43070	LE	EFPC	FGB	PTR	GWR
43012	LA	EFPC	FGB	ANG	GWR	43071	LE	EFPC	FGB	PTR	GWR
43015	LA	EFPC	FGB	ANG	GWR	43078	LE	EFPC	FGB	PTR	GWR
43016	LA	EFPC	FGB	ANG	GWR	43079	LE	EFPC	FGB	PTR	GWR
43017	LA	EFPC	FGB	ANG	GWR	43086	LE	EFPC	FGB	PTR	GWR
43018	LA	EFPC	FGB	ANG	GWR	43087	LE	EFPC	FGB	PTR	GWR
43020	LA	EFPC	FGB	ANG	GWR	43088	LE	EFPC	FGB	PTR	GWR
43021	LA	EFPC	FGB	ANG	GWR	43091	LE	EFPC	FGB	PTR	GWR
43022	LA	EFPC	FGB	ANG	GWR	43092	LE	EFPC	FGB	PTR	GWR
43023	LA	EFPC	FGB	ANG	GWR	43093	LE	EFPC	FGB	PTR	GWR
43024	LA	EFPC	FGB	ANG	GWR	43094	LE	EFPC	FGB	PTR	GWR
43025	LA	EFPC	FGB	ANG	GWR	43097	LE	EFPC	FGB	PTR	GWR
43026	LA	EFPC	FGB	ANG	GWR	43098	LE	EFPC	FGB	PTR	GWR
43027	LA	EFPC	FGA¶	ANG	GWR	43122	LE	EFPC	FGB	FGP	GWR
43028	LA	EFPC	FGB	ANG	GWR	43124	LE	EFPC	FGB	ANG	GWR
43029	LA	EFPC	FGB	ANG	GWR	43125	LE	EFPC	FGB	ANG	GWR
43030	LA	EFPC	FGB	ANG	GWR	43126	LE	EFPC	FGB	ANG	GWR
43031	LA	EFPC	FGB	ANG	GWR	43127	LE	EFPC	FGB	ANG	GWR
43032	LA	EFPC	FGB	ANG	GWR	43128	LE	EFPC	FGB	ANG	GWR
43033	LA	EFPC	FGB	ANG	GWR	43129	LE	EFPC	FGB	ANG	GWR
43034	LA	EFPC	FGB	ANG	GWR	43130	LE	EFPC	FGB	ANG	GWR
43035	LA	EFPC	FGB	ANG	GWR	43131	LE	EFPC	FGB	ANG	GWR
43036	LA	EFPC	FGB	ANG	GWR	43132	LE	EFPC	FGB	ANG	GWR
43037	LA	EFPC	FGB	ANG	GWR	43133	LE	EFPC	FGB	ANG	GWR
43040	LA	EFPC	FGB	ANG	GWR	43134	LE	EFPC	FGB	ANG	GWR
43041	LE	EFPC	GWG	ANG	GWR	43135	LE	EFPC	FGB	ANG	GWR
						43136	LE	EFPC	FGB	ANG	GWR

Below: *When this issue of the* abc Rail Guide *went to press in January 2017, Great Western still had a fleet of 119 Class 43s on its books, but this number is set to drop during the year as the first IEP trains enter service. Four Class 43s carry the latest GWR green livery, while No. 43002 has been returned to original yellow blue colours and 43185 carries 1980s InterCity 'Swallow' livery. Several others carry advertising colours. GWR green power cars Nos. 43187 and 43188 with HST set LA15 in like livery pass along the Dawlish sea wall in mid-2016.* **CJM**

43137	LE	EFPC	FGB	ANG	GWR	43168	OO	EFPC	FGB	ANG	GWR
43138	LE	EFPC	FGB	ANG	GWR	43169	OO	EFPC	FGB	ANG	GWR
43139	LE	EFPC	FGB	ANG	GWR	43170	OO	EFPC	FGB	ANG	GWR
43140	LE	EFPC	FGB	ANG	GWR	43171	OO	EFPC	FGB	ANG	GWR
43141	LE	EFPC	FGB	ANG	GWR	43172	OO	EFPC	SPL	ANG	GWR
43142	LE	EFPC	FGB	ANG	GWR	43174	OO	EFPC	FGB	ANG	GWR
43143	LE	EFPC	FGB	ANG	GWR	43175	OO	EFPC	FGB	ANG	GWR
43144	LE	EFPC	FGA±	ANG	GWR	43176	OO	EFPC	FGB	ANG	GWR
43145	LE	EFPC	FGB	ANG	GWR	43177	OO	EFPC	FGB	ANG	GWR
43146	LE	EFPC	FGA±	ANG	GWR	43179	OO	EFPC	FGB	ANG	GWR
43147	LE	EFPC	FGB	ANG	GWR	43180	OO	EFPC	FGB	PTR	GWR
43148	LE	EFPC	FGB	ANG	GWR	43181	OO	EFPC	FGB	ANG	GWR
43149	LE	EFPC	FGB	ANG	GWR	43182	OO	EFPC	FGB	ANG	GWR
43150	LE	EFPC	FGB	ANG	GWR	43183	OO	EFPC	FGB	ANG	GWR
43151	LE	EFPC	FGB	ANG	GWR	43185	OO	EFPC	ICS	ANG	GWR
43152	LE	EFPC	FGB	ANG	GWR	43186	OO	EFPC	FGB	ANG	GWR
43153	OO	EFPC	FGB	FGP	GWR	43187	OO	EFPC	GWR	ANG	GWR
43154	OO	EFPC	FGB	FGP	GWR	43188	OO	EFPC	GWR	ANG	GWR
43155	OO	EFPC	FGB	FGP	GWR	43189	OO	EFPC	FGB	ANG	GWR
43156	OO	EFPC	FGB	PTR	GWR	43190	OO	EFPC	FGB	ANG	GWR
43158	OO	EFPC	FGB	FGP	GWR	43191	OO	EFPC	FGB	ANG	GWR
43159	OO	EFPC	FGB	PTR	GWR	43192	OO	EFPC	FGB	ANG	GWR
43160	OO	EFPC	FGB	PTR	GWR	43193	OO	EFPC	FGB	PTR	GWR
43161	OO	EFPC	FGB	PTR	GWR	43194	OO	EFPC	FGB	FGP	GWR
43162	OO	EFPC	FGB	ANG	GWR	43195	OO	EFPC	FGB	PTR	GWR
43163	OO	EFPC	FGA§	ANG	GWR	43196	OO	EFPC	FGB	PTR	GWR
43164	OO	EFPC	FGB	ANG	GWR	43197	OO	EFPC	FGB	PTR	GWR
43165	OO	EFPC	FGB	ANG	GWR	43198	OO	EFPC	FGB	FGP	GWR

FGA§ - Visit Plymouth branding, FGA± - Building a Greater West branding, FGA¶ - 90 Glorious Years branding

Names applied

43002	*Sir Kenneth Grange*
43003	*Isambard Kingdom Brunel*
43004	*First for the Future / First ar gyfer y dyfodol*
43012	*Exeter Panel Signal Box 21st Anniversary 2009*
43017	*Hannahs discoverhannahs.org*
43020	*MTU Power Passion Partnership*
43021	*David Austin – Cartoonist*
43022	*The Duke of Edinburgh's Award Diamond Anniversary 1956-2016*
43023	*Sqn Ldr Harold Starr One of the Few*
43024	*Great Western Society 1961-2011 Didcot Railway Centre*
43025	*The Institution of Railway Operators*
43026	*Michael Eavis*
43030	*Christian Lewis Trust*
43033	*Driver Brian Cooper 15 June 1947 – 5 October 1999*
43037	*Penydarren*
43040	*Bristol St Philip's Marsh*
43041	*Meningitis Trust Support for Life*
43053	*University of Worcester*
43056	*The Royal British Legion*
43070	*The Corps of Royal Electrical and Mechanical Engineers*
43087	*11 Explosive Ordnance Disposal Regiment Royal Logistic Corps*
43097	*Environment Agency*
43127	*Sir Peter Parker 1924-2002 – Cotswold Line 150*
43132	*We Save the Children - Will You?*
43137	*Newton Abbot 150*
43139	*Driver Stan Martin 25 June 1960 – 6 November 2004*
43140	*Depo Diesel Glandŵr 1963 Dathlu 50 Mlynedd 2013 Landore Diesel Depot 1963 Celebrating 50 Years 2013*
43141	*Cardiff Panel Signal Box 1966-2016 / Blwch Signalau Panel Caerdydd 1966-2016*
43142	*Reading Panel Signal Box 1965 - 2010*
43143	*Stroud 700*
43147	*Royal Marines Celebrating 300 Years*
43149	*University of Plymouth*
43155	*The Red Arrows 50 Seasons of Excellence*
43156	*Dartington International Summer School*
43160	*Sir Moir Lockhead OBE*
43165	*Prince Michael of Kent*
43169	*The National Trust*
43172	*Harry Patch The last survivor of the trenches*
43175	*GWR 175th Anniversary*
43179	*Pride of Laira*
43185	*Great Western*
43189	*Railway Heritage Trust*
43198	*Oxfordshire 2007*

Right: *A number of GWR Class 43s carry cast nameplates, commemorating people or features/areas of the GW route. No. 43012 twins with Exeter Panel Signal Box, forming a bond between the TOC and Network Rail.* **CJM**

Exeter Panel Signal Box 21st Anniversary 2009

Great Western Railway

Class 57/6

Vehicle Length: 63ft 6in (19.38m)			Engine: EMD 645-12E3			
Height: 12ft 10¹⁄₂in (3.91m)			Horsepower: 2,500hp (1,860kW)			
Width: 9ft 2in (2.79m)			Electrical Equipment: Brush			

Number	Depot	Pool	Livery	Owner	Operator	Name
57602 (47337)	OO	EFOO	gwg	PTR	GWR	*Restormel Castle*
57603 (47349)	OO	EFOO	GWG	PTR	GWR	*Tintagel Castle*
57604 (47209)	OO	EFOO	GWR	PTR	GWR	*Pendennis Castle*
57605 (47206)	OO	EFOO	GWG	PTR	GWR	*Totnes Castle*

Left: To operate the 'Night Riviera' sleeper service between Paddington and Penzance, a fleet of four Class 57/6 locos is based at Old Oak Common. All except No. 57604 carry the new Great Western Railway green livery, while No. 57604 is painted in lined BR Western Region colours of the 1950s. No. 57605 Totnes Castle *is shown powering a summer relief Exeter to Penzance service away from Dawlish on 28 May 2016.* **CJM**

HST Passenger Fleet

Vehicle Length: 75ft 0in (22.86m)		Width: 8ft 11in (2.71m)	
Height: 12ft 9in (3.88m)		Bogie Type: BT10	

GN2G - TSRMB *Seating 70S*

Number	Depot	Livery	Owner
40101 (42170)	LA	FGW	PTR
40102 (42223)	LA	FGW	PTR
40103 (42316)	LA	FGW	PTR
40104 (42254)	LA	FGW	PTR
40105 (42084)	LA	FGW	PTR
40106 (42162)	LA	FGW	PTR
40107 (42334)	LA	FGW	PTR
40108 (42314)	LA	FGW	PTR
40109 (42262)	LA	FGW	PTR
40110 (42187)	LA	FGW	PTR
40111 (42248)	LA	FGW	PTR
40112 (42336)	LA	FGW	PTR
40113 (42309)	LA	FGW	PTR
40114 (42086)	LA	FGW	PTR
40115 (42320)	LA	FGW	PTR
40116 (42147)	LA	FGW	PTR
40117 (42249)	LA	FGW	PTR
40118 (42338)	LA	FGW	PTR
40119 (42090)	LA	FGW	PTR

GN1G - TRFB *Seating 23F*

Number	Depot	Livery	Owner
40204	LA	FGW	ANG
40205	LA	FGW	ANG
40207	LA	FGW	ANG
40210	LA	FGW	ANG
40221	LA	FGW	ANG
40231	LA	FGW	ANG

GK1G - TRFB *Seating 17F*

Number	Depot	Livery	Owner
40703	LA	FGW	ANG
40707	LA	FGW	ANG
40710	LA	FGW	ANG
40713	LA	FGW	ANG
40715	LA	GWG	ANG
40716	LA	FGW	ANG
40718	OO	FGW	ANG
40721	LA	FGW	ANG
40722	LA	FGW	ANG
40727	LA	FGW	ANG

Number	Depot	Livery	Owner
40733	LA	FGW	ANG
40734	LA	FGW	ANG
40739	LA	FGW	ANG
40743	LA	GWG	ANG
40752	LA	FGW	ANG
40755	LA	FGW	ANG
40757	LA	FGW	ANG

GL1G - TRFB *Seating 17F*

Number	Depot	Livery	Owner
40801	OO	FGW	PTR
40802	OO	FGW	PTR
40803	OO	FGW	PTR
40806	OO	FGW	PTR
40807	OO	FGW	PTR
40808	OO	FGW	PTR
40809	OO	FGW	PTR
40810	OO	FGW	PTR
40811	OO	FGW	PTR

Left: The massive fleet of Mk3 HST stock operated by Great Western is set to reduce from 2017 as IEP stock comes on stream. At the start of 2017 a fleet of 51 catering vehicles was in service of four different types, providing a wide range of services from a counter and trolley service to full at-seat silver service dining. TRFB No. 40752 is illustrated from its counter and kitchen end. These vehicles provide 17 first class seats in the 2+1 layout. **Antony Christie**

GN1G - TRB *Seating 23F*

Number	Depot	Livery	Owner
40900	LA	FGW	FGP
40901	LA	FGW	FGP
40902	LA	FGW	FGP
40903	LA	FGW	FGP
40904	LA	FGW	FGP

GH1G - TF *Seating 48F*

Number	Depot	Livery	Owner
41004	OO	FGW	ANG
41006	OO	FGW	ANG
41008	OO	FGW	ANG
41010	LA	FGW	ANG
41012	LA	FGW	ANG
41016	LA	FGW	ANG
41018	OO	FGW	ANG
41020	LA	FGW	ANG
41022	LA	FGW	ANG
41024	LA	FGW	ANG
41028	OO	FGW	ANG
41030	OO	FGW	ANG
41032	LA	FGW	ANG
41034	OO	FGW	ANG
41038	LA	FGW	ANG
41052	LA	FGW	ANG
41056	OO	FGW	ANG
41059	LA	FGW	FGP
41089	OO	FGW	ANG
41094	LA	FGW	ANG
41102	OO	FGW	ANG
41103	LA	FGW	ANG
41104	LA	FGW	ANG
41106	OO	FGW	ANG
41108	OO	FGW	PTR
41110	OO	FGW	ANG
41116	LA	FGW	ANG
41122	LA	FGW	ANG
41124	LA	FGW	ANG
41126	OO	FGW	ANG
41128	OO	FGW	ANG
41130	LA	FGW	ANG
41132	LA	FGW	ANG
41134	LA	FGW	ANG
41135	LA	FGW	ANG
41136	LA	FGW	ANG
41137	OO	FGW	ANG
41138	OO	FGW	ANG
41140	OO	FGW	ANG
41142	LA	FGW	ANG
41144	LA	FGW	ANG
41146	LA	GWG	ANG
41149	OO	FGW	PTR
41158	LA	GWG	ANG
41160	LA	FGW	FGP
41161	OO	FGW	PTR
41162	LA	FGW	FGP
41166	LA	FGW	FGP
41167	LA	FGW	FGP
41169	OO	FGW	PTR
41176	OO	FGW	PTR
41180	OO	FGW	ANG
41182	OO	FGW	PTR
41183	OO	FGW	PTR
41186	OO	FGW	PTR
41187	OO	FGW	PTR
41189	OO	FGW	PTR
41192	OO	FGW	PTR

GH2G - TS *Seating 68-84S*

Number	Depot	Livery	Owner
42003	OO	FGW	ANG
42004	LA	FGW	ANG
42005	LA	FGW	ANG
42006	LA	FGW	ANG
42007	LA	FGW	ANG
42008	OO	FGW	ANG
42009	LA	FGW	ANG
42010	LA	FGW	ANG
42012	LA	FGW	ANG
42013	LA	FGW	ANG
42014	LA	FGW	ANG
42015	LA	FGW	ANG
42016	LA	FGW	ANG
42019	LA	FGW	ANG
42021	LA	FGW	ANG
42023	LA	FGW	ANG
42024	OO	FGW	ANG
42025	OO	FGW	ANG
42026	OO	FGW	ANG
42027	OO	FGW	ANG
42028	LA	FGW	ANG
42029	LA	FGW	ANG
42030	LA	FGW	ANG
42031	LA	FGW	ANG
42032	LA	FGW	ANG
42033	LA	FGW	ANG
42034	LA	FGW	ANG
42035	LA	FGW	ANG
42039	OO	FGW	ANG
42040	OO	FGW	ANG
42041	OO	FGW	ANG
42042	OO	FGW	ANG
42043	OO	FGW	ANG
42044	OO	FGW	ANG
42045	LA	FGW	ANG
42046	LA	FGW	ANG
42047	LA	FGW	ANG
42048	OO	FGW	ANG
42049	OO	FGW	ANG
42050	OO	FGW	ANG
42054	LA	FGW	ANG
42055	LA	FGW	ANG
42056	LA	FGW	ANG
42060	OO	FGW	ANG
42061	OO	FGW	ANG
42062	OO	FGW	ANG
42066	OO	FGW	ANG
42067	OO	FGW	ANG
42068	OO	FGW	ANG
42069	OO	FGW	ANG
42070	OO	FGW	ANG
42071	OO	FGW	ANG
42072	LA	FGW	ANG
42073	OO	FGW	ANG
42074	OO	FGW	ANG
42075	LA	FGW	ANG
42076	LA	FGW	ANG
42077	LA	FGW	ANG
42078	LA	FGW	ANG
42079	OO	FGW	ANG
42080	OO	FGW	ANG
42081	OO	FGW	ANG
42083	OO	FGW	ANG
42085	OO	FGW	ANG
42087	OO	FGW	ANG
42089	OO	FGW	ANG
42092	LA	FGW	FGP
42093	LA	FGW	FGP
42094	LA	FGW	FGP
42095	LA	FGW	FGP
42096	LA	FGW	ANG
42098	OO	FGW	ANG
42099	OO	FGW	ANG
42101	OO	FGW	PTR
42102	OO	FGW	PTR
42103	LA	FGW	FGP
42105	LA	FGW	FGP
42107	LA	FGW	ANG
42108	LA	FGW	FGP
42115	OO	FGW	PTR
42118	OO	FGW	ANG
42126	OO	FGW	ANG
42129	LA	GWG	ANG
42138	OO	FGW	ANG
42143	LA	FGW	ANG
42144	LA	FGW	ANG
42145	LA	FGW	ANG
42166	OO	FGW	PTR
42167	LA	FGB	FGP
42168	LA	FGB	FGP
42169	LA	FGB	FGP
42173	OO	FGW	PTR
42174	OO	FGW	PTR
42175	LA	FGW	FGP

Right: *When the Great Western Trailer Standard (TS) vehicles were refurbished different interior layouts were incorporated with medium and high-density seating, with between 68 and 84 seats in the 2+2, mainly airline style. Car No. 42213 is illustrated.*
CJM

Great Western Railway

42176	LA	FGW	FGP	42265	LA	FGW	ANG	42347	OO	GWG	ANG
42177	LA	FGW	FGP	42266	OO	FGW	PTR	42348	OO	FGW	ANG
42178	OO	FGW	PTR	42267	LA	FGW	ANG	42349	OO	FGW	ANG
42183	LA	FGW	ANG	42268	LA	FGW	ANG	42350	LA	FGW	ANG
42184	LA	FGW	ANG	42269	LA	FGW	ANG	42351	LA	GWG	ANG
42185	LA	FGW	ANG	42271	OO	FGW	ANG	42353	LA	FGW	FGP
42195	OO	FGW	PTR	42272	OO	FGW	ANG	42356	OO	FGW	ANG
42196	OO	FGW	ANG	42273	OO	FGW	ANG	42360	LA	FGW	ANG
42197	OO	FGW	ANG	42275	LA	FGW	ANG	42361	LA	FGW	ANG
42200	LA	GWG	ANG	42276	LA	FGW	ANG	42362	OO	FGW	ANG
42201	OO	FGW	ANG	42277	LA	FGW	ANG	42364	OO	FGW	PTR
42202	OO	FGW	ANG	42279	LA	FGW	ANG	42365	OO	FGW	PTR
42203	OO	FGW	ANG	42280	LA	FGW	ANG	42381 (41058)	OO	FGW	PTR
42204	OO	FGW	ANG	42281	LA	FGW	ANG	42382 (12128)	OO	FGW	PTR
42206	LA	FGW	ANG	42283	OO	FGW	ANG	42383 (12172)	OO	FGW	PTR
42207	LA	FGW	ANG	42284	OO	FGW	ANG	42501 (40744)	OO	FGW	ANG
42208	LA	FGW	ANG	42285	OO	FGW	ANG	42502 (40731)	OO	FGW	ANG
42209	LA	FGW	ANG	42287	OO	FGW	ANG	42503 (40712)	OO	FGW	ANG
42211	OO	FGW	ANG	42288	OO	FGW	ANG	42504 (40714)	OO	FGW	ANG
42212	OO	FGW	ANG	42289	OO	FGW	ANG	42505 (40228)	OO	FGW	ANG
42213	OO	FGW	ANG	42291	LA	FGW	ANG	42506 (40724)	OO	FGW	ANG
42214	OO	FGW	ANG	42292	LA	FGW	ANG	42507 (40209)	OO	FGW	ANG
42216	OO	FGW	ANG	42293	LA	FGW	ANG	42508 (40725)	OO	FGW	ANG
42217	OO	FGW	PTR	42294	OO	FGW	PTR	42509 (40736)	OO	FGW	ANG
42218	OO	FGW	PTR	42295	LA	FGW	ANG	42510 (40717)	OO	FGW	ANG
42221	OO	FGW	ANG	42296	LA	FGW	ANG	42511 (40709)	OO	FGW	ANG
42222	OO	FGW	PTR	42297	LA	FGW	ANG	42512 (40208)	OO	FGW	ANG
42224	OO	FGW	PTR	42299	LA	GWG	ANG	42513 (40738)	OO	FGW	ANG
42231	LA	FGW	FGP	42300	LA	GWG	ANG	42514 (40726)	OO	FGW	ANG
42232	LA	FGW	FGP	42301	LA	GWG	ANG	42515 (40747)	LA	FGW	ANG
42233	LA	FGW	FGP	42302	LA	FGW	FGP	42516 (40723)	LA	FGW	ANG
42236	OO	FGW	ANG	42303	LA	FGW	FGP	42517 (40745)	LA	FGW	ANG
42245	LA	GWG	ANG	42304	LA	FGW	FGP	42518 (40403)	LA	FGW	ANG
42247	OO	FGW	PTR	42305	LA	FGW	FGP	42519 (40416)	LA	FGW	ANG
42250	LA	GWG	ANG	42308	OO	FGW	PTR	42520 (40434)	LA	FGW	ANG
42251	OO	FGW	ANG	42310	OO	FGW	PTR	42551 (41003)	LA	FGW	ANG
42252	LA	FGW	ANG	42315	OO	FGW	PTR	42552 (41007)	LA	FGW	ANG
42253	LA	FGW	ANG	42317	OO	FGW	PTR	42553 (41009)	LA	FGW	ANG
42255	LA	FGW	ANG	42319	OO	FGW	PTR	42554 (41011)	LA	FGW	ANG
42256	LA	FGW	ANG	42321	OO	FGW	PTR	42555 (41015)	LA	FGW	ANG
42257	LA	FGW	ANG	42325	LA	FGW	ANG	42556 (41017)	LA	FGW	ANG
42258	OO	FGW	PTR	42332	LA	FGW	ANG	42557 (41019)	LA	FGW	ANG
42259	LA	FGW	ANG	42333	LA	FGW	ANG	42558 (41021)	LA	FGW	ANG
42260	OO	FGW	ANG	42343	LA	FGW	ANG	42559 (41023)	LA	FGW	ANG
42261	OO	FGW	ANG	42344	OO	FGW	ANG	42560 (41027)	LA	FGW	ANG
42263	LA	FGW	ANG	42345	LA	FGW	ANG	42561 (41031)	LA	FGW	ANG
42264	OO	FGW	ANG	42346	OO	FGW	ANG	42562 (41037)	LA	FGW	ANG

Left: *Originally all Great Western HST consists were formed with two first class carriages; this has now been reduced to one, with a number of former first class vehicles rebuilt to standard class standards. The TF vehicles seat 48 in the low-density 2+1 style and are identified from the outside by a yellow band at cantrail height. Vehicle No. 41126 is illustrated.* **CJM**

■ In 2017-18, 11 four-car HSTs are to be formed to operate local services between Cardiff and Taunton and Exeter-Penzance. These will be formed of 24 Class 43s and 48 standard class HST coaches.

42563 (41045)	LA	FGW	FGP
42564 (41051)	LA	FGW	ANG
42565 (41085)	LA	FGB	FGP
42566 (41086)	LA	FGW	FGP
42567 (41093)	LA	FGW	ANG
42568 (41101)	LA	FGW	ANG
42569 (41105)	LA	FGW	ANG
42570 (41114)	LA	FGW	FGP
42571 (41121)	LA	FGW	ANG
42572 (41123)	LA	FGW	ANG
42573 (41127)	LA	FGW	ANG
42574 (41129)	LA	FGW	ANG
42575 (41131)	LA	FGW	ANG
42576 (41133)	LA	FGW	ANG
42577 (41141)	LA	FGW	ANG
42578 (41143)	LA	FGW	ANG
42579 (41145)	LA	GWG	ANG
42580 (41155)	LA	FGW	PTR
42581 (41157)	LA	GWG	ANG
42582 (41163)	LA	FGW	FGP
42583 (42385)	LA	FGW	PTR

GJ2G - TGS *Seating 67-71S*

Number	Depot	Livery	Owner
44000	OO	FGW	PTR
44001	LA	FGW	ANG
44002	OO	FGW	ANG
44003	OO	FGW	ANG
44004	LA	FGW	ANG
44005	LA	FGW	ANG
44007	LA	FGW	ANG
44008	OO	FGW	ANG
44009	LA	FGW	ANG
44010	LA	FGW	ANG
44011	LA	FGW	ANG

44013	OO	FGW	ANG
44014	OO	FGW	ANG
44015	LA	FGW	ANG
44016	OO	FGW	ANG
44018	LA	FGW	ANG
44020	OO	FGW	ANG
44022	OO	FGW	ANG
44023	OO	FGW	ANG
44024	OO	FGW	ANG
44025	LA	FGW	ANG
44026	OO	FGW	ANG
44028	LA	FGW	ANG
44029	LA	FGW	ANG
44030	OO	FGW	ANG
44032	LA	FGW	ANG
44033	OO	FGW	ANG
44034	LA	FGW	ANG
44035	LA	FGW	ANG
44036	LA	FGW	ANG
44037	OO	FGW	ANG
44038	LA	FGW	ANG
44039	LA	FGW	ANG
44040	LA	GWG	ANG
44042	OO	FGW	PTR
44043	OO	FGW	ANG
44049	LA	FGW	ANG
44055	LA	FGB	FGP
44059	LA	FGW	ANG
44060	OO	FGW	PTR
44064	OO	FGW	ANG
44066	LA	FGW	ANG
44067	OO	FGW	ANG
44068	LA	FGW	FGP
44069	OO	FGW	PTR
44074	LA	FGW	FGP

44076	LA	FGW	FGP
44078	OO	FGW	PTR
44079	OO	FGW	PTR
44081	LA	FGW	FGP
44083	OO	FGW	PTR
44086	LA	GWG	ANG
44090	OO	FGW	PTR
44091	OO	FGW	PTR
44093	OO	FGW	ANG
44097	OO	FGW	PTR
44100	LA	FGW	FGP
44101	OO	FGW	PTR

GH3A - TC *Seating 24F/39S*

Number	Depot	Livery	Owner
46001 (41005)	LA	FGW	ANG
46002 (41029)	LA	FGW	ANG
46003 (41033)	LA	FGW	ANG
46004 (41055)	LA	FGW	ANG
46005 (41065)	LA	FGW	ANG
46006 (41081)	LA	FGW	PTR
46007 (41096)	LA	FGW	PTR
46008 (41109)	LA	FGW	PTR
46009 (41119)	LA	FGW	PTR
46010 (41125)	LA	FGW	ANG
46011 (41139)	LA	FGW	PTR
46012 (41147)	LA	FGW	PTR
46013 (41148)	LA	FGW	PTR
46014 (41168)	LA	FGW	PTR
46015 (41179)	LA	FGW	ANG
46016 (41181)	LA	FGW	PTR
46017 (41184)	LA	FGW	PTR
46018 (41191)	LA	FGW	PTR

Class 143
Pacer

Vehicle Length: 51ft 0½in (15.55m)
Height: 12ft 2¼in (3.73m)
Width: 8ft 10½in (2.70m)
Engine: 1 x Cummins LTA10-R per vehicle
Horsepower: 460hp (343kW)
Seats (total/car): 92S, 48S/44S

Number	Formation DMS+DMSL	Depot	Livery	Owner	Operator
143603	55658+55689	EX	FGL	PTR	FGW
143611	55652+55677	EX	FGL	PTR	FGW
143612	55653+55678	EX	FGL	PTR	FGW
143617	55644+55683	EX	FGL	PTR	FGW
143618	55659+55684	EX	FGL	PTR	FGW
143619	55660+55685	EX	FGL	PTR	FGW
143620	55661+55686	EX	FGL	PTR	FGW
143621	55662+55687	EX	FGL	PTR	FGW

Right: *Scheduled for early withdrawal following a cascade of stock from the Bristol area are the eight Class 143s based at Exeter for Devon branch-line services. The sets, usually operated in pairs or with a Class 150 or 153, operate on the Exeter-Paignton, Barnstaple and Exmouth routes. A four-car formation is seen led by set No. 143621.* **CJM**

Class 150/0
Sprinter

Vehicle Length: (Driving) 65ft 9¾in (20.05m), (Inter) 66ft 2½in (20.18m)
Height: 12ft 4½in (3.77m)
Width: 9ft 3⅛in (2.82m)
Engine: 1 x Cummins NT855R4 of 285hp per vehicle
Horsepower: 855hp (638kW)
Seats (total/car): 240S, 72S/92S/76S

Number	Formation DMSL+MS+DMS	Depot	Livery	Owner	Op'r
150001	55200+55400+55300	RG	GWG	ANG	GWR
150002	55201+55401+55301	RG	GWG	ANG	GWR

Great Western Railway

Class 150/1
Sprinter

Vehicle Length: 64ft 9¾in (19.74m)
Height: 12ft 4½in (3.77m)
Width: 9ft 3⅛in (2.82m)

Engine: 1 x NT855R5 of 285hp per vehicle
Horsepower: 570hp (425kW)
Seats (total/car): 141S, 71S/70S

Two-car sets

Number	Formation DMSL+DMS	Depot	Livery	Owner	Operator
150101	52101+57101	PM	FGB	PTR	GWR
150102	52102+57102	PM	FGB	PTR	GWR
150104	52104+57104	PM	FGB	PTR	GWR
150106	52106+57106	PM	FGB	PTR	GWR
150108	52108+57108	PM	FGB	PTR	GWR
150120	52120+57120	EX	FGB	PTR	GWR
150121	52121+57121	EX	FGB	PTR	GWR
150122	52122+57122	EX	FGB	PTR	GWR
150123	52123+57123	EX	FGB	PTR	GWR
150124	52124+57124	EX	FGB	PTR	GWR
150127	52127+57127	EX	FGB	PTR	GWR
150128	52128+57128	EX	FGB	PTR	GWR
150129	52129+57129	EX	FGB	PTR	GWR
150130	52130+57130	EX	FGB	PTR	GWR
150131	52130+57130	EX	FGB	PTR	GWR

Three-car sets

Number	Formation DMSL+DMS+DMS	Depot	Livery	Owner	Op'r
150925	52125+57209+57125	EX	FGB	PTR	GWR
150926	52126+57212+57126	EX	FGB	PTR	GWR

Names applied
150925 *The Heart of Wessex Line*
150129 *Devon & Cornwall Rail Partnership*
150130 *Severnside Community Rail Partnership*

Left: *Another class of DMUs set to disappear from the West Country scene are the 17 Class 150/1 sets allocated to Bristol and Exeter. These will be replaced in the cascade following introduction of GWR EMUs in the London area. Two-car set No. 150127 is illustrated. These '150s' still retain their high-density 2+3 seating.* **CJM**

Class 150/2
Sprinter

Vehicle Length: 64ft 9¾in (19.74m)
Height: 12ft 4½in (3.77m)
Width: 9ft 3⅛in (2.82m)

Engine: 1 x NT855R5 of 285hp per vehicle
Horsepower: 570hp (425kW)
Seats (total/car): 116S, 60S/56S
Refurbished * 108S 50S/58S

Number	Formation DMSL+DMS	Depot	Livery	Owner	Operator
150202	52202+57202	PM	FGB	ANG	GWR
150216	52216+57216	PM	FGB	ANG	GWR
150219*	52219+57219	PM	FGB	PTR	GWR
150221	52221+57221	PM	FGL	PTR	GWR
150232	52232+57232	PM	GWG	PTR	GWR
150233	52233+57233	PM	GWG	PTR	GWR
150234	52234+57234	PM	GWG	PTR	GWR
150238*	52238+57238	PM	FGB	PTR	GWR
150239	52239+57239	PM	FGL	PTR	GWR
150243	52243+57243	PM	FGL	PTR	GWR
150244	52244+57244	PM	FGL	PTR	GWR
150246	52246+57246	PM	FGL	PTR	GWR
150247	52247+57247	PM	GWG	PTR	GWR
150248	52248+57248	PM	GWG	PTR	GWR
150249	52249+57249	PM	FGL	PTR	GWR
150261	52261+57261	PM	FGB	PTR	GWR
150263	52263+57263	PM	GWG	PTR	GWR
150265	52265+57265	PM	FGL	PTR	GWR
150266	52266+57266	PM	GWG	PTR	GWR

Name applied
150261 *The Tarka Line The First 25 Years 1989-2014*

Left: *A start was made in 2016 to repaint the Class 150/2 sets operated by GWR into the latest GWR green colours, carried out when sets have been refurbished with revised disabled access toilets, a cleaned-up interior and wifi facilities. Sporting GWR branding and a bicycle sign on the gangway door, set No. 150247 is seen along the South Devon coast.* **CJM**

Class 153

Vehicle Length: 76ft 5in (23.29m)
Height: 12ft 3⅛in (3.75m)
Width: 8ft 10in (2.70m)

Engine: 1 x NT855R5 of 285hp
Horsepower: 285hp (213kW)
Seats (total/car): 72S

Number	Formation DMSL	Depot	Livery	Owner	Operator
153305	52305	EX	FGL	ANG	GWR
153318	52318	EX	FGL	ANG	GWR
153325	52325	EX	ADV	PTR	GWR
153329	52329	EX	FGB	ANG	GWR
153333	52333	EX	ADV	PTR	GWR
153361	57361	EX	FGB	ANG	GWR
153368	57368	EX	FGL	ANG	GWR
153369	57369	EX	FGB	ANG	GWR
153370	57370	EX	FGL	ANG	GWR
153372	57372	EX	FGL	ANG	GWR
153373	57373	EX	FGB	ANG	GWR
153377	57377	EX	FGL	ANG	GWR
153380	57380	EX	FGB	ANG	GWR
153382	57382	EX	FGL	ANG	GWR

Right: *Currently GWR operates a fleet of 14 Class 153 single-car DMUs, but these will be removed from service in the West Country following stock cascades in 2017-2018. The vehicles are allocated to Exeter depot and operate on a wide variety of routes in Wiltshire, Avon, Gloucestershire, Somerset, Devon and Cornwall. Various liveries are applied including First Great Western, Great Western blue and advertising branding. GW blue-liveried set No. 153329 is seen at Westbury.* **CJM**

Class 158/0 (2-car)

Vehicle Length: 76ft 1¾in (23.21m)
Height: 12ft 6in (3.81m)
Width: 9ft 3¾in (2.82m)

Engine: 1 x Cummins NTA855R of 350hp per vehicle
Horsepower: 700hp (522kW)
Seats (total/car): 134S, 66S/68S

Number	Formation DMSL+DMSL	Depot	Livery	Owner	Operator
158763	52763+57763	PM	FGL	PTR	GWR
158766	52766+57766	PM	FGL	PTR	GWR

Class 158/0 (3-car)

158798
Vehicle Length: 76ft 1¾in (23.21m)
Height: 12ft 6in (3.81m)
Width: 9ft 3¼in (2.82m)

Engine: 1 x Cummins NTA855R of 350hp per vehicle
Horsepower: 1,050hp (783kW)
Seats (total/car): 200S, 66S/66S/68S

158950 - 158961
Vehicle Length: 76ft 1¾in (23.21m)
Height: 12ft 6in (3.81m)
Width: 9ft 3¼in (2.82m)

Engine: 1 x Cummins NTA855R of 350hp per vehicle
Horsepower: 1,050hp (783kW)
Seats (total/car): 204S, 66S/70S/68S

Number	Formation DMSL+MSL+DMSL		Depot	Livery	Owner	Operator
158798	52798+58715+57798		PM	ADV	PTR	GWR

Number	Formation DMSL+DMSL+DMSL		Depot	Livery	Owner	Operator
158950	(158751/761)	57751+52761+57761	PM	FGL	PTR	GWR
158951	(158751/764)	52751+52764+57764	PM	FGL	PTR	GWR
158952	(158745/762)	57745+52762+57762	PM	FGL	PTR	GWR
158953	(158745/750)	52745+52750+57750	PM	FGL	PTR	GWR
158954	(158747/760)	57747+52760+57760	PM	FGL	PTR	GWR
158955	(158747/765)	52747+52765+57765	PM	FGL	PTR	GWR
158956	(158748/768)	57748+52768+57768	PM	GWG	PTR	GWR
158957	(158748/771)	52748+52771+57771	PM	GWG	PTR	GWR
158958	(158746/776)	57746+52776+57776	PM	FGL	PTR	GWR
158959	(158746/778)	52746+52778+57778	PM	FGL	PTR	GWR
158960	(158769/749)	57769+52769+57749	PM	FGL	PTR	GWR
158961	(158767/749)	57767+52767+52749	PM	FGL	PTR	GWR

Left: *Soon to see more wider use in the West Country, the two- and three-car Class 158s are scheduled to be replaced in the Bristol area by cascaded Class 165s from Reading. In 2016 a slow start was made at repainting the '158s' into the new GWR green livery. Painted in FGW colours, set No. 158950 is seen at Westbury on a Portsmouth to Cardiff service.* **CJM**

Class 165/1 (3-car)
Networker Turbo

Vehicle Length: (Driving) 75ft 2½in (22.91m), (Inter) 74ft 6½in (22.72m)
Height: 12ft 5¼in (3.79m)
Width: 9ft 5½in (2.81m)
Engine: 1 x Perkins 2006TWH of 350hp per car
Horsepower: 1,050hp (783kW)
Seats (total/car): 286S, 82S/106S/98S

Number	Formation DMSL+MS+DMS	Depot	Livery	Owner	Operator
165101	58953+55415+58916	RG	GWG	ANG	GWR
165102	58954+55416+58917	RG	GWG	ANG	GWR
165103	58955+55417+58918	RG	GWG	ANG	GWR
165104	58956+55418+58919	RG	GWG	ANG	GWR
165105	58957+55419+58920	RG	GWG	ANG	GWR
165106	58958+55420+58921	RG	FGT	ANG	GWR
165107	58959+55421+58922	RG	FGT	ANG	GWR
165108	58960+55422+58923	RG	FGT	ANG	GWR
165109	58961+55423+58924	RG	FGT	ANG	GWR
165110	58962+55424+58925	RG	FGT	ANG	GWR
165111	58963+55425+58926	RG	FGT	ANG	GWR
165112	58964+55426+58927	RG	FGT	ANG	GWR
165113	58965+55427+58928	RG	FGT	ANG	GWR
165114	58966+55428+58929	RG	FGT	ANG	GWR
165116	58968+55430+58931	RG	FGT	ANG	GWR
165117	58969+55431+58932	RG	FGT	ANG	GWR

Left: *Scheduled to be replaced by new Class 387 EMUs, the Class 165s continue at present to be the backbone of London area local services, alongside the Class 166 fleet. Currently 16 three-car and 20 two-car sets are allocated to Reading. Sets will be repainted in the new GWR green livery and a start on this operation was made at the end of 2016. Set No. 165102 is seen at Oxford with a service bound for Paddington.* **Nathan Williamson**

Class 165/1 (2-car)
Networker Turbo

Vehicle Length: 75ft 2½in (22.91m)
Height: 12ft 5¼in (3.79m)
Width: 9ft 5½in (2.81m)
Engine: 1 x Perkins 2006TWH of 350hp per car
Horsepower: 700hp (522kW)
Seats (total/car): 16F/170S, 16F-72S/98S

Number	Formation DMCL+DMS	Depot	Livery	Owner	Operator
165118	58879+58933	RG	FGT	ANG	GWR
165119	58880+58934	RG	FGT	ANG	GWR
165120	58881+58935	RG	FGT	ANG	GWR
165121	58882+58936	RG	FGT	ANG	GWR
165122	58883+58937	RG	FGT	ANG	GWR
165123	58884+58938	RG	FGT	ANG	GWR
165124	58885+58939	RG	FGT	ANG	GWR
165125	58886+58940	RG	FGT	ANG	GWR
165126	58887+58941	RG	FGT	ANG	GWR
165127	58888+58942	RG	FGT	ANG	GWR

165128	58889+58943	RG	FGT	ANG	GWR	165133	58894+58948	RG	FGT	ANG	GWR
165129	58890+58944	RG	FGT	ANG	GWR	165134	58895+58949	RG	FGT	ANG	GWR
165130	58891+58945	RG	FGT	ANG	GWR	165135	58896+58950	RG	FGT	ANG	GWR
165131	58892+58946	RG	FGT	ANG	GWR	165136	58897+58951	RG	FGT	ANG	GWR
165132	58893+58947	RG	FGT	ANG	GWR	165137	58898+58952	RG	FGT	ANG	GWR

Class 166
Networker Turbo Express

Vehicle Length: (Driving) 75ft 2½in (22.91m), (Inter) 74ft 6½in (22.72m)
Height: 12ft 5¼in (3.79m)   Engine: 1 x Perkins 2006TWH of 350hp per car
Width: 9ft 5½in (2.81m)   Horsepower: 1,050hp (783kW)
Seats (total/car): 16F/258S, 90S/96S/16F-72S

Number	Formation DMSL+MS+DMCL	Depot	Livery	Owner	Operator	Name
166201	58101+58601+58122	RG	FGB	ANG	GWR	
166202	58102+58602+58123	RG	FGB	ANG	GWR	
166203	58103+58603+58124	RG	FGB	ANG	GWR	
166204	58104+58604+58125	RG	GWG	ANG	GWR	*Norman Topsom MBE*
166205	58105+58605+58126	RG	GWG	ANG	GWR	
166206	58106+58606+58127	RG	GWG	ANG	GWR	
166207	58107+58607+58128	RG	FGB	ANG	GWR	
166208	58108+58608+58129	RG	GWG	ANG	GWR	
166209	58109+58609+58130	RG	FGB	ANG	GWR	
166210	58110+58610+58131	RG	GWG	ANG	GWR	
166211	58111+58611+58132	RG	FGB	ANG	GWR	
166212	58112+58612+58133	RG	GWG	ANG	GWR	
166213	58113+58613+58134	RG	GWG	ANG	GWR	
166214	58114+58614+58135	RG	GWG	ANG	GWR	
166215	58115+58615+58136	RG	FGB	ANG	GWR	
166216	58116+58616+58137	RG	GWG	ANG	GWR	
166217	58117+58617+58138	RG	GWG	ANG	GWR	
166218	58118+58618+58139	RG	GWG	ANG	GWR	
166219	58119+58619+58140	RG	GWG	ANG	GWR	
166220	58120+58620+58141	RG	GWG	ANG	GWR	
166221	58121+58621+58142	RG	FGB	ANG	GWR	*Reading Train Care Depot*

Right: *A fleet of 21 three-car Class 166 'Networker Turbo Express' sets is based at Reading, and will soon be moved to the Bristol area. At present the sets, now sporting either Great Western blue or the latest GWR green livery, operate outer-suburban services on the London-Oxford corridor. Recently sets have had the first class accommodation removed from one driving car, thus increasing the second class seating. Set No. 166214 is shown.*
Nathan Williamson

Class 180
Adelante

Vehicle Length: (Driving) 75ft 7in (23.71m), (Inter) 75ft 5in (23.03m)
Height: 12ft 4in (3.75m)   Engine: 1 x Cummins QSK19 of 750hp per car
Width: 9ft 2in (2.80m)   Horsepower: 3,750hp (2,796kW)
Seats (total/car): 42F/226S, 46S/42F/68S/56S/56S

Number	Formation DMSL(A)+MFL+MSL+MSLRB+DMSL(B)	Depot	Livery	Owner	Operator	
180102	50902+54902+55902+56902+59902	OO	FGW	ANG	GWR	To be fitted with Alstom Atlas 200 ETCS system
180103	50903+54903+55903+56903+59903	OO	FGW	ANG	GWR	
180104	50904+54904+55904+56904+59904	OO	FGW	ANG	GWR	
180106	50906+54906+55906+56906+59906	OO	FGW	ANG	GWR	
180108	50908+54908+55908+56908+59908	OO	FGW	ANG	GWR	

Left: *Scheduled to be transferred to Grand Central, once sufficient new stock has been commissioned by GWR, the five Class 180s are currently based at Old Oak Common and operate on the London Paddington to Oxford and Worcester route. Sets are finished in First GW 'dynamic lines' colours. Set No. 180104 is shown under the Brunel roof at Paddington in August 2016.* **CJM**

Class 387
Electrostar

Vehicle Length: (Driving) 66ft 9in (20.3m) Width: 9ft 2in (2.79m)
(Inter) 65ft 6in (19.96m) Horsepower: 2,012hp (1,500kW)
Height: 12ft 4in (3.75m) Seats (total/car): 223S. 56S/62S/45S/60S

Number	Formation DMSO(A)+MSO+TSO+DMSO(B)	Depot	Livery	Owner	Operator
387130	421130+422130+423130+424130	RG	GWR	PTR	GWR
387131	421131+422131+423131+424131	RG	GWR	PTR	GWR
387132	421132+422132+423132+424132	RG	GWR	PTR	GWR
387133	421133+422133+423133+424133	RG	GWR	PTR	GWR
387134	421134+422134+423134+424134	RG	GWR	PTR	GWR
387135	421135+422135+423135+424135	RG	GWR	PTR	GWR
387136	421136+422136+423136+424136	RG	GWR	PTR	GWR
387137	421137+422137+423137+424137	RG	GWR	PTR	GWR
387138	421138+422138+423138+424138	RG	GWG	PTR	GWR
387139	421139+422139+423139+424139	RG	GWG	PTR	GWR
387140	421140+422140+423140+424140	RG	GWG	PTR	GWR
387141	421141+422141+423141+424141	RG	GWG	PTR	GWR
387142	421142+422142+423142+424142	RG	GWG	PTR	GWR
387143	421143+422143+423143+424143	RG	GWG	PTR	GWR
387144	421144+422144+423144+424144	RG	GWG	PTR	GWR
387145	421145+422145+423145+424145	RG	GWG	PTR	GWR
387146	421146+422146+423146+424146	RG	GWG	PTR	GWR
387147	421147+422147+423147+424147	RG	GWG	PTR	GWR
387148	421148+422148+423148+424148	RG	GWG	PTR	GWR
387149	421149+422149+423149+424149	RG	GWG	PTR	GWR
387150	421150+422150+423150+424150	RG	GWG	PTR	GWR
387151	421151+422151+423151+424151	RG	GWG	PTR	GWR
387152	421152+422152+423152+424152	RG	GWG	PTR	GWR
387153	421153+422153+423153+424153	RG	GWG	PTR	GWR
387154	421154+422154+423154+424154	RG	GWG	PTR	GWR
387155	421155+422155+423155+424155	RG	GWG	PTR	GWR
387156	421156+422156+423156+424156	RG	GWG	PTR	GWR
387157	421157+422157+423157+424157	RG	GWG	PTR	GWR
387158	421158+422158+423158+424158	RG	GWG	PTR	GWR
387159	421159+422159+423159+424159	RG	GWG	PTR	GWR
387160	421160+422160+423160+424160	RG	GWG	PTR	GWR
387161	421161+422161+423161+424161	RG	GWG	PTR	GWR
387162	421162+422162+423162+424162	RG	GWG	PTR	GWR
387163	421163+422163+423163+424163	RG	GWG	PTR	GWR
387164	421164+422164+423164+424164	RG	GWG	PTR	GWR
387165	421165+422165+423165+424165	RG	GWG	PTR	GWR
387166	421166+422166+423166+424166	RG	GWG	PTR	GWR
387167	421167+422167+423167+424167	RG	GWG	PTR	GWR
387168	421168+422168+423168+424168	RG	GWG	PTR	GWR
387169	421169+422169+423169+424169	RG	GWG	PTR	GWR
387170	421170+422170+423170+424170	RG	GWG	PTR	GWR
387171	421171+422171+423171+424171	RG	GWG	PTR	GWR
387172	421172+422172+423172+424172	RG	GWG	PTR	GWR
387173	421173+422173+423173+424173	RG	GWG	PTR	GWR
387174	421174+422174+423174+424174	RG	GWG	PTR	GWR

Passenger Train Operating Companies - Great Western Railway

Right: *In August 2016 the first of a fleet of 45 four-car Class 387 'Electrostar' sets built by Bombardier and owned by Porterbrook entered service on Paddington suburban services. The '387s' finished in the new GWR green livery will replace the Class 165 and 166 stock currently in use when electrification has been extended from Airport Junction to Reading, Oxford and Newbury. Set No. 387131 is seen at Paddington.* **CJM**

Mk3 Hauled Stock

Vehicle Length: 75ft 0in (22.86m)   Width: 8ft 11in (2.71m)
Height: 12ft 9in (3.88m)   Bogie Type: BT10

AJ1G - RFB *Seating 18F*

Number	Depot	Livery	Owner
10217§	PZ	GWG	PTR
10219	PZ	GWG	PTR
10225	PZ	GWG	PTR
10232§	PZ	FGW	PTR

AU4G - SLEP *Comps 12*

Number	Depot	Livery	Owner
10532	PZ	GWG	PTR
10534	PZ	GWG	PTR
10563	PZ	GWG	PTR

Number	Depot	Livery	Owner
10584	PZ	GWG	PTR
10589	PZ	FGW	PTR
10590	PZ	GWG	PTR
10594	PZ	GWG	PTR
10596	ZN	GWG	PTR
10601	PZ	GWG	PTR
10612	PZ	GWG	PTR
10616	PZ	GWG	PTR

AC2G - TSO *Seating 45S*

Number	Depot	Livery	Owner
12100	PZ	FGW	PTR

Number	Depot	Livery	Owner
12142	PZ	GWG	PTE
12161	PZ	FGW	PTR

AE1H - BFO *Seating 36F*

Number	Depot	Livery	Owner
17173	PZ	GWG	PTR
17174	PZ	GWG	PTR
17175	PZ	GWG	PTR

§ 10217 currently being overhauled will replace 10232 to go off lease.

Right: *The 20-strong Mk3 loco-hauled fleet, allocated to Penzance, is used on the 'Night Riviera' services between London and Penzance. The fleet consists of 11 sleeping cars, three catering vehicles, three seating saloons and three seating brake vehicles. Vehicles are currently being repainted in GWR green livery, as displayed by coach No. 10219, an RFB coach, seen from its seating end.* **CJM**

Service Stock

HST Barrier Vehicles

Number	Depot	Livery	Owner	Former Identity
6330	LA	FGB	ANG	BFK - 14084
6336(S)	PM	FGB	ANG	BG - 81591/92185
6338	LA	FGB	ANG	BG - 81581/92180
6348(S)	PM	FGB	ANG	BG - 81233/92963

Right: *When HST Mk3 stock is required to be moved by a locomotive, barrier vehicles are needed as the buckeye couplings of the trailer stock are not compatible with locomotives. For this work, four barriers are owned by Angel Trains and based on GWR. Two vehicles are stored and two are operational and painted in First GW blue livery. Vehicle No. 6338, a rebuild from parcels van 92180, is shown attached to a Mk3.* **CJM**

Great Western Railway

Class 800/0 Bi-Mode 'IEP' stock

5-car sets

Vehicle Length: (Driving) 85ft 4in (26m)	Width: 8ft 10in (2.7m)
Height: 12ft 4in (3.75m)	Horsepower: Electric 3,636hp (2,712kW)
Engine: MTU 12V 1600R80L of 750hp (560kW) x 3	Seats (total/car): 45F/270S - 56S, 88S,88S,30F/38S,15F

Number	Formation DPTS+MS+MS+MC+DPTF	Depot	Livery	Owner	Operator	Name
800001 (T1)*	811001+812001+813001+814001+815001	NP	SPL	EVL	HIT	
800002 (T2)*	811002+812002+813002+814002+815002	NP	SPL	EVL	HIT	
800003 (T3)*	811003+812003+813003+814003+815003	NP	SPL	EVL	HIT	
800004 (T4)*	811004+812004+813004+814004+815004	NP	GWG	EVL	HIT	*Sir Daniel Gooch /*
						Isambard Kingdom Brunel
800005 (T5)	811005+812005+813005+814005+815005	NP	SPL	EVL	HIT	
800006	811006+812006+813006+814006+815006	NP	GWG	EVL	-	
800007	811007+812007+813007+814007+815007	NP	GWG	EVL	-	
800008	811008+812008+813008+814008+815008	NP	GWG	EVL	-	
800009	811009+812009+813009+814009+815009	NP	GWG	EVL	-	
800010	811010+812010+813010+814010+815010	NP	GWG	EVL	-	
800011	811011+812011+813011+814011+815011	NP	GWG	EVL	-	
800012	811012+812012+813012+814012+815012	NP	GWG	EVL	-	
800013	811013+812013+813013+814013+815013	NP	GWG	EVL	-	
800014	811014+812014+813014+814014+815014	NP	GWG	EVL	-	
800015	811015+812015+813015+814015+815015	NP	GWG	EVL	-	
800016	811016+812016+813016+814016+815016	NP	GWG	EVL	-	
800017	811017+812017+813017+814017+815017	NP	GWG	EVL	-	
800018	811018+812018+813018+814018+815018	NP	GWG	EVL	-	
800019	811019+812019+813019+814019+815019	NP	GWG	EVL	-	
800020	811020+812020+813020+814020+815020	NP	GWG	EVL	-	
800021	811021+812021+813021+814021+815021	NP	GWG	EVL	-	
800022	811022+812022+813022+814022+815022	NP	GWG	EVL	-	
800023	811023+812023+813023+814023+815023	NP	GWG	EVL	-	
800024	811024+812024+813024+814024+815024	NP	GWG	EVL	-	
800025	811025+812025+813025+814025+815025	NP	GWG	EVL	-	
800026	811026+812026+813026+814026+815026	NP	GWG	EVL	-	
800027	811027+812027+813027+814027+815027	NP	GWG	EVL	-	
800028	811028+812028+813028+814028+815028	NP	GWG	EVL	-	
800029	811029+812029+813029+814029+815029	NP	GWG	EVL	-	
800030	811030+812030+813030+814030+815030	NP	GWG	EVL	-	
800031	811031+812031+813031+814031+815031	NP	GWG	EVL	-	
800032	811032+812032+813032+814032+815032	NP	GWG	EVL	-	
800033	811033+812033+813033+814033+815033	NP	GWG	EVL	-	
800034	811034+812034+813034+814034+815034	NP	GWG	EVL	-	
800035	811035+812035+813035+814035+815035	NP	GWG	EVL	-	
800036	811036+812036+813036+814036+815036	NP	GWG	EVL	-	

* Built in Japan, delivered to the the UK

Left: *Throughout 2016 testing of the first delivered Class 800 and 801 stock was under way on both the Great Western and East Coast routes. The first five-car set to sport full Great Western livery, No. 800004, took to the main line in mid-2016 and was used for type test approval, equipment testing and training. The set is seen under the great Brunel roof at London Paddington.* **Antony Christie**

Class 800/3 Bi-Mode 'IEP' stock
9-car sets

Vehicle Length: (Driving) 85ft 4in (26m)	*Width: 8ft 10in (2.7m)*
Height: 12ft 4in (3.75m)	*Horsepower: Electric 6,061hp (4,520kW)*
Engine: MTU 12V 1600R80L of 750hp (560kW) x 5	*Seats (total/car): 93F/534S -*
	56S, 88S, 88S, 88S, 88S, 88S,30F/38S, 48F, 15F

Number	Formation	Depot	Livery	Owner	Operator
800301	821001+822001+823001+824001+825001+826001+827001+828001+829001	NP	GWG	EVL	-
800302	821002+822002+823002+824002+825002+826002+827002+828002+829002	NP	GWG	EVL	-
800303	821003+822003+823003+824003+825003+826003+827003+828003+829003	NP	GWG	EVL	-
800304	821004+822004+823004+824004+825004+826004+827004+828004+829004	NP	GWG	EVL	-
800305	821005+822005+823005+824005+825005+826005+827005+828005+829005	NP	GWG	EVL	-
800306	821006+822006+823006+824006+825006+826006+827006+828006+829006	NP	GWG	EVL	-
800307	821007+822007+823007+824007+825007+826007+827007+828007+829007	NP	GWG	EVL	-
800308	821008+822008+823008+824008+825008+826008+827008+828008+829008	NP	GWG	EVL	-
800309	821009+822009+823009+824009+825009+826009+827009+828009+829009	NP	GWG	EVL	-
800310	821010+822010+823010+824010+825010+826010+827010+828003+829010	NP	GWG	EVL	-
800311	821011+822011+823011+824011+825011+826011+827011+828011+829011	NP	GWG	EVL	-
800312	821012+822012+823012+824012+825012+826012+827012+828012+829012	NP	GWG	EVL	-
800313	821013+822013+823013+824013+825013+826013+827013+828013+829013	NP	GWG	EVL	-
800314	821014+822014+823014+824014+825014+826014+827014+828014+829014	NP	GWG	EVL	-
800315	821015+822015+823015+824015+825015+826015+827015+828015+829015	NP	GWG	EVL	-
800316	821016+822016+823016+824016+825016+826016+827016+828016+829016	NP	GWG	EVL	-
800317	821017+822017+823017+824017+825017+826017+827017+828017+829017	NP	GWG	EVL	-
800318	821018+822018+823018+824018+825018+826018+827018+828018+829018	NP	GWG	EVL	-
800319	821019+822019+823019+824019+825019+826019+827019+828019+829019	NP	GWG	EVL	-
800320	821020+822020+823020+824020+825020+826020+827020+828020+829020	NP	GWG	EVL	-
800321	821021+822021+823021+824021+825021+826021+827021+828021+829021	NP	GWG	EVL	-

Right: *This is the interior carried by No. 800004 during its media launch at London Paddington in summer 2016. It is likely to be further refined when a production standard is set. This view shows the first class in the DPTF.*
Antony Christie

Class 802 Bi-Mode 'IEP' stock
5- and 9-car 'West of England' sets

On 30 July 2015 a contract was signed between Great Western, the UK Government, Eversholt Leasing and Hitachi Rail for the supply of HST replacement stock for the West of England routes to Exeter, Paignton, Plymouth and Penzance, when a fleet of 29 Hitachi AT300 train sets was ordered. In summer 2016 a follow-on order for an extra seven nine-car sets was made. The overall fleet will comprise 14 nine-car and 22 five-car units.

These trains will be closely related to the previously ordered 'IEP' Class 800 and 801 stock, but will have some detail differences, such as larger fuel tanks, revised brake resistors and improved performance of the engines when working over the undulating Devon and Cornwall main line.

These sets will be built it Italy at the former Ansaldo/Breda plant, which is now owned by Hitachi.

Passenger Train Operating Companies - Great Western Railway

First Hull Trains

Address:	✉ Europa House, 184 Ferensway, Kingston-upon-Hull, HU1 3UT
	✎ customer.services@hulltrains.co.uk
	ℂ 0845 676 9905
	① www.hulltrains.co.uk

Managing Director:	Will Dunnett	**General Manager:**	Cath Bellamy
Franchise Dates:	Private Open Access Operator, agreement to December 2029		
Principal Route:	London King's Cross - Hull		
Depots:	Old Oak Common (OO) [Operated by FGW], Crofton (XW)		
Parent Company:	First Group PLC		

Hull — Brough — Howden — Selby — Doncaster — Retford — Grantham — Stevenage — London King's Cross

© TRC.Com Ltd 2013

Class 180
Adelante

Vehicle Length: (Driving) 75ft 7in (23.71m), (Inter) 75ft 5in (23.03m)
Height: 12ft 4in (3.75m)
Width: 9ft 2in (2.80m)
Engine: 1 x Cummins OSK19 of 750hp per vehicle
Horsepower: 3,750hp (2,796kW)
Seats (total/car): 42F/226S, 46S/42F/68S/56S/56S

Number	Formation DMSL(A)+MFL+MSF+MSLRB+DMSL(B)	Depot	Livery	Owner	Operator
180109	50909+54909+55909+56909+59909	OO/XW	FHT	ANG	FHT
180110	50910+54910+55910+56910+59910	OO/XW	FHT	ANG	FHT
180111	50911+54911+55911+56911+59911	OO/XW	FHT	ANG	FHT
180113	50913+54913+55913+56913+59913	OO/XW	FHT	ANG	FHT

Hull Trains has ordered five five-car bi-mode AT300s from Hitachi through Angel Trains, as replacement for the Class 180s. Each new train will seat 327 and the sets are due for delivery to Bounds Green in 2019.

Below: *Hull Trains, operated by First Group as an 'open access' operation, currently uses four Class 180 five-car sets on its London King's Cross to Hull service. Sets are painted in First dynamic lines colours and allocated jointly to Old Oak Common and Crofton depots. Set No. 180109 is seen at Doncaster.*
Antony Christie

■ Sets to be fitted
with Alstom Atlas
200 ETCS systems.

First TransPennine Express

Address: ✉ Floor 7, Bridgewater House, 60 Whitworth Street, Manchester, M1 6LT
✆ tpecustomer.relations@firstgroup.com
✆ 0845 600 1671
ⓘ www.tpexpress.co.uk

Managing Director: Leo Goodwin
Franchise Dates: 1 February 2004 - 31 March 2023
Principal Routes: Newcastle, Middlesbrough, Scarborough, Hull, Cleethorpes
to Manchester, Liverpool, Barrow, Carlisle, Edinburgh and
Glasgow
Depots: Ardwick (AK) (Siemens-operated), York (YK), Crofton (XW)
Parent Company: First Group PLC

During this franchise FTPE will introduce 220 vehicles (44 train sets) with a top speed of 125mph and introduce several new routes and expand services on all lines.

The rolling stock order covers 19 five-car Class 802/2 bi-mode sets by Hitachi, 12 CAF-built five-car 'Cavity' Class 397 EMUs to replace the '350s' (funded by Eversholt), and 13 CAF-built loco-hauled sets to be powered by DRS Class 68s (funded by Beacon Rail).

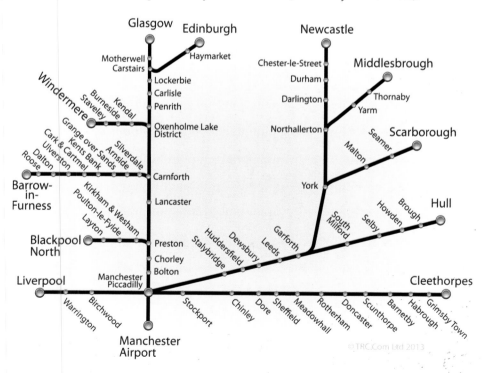

First TransPennine Express

Class 185
Desiro

Vehicle Length: (Driving) 77ft 11in (23.76m), (Inter) 77ft 10½in (23.75m)	
Height: 12ft 4in (3.75m)	Engine: 1 x Cummins QSK19 of 750hp per vehicle
Width: 9ft 3in (2.81m)	Horsepower: 2,250hp (1,680kW)
	Seats (total/car): 15F/154S, 15F-18S/72S/64S

Number	Formation DMCL+MSL+DMS	Depot	Livery	Owner	Operator
185101	51101+53101+54101	AK	FTP	EVL	FTP
185102	51102+53102+54102	AK	FTP	EVL	FTP
185103	51103+53103+54103	AK	FTP	EVL	FTP
185104	51104+53104+54104	AK	FTP	EVL	FTP
185105	51105+53105+54105	AK	FTP	EVL	FTP
185106	51106+53106+54106	AK	FTP	EVL	FTP
185107	51107+53107+54107	AK	FTP	EVL	FTP
185108	51108+53108+54108	AK	FTN	EVL	FTP
185109	51109+53109+54109	AK	FTP	EVL	FTP
185110	51110+53110+54110	AK	FTP	EVL	FTP
185111	51111+53111+54111	AK	FTP	EVL	FTP
185112	51112+53112+54112	AK	FTP	EVL	FTP
185113	51113+53113+54113	AK	FTP	EVL	FTP
185114	51114+53114+54114	AK	FTN	EVL	FTP
185115	51115+53115+54115	AK	FTN	EVL	FTP
185116	51116+53116+54116	AK	FTP	EVL	FTP
185117	51117+53117+54117	AK	FTP	EVL	FTP
185118	51118+53118+54118	AK	FTP	EVL	FTP
185119	51119+53119+54119	AK	FTP	EVL	FTP
185120	51120+53120+54120	AK	FTP	EVL	FTP
185121	51121+53121+54121	AK	FTP	EVL	FTP
185122	51122+53122+54122	AK	FTP	EVL	FTP
185123	51123+53123+54123	AK	FTN	EVL	FTP
185124	51124+53124+54124	AK	FTP	EVL	FTP
185125	51125+53125+54125	AK	FTP	EVL	FTP
185126	51126+53126+54126	AK	FTP	EVL	FTP
185127	51127+53127+54127	AK	FTN	EVL	FTP
185128	51128+53128+54128	AK	FTP	EVL	FTP
185129	51129+53129+54129	AK	FTP	EVL	FTP
185130	51130+53130+54130	AK	FTP	EVL	FTP
185131	51131+53131+54131	AK	FTN	EVL	FTP
185132	51132+53132+54132	AK	FTP	EVL	FTP
185133	51133+53133+54133	AK	FTN	EVL	FTP
185134	51134+53134+54134	AK	FTP	EVL	FTP
185135	51135+53135+54135	AK	FTP	EVL	FTP
185136	51136+53136+54136	AK	FTP	EVL	FTP

■ Following introduction of new stock, 22 Class 185s will be taken off lease.

Below: *At present, the core FTPE operation uses a fleet of 51 Siemens 'Desiro' three-car Class 185s based in Manchester. In 2016 it was announced that new CAF and Hitachi stock had been ordered to increase and improve services. In First livery, set No. 185125 is seen at Doncaster forming a Manchester-Cleethorpes service.* **CJM**

185137	51137+53137+54137	AK	FTP	EVL	FTP
185138	51138+53138+54138	AK	FTP	EVL	FTP
185139	51139+53139+54139	AK	FTN	EVL	FTP
185140	51140+53140+54140	AK	FTP	EVL	FTP
185141	51141+53141+54141	AK	FTP	EVL	FTP
185142	51142+53142+54142	AK	FTA	EVL	FTP
185143	51143+53143+54143	AK	FTP	EVL	FTP
185144	51144+53144+54144	AK	FTN	EVL	FTP
185145	51145+53145+54145	AK	FTP	EVL	FTP
185146	51146+53146+54146	AK	FTP	EVL	FTP
185147	51147+53147+54147	AK	FTP	EVL	FTP
185148	51148+53148+54148	AK	FTP	EVL	FTP
185149	51149+53149+54149	AK	FTP	EVL	FTP
185150	51150+53150+54150	AK	FTP	EVL	FTP
185151	51151+53151+54151	AK	FTP	EVL	FTP

Class 350/4
Desiro

Vehicle Length: 66ft 9in (20.4m)
Height: 12ft 1½in (3.78m)
Width: 9ft 2in (2.7m)
Horsepower: 1,341hp (1,000kW)
Seats (total/car): 19F/178S

Number	Formation DMSO(A)+TCO+PTSO+DMSO(B)	Depot	Livery	Owner	Operator
350401	60691+60901+60941+60671	AK	FTP	ANG	FTP
350402	60692+60902+60942+60672	AK	FTP	ANG	FTP
350403	60693+60903+60943+60673	AK	FTP	ANG	FTP
350404	60694+60904+60944+60674	AK	FTP	ANG	FTP
350405	60695+60905+60945+60675	AK	FTP	ANG	FTP
350406	60696+60906+60946+60676	AK	FTP	ANG	FTP
350407	60697+60907+60947+60677	AK	FTP	ANG	FTP
350408	60698+60908+60948+60678	AK	FTP	ANG	FTP
350409	60699+60909+60949+60679	AK	FTP	ANG	FTP
350410	60700+60910+60950+60680	AK	FTP	ANG	FTP

Following introduction of new stock, these sets will be transferred to London Midland.

Right: *To operate a more efficient service under the wires on the West Coast route a fleet of 10 Class 350 'Desiro' EMUs was introduced in 2014 and currently operates Manchester to Edinburgh/ Glasgow services. Set No. 350404 is seen arriving at Preston. Following introduction of new First TransPennine Express stock, the 10 Class 350s will move south to Northampton depot and strengthen the existing London Midland Class 350 fleet.* **CJM**

Mk3 Hauled Stock

Vehicle Length: 75ft 0in (22.86m)
Height: 12ft 9in (3.88m)
Width: 8ft 11in (2.71m)
Bogie Type: BT10

These Mk3 vehicles are on short-term lease to First TransPennine to operate a loco-hauled service and provide staff training.

AJ1G - RFB *Seating 18F*

Number	Depot	Livery	Owner
10212	LA	-	PTR

AD1G - FO *Seating 48F*

Number	Depot	Livery	Owner
11007	LA	-	PTR
11018	LA	-	PTR
11048	LA	-	PTR

AC2G - TS0 (*TSOD) *Seating 76/70*S*

Number	Depot	Livery	Owner
12011	LA	-	PTR
12078	LA	-	PTR
12122*	LA	-	PTR
12133	LA	-	PTR
12138	LA	-	PTR

Grand Central

Address: ✉ River House, 17 Museum Street, York, YO1 7DJ
ℳ info@grandcentral.com
© 0845 603 4852
ⓘ www.grandcentral.co.uk

Managing Director: Richard McLean
Franchise Dates: Open Access Operator, to December 2026
Principal Routes: London King's Cross - Sunderland/Bradford
Depots: Heaton (HT)
Parent Company: Arriva PLC

Below: *During 2017 the six buffer-fitted Class 43s remain in service with Grand Central based at Heaton and used on the London King's Cross-Sunderland route. These HST sets are due to be replaced when extra Class 180s are made available to Grand Central. No. 43465 is seen on the rear of a northbound train at Doncaster.* **CJM**

Class 43 – HST

Vehicle Length: 58ft 5in (18.80m)
Height: 12ft 10in (3.90m)
Width: 8ft 11in (2.73m)
Engine: MTU 16V4000 R41R
Horsepower: 2,250hp (1,680kW)
Electrical Equipment: Brush

Number	Depot	Pool	Livery	Owner	Operator
43423 (43123)	HT	GCHP	GTO	ANG	GTL
43465 (43065)	HT	GCHP	GTO	ANG	GTL
43467 (43067)	HT	GCHP	GTO	ANG	GTL
43468 (43068)	HT	GCHP	GTO	ANG	GTL
43480 (43080)	HT	GCHP	GTO	ANG	GTL
43484 (43084)	HT	GCHP	GTO	ANG	GTL

Names applied
43423 *'Valenta' 1972 - 2010*
43484 *Peter Fox 1942 - 2011*

Class 180
Zephyr

Vehicle Length: (Driving) 75ft 7in (23.71m), (Inter) 75ft 5in (23.03m)
Height: 12ft 4in (3.75m)
Width: 9ft 2in (2.80m)
Engine: 1 x Cummins OSK19 of 750hp per vehicle
Horsepower: 3,750hp (2,796kW)
Seats (total/car): 42F/226S, 46S/42F/68S/56S/56S

Number	Formation DMSL(A)+MFL+MSL+MSLRB+DMSL(B)	Depot	Livery	Owner	Operator	Name
180101	50901+54901+55901+56901+59901	HT	GTO	ANG	GTL	
180105	50905+54905+55905+56905+59905	HT	GTO	ANG	GTL	*The Yorkshire Artist Ashley Jackson*
180107	50907+54907+55907+56907+59907	HT	GTO	ANG	GTL	*Hart of the North*
180112	50912+54912+55912+56912+59912	HT	GTO	ANG	GTL	*James Herriot Celebrating 100 Years 1916-2016*
180114	50914+54914+55914+56914+59914	HT	GTO	ANG	GTL	

Above: *At the start of 2017 Grand Central operates a fleet of five Class 180 five-car sets known as 'Zephyrs'. Allocated to Heaton depot, the sets have all been refurbished and carry the smart-looking black and orange livery of GC. To identify passenger class, standard class carriages have silver doors and first class coaches have gold doors. Set No. 180114 is seen near Colton Junction, York.* **Antony Christie**

To be fitted with Alstom Atlas 200 ETCS system

■ Grand Central has announced that it will take over five Class 180s from Great Western Railway in 2017, allowing it to cease using HSTs. A major refurbishing project for all 10 Class 180s would then be undertaken. ■

Mk3 HST Stock

Vehicle Length: 75ft 0in (22.86m)	Width: 8ft 11in (2.71m)
Height: 12ft 9in (3.88m)	Bogie Type: BT10

GK2G - TRSB *Seating 33S*

Number		Depot	Livery	Owner
40424	(40024)	HT	GTO	ANG
40426	(40026)	HT	GTO	ANG
40433	(40033)	HT	GTO	ANG

GH1G - TF *Seating 48F*

Number		Depot	Livery	Owner
41201	(11045)	HT	GTO	ANG
41202	(11017)	HT	GTO	ANG
41203	(11038)	HT	GTO	ANG
41204	(11023)	HT	GTO	ANG
41205	(11036)	HT	GTO	ANG
41206	(11055)	HT	GTO	ANG

GH2G - TS *Seating 64S* *TSD Seating 60S*

Number		Depot	Livery	Owner
42401	(12149)	HT	GTO	ANG
42402	(12155)	HT	GTO	ANG
42403*	(12033)	HT	GTO	ANG
42404	(12152)	HT	GTO	ANG
42405	(12136)	HT	GTO	ANG
42406*	(12112)	HT	GTO	ANG
42407	(12044)	HT	GTO	ANG
42408	(12121)	HT	GTO	ANG
42409*	(12088)	HT	GTO	ANG

GJ2G - TGS *Seating 67S*

Number	Depot	Livery	Owner
44065 (S)	LM	VIR	AUT
44089 (S)	LM	VIT	AUT

Right: *A fleet of 18 operational Mk3 vehicles operates with the Grand Central HST power cars. All except the three catering vehicles are rebuilds from Mk3 loco-hauled stock. Coaches are finished in GC black and orange with silver doors on standard class and gold doors on first class coaches. Two former HST Trailer Guards Standards are also on the books of GC/Arriva Trains but are not in use and stored at Long Marston. TRSB No. 40433 is shown.* **Antony Christie**

Greater Anglia

Address: ✉ 2nd Floor, East Anglia House, 12-34 Great Eastern Street,
London, EC2A 3EH
✆ contactcentre@greateranglia.co.uk
✆ 0845 600 7245
ⓘ www.greateranglia.co.uk

Managing Director: Jamie Burles
Franchise Dates: 1 February 2012 - October 2025
Principal Routes: London Liverpool Street to Norwich, Cambridge, Enfield
Town, Hertford East, Upminster, Southend Victoria,
Southminster, Braintree, Sudbury, Clacton, Walton, Harwich
Town, Felixstowe, Lowestoft, Great Yarmouth, Sheringham,
Stansted Airport and Peterborough
Depots: Ilford (IL), Norwich (NC), Clacton (CC)
Parent Company: Abellio (60%), Mitsui (40%)

Class 90/0

Vehicle Length: 61ft 6in (18.74m)   Power Collection: 25kV ac overhead
Height: 13ft 0¼in (3.96m)   Horsepower: 7,860hp (5,860kW)
Width: 9ft 0in (2.74m)   Electrical Equipment: GEC

Number	Depot	Pool	Livery	Owner	Operator	Name
90001	NC	IANA	AWT	PTR	GAR	Crown Point
90002	NC	IANA	AWT	PTR	GAR	Eastern Daily Press 1870-2010 Serving Norfolk for 140 years
90003	NC	IANA	AWT	PTR	GAR	Raedwald of East Anglia
90004	NC	IANA	AWT	PTR	GAR	City of Chelmsford
90005	NC	IANA	AWT	PTR	GAR	Vice-Admiral Lord Nelson
90006	NC	IANA	AWT	PTR	GAR	Roger Ford / Modern Railways Magazine
90007	NC	IANA	AWT	PTR	GAR	Sir John Betjeman
90008	NC	IANA	AWT	PTR	GAR	The East Anglian
90009	NC	IANA	AWT	PTR	GAR	
90010	NC	IANA	AWT	PTR	GAR	Bressingham Steam and Gardens
90011	NC	IANA	AWT	PTR	GAR	East Anglian Daily Times Suffolk & Proud
90012	NC	IANA	AWT	PTR	GAR	Royal Anglian Regiment
90013	NC	IANA	AWT	PTR	GAR	The Evening Star
90014	NC	IANA	AWT	PTR	GAR	Norfolk and Norwich Festival
90015	NC	IANA	AWT	PTR	GAR	Colchester Castle

Left: *Soon to be replaced by high-specification Stadler-built multiple units, the Class 90s are still in charge of the London Liverpool Street to Norwich route for the next couple of years. The 15 former West Coast locos are now based at Norwich and exclusively operate on the Norwich-London corridor. Locos are all finished in Abellio Greater Anglia white colours. No. 90014* Norwich and Norwich Festival *is seen departing from Norwich.* **Antony Christie**

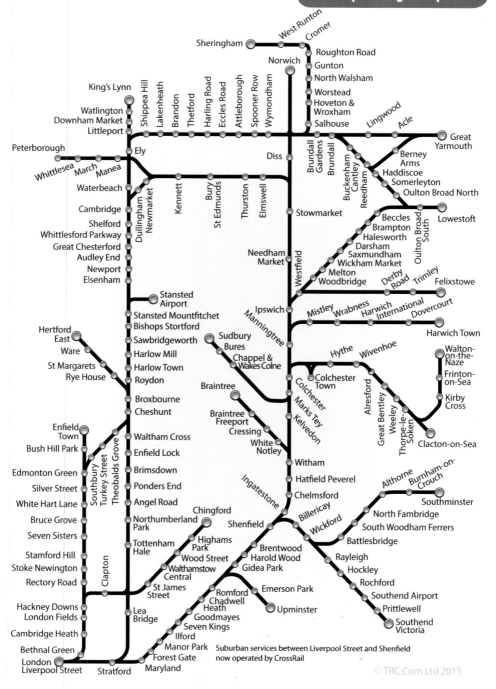

Suburban services between Liverpool Street and Shenfield now operated by CrossRail

© TRC.Com Ltd 2015

Mk3 Hauled Stock

Vehicle Length: 75ft 0in (22.86m)	Width: 8ft 11in (2.71m)
Height: 12ft 9in (3.88m)	Bogie Type: BT10

AJ1G - RFM *Seating 24F*

Number	Depot	Livery	Owner
10228 (11035)	NC	AWT	PTR

AN2G - TSOB *Seating 52S*

10401 (12168)	NC	AWT	PTR
10402 (12010)	NC	AWT	PTR
10403 (12135)	NC	AWT	PTR
10404 (12068)	NC	AWT	PTR
10405 (12137)	NC	AWT	PTR
10406 (12020)	NC	AWT	PTR
10411 (10200)	NC	AWT	PTR
10412 (10203)	NC	AWT	PTR
10413 (10214)	NC	AWT	PTR
10414 (10216)	NC	AWT	PTR
10415 (10223)	NC	AWT	PTR
10416 (10228)	NC	AWT	PTR
10417 (10247)	NC	AWT	PTR

AD1G - FO, *FOD *Seating 48F/37F*

11066	NC	AWT	PTR
11067	NC	AWT	PTR
11068	NC	AWT	PTR
11069	NC	AWT	PTR
11070	NC	AWT	PTR
11072*	NC	AWT	PTR
11073*	NC	AWT	PTR
11075	NC	AWT	PTR
11076	NC	AWT	PTR
11077	NC	AWT	PTR
11078*	NC	AWT	PTR
11080	NC	AWT	PTR
11081	NC	AWT	PTR
11082	NC	AWT	PTR
11085*	NC	AWT	PTR
11087*	NC	AWT	PTR
11088*	NC	AWT	PTR
11090*	NC	AWT	PTR
11091*	NC	AWT	PTR
11092	NC	AWT	PTR
11093*	NC	AWT	PTR
11094*	NC	AWT	PTR
11095*	NC	AWT	PTR
11096*	NC	AWT	PTR
11098*	NC	AWT	PTR
11099*	NC	AWT	PTR
11100*	NC	AWT	PTR
11101*	NC	AWT	PTR

AC2G - TSO *Seating 80S*

12005	NC	AWT	PTR
12009	NC	AWT	PTR
12012	NC	AWT	PTR
12013	NC	AWT	PTR
12015	NC	AWT	PTR
12016	NC	AWT	PTR
12019	NC	AWT	PTR
12021	NC	AWT	PTR
12024	NC	AWT	PTR
12026	NC	AWT	PTR
12027	NC	AWT	PTR
12030	NC	AWT	PTR
12031	NC	AWT	PTR
12032	NC	AWT	PTR
12034	NC	AWT	PTR
12035	NC	AWT	PTR
12037	NC	AWT	PTR
12040	NC	AWT	PTR
12041	NC	AWT	PTR
12042	NC	AWT	PTR
12046	NC	AWT	PTR
12049	NC	AWT	PTR
12051	NC	AWT	PTR
12056	NC	AWT	PTR
12057	NC	AWT	PTR
12060	NC	AWT	PTR
12061	NC	AWT	PTR
12062	NC	AWT	PTR
12064	NC	AWT	PTR
12066	NC	AWT	PTR
12067	NC	AWT	PTR
12073	NC	AWT	PTR
12079	NC	AWT	PTR
12081	NC	AWT	PTR
12082	NC	AWT	PTR
12084	NC	AWT	PTR
12089	NC	AWT	PTR
12090	NC	AWT	PTR
12091	NC	AWT	PTR
12093	NC	AWT	PTR
12097	NC	AWT	PTR
12098	NC	AWT	PTR
12099	NC	AWT	PTR
12103	NC	AWT	PTR
12105	NC	AWT	PTR
12107	NC	AWT	PTR
12108	NC	AWT	PTR

12109	NC	AWT	PTR
12110	NC	AWT	PTR
12111	NC	AWT	PTR
12114	NC	AWT	PTR
12115	NC	AWT	PTR
12116	NC	AWT	PTR
12118	NC	AWT	PTR
12120	NC	AWT	PTR
12125	NC	AWT	PTR
12126	NC	AWT	PTR
12129	NC	AWT	PTR
12130	NC	AWT	PTR
12132	NC	AWT	PTR
12137	NC	AWT	PTR
12139	NC	AWT	PTR
12141	NC	AWT	PTR
12143	NC	AWT	PTR
12146	NC	AWT	PTR
12147	NC	AWT	PTR
12148	NC	AWT	PTR
12150	NC	AWT	PTR
12151	NC	AWT	PTR
12153	NC	AWT	PTR
12154	NC	AWT	PTR
12159	NC	AWT	PTR
12164	NC	AWT	PTR
12166	NC	AWT	PTR
12167	NC	AWT	PTR
12170	NC	AWT	PTR
12171	NC	AWT	PTR

NZAH - DVT

82102	NC	AWT	PTR
82103§	NC	AWT	PTR
82105	NC	AWT	PTR
82107	NC	AWT	PTR
82112	NC	AWT	PTR
82114	NC	AWT	PTR
82118	NC	AWT	PTR
82121	NC	AWT	PTR
82127	NC	AWT	PTR
82132	NC	AWT	PTR
82133	NC	AWT	PTR
82136	NC	AWT	PTR
82139	NC	AWT	PTR
82143	NC	AWT	PTR
82152	NC	AWT	PTR

§ Fitted with de-icing equipment

Left: *Now all refurbished and carrying the Abellio Greater Anglia white livery, the Norwich-based Mk3 fleet will remain in traffic until new Stadler-built multiple unit trains enter service from 2019. First Open Disabled (FOD) No. 11093 is illustrated. The fleet of FOD vehicles have 37 first class seats in the 2+1 style with a disabled access toilet compartment at one end.*
Antony Christie

Right: *To operate at the remote end of Class 90-powered Abellio Anglia main-line services, a fleet of 15 Mk3 Driving Van Trailers (DVT) is allocated to Norwich; like the Class 90s, these came second-hand from the West Coast Main Line, but have been considerably refurbished. Painted in Abellio white livery, vehicle No. 82152 is seen arriving at Norwich.*
Antony Christie

Class 153

	Vehicle Length: 76ft 5in (23.29m)	Engine: 1 x NT855R5 of 285hp
	Height: 12ft 3⅛in (3.75m)	Horsepower: 285hp (213kW)
	Width: 8ft 10in (2.70m)	Seats (total/car): 72S

Number	Formation DMSL	Depot	Livery	Owner	Operator	Name
153306	52306	NC	AWT	PTR	GAR	
153309	52309	NC	AWT	PTR	GAR	*Gerard Fiennes*
153314	52314	NC	AWT	PTR	GAR	
153322	52322	NC	AWT	PTR	GAR	*Benjamin Britten*
153335	52335	NC	AWT	PTR	GAR	*Michael Palin*

Right: *Five Class 153 'Bubble cars' are allocated to Norwich Crown Point for Anglia rural branch-line use. Seating 72 standard class passengers in the 2+2 style, with a toilet compartment at one end of the vehicle, the '153s' provide a good service. Under the Abellio route modernisation, they will be replaced by new Stadler DMU sets. Class 153 No. 153335* Michael Palin *is seen at Brundall.* **Antony Christie**

Class 156

	Vehicle Length: 75ft 6in (23.03m)	Engine: 1 x Cummins NT855R5 of 285hp per car
	Height: 12ft 6in (3.81m)	Horsepower: 570hp (425kW)
	Width: 8ft 11in (2.73m)	Seats (total/car): 136S, 62S/74S

Number	Formation DMSL+DMS	Depot	Livery	Owner	Operator
156402	52402+57402	NC	AWT	PTR	GAR
156407	52407+57407	NC	AWT	PTR	GAR
156409	52409+57409	NC	AWT	PTR	GAR
156412	52412+57412	NC	AWT	PTR	GAR
156416	52416+57416	NC	AWT	PTR	GAR
156417	52417+57417	NC	AWT	PTR	GAR
156418	52418+57418	NC	AWT	PTR	GAR
156419	52419+57419	NC	AWT	PTR	GAR
156422	52422+57422	NC	AWT	PTR	GAR

Names applied
156416 *Saint Edmund*
156418 *ESTA 1965-2015*

Right: *Longer-distance Norwich-based Anglia rural services are in the hands of a fleet of nine two-car Class 156s. These have recently been refurbished to include a disabled access toilet in one vehicle. All sets carry Abellio white livery offset by orange passenger doors. Set No. 156419 is illustrated.*
Antony Christie

Passenger Train Operating Companies - Greater Anglia

Greater Anglia

Class 170/2
Turbostar

Vehicle Length: 77ft 6in (23.62m)			Engine: 1 x MTU 6R 183TD13H of 422hp per vehicle			
Height: 12ft 4½in (3.77m)			Horsepower: 1,266hp (944kW)			
Width: 8ft 10in (2.69m)			Seats (total/car): 7F-173S 7F-39S/68S/66S			

Number	Formation DMCL+MSL+DMSL	Depot	Livery	Owner	Operator
170201	50201+56201+79201	NC	ORA	PTR	GAR
170202	50202+56202+79202	NC	ORA	PTR	GAR
170203	50203+56203+79203	NC	ORA	PTR	GAR
170204	50204+56204+79204	NC	ORA	PTR	GAR
170205	50205+56205+79205	NC	ORA	PTR	GAR
170206	50206+56206+79206	NC	ORA	PTR	GAR
170207	50207+56207+79207	NC	ORA	PTR	GAR
170208	50208+56208+79208	NC	ADV	PTR	GAR

Vehicle Length: 77ft 6in (23.62m)		Engine: 1 x MTU 6R 183TD13H of 422hp per vehicle
Height: 12ft 4½in (3.77m)		Horsepower: 844hp (629kW)
Width: 8ft 10in (2.69m)		Seats (total/car): 9F-110S 57S/9F-53S

Number	Formation DMSL+DMCL	Depot	Livery	Owner	Operator
170270	50270+79270	NC	ORA	PTR	GAR
170271	50271+79271	NC	ANN	PTR	GAR
170272	50272+79272	NC	ANN	PTR	GAR
170273	50273+79273	NC	ANN	PTR	GAR

Left: *Class 170/2s in both two- and three-car formations are operated by Anglia on long-distance services. A total of eight three-car and four two-car sets are in use, allocated to Norwich and still displaying the older turquoise and black livery. Three-car set No. 170202 is illustrated at Norwich.*
Antony Christie

Class 317/5

Vehicle Length: (Driving) 65ft 0¾in (19.83m)	Width: 9ft 3in (2.82m)	
(Inter) 65ft 4¼in (19.92m)	Horsepower: 1,000hp (746kW)	
Height: 12ft 1½in (3.58m)	Seats (total/car): 291S, 74S/79S/68S/70S	

Number	Former Number	Formation DTSO(A)+MSO+TCO+DTSO(B)	Depot	Livery	Owner	Operator	Name
317501	(317301)	77024+62661+71577+77048	IL	AWT	ANG	GAR	
317502	(317302)	77001+62662+71578+77049	IL	AWT	ANG	GAR	
317503	(317303)	77002+62663+71579+77050	IL	AWT	ANG	GAR	
317504	(317304)	77003+62664+71580+77051	IL	AWT	ANG	GAR	
317505	(317305)	77004+62665+71581+77052	IL	AWT	ANG	GAR	
317506	(317306)	77005+62666+71582+77053	IL	AWT	ANG	GAR	
317507	(317307)	77006+62667+71583+77054	IL	AWT	ANG	GAR	*University of Cambridge 800 years 1209-2009*

Left: *A fleet of 15 earlier body-styled Class 317s operates London outer suburban services for Abellio Anglia, based at Ilford. In the process of being repainted into Abellio white livery, these sets will by around 2020 be replaced by new Bombardier-built 'Aventra' EMUs. Class 317/5 No. 317501 is shown at London Liverpool Street. This was the very first set of the 'Bed-Pan' electric stock, then numbered as 317301, built in 1981.*
Antony Christie

317508	(317311)	77010+62697+71587+77058	IL	AWT	ANG	GAR	
317509	(317312)	77011+62672+71588+77059	IL	AWT	ANG	GAR	
317510	(317313)	77012+62673+71589+77060	IL	AWT	ANG	GAR	
317511	(317315)	77014+62675+71591+77062	IL	AWT	ANG	GAR	
317512	(317316)	77015+62676+71592+77063	IL	AWT	ANG	GAR	
317513	(317317)	77016+62677+71593+77064	IL	AWT	ANG	GAR	
317514	(317318)	77017+62678+71594+77065	IL	AWT	ANG	GAR	
317515	(317320)	77019+62680+71596+77067	IL	AWT	ANG	GAR	

Class 317/6

Vehicle Length: (Driving) 65ft 0¾in (19.83m) Width: 9ft 3in (2.82m)
(Inter) 65ft 4¼in (19.92m) Horsepower: 1,000hp (746kW)
Height: 12ft 1½in (3.58m) Seats (total/car): 24F/244S, 64S/70S/62S/24F-48S

Number	Former Number	Formation DTSO+MSO+TSO+DTCO	Depot	Livery	Owner	Operator	Name
317649	(317349)	77200+62846+71734+77220	IL	NXU	ANG	GAR	
317650	(317350)	77201+62847+71735+77221	IL	NXU	ANG	GAR	
317651	(317351)	77202+62848+71736+77222	IL	NXU	ANG	GAR	
317652	(317352)	77203+62849+71739+77223	IL	NXU	ANG	GAR	
317653	(317353)	77204+62850+71738+77224	IL	NXU	ANG	GAR	
317654	(317354)	77205+62851+71737+77225	IL	NXU	ANG	GAR	*Richard Wells*
317655	(317355)	77206+62852+71740+77226	IL	AWT	ANG	GAR	
317656	(317356)	77207+62853+71742+77227	IL	AWT	ANG	GAR	
317657	(317357)	77208+62854+71741+77228	IL	NXU	ANG	GAR	
317658	(317358)	77209+62855+71743+77229	IL	AWT	ANG	GAR	
317659	(317359)	77210+62856+71744+77230	IL	AWT	ANG	GAR	
317660	(317360)	77211+62857+71745+77231	IL	AWT	ANG	GAR	
317661	(317361)	77212+62858+71746+77232	IL	AWT	ANG	GAR	
317662	(317362)	77213+62859+71747+77233	IL	AWT	ANG	GAR	
317663	(317363)	77214+62860+71748+77234	IL	AWT	ANG	GAR	
317664	(317364)	77215+62861+71749+77235	IL	AWT	ANG	GAR	
317665	(317365)	77216+62862+71750+77236	IL	AWT	ANG	GAR	
317666	(317366)	77217+62863+71752+77237	IL	NXU	ANG	GAR	
317667	(317367)	77218+62864+71751+77238	IL	AWT	ANG	GAR	
317668	(317368)	77219+62865+71753+77239	IL	AWT	ANG	GAR	
317669	(317369)	77280+62886+71762+77284	IL	NXU	ANG	GAR	
317670	(317370)	77281+62887+71763+77285	IL	AWT	ANG	GAR	
317671	(317371)	77282+62888+71764+77286	IL	AWT	ANG	GAR	
317672	(317372)	77283+62889+71765+77287	IL	AWT	ANG	GAR	

Class 317/8

Vehicle Length: (Driving) 65ft 0¾in (19.83m) Width: 9ft 3in (2.82m)
(Inter) 65ft 4¼in (19.92m) Horsepower: 1,000hp (746kW)
Height: 12ft 1½in (3.58m) Seats (total/car): 20F/265S, 74S/79S/20F-42S/70S

Number	Former Number	Formation DTSO(A)+MSO+TCO+DTSO(B)	Depot	Livery	Owner	Operator	
317881	(317321)	77020+62681+71597+77068	IL	AWT	ANG	GAR	12 additional Class 317s,
317882	(317324)	77023+62684+71600+77071	IL	NXU	ANG	GAR	Nos. 317337-317348, and
317883	(317325)	77000+62685+71601+77072	IL	AWT	ANG	GAR	six unspecified Class
317884	(317326)	77025+62686+71602+77073	IL	NXU	ANG	GAR	321s will transfer from
317885	(317327)	77026+62687+71603+77074	IL	NXU	ANG	GAR	Thameslink to Greater
317886	(317328)	77027+62688+71604+77075	IL	NXU	ANG	GAR	Anglia in January 2017.

Right: *Six members of Class 317/8, sets which were refurbished by Wabtec in 2006 and of phase 1 design, are in traffic. Painted in Abellio white livery with blue passenger doors, set No. 317885 is seen at London Liverpool Street.* **Antony Christie**

■ Class 317/7 No. 317722 is in traffic based at Ilford as a traction and rolling stock development train, fitted with different interior layouts. The set is formed of vehicles 77021+62682+71598+77069.

Greater Anglia

Class 321/3

Vehicle Length: (Driving) 65ft 0¾in (19.83m)	Width: 9ft 3in (2.82m)			
(Inter) 65ft 4¼in (19.92m)	Horsepower: 1,328hp (996kW)			
Height: 12ft 4¾in (3.78m)	Seats (total/car): 16F/292S, 16F-57S/82S/75S/78S			

Number	Formation DTCO+MSO+TSO+DTSO	Depot	Livery	Owner	Operator	Name
321301	78049+62975+71880+77853	IL	GAZ	EVL	GAR	
321302	78050+62976+71881+77854	IL	GAZ	EVL	GAR	
321303	78051+62977+71882+77855	IL	GAZ	EVL	GAR	
321304	78052+62978+71883+77856	IL	GAZ	EVL	GAR	
321305	78053+62979+71884+77857	IL	GAR	EVL	GAR	
321306	78054+62980+71885+77858	IL	GAR	EVL	GAR	
321307	78055+62981+71886+77859	IL	GAR	EVL	GAR	
321308	78056+62982+71887+77860	IL	GAR	EVL	GAR	
321309	78057+62983+71888+77861	IL	GAR	EVL	GAR	
321310	78058+62984+71889+77862	IL	NGE	EVL	GAR	
321311	78059+62985+71890+77863	IL	GAR	EVL	GAR	
321312	78060+62986+71891+77864	IL	GAR	EVL	GAR	Southend-on-Sea
321313	78061+62987+71892+77865	IL	GAR	EVL	GAR	University of Essex
321314	78062+62988+71893+77866	IL	NGE	EVL	GAR	
321315	78063+62989+71894+77867	IL	GAR	EVL	GAR	
321316	78064+62990+71895+77868	IL	GAR	EVL	GAR	
321317	78065+62991+71896+77869	IL	GAR	EVL	GAR	
321318	78066+62992+71897+77870	IL	GAR	EVL	GAR	
321319	78067+62993+71898+77871	IL	GAR	EVL	GAR	
321320	78068+62994+71899+77872	IL	GAR	EVL	GAR	
321321	78069+62995+71900+77873	IL	GAR	EVL	GAR	NSPCC Essex Full Stop
321322	78070+62996+71901+77874	IL	GAR	EVL	GAR	
321323	78071+62997+71902+77875	IL	GAR	EVL	GAR	
321324	78072+62998+71903+77876	IL	GAR	EVL	GAR	
321325	78073+62999+71904+77877	IL	GAR	EVL	GAR	
321326	78074+63000+71905+77878	IL	GAR	EVL	GAR	
321327	78075+63001+71906+77879	IL	NXU	EVL	GAR	
321328	78076+63002+71907+77880	IL	GAR	EVL	GAR	
321329	78077+63003+71908+77881	IL	GAR	EVL	GAR	
321330	78078+63004+71909+77882	IL	NXU	EVL	GAR	
321331	78079+63005+71910+77883	IL	NXU	EVL	GAR	
321332	78080+63006+71911+77884	IL	NXU	EVL	GAR	
321333	78081+63007+71912+77885	IL	NXU	EVL	GAR	Amsterdam
321334	78082+63008+71913+77886	IL	NXU	EVL	GAR	
321335	78083+63009+71914+77887	IL	NXU	EVL	GAR	Geoffrey Freeman Allen
321336	78084+63010+71915+77888	IL	NXU	EVL	GAR	
321337	78085+63011+71916+77889	IL	NXU	EVL	GAR	
321338	78086+63012+71917+77890	IL	NXU	EVL	GAR	
321339	78087+63013+71918+77891	IL	NXU	EVL	GAR	
321340	78088+63014+71919+77892	IL	NXU	EVL	GAR	
321341	78089+63015+71920+77893	IL	NXU	EVL	GAR	
321342	78090+63016+71921+77894	IL	NXU	EVL	GAR	R Barnes
321343	78091+63017+71922+77895	IL	NXU	EVL	GAR	
321344	78092+63018+71923+77896	IL	NXU	EVL	GAR	
321345	78093+63019+71924+77897	IL	NXU	EVL	GAR	
321346	78094+63020+71925+77898	IL	NGU	EVL	GAR	
321347	78131+63105+71991+78280	IL	NXU	EVL	GAR	
321348	78132+63106+71992+78281	IL	NXU	EVL	GAR	
321349	78133+63107+71993+78282	IL	NGE	EVL	GAR	
321350	78134+63108+71994+78283	IL	NXU	EVL	GAR	Gurkha
321351	78135+63109+71995+78284	IL	NXU	EVL	GAR	London Southend Airport
321352	78136+63110+71996+78285	IL	NXU	EVL	GAR	
321353	78137+63111+71997+78286	IL	NXU	EVL	GAR	
321354	78138+63112+71998+78287	IL	NXU	EVL	GAR	
321355	78139+63113+71999+78288	IL	NXU	EVL	GAR	
321356	78140+63114+72000+78289	IL	NGU	EVL	GAR	
321357	78141+63115+72001+78290	IL	NGE	EVL	GAR	
321358	78142+63116+72002+78291	IL	NXU	EVL	GAR	
321359	78143+63117+72003+78292	IL	AWT	EVL	GAR	
321360	78144+63118+72004+78293	IL	NXU	EVL	GAR	Phoenix

321361	78145+63119+72005+78294	IL	AWT	EVL	GAR
321362	78146+63120+72006+78295	IL	AWT	EVL	GAR
321363	78147+63121+72007+78296	IL	AWT	EVL	GAR
321364	78148+63122+72008+78297	IL	AWT	EVL	GAR
321365	78149+63123+72009+78298	IL	AWT	EVL	GAR
321366	78150+63124+72010+78299	IL	AWT	EVL	GAR

Between 2015 and 2018 up to 30 Class 321/3 sets are being fully refurbished under the 'Renatus Project', a joint initiative between Eversholt Leasing and Wabtec. With the 2016 announcement of a complete new fleet for Abellio, it is not clear how many sets will be overhauled.

Right: *The backbone of the Abellio outer-suburban passenger network is two fleets of Class 321/3 and 321/4 sets allocated to Ilford. The '321/3s' were introduced by NSE for Great Eastern service, while the 321/4s were originally used on the Euston line. Painted in Abellio white livery with blue doors, set No. 321349 is shown.*
Ron Cover

Class 321/4

Vehicle Length: (Driving) 65ft 0¾in (19.83m)	*Width:* 9ft 3in (2.82m)	
(Inter) 65ft 4¼in (19.92m)	*Horsepower:* 1,328hp (996kW)	
Height: 12ft 4¾in (3.78m)	*Seats (total/car):* 16F/283S, 16F-52S/79S/74S/78S	

Number	Formation DTCO+MSO+TSO+DTSO	Depot	Livery	Owner	Operator	Name
321421	78115+63083+71969+77963	IL	NXU	EVL	GAR	
321422	78116+63084+71970+77964	IL	NXU	EVL	GAR	
321423	78117+63085+71971+77965	IL	NXU	EVL	GAR	
321424	78118+63086+71972+77966	IL	GAR	EVL	GAR	
321425	78119+63087+71973+77967	IL	AWT	EVL	GAR	
321426	78120+63088+71974+77968	IL	GAR	EVL	GAR	
321427	78121+63089+71975+77969	IL	GAR	EVL	GAR	
321428	78122+63090+71976+77970	IL	AWT	EVL	GAR	*The Essex Commuter*
321429	78123+69031+71977+77971	IL	GAR	EVL	GAR	
321430	78124+63092+71978+77972	IL	GAR	EVL	GAR	
321431	78151+63125+72011+78300	IL	GAR	EVL	GAR	
321432	78152+63126+72012+78301	IL	NXU	EVL	GAR	
321433	78153+63127+72013+78302	IL	NXU	EVL	GAR	
321434	78154+63128+72014+78303	IL	NXU	EVL	GAR	
321435	78155+63129+72015+78304	IL	NXU	EVL	GAR	
321436	78156+63130+72016+78305	IL	NXU	EVL	GAR	
321437	78157+63131+72017+78306	IL	NXU	EVL	GAR	
321438	78158+63132+72018+78307	IL	AWT	EVL	GAR	
321439	78159+63133+72019+78308	IL	AWT	EVL	GAR	
321440	78160+63134+72020+78309	IL	AWT	EVL	GAR	
321441	78161+63135+72021+78310	IL	AWT	EVL	GAR	
321442	78162+63136+72022+78311	IL	AWT	EVL	GAR	*Crouch Valley 1889-2014*
321443	78125+63099+71985+78274	IL	AWT	EVL	GAR	
321444	78126+63100+71986+78275	IL	AWT	EVL	GAR	*Essex Lifeboats*
321445	78127+63101+71987+78276	IL	AWT	EVL	GAR	
321446	78128+63102+71988+78277	IL	AWT	EVL	GAR	*George Mullings*
321447	78129+63103+71989+78278	IL	AWT	EVL	GAR	
321448	78130+63104+71990+78279	IL	ADV	EVL	§	

§ Eversholt development train consisting of two vehicles with Metro interior and two with suburban, seating 246 passengers and allocated to Ilford for demonstration running on Abellio Greater Anglia services.

Left: *This fleet of 28 Class 321/4 sets was originally introduced in the 1980s for NSE's Euston outer-suburban network. Allocated to Ilford, these sets still have slightly different passenger interiors from the 321/3 sets. Unit No. 321443 is seen at Stratford showing the white with orange doors livery style.* **Antony Christie**

Class 360/1
Desiro

Vehicle Length: 66ft 9in (20.4m)	Horsepower: 1,341hp (1,000kW)
Height: 12ft 1½in (3.7m)	Seats (total/car): 16F/265S, 8F-59S/69S/78S/8F-59S
Width: 9ft 2in (2.79m)	

Number	Formation DMCO(A)+PTSO+TSO+DMCO(B)	Depot	Livery	Owner	Operator
360101	65551+72551+74551+68551	IL	FNA	ANG	GAR
360102	65552+72552+74552+68552	IL	FNA	ANG	GAR
360103	65553+72553+74553+68553	IL	FNA	ANG	GAR
360104	65554+72554+74554+68554	IL	FNA	ANG	GAR
360105	65555+72555+74555+68555	IL	FNA	ANG	GAR
360106	65556+72556+74556+68556	IL	FNA	ANG	GAR
360107	65557+72557+74557+68557	IL	FNA	ANG	GAR
360108	65558+72558+74558+68558	IL	FNA	ANG	GAR
360109	65559+72559+74559+68559	IL	FNA	ANG	GAR
360110	65560+72560+74560+68560	IL	FNA	ANG	GAR
360111	65561+72561+74561+68561	IL	FNA	ANG	GAR
360112	65562+72562+74562+68562	IL	FNA	ANG	GAR
360113	65563+72563+74563+68563	IL	FNA	ANG	GAR
360114	65564+72564+74564+68564	IL	FNA	ANG	GAR
360115	65565+72565+74565+68565	IL	FNA	ANG	GAR
360116	65566+72566+74566+68566	IL	FNA	ANG	GAR
360117	65567+72567+74567+68567	IL	FNA	ANG	GAR
360118	65568+72568+74568+68568	IL	FNA	ANG	GAR
360119	65569+72569+74569+68569	IL	FNA	ANG	GAR
360120	65570+72570+74570+68570	IL	FNA	ANG	GAR
360121	65571+72571+74571+68571	IL	FNA	ANG	GAR

Below: *Post-privatisation, First Group, the then operator of the Anglia franchise was keen to introduce new stock, and through a funding package with Angel Trains obtained a fleet of 21 four-car Class 360/1 Siemens 'Desiro' sets for longer-distance outer-suburban use. All sets still carry a version of First blue with Abellio branding. Set No. 360115 is seen at Stratford with a service bound for London Liverpool Street.* **Ron Cover**

Class 379
Electrostar

Vehicle Length: (Driving) 66ft 9in (20.40m)		Width: 9ft 2in (2.80m)		
(Inter) 65ft 6in (19.99m)		Horsepower: 2,010hp (1,500kW)		
Height: 12ft 4in (3.77m)		Seats (total/car): 20F/189S, 60S/62S/43S/20F-24S		

Number	Formation DMSO(A)+MSO+TSO+DMCO	Depot	Livery	Owner	Operator	Name
379001	61201+61701+61901+62101	IL	NXU	MAG	GAR	
379002	61202+61702+61902+62102	IL	NXU	MAG	GAR	
379003	61203+61703+61903+62103	IL	NXU	MAG	GAR	
379004	61204+61704+61904+62104	IL	NXU	MAG	GAR	
379005	61205+61705+61905+62105	IL	NXU	MAG	GAR	*Stansted Express*
379006	61206+61706+61906+62106	IL	NXU	MAG	GAR	
379007	61207+61707+61907+62107	IL	NXU	MAG	GAR	
379008	61208+61708+61908+62108	IL	NXU	MAG	GAR	
379009	61209+61709+61909+62109	IL	NXU	MAG	GAR	
379010	61210+61710+61910+62110	IL	NXU	MAG	GAR	
379011	61211+61711+61911+62111	IL	NXU	MAG	GAR	*Ely Cathedral*
379012	61212+61712+61912+62112	IL	NXU	MAG	GAR	*The West Anglian*
379013	61213+61713+61913+62113	IL	NXU	MAG	GAR	
379014	61214+61714+61914+62114	IL	NXU	MAG	GAR	
379015	61215+61715+61915+62115	IL	NXU	MAG	GAR	*City of Cambridge*
379016	61216+61716+61916+62116	IL	NXU	MAG	GAR	
379017	61217+61717+61917+62117	IL	NXU	MAG	GAR	
379018	61218+61718+61918+62118	IL	NXU	MAG	GAR	
379019	61219+61719+61919+62119	IL	NXU	MAG	GAR	
379020	61220+61720+61920+62120	IL	NXU	MAG	GAR	
379021	61221+61721+61921+62121	IL	NXU	MAG	GAR	
379022	61222+61722+61922+62122	IL	NXU	MAG	GAR	
379023	61223+61723+61923+62123	IL	NXU	MAG	GAR	
379024	61224+61724+61924+62124	IL	NXU	MAG	GAR	
379025	61225+61725+61925+62125	IL	NXU	MAG	GAR	*Go Discover*
379026	61226+61726+61926+62126	IL	NXU	MAG	GAR	
379027	61227+61727+61927+62127	IL	NXU	MAG	GAR	
379028	61228+61728+61928+62128	IL	NXU	MAG	GAR	
379029	61229+61729+61929+62129	IL	NXU	MAG	GAR	
379030	61230+61730+61930+62130	IL	NXU	MAG	GAR	

Right: *Despite being introduced as recently as 2011, the 30-strong fleet of four-car Bombardier Class 379 'Electrostar' units operated by Abellio Greater Anglia on the London Liverpool Street to Cambridge / Stansted Airport route is due to be replaced by new Stadler Flirt EMUs from 2019. On 14 September 2016, Nos. 379025 and 379024 form an eight-car service passing Sawbridgeworth.*
John Binch

New Abellio Greater Anglia rolling stock orders

As part of a new franchise agreement, Abellio will continue to operate the Greater Anglia franchise until October 2026 and new train orders were announced at the contract signing.

The new order consists of 22 ten-car and 89 five-car Bombardier 'Aventra' EMUs for suburban line operations to be funded by Angel Trains and the Commonwealth Bank of Australia. These will be built in Derby, UK.

For main-line and longer-distance services a fleet of Stadler 'Flirt' multiple units have been ordered; these will be formed as ten 12-car electric sets for InterCity operations, ten 12-car sets for Stansted Airport operations, 24 four-car bi-mode (electric/diesel) sets for regional operations and 14 three-car bi-mode sets for branch line use. These sets will be funded by Rock Rail/SL Capital Partners.

The Stadler sets are scheduled for delivery and introduction between 2019 and 2020 and the suburban sets between 2020 and 2021. Norwich and Ilford depots will remain, with a new depot built at Manningtree.

Heathrow Express / Heathrow Connect

Address: ✉ 6th Floor, 50 Eastbourne Terrace, Paddington, London, W2 6LX

✆ queries@heathrowexpress.com or queries@heathrowconnect.com

☏ 020 8750 6600

ⓘ www.heathrowexpress.com or www.heathrowconnect.com

Managing Director:	Keith Greenfield
Franchise Dates:	Private Open Access Operator
Principal Routes:	London Paddington - Heathrow Airport
Owned Stations:	Heathrow Central, Heathrow Terminal 4, Heathrow Terminal 5
Depots:	Old Oak Common HEX (OH)
Parent Company:	Heathrow Express - Heathrow Airport Ltd
	Heathrow Connect - Heathrow Airport Ltd / First Group

Heathrow Express

© TRC.Com Ltd 2013

Heathrow Airport Terminal 5 — Heathrow Airport Terminals 1-3 — London Paddington

Heathrow Connect

Heathrow Airport Terminal 4 — Heathrow Airport Terminals 1-3 — Hayes — Southall — Hanwell — West Ealing — Ealing Broadway — London Paddington

Shuttle

Left: *A fleet of 14 four- and five-car Class 332s operates the dedicated Heathrow Express service from London Paddington to Heathrow Airport, operating a 15-minute-interval service. The sets based at Old Oak Common usually operate in nine-car formations. Additional income is generated for the Heathrow Express airport service by train-length advertising contracts. At present sets carry Tata Communications colours. Set No. 332002, a four-car set, is seen at Paddington.*
Antony Christie

Class 332

		Vehicle Length: (Driving) 77ft 10¾in (23.74m)	Width: 9ft 1in (2.75m)
		(Inter) 75ft 11in (23.143m)	Horsepower: 1,876hp (1,400kW)
		Height: 12ft 1½in (3.70m)	Seats 4-car (total/car): 26F-148S, 26F/56S/44S/48S
			5-car (total/car): 26F-204S, 26F/56S/44S/56S/48S

Number	Formation	Depot	Livery	Owner	Operator
	DMFO+TSO+PTSO+(TSO)+DMSO				
332001	78400+72412+63400+ - +78401	OH	HEX	BAA	HEX
332002	78402+72409+63406+ - +78403	OH	HEX	BAA	HEX
332003	78404+72407+63402+ - +78405	OH	HEX	BAA	HEX
332004	78406+72406+63403+ - +78407	OH	HEX	BAA	HEX
332005	78408+72411+63404+72417+78409	OH	HEX	BAA	HEX
332006	78410+72410+63405+72415+78411	OH	HEX	BAA	HEX
332007	78412+72401+63401+72414+78413	OH	HEX	BAA	HEX

		Vehicle Length: (Driving) 77ft 10¾in (23.74m)	Width: 9ft 1in (2.75m)
		(Inter) 75ft 11in (23.143m)	Horsepower: 1,876hp (1,400kW)
		Height: 12ft 1½in (3.70m)	Seats 4-car (total/car): 14F-148S, 48S/56S/44S/14F
			5-car (total/car): 14F-204S, 48S/56S/44S/56S/14F

Number	Formation	Depot	Livery	Owner	Operator
	DMSO+TSO+PTSO+(TSO)+DMFLO				
332008	78414+72413+63407+72418+78415	OH	HEX	BAA	HEX
332009	78416+72400+63408+72416+78417	OH	HEX	BAA	HEX
332010	78418+72402+63409+ - +78419	OH	HEX	BAA	HEX
332011	78420+72403+63410+ - +78421	OH	HEX	BAA	HEX
332012	78422+72404+63411+ - +78423	OH	HEX	BAA	HEX
332013	78424+72408+63412+ - +78425	OH	HEX	BAA	HEX
332014	78426+72406+63413+ - +78427	OH	HEX	BAA	HEX

Class 360/2
Desiro

		Vehicle Length: 66ft 9in (20.4m)	Horsepower: 1,341hp (1,000kW)
		Height: 12ft 1½in (3.7m)	Seats (total/car): 340S, 63S/66S/74S/74S/63S
		Width: 9ft 2in (2.79m)	(360205 - 280S using 2+2 seats)

Number	Formation	Depot	Livery	Owner	Operator
	DMSO(A)+PTSO+TSO+TSO+DMSO(B)				
360201	78431+63421+72431+72421+78441	OH	HEC	BAA	HEC
360202	78432+63422+72432+72422+78442	OH	HEC	BAA	HEC
360203	78433+63423+72433+72423+78443	OH	HEC	BAA	HEC
360204	78434+63424+72434+72424+78444	OH	HEC	BAA	HEC
360205	78435+63425+72435+72425+78445	OH	HEL	BAA	HEC

Below: *GWR/Heathrow Airport Ltd operates the Connect all-stations service between London Paddington to Heathrow Airport. With GWR electrification and the introduction of Class 387s on London local services, the Class 360 fleet will soon be replaced by new Class 387s. Set No. 360202 is shown at Paddington.* **Antony Christie**

Island Line

Address: ✉ Ryde St Johns Road Station, Ryde, Isle of Wight, PO33 2BA
📧 info@island-line.co.uk ✆ 01983 812591 ⓘ www.island-line.co.uk
Managing Director: Tim Shoveller (South West Trains) **General Manager:** Andy Naylor
Franchise Dates: Part of SWT franchise 2 February 2007 - 3 February 2017
Principal Route: Ryde Pier Head - Shanklin
Owned Stations: All
Depots: Ryde St Johns Road (RY)
Parent Company: Stagecoach

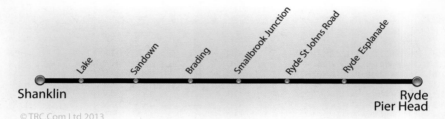

© TRC.Com Ltd 2013

Class 483

Vehicle Length: 52ft 4in (15.95m)	Horsepower: 670hp (500kW)
Height: 9ft 5½in (2.88m)	Seats (total/car): 82S, 40S/42S
Width: 8ft 8½in (2.65m)	

Number	Formation DMSO+DMSO	Depot	Livery	Owner	Operator		Number	Formation	Depot	Livery	Owner	Operator
							483006	126+226	RY	LUL	SWT	SIL
							483007	127+227	RY	LUL	SWT	SIL
483002	122+224	RY	LUL	SWT	SIL		483008	128+228	RY	LUL	SWT	SIL
483004	124+224	RY	LUL	SWT	SIL		483009	129+229	RY	LUL	SWT	SIL

Below: *The little self-contained 'Island Line' still continues to operate a regular service between Ryde Pier Head and Shanklin using Class 483 two-car ex-London Underground stock. Painted in heritage LU red livery, the sets are needing replacement and the long-term future of rails on the Island is currently under review. Set No. 009 is seen at Smallbrook Junction.* **CJM**

London Midland

Address:	✉ 102 New Street, Birmingham, B2 4JB
	✉ comments@londonmidland.com
	✆ 0844 811 0133
	ⓘ www.londonmidland.com
Managing Director:	Patrick Verwer
Franchise Dates:	11 November 2007 - October 2017
Principal Routes:	London Euston - Liverpool Lime Street, West Midlands routes to Stratford-upon-Avon, Worcester, Hereford, Shrewsbury, plus Bedford and St Albans Abbey branches
Depots:	Northampton (NN)§, Soho (SI), Tyseley (TS), Stourbridge Junction (SJ) § Operated by Siemens
Parent Company:	Govia

Passenger Train Operating Companies - London Midland

Class 08

Vehicle Length: 29ft 3in (8.91m)
Height: 12ft 8⅝in (3.87m)
Width: 8ft 6in (2.59m)

Engine: English Electric 6K
Horsepower: 400hp (298kW)
Electrical Equipment: English Electric

Number	Depot	Pool	Livery	Owner	Operator	Name
08616 (3783)	TS	EJLO	LMI	LMI	LMI	*Tyseley 100*
08805	SI	EJLO	GRY	LMI	LMI	

Class 139

Vehicle Length: 28ft 6in (8.7m)
Width: 7ft 6in (2.4m)

Engine: 1 x MVH420 2.0ltr LPG, flywheel hybrid
Seats (total/car): 18S

Number	Formation DMS	Depot	Livery	Owner	Operator		Number	Formation DMS	Depot	Livery	Owner	Operator
139001	39001	SJ	LMI	LMI	LMI		139002	39002	SJ	LMI	LMI	LMI

Below: *London Midland continues to operate two Parry People Mover vehicles on the short Stourbridge Junction to Stourbridge Town 'shuttle' service. Painted in London Midland grey, green and grey livery, vehicle No. 39002 (139002) is shown approaching Stourbridge Junction.* **CJM**

London Midland

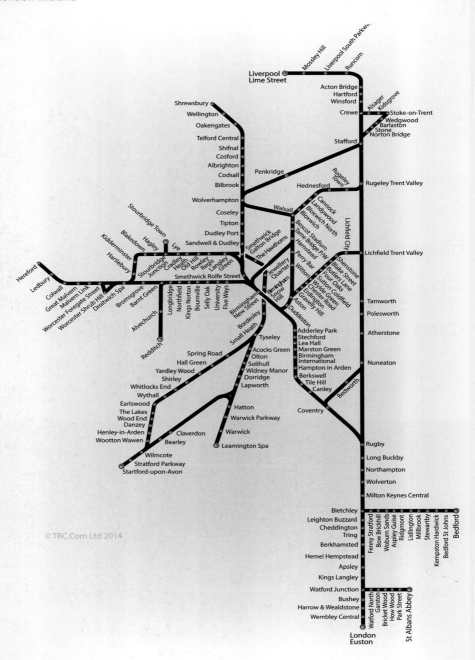

©TRC.Com Ltd 2014

Class 150/1
Sprinter

Vehicle Length: 64ft 9¾in (19.74m)			Engine: 1 x NT855R5 of 285hp per vehicle		
Height: 12ft 4½in (3.77m)			Horsepower: 570hp (425kW)		
Width: 9ft 3⅛in (2.82m)			Seats (total/car): 148S, 76S/72S		

Number	Formation	Depot	Livery	Owner	Operator
	DMSL+DMS				
150105	52105+57105	TS	CTL	ANG	LMI
150107	52107+57107	TS	LMI	ANG	LMI
150109	52109+57109	TS	CTL	ANG	LMI

Right: *Three refurbished Class 150/1 sets operate for London Midland, based at Tyseley and deployed on the Bedford-Bletchley route as well as on limited Midlands services often on the Birmingham-Hereford corridor. Set No. 150109 is captured on the Bedford-Bletchley route at Millbrook in May 2016.* **Antony Christie**

Scheduled for transfer to Northern

Class 153

Vehicle Length: 76ft 5in (23.29m)			Engine: 1 x NT855R5 of 285hp							
Height: 12ft 3⅛in (3.75m)			Horsepower: 285hp (213kW)							
Width: 8ft 10in (2.70m)			Seats (total/car): 72S							

Number	Formation	Depot	Livery	Owner	Operator		Number	Formation	Depot	Livery	Owner	Operator
	DMSL						153364	57364	TS	LMI	PTR	LMI
							153365	57365	TS	LMI	PTR	LMI
153334	52334	TS	LMI	PTR	LMI		153366	57366	TS	LMI	PTR	LMI
153354	57354	TS	LMI	PTR	LMI		153371	57371	TS	LMI	PTR	LMI
153356	57356	TS	LMI	PTR	LMI		153375	57375	TS	LMI	PTR	LMI

Right: *For deployment on low-patronage lines such as Bedford-Bletchley and Coventry-Nuneaton, London Midland operates a fleet of eight Class 153 'Bubble cars'. The operator is set to cease using '153s' on the Coventry to Nuneaton line following proposed introduction of Vivarail Class 230 ex-London Underground stock. On 1 September 2016, No. 153375 arrives alongside the new platform extension at Bedworth with the 17.14 Nuneaton to Coventry service.* **John Binch**

Class 170/5
Turbostar

Vehicle Length: 77ft 6in (23.62m)			Engine: 1 x MTU 6R 183TD13H of 422hp per vehicle							
Height: 12ft 4½in (3.77m)			Horsepower: 844hp (629kW)							
Width: 8ft 10in (2.69m)			Seats (total/car): 122S 55S/67S							

Number	Formation	Depot	Livery	Owner	Operator		Number	Formation	Depot	Livery	Owner	Operator
	DMSL+DMSL						170504	50504+79504	TS	LMI	PTR	LMI
							170505	50505+79505	TS	LMI	PTR	LMI
170501	50501+79501	TS	LMI	PTR	LMI		170506	50506+79506	TS	LMI	PTR	LMI
170502	50502+79502	TS	LMI	PTR	LMI		170507	50507+79507	TS	LMI	PTR	LMI
170503	50503+79503	TS	LMI	PTR	LMI		170508	50508+79508	TS	LMI	PTR	LMI

London Midland

170509	50509+79509	TS	LMI	PTR	LMI	170514	50514+79514	TS	LMI	PTR	LMI
170510	50510+79510	TS	LMI	PTR	LMI	170515	50515+79515	TS	LMI	PTR	LMI
170511	50511+79511	TS	LMI	PTR	LMI	170516	50516+79516	TS	LMI	PTR	LMI
170512	50512+79512	TS	LMI	PTR	LMI	170517	50517+79517	TS	LMI	PTR	LMI
170513	50513+79513	TS	LMI	PTR	LMI						

Class 170/6
Turbostar

Vehicle Length: 77ft 6in (23.62m)	Engine: 1 x MTU 6R 183TD13H of 422hp per vehicle
Height: 12ft 4½in (3.77m)	Horsepower: 1,266hp (944kW)
Width: 8ft 10in (2.69m)	Seats (total/car): 196S 55S/74S/67S

Number	Formation DMSL+MS+DMSL	Depot	Livery	Owner	Operator
170630	50630+56630+79630	TS	LMI	PTR	LMI
170631	50631+56631+79631	TS	LMI	PTR	LMI
170632	50632+56632+79632	TS	LMI	PTR	LMI
170633	50633+56633+79633	TS	LMI	PTR	LMI
170634	50634+56634+79634	TS	LMI	PTR	LMI
170635	50635+56635+79635	TS	LMI	PTR	LMI

Left: A fleet of 17 two-car and six three-car Class 170 'Turbostar' sets is operated by London Midland; based at Tyseley the sets operate longer-distance outer-suburban duties. All sets are refurbished and set out for standard class only occupancy. Sets are painted in standard London Midland livery. Three-car set No. 170634 is seen at Malvern. **Antony Christie**

Class 172/2
Turbostar

Vehicle Length: 73ft 4in (22.37m)	Engine: MTU 6H1800 of of 482hp (360kW) per vehicle
Height: 12ft 4½in (3.77m)	Horsepower: 964hp (720kW)
Width: 8ft 8in (2.69m)	Seats (total/car): 121S, 53S/68S

Number	Formation DMS+DMS	Depot	Livery	Owner	Operator						
						172216	50216+79216	TS	LMI	PTR	LMI
						172217	50217+79217	TS	LMI	PTR	LMI
172211	50211+79211	TS	LMI	PTR	LMI	172218	50218+79218	TS	LMI	PTR	LMI
172212	50212+79212	TS	LMI	PTR	LMI	172219	50219+59219	TS	LMI	PTR	LMI
172213	50213+79213	TS	LMI	PTR	LMI	172220	50220+79220	TS	LMI	PTR	LMI
172214	50214+79214	TS	LMI	PTR	LMI	172221	50221+79221	TS	LMI	PTR	LMI
172215	50215+79215	TS	LMI	PTR	LMI	172222	50222+79222	TS	LMI	PTR	LMI

Left: Currently the most modern stock operated by London Midland is a fleet of two- and three-car Class 172s, with 12 two-car and 15 three-car sets based at Tyseley. Painted in standard LM livery, these sets operate on the outer-suburban services. Three-car set No. 172334 is seen at Kidderminster. **CJM**

Class 172/3
Turbostar

Vehicle Length: (Driving) 73ft 4in (22.37m)			Engine: MTU 6H1800 of 482hp (360kW) per vehicle		
(Inter): 76ft 7in (23.36m)			Horsepower: 1,446hp (1,080kW)		
Height: 12ft 4½in (3.77m)			Seats (total/car): 193S, 53S/72S/68S		
Width: 8ft 8in (2.69m)					

Number	Formation DMSO+MS+DMSO	Depot	Livery	Owner	Operator
172331	50331+56331+79331	TS	LMI	PTR	LMI
172332	50332+56332+79332	TS	LMI	PTR	LMI
172333	50333+56333+79333	TS	LMI	PTR	LMI
172334	50334+56334+79334	TS	LMI	PTR	LMI
172335	50335+56335+79335	TS	LMI	PTR	LMI
172336	50336+56336+79336	TS	LMI	PTR	LMI
172337	50337+56337+79337	TS	LMI	PTR	LMI
172338	50338+56338+79338	TS	LMI	PTR	LMI
172339	50339+56339+79339	TS	LMI	PTR	LMI
172340	50340+56340+79340	TS	LMI	PTR	LMI
172341	50341+56341+79341	TS	LMI	PTR	LMI
172342	50342+56342+79342	TS	LMI	PTR	LMI
172343	50343+56343+79343	TS	LMI	PTR	LMI
172344	50344+56344+79344	TS	LMI	PTR	LMI
172345	50345+56345+79345	TS	LMI	PTR	LMI

Class 319

Vehicle Length: (Driving) 65ft 0¾in (19.83m)		Width: 9ft 3in (2.82m)	
(Inter) 65ft 4¼in (19.92m)		Horsepower: 1,326hp (990kW)	
Height: 11ft 9in (3.58m)		Seats (total/car): 12F/277S, 12F-54S/77S/72S/74S	

Number	Formation DTSO(A)+MSO+TSO+DTSO(B)	Depot	Livery	Owner	Operator
319013	77315+62903+71784+77314	NN	LMI	PTR	LMI
319216	77321+62906+71787+77320	NN	LMW	PTR	LMI
319429	77347+62919+71800+77346	NN	LMW	PTR	LMI
319441	77371+62931+71812+77370	NN	LMW	PTR	LMI
319455	77447+62969+71874+77446	NN	LMW	PTR	LMI
319457	77451+62971+71876+77450	NN	LMW	PTR	LMI
319460	77457+62974+71879+77456	NN	WHT	PTR	LMI

Right: *Shuffling of rolling stock, which saw the LM Class 321s transferred away, led to a fleet of seven Class 319s, previously used on Thameslink, being transferred to Northampton depot for peak-hour services to augment the main fleet of '350s'. Painted in LM livery, set No. 319013 is seen at Harrow & Wealdstone.* **Antony Christie**

Class 323

Vehicle Length: (Driving) 76ft 8¼in (23.37m)	Width: 9ft 2¼in (2.80m)	
(Inter) 76ft 10¾in (23.44m)	Horsepower: 1,565hp (1,168kW)	
Height: 12ft 4¾in (3.78m)	Seats (total/car): 284S, 98S/88S/98S	

Number	Formation DMSO(A)+PTSO+DMSO(B)	Depot	Livery	Owner	Op'r
323201	64001+72201+65001	SI	LMI	PTR	LMI
323202	64002+72202+65002	SI	LMI	PTR	LMI
323203	64003+72203+65003	SI	LMI	PTR	LMI
323204	64004+72204+65004	SI	LMI	PTR	LMI
323205	64005+72205+65005	SI	LMI	PTR	LMI
323206	64006+72206+65006	SI	LMI	PTR	LMI
323207	64007+72207+65007	SI	LMI	PTR	LMI
323208	64008+72208+65008	SI	LMI	PTR	LMI
323209	64009+72209+65009	SI	LMI	PTR	LMI
323210	64010+72210+65010	SI	LMI	PTR	LMI
323211	64011+72211+65011	SI	LMI	PTR	LMI
323212	64012+72212+65012	SI	LMI	PTR	LMI
323213	64013+72213+65013	SI	LMI	PTR	LMI
323214	64014+72214+65014	SI	LMI	PTR	LMI
323215	64015+72215+65015	SI	LMI	PTR	LMI
323216	64016+72216+65016	SI	LMI	PTR	LMI
323217	64017+72217+65017	SI	LMI	PTR	LMI
323218	64018+72218+65018	SI	LMI	PTR	LMI
323219	64019+72219+65019	SI	LMI	PTR	LMI
323220	64020+72220+65020	SI	LMI	PTR	LMI
323221	64021+72221+65021	SI	ADV	PTR	LMI

London Midland

323222	64022+72222+65022 SI	LMI	PTR	LMI	
323240	64040+72340+65040 SI	LMI	PTR	LMI	
323241	64041+72341+65041 SI	LMI	PTR	LMI	

323242	64042+72342+65042 SI	LMI	PTR	LMI
323243	64043+72343+65043 SI	LMI	PTR	LMI

Left: The Birmingham area suburban services are in the hands of a fleet of 26 Class 323 three-car sets based at Soho depot. Owned by Porterbrook, these sets can accommodate 284 seated and an equal number standing. Set No. 323243 is seen at Tipton. In 2017-18 the Class 323s presently operated by Northern in the Manchester area are scheduled to cascade to the Birmingham area as new stock is introduced. **John Binch**

Class 350/1
Desiro

Vehicle Length: 66ft 9in (20.4m)
Height: 12ft 1½in (3.78m)
Width: 9ft 2in (2.7m)

Horsepower: 1,341hp (1,000kW)
Seats (total/car): 24F-209S, 60S/24F-32S/57S/60S
110mph max speed

Number	Formation DMSO(A)+TCO+PTSO+DMSO(B)	Depot	Livery	Owner	Operator
350101	63761+66811+66861+63711	NN	LMI	ANG	LMI
350102	63762+66812+66862+63712	NN	LMI	ANG	LMI
350103	63765+66813+66863+63713	NN	LMI	ANG	LMI
350104	63764+66814+66864+63714	NN	LMI	ANG	LMI
350105	63763+66815+66868+63715	NN	LMI	ANG	LMI
350106	63766+66816+66866+63716	NN	LMI	ANG	LMI
350107	63767+66817+66867+63717	NN	LMI	ANG	LMI
350108	63768+66818+66865+63718	NN	LMI	ANG	LMI
350109	63769+66819+66869+63719	NN	LMI	ANG	LMI
350110	63770+66820+66870+63720	NN	LMA	ANG	LMI
350111	63771+66821+66871+63721	NN	LMI	ANG	LMI
350112	63772+66822+66872+63722	NN	LMI	ANG	LMI
350113	63773+66823+66873+63723	NN	LMI	ANG	LMI
350114	63774+66824+66874+63724	NN	LMI	ANG	LMI
350115	63775+66825+66875+63725	NN	LMI	ANG	LMI
350116	63776+66826+66876+63726	NN	LMI	ANG	LMI
350117	63777+66827+66877+63727	NN	LMI	ANG	LMI
350118	63778+66828+66878+63728	NN	LMI	ANG	LMI
350119	63779+66829+66879+63729	NN	LMI	ANG	LMI
350120	63780+66830+66880+63730	NN	LMI	ANG	LMI
350121	63781+66831+66881+63731	NN	LMI	ANG	LMI
350122	63782+66832+66882+63732	NN	LMI	ANG	LMI
350123	63783+66833+66883+63733	NN	LMI	ANG	LMI
350124	63784+66834+66884+63734	NN	LMI	ANG	LMI
350125	63785+66835+66885+63735	NN	LMI	ANG	LMI
350126	63786+66836+66886+63736	NN	LMI	ANG	LMI
350127	63787+66837+66887+63737	NN	LMI	ANG	LMI
350128	63788+66838+66888+63738	NN	LMI	ANG	LMI
350129	63789+66839+66889+63739	NN	LMI	ANG	LMI
350130	63790+66840+66890+63740	NN	LMI	ANG	LMI

Class 350/2
Desiro

Vehicle Length: 66ft 9in (20.4m)
Height: 12ft 1½in (3.78m)
Width: 9ft 2in (2.7m)

Horsepower: 1,341hp (1,000kW)
Seats (total/car): 24F-243S, 70S/24F-42S/61S/70S
100mph max speed

Number	Formation DMSO(A)+TCO+PTSO+DMSO(B)	Depot	Livery	Owner	Operator	Name
350231	61431+65231+67531+61531	NN	LMI	PTR	LMI	
350232	61432+65232+67532+61532	NN	LMI	PTR	LMI	*Chad Varah*
350233§	61433+65233+67533+61533	NN	LMI	PTR	LMI	
350234	61434+65234+67534+61534	NN	LMI	PTR	LMI	

350235	61435+65235+67535+61535	NN	LMI	PTR	LMI
350236	61436+65236+67536+61536	NN	LMI	PTR	LMI
350237	61437+65237+67537+61537	NN	LMI	PTR	LMI
350238	61438+65238+67538+61538	NN	LMI	PTR	LMI
350239	61439+65239+67539+61539	NN	LMI	PTR	LMI
350240	61440+65240+67540+61540	NN	LMI	PTR	LMI
350241	61441+65241+67541+61541	NN	LMI	PTR	LMI
350242	61442+65242+67542+61542	NN	LMI	PTR	LMI
350243	61443+65243+67543+61543	NN	LMI	PTR	LMI
350244	61444+65244+67544+61544	NN	LMI	PTR	LMI
350245	61445+65245+67545+61545	NN	LMI	PTR	LMI
350246	61446+65246+67546+61546	NN	LMI	PTR	LMI
350247	61447+65247+67547+61547	NN	LMI	PTR	LMI
350248	61448+65248+67548+61548	NN	LMI	PTR	LMI
350249	61449+65249+67549+61549	NN	LMI	PTR	LMI
350250	61450+65250+67550+61550	NN	LMI	PTR	LMI
350251	61451+65251+67551+61551	NN	LMI	PTR	LMI
350252	61452+65252+67552+61552	NN	LMI	PTR	LMI
350253	61453+65253+67553+61553	NN	LMI	PTR	LMI
350254	61454+65254+67554+61554	NN	LMI	PTR	LMI
350255	61455+65255+67555+61555	NN	LMI	PTR	LMI
350256	61456+65256+67556+61556	NN	LMI	PTR	LMI
350257	61457+65257+67557+61557	NN	LMI	PTR	LMI
350258	61458+65258+67558+61558	NN	LMI	PTR	LMI
350259	61459+65259+67559+61559	NN	LMI	PTR	LMI
350260	61460+65260+67560+61560	NN	LMI	PTR	LMI
350261	61461+65261+67561+61561	NN	LMI	PTR	LMI
350262	61462+65262+67562+61562	NN	LMI	PTR	LMI
350263	61463+65263+67563+61563	NN	LMI	PTR	LMI
350264§	61464+65264+67564+61564	NN	LMI	PTR	LMI
350265	61465+65265+67565+61565	NN	LMI	PTR	LMI
350266	61466+65266+67566+61566	NN	LMI	PTR	LMI
350267	61467+65267+67567+61567	NN	LMI	PTR	LMI

§ Stored at Siemens Germany with serious collision damage.

Right: *Long-distance London Midland electric services are in the hands of a fleet of 77 Class 350 'Desiro' four-car sets based at Northampton. Sets come in three different sub-classes, each with slightly different interiors. In the future when First TransPennine take delivery of new stock, the 10 Class 350/4 sets will move to join the LM fleet. Set No. 350244 is seen at Birmingham International.* **CJM**

Class 350/3
Desiro

Vehicle Length: 66ft 9in (20.4m)
Height: 12ft 1½in (3.78m)
Width: 9ft 2in (2.7m)

Horsepower: 1,341hp (1,000kW)
Seats (total/car): 24F-209S, 60S/24F-32S/57S/60S
110mph max speed

Number	Formation DMSO(A)+TCO+PTSO+DMSO(B)	Depot	Livery	Owner	Operator	Name
350368	60141+60511+60651+60151	NN	LMI	ANG	LMI	
350369	60142+60512+60652+60152	NN	LMI	ANG	LMI	
350370	60143+60513+60653+60153	NN	LMI	ANG	LMI	*Lichfield Festival*
350371	60144+60514+60654+60154	NN	LMI	ANG	LMI	
350372	60145+60515+60655+60155	NN	LMI	ANG	LMI	
350373	60146+60516+60656+60156	NN	LMI	ANG	LMI	
350374	60147+60517+60657+60157	NN	LMI	ANG	LMI	
350375	60148+60518+60658+60158	NN	LMI	ANG	LMI	
350376	60149+60519+60659+60159	NN	LMI	ANG	LMI	
350377	60150+60520+60660+60160	NN	LMI	ANG	LMI	

Passenger Train Operating Companies - London Midland

London Overground

Address: ✉ 125 Finchley Road, London, NW3 6H
✆ overgroundinfo@tfl.gov.uk, ✆ 0845 601 4867, ⓘ www.tfl.gov.uk/overground
Managing Director: Steve Murphy
Principal Routes: Clapham Junction - Willesden, Richmond - Stratford
Gospel Oak - Barking, Euston - Watford
East London Line - Dalston - West Croydon
Depots: Willesden (WN), New Cross Gate (NX), Silwood Sidings
Parent Company: Transport for London (TfL), operated by Arriva

Passenger Train Operating Companies - London Overground

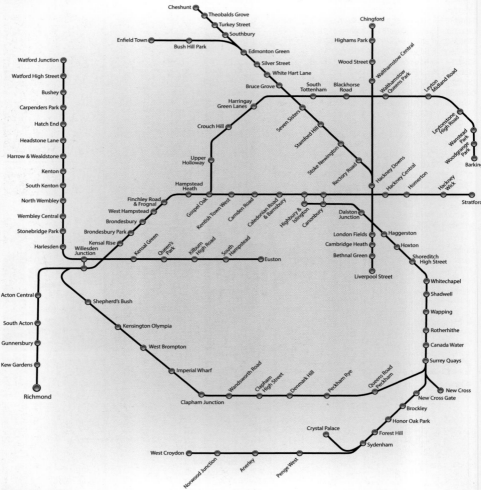

45 Bombardier 'Aventra' Class 710 four-car EMUs Nos. 710001-710045, are on order to replace Class 315/317 stock. Thirty-one sets are for West Anglia routes and eight will operate the electrified Gospel Oak-Barking line. Thirty-one sets will be ac power ony and 14 sets dual ac/dc power. An option exists on a further 34 sets. Stock funded by Rock Rail.

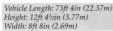

Class 09/0

Vehicle Length: 29ft 3in (8.91m)		Engine: English Electric 6K			
Height: 12ft 8⅝in (3.87m)		Horsepower: 400hp (298kW)			
Width: 8ft 6in (2.59m)		Electrical Equipment: English Electric			

Number	Depot	Pool	Livery	Owner	Operator
09007 (D3671)	WN	-	GRN	LOG	LOG

Class 172/0
Turbostar

Vehicle Length: 73ft 4in (22.37m)		Engine: MTU 6H1800R83 of 360kW (483hp) per car		
Height: 12ft 4⅓in (3.77m)		Horsepower: 966hp (720kW)		
Width: 8ft 8in (2.69m)		Seats (total/car): 124S, 60S/64S		

Number	Formation DMS+DMS	Depot	Livery	Owner	Operator
172001	59311+59411	WN	LOG	ANG	LOG
172002	59312+59412	WN	LOG	ANG	LOG
172003	59313+59413	WN	LOG	ANG	LOG
172004	59314+59414	WN	LOG	ANG	LOG
172005	59315+59415	WN	LOG	ANG	LOG
172006	59316+59416	WN	LOG	ANG	LOG
172007	59317+59417	WN	LOG	ANG	LOG
172008	59318+59418	WN	LOG	ANG	LOG

Right: *Eight two-car Class 172/0 sets are currently on the books of London Overground and were used on the non-electrified Gospel Oak to Barking route, but as that route is now being electrified the sets are likely to be displaced. Presently they are based at Willesden depot. Set No. 172005 is seen at Blackhorse Road.*
Antony Christie

Class 315

Vehicle Length: (Driving) 64ft 11½in (19.80m)	Width: 9ft 3in (2.82m)	
(Inter) 65ft 4½in (19.92m)	Horsepower: 880hp (656kW)	
Height: 11ft 6½in (3.58m)	Seats (total/car): 318S, 74S/86S/84S/74S	

Number	Formation DMSO(A)+TSO+PTSO+DMSO(B)	Depot	Livery	Owner	Operator	Name
315801	64461+71281+71389+64462	IL	TFL	EVL	LOG	
315802	64463+71282+71390+64464	IL	TFL	EVL	LOG	
315803	64465+71283+71391+64466	IL	TFL	EVL	LOG	
315804	64467+71284+71392+64468	IL	TFL	EVL	LOG	
315805	64469+71285+71393+64470	IL	TFL	EVL	LOG	
315806	64471+71286+71394+64472	IL	TFL	EVL	LOG	
315807	64473+71287+71395+64474	IL	TFL	EVL	LOG	
315808	64475+71288+71396+64476	IL	TFL	EVL	LOG	
315809	64477+71289+71397+64478	IL	TFL	EVL	LOG	
315810	64479+71290+71398+64480	IL	TFL	EVL	LOG	
315811	64481+71291+71399+64482	IL	TFL	EVL	LOG	
315812	64483+71292+71400+64484	IL	TFL	EVL	LOG	
315813	64485+71293+71401+64486	IL	TFL	EVL	LOG	
315814	64487+71294+71402+64488	IL	TFL	EVL	LOG	
315815	64489+71295+71403+64490	IL	TFL	EVL	LOG	
315816	64491+71296+71404+64492	IL	TFL	EVL	LOG	
315817	64493+71297+71405+64494	IL	TFL	EVL	LOG	*Transport for London*

Right: *A fleet of 17 Class 315s, now all sporting TfL livery, is based at Ilford and used on the TfL route from London Liverpool Street to Chingford, Cheshunt and Enfield Town. These sets will be replaced by new Class 710 Bombardier 'Aventra' sets. Unit No. 315801 rests under the roof at London Liverpool Street.* **Antony Christie**

London Overground

Class 317/7

Vehicle Length: (Driving) 65ft 0¾in (19.83m)   Width: 9ft 3in (2.82m)
(Inter) 65ft 4¼in (19.92m)   Horsepower: 1,000hp (746kW)
Height: 12ft 1½in (3.58m)   Seats (total/car): 22F/172S, 52S/62S/42S/22F-16S

Number	Former Number	Formation DTSO+MSO+TSO+DTCO	Depot	Livery	Owner	Operator
317708	(317308)	77007+62668+71584+77055	IL	TFL	ANG	LOG
317709	(317309)	77008+62669+71585+77056	IL	TFL	ANG	LOG
317710	(317310)	77009+62670+71586+77057	IL	TFL	ANG	LOG
317714	(317314)	77013+62674+71590+77061	IL	TFL	ANG	LOG
317719	(317319)	77018+62679+71595+77066	IL	TFL	ANG	LOG
317723	(317323/393)	77022+62683+71599+77070	IL	TFL	ANG	LOG
317729	(317329)	77028+62689+71605+77076	IL	TFL	ANG	LOG
317732	(317332)	77031+62692+71608+77079	IL	TFL	ANG	LOG

Left: *For longer-distance West Anglia TfL services a fleet of 14 Ilford-based Class 317s is operated by TfL and is in the process of being redecorated in TfL colours. Former Stansted Airport set No. 317729 with revised front end is seen in TfL livery at Liverpool Street.* **Antony Christie**

Class 317/8

Vehicle Length: (Driving) 65ft 0¾in (19.83m)   Width: 9ft 3in (2.82m)
(Inter) 65ft 4¼in (19.92m)   Horsepower: 1,000hp (746kW)
Height: 12ft 1½in (3.58m)   Seats (total/car): 20F/265S, 74S/79S/20F-42S/70S

317887	(317330)	77043+62704+71606+77077	IL	NXU	ANG	LOG	
317888	(317331)	77030+62691+71607+77078	IL	TFL	ANG	LOG	
317889	(317333)	77032+62693+71609+77080	IL	TFL	ANG	LOG	
317890	(317334)	77033+62694+71610+77081	IL	GAR	ANG	LOG	
317891	(317335)	77034+62695+71611+77082	IL	GAR	ANG	LOG	
317892	(317336)	77035+62696+71612+77083	IL	GAR	ANG	LOG	*Ilford Depot*

Class 378/1
Capitalstar

Vehicle Length: (Driving) 20.46m, (Inter) 20.14m   Width: 9ft 2in (2.80m)
Height: 11ft 9in (3.58m)   Horsepower: 2,010hp (1,500kW)
750V dc sets   Seats (total/car): 146S, 36S/40S/34S/36S

Number	Formation DMSO+MSO+TSO+MSO+DMSO	Depot	Livery	Owner	Operator
378135	38035+38235+38335+38435+38135	NG	LOG	QWR	LOG
378136	38036+38236+38336+38436+38136	NG	LOG	QWR	LOG
378137	38037+38237+38337+38437+38137	NG	LOG	QWR	LOG
378138	38038+38238+38338+38438+38138	NG	LOG	QWR	LOG
378139	38039+38239+38339+38439+38139	NG	LOG	QWR	LOG
378140	38040+38240+38340+38440+38140	NG	LOG	QWR	LOG
378141	38041+38241+38341+38441+38141	NG	LOG	QWR	LOG
378142	38042+38242+38342+38442+38142	NG	LOG	QWR	LOG
378143	38043+38243+38343+38443+38143	NG	LOG	QWR	LOG
378144	38044+38244+38344+38444+38144	NG	LOG	QWR	LOG
378145	38045+38245+38345+38445+38145	NG	LOG	QWR	LOG
378146	38046+38246+38346+38446+38146	NG	LOG	QWR	LOG
378147	38047+38247+38347+38447+38147	NG	LOG	QWR	LOG
378148	38048+38248+38348+38448+38148	NG	LOG	QWR	LOG
378149	38049+38249+38349+38449+38149	NG	LOG	QWR	LOG
378150	38050+38250+38350+38450+38150	NG	LOG	QWR	LOG
378151	38051+38251+38351+38451+38151	NG	LOG	QWR	LOG

378152	38052+38252+38352+38452+38152	NG	LOG	QWR	LOG
378153	38053+38253+38353+38453+38153	NG	LOG	QWR	LOG
378154	38054+38254+38354+38454+38154	NG	LOG	QWR	LOG

Class 378/2
Capitalstar

Vehicle Length: (Driving) 20.46m, (Inter) 20.14m	Width: 9ft 2in (2.80m)
Height: 11ft 9in (3.58m)	Horsepower: 2,010hp (1,500kW)
Dual voltage - 750V dc third rail and 25kV ac overhead	Seats (total/car): 146S, 36S/40S/34S/36S

Sets built as three-car units as Class 378/0, MSO added and reclassified as 378/2

Number	Formation	Depot	Livery	Owner	Operator	Name
	DMSO+MSO+PTSO+MSO+DMSO					
378201 (378001)	38001+38201+38301+38401+38101	NG	LOG	QWR	LOG	
378202 (378002)	38002+38202+38302+38402+38102	NG	LOG	QWR	LOG	
378203 (378003)	38003+38203+38303+38403+38103	NG	LOG	QWR	LOG	
378204 (378004)	38004+38204+38304+38404+38104	NG	LOG	QWR	LOG	*Professor Sir Peter Hall*
378205 (378005)	38005+38205+38305+38405+38105	NG	LOG	QWR	LOG	
378206 (378006)	38006+38206+38306+38406+38106	NG	LOG	QWR	LOG	
378207 (378007)	38007+38207+38307+38407+38107	NG	LOG	QWR	LOG	
378208 (378008)	38008+38208+38308+38408+38108	NG	LOG	QWR	LOG	
378209 (378009)	38009+38209+38309+38409+38109	NG	LOG	QWR	LOG	
378210 (378010)	38010+38210+38310+38410+38110	NG	LOG	QWR	LOG	
378211 (378011)	38011+38211+38311+38411+38111	NG	LOG	QWR	LOG	
378212 (378012)	38012+38212+38312+38412+38112	NG	LOG	QWR	LOG	
378213 (378013)	38013+38213+38313+38413+38113	NG	LOG	QWR	LOG	
378214 (378014)	38014+38214+38314+38414+38114	NG	LOG	QWR	LOG	
378215 (378015)	38015+38215+38315+38415+38115	NG	LOG	QWR	LOG	
378216 (378016)	38016+38216+38316+38416+38116	NG	LOG	QWR	LOG	
378217 (378017)	38017+38217+38317+38417+38117	NG	LOG	QWR	LOG	
378218 (378018)	38018+38218+38318+38418+38118	NG	LOG	QWR	LOG	
378219 (378019)	38019+38219+38319+38419+38119	NG	LOG	QWR	LOG	
378220 (378020)	38020+38220+38320+38420+38120	NG	LOG	QWR	LOG	
378221 (378021)	38021+38221+38321+38421+38121	NG	LOG	QWR	LOG	
378222 (378022)	38022+38222+38322+38422+38122	NG	LOG	QWR	LOG	
378223 (378023)	38023+38223+38323+38423+38123	NG	LOG	QWR	LOG	
378224 (378024)	38024+38224+38324+38424+38124	NG	LOG	QWR	LOG	

Sets 378216-378220 fitted with de-icing equipment

Number	Formation	Depot	Livery	Owner	Operator	Name
	DMSO+MSO+TSO+MSO+DMSO					
378225	38025+38225+38325+38425+38125	NG	LOG	QWR	LOG	
378226	38026+38226+38326+38426+38126	NG	LOG	QWR	LOG	
378227	38027+38227+38327+38427+38127	NG	LOG	QWR	LOG	
378228	38028+38228+38328+38428+38128	NG	LOG	QWR	LOG	
378229	38029+38229+38329+38429+38129	NG	LOG	QWR	LOG	
378230	38030+38230+38330+38430+38130	NG	LOG	QWR	LOG	
378231	38031+38231+38331+38431+38131	NG	LOG	QWR	LOG	
378232	38032+38232+38332+38432+38132	NG	LOG	QWR	LOG	
378233	38033+38233+38333+38433+38133	NG	LOG	QWR	LOG	*Ian Brown CBE*
378234	38034+38234+38334+38434+38134	NG	LOG	QWR	LOG	
378255	38055+38255+38355+38455+38155	NG	LOG	QWR	LOG	
378256	38056+38256+38356+38456+38156	NG	LOG	QWR	LOG	
378257	38057+38257+38357+38457+38157	NG	LOG	QWR	LOG	

Right: *The core TfL EMU fleet consists of 57 five-car Class 378 'Capitalstar' sets. Members of Class 378/1 are equipped for dc third rail power collection only, while members of Class 387/2 are fitted with dual ac/ dc power collection. When originally built these were three-car sets, but due to passenger growth were quickly strengthened to four-car sets and eventually to the present five-car formations. Set No. 378204 is seen at Clapham Junction.* **CJM**

Merseyrail

Address: ✉ Rail House, Lord Nelson Street, Liverpool, L1 1JF
✎ comment@merseyrail.org
✆ 0151 702 2534
ⓘ www.merseyrail.org

Managing Director: Jan Chaudhry
Franchise Dates: 20 July 2003 - 19 July 2028
Principal Routes: All non-main-line services in Liverpool area
Depots: Birkenhead North (BD)
Parent Company: Serco / Abellio

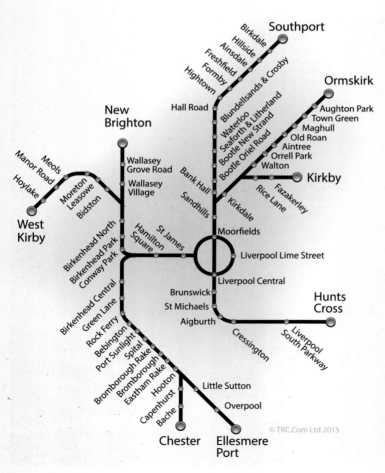

■ A new fleet of 52 Stadlet four-coach articulated sets were ordered in December 2016 for delivery in 2019-2020.

Right: *The Merseyrail electric network around Liverpool presently uses a fleet of 1972-designed Class 507 and 508 EMUs, which are scheduled to be replaced by new trains in the near future. Painted in the distinctive Merseyrail yellow livery, set No. 507004 is seen at Hall Road.* **Tim Easter**

© TRC.Com Ltd 2015

Class 507

	Vehicle Length: (Driving) 64ft 11½in (19.80m)	Width: 9ft 3in (2.82m)
	(Inter) 65ft 4¼in (19.92m)	Horsepower: 880hp (656kW)
	Height: 11ft 6½in (3.58m)	Seats (total/car): 186S, 56S/74S/56S

Number	Formation DMSO+TSO+DMSO	Depot	Livery	Owner	Operator	Name
507001	64367+71342+64405	BD	MEY	ANG	MER	
507002	64368+71343+64406	BD	ADV	ANG	MER	
507003	64369+71344+64407	BD	MEY	ANG	MER	
507004	64388+71345+64408	BD	MEY	ANG	MER	Bob Paisley
507005	64371+71346+64409	BD	MEY	ANG	MER	
507006	64372+71347+64410	BD	MEY	ANG	MER	
507007	64373+71348+64411	BD	MEY	ANG	MER	
507008	64374+71349+64412	BD	MEY	ANG	MER	Harold Wilson
507009	64375+71350+64413	BD	MEY	ANG	MER	Dixie Dean
507010	64376+71351+64414	BD	MEY	ANG	MER	
507011	64377+71352+64415	BD	MEY	ANG	MER	
507012	64378+71353+64416	BD	MEY	ANG	MER	
507013	64379+71354+64417	BD	MEY	ANG	MER	
507014	64380+71355+64418	BD	MEY	ANG	MER	
507015	64381+71356+64419	BD	MEY	ANG	MER	
507016	64382+71357+64420	BD	MEY	ANG	MER	Merseyrail - celebrating the first ten years 2003-2013
507017	64383+71358+64421	BD	MEY	ANG	MER	
507018	64384+71359+64422	BD	MEY	ANG	MER	
507019	64385+71360+64423	BD	MEY	ANG	MER	
507020	64386+71361+64424	BD	MEY	ANG	MER	John Peel
507021	64387+71362+64425	BD	MEY	ANG	MER	Red Rum
507023	64389+71364+64427	BD	MEY	ANG	MER	Operating Inspector Stuart Mason
507024	64390+71365+64428	BD	MEY	ANG	MER	
507025	64391+71366+64429	BD	MEY	ANG	MER	
507026	64392+71367+64430	BD	MEY	ANG	MER	Councillor George Howard
507027	64393+71368+64431	BD	MEY	ANG	MER	
507028	64394+71369+64432	BD	MEY	ANG	MER	
507029	64395+71370+64433	BD	MEY	ANG	MER	
507030	64396+71371+64434	BD	MEY	ANG	MER	
507031	64397+71372+64435	BD	MEY	ANG	MER	
507032	64398+71373+64436	BD	MEY	ANG	MER	
507033	64399+71374+64437	BD	MEY	ANG	MER	

Passenger Train Operating Companies - Merseyrail

Merseyrail

Class 508/1

Vehicle Length: (Driving) 64ft 11½in (19.80m)			Width: 9ft 3in (2.82m)	
(Inter) 65ft 4¼in (19.92m)			Horsepower: 880hp (656kW)	
Height: 11ft 6½in (3.58m)			Seats (total/car): 186S, 56S/74S/56S	

Number	Formation DMSO+TSO+DMSO	Depot	Livery	Owner	Operator	Name
508103	64651+71485+64694	BD	MEY	ANG	MER	
508104	64652+71486+64964	BD	MEY	ANG	MER	
508108	64656+71490+64699	BD	MEY	ANG	MER	
508110	64658+71492+64701	BD	MEY	ANG	MER	
508111	64659+71493+64702	BD	SPL	ANG	MER	The Beatles
508112	64660+71494+64703	BD	MEY	ANG	MER	
508114	64662+71496+64705	BD	MEY	ANG	MER	
508115	64663+71497+64708	BD	MEY	ANG	MER	
508117	64665+71499+64908	BD	MEY	ANG	MER	
508120	64668+71502+64711	BD	MEY	ANG	MER	
508122	64670+71504+64713	BD	MEY	ANG	MER	
508123	64671+71505+64714	BD	MEY	ANG	MER	William Roscoe
508124	64672+71506+64715	BD	MEY	ANG	MER	
508125	64673+71507+64716	BD	MEY	ANG	MER	
508126	64674+71508+64717	BD	MEY	ANG	MER	
508127	64675+71509+64718	BD	MEY	ANG	MER	
508128	64676+71510+64719	BD	MEY	ANG	MER	
508130	64678+71512+64721	BD	MEY	ANG	MER	
508131	64679+71513+64722	BD	MEY	ANG	MER	
508134	64682+71516+64725	BD	MEY	ANG	MER	
508136	64684+71518+64727	BD	MEY	ANG	MER	
508137	64685+71519+64728	BD	MEY	ANG	MER	
508138	64686+71520+64729	BD	MEY	ANG	MER	
508139	64687+71521+64730	BD	MEY	ANG	MER	
508140	64688+71522+64731	BD	MEY	ANG	MER	
508141	64689+71523+64732	BD	MEY	ANG	MER	
508143	64691+71525+64734	BD	MEY	ANG	MER	

Above: *Working alongside the Class 507s is a fleet of 27 Class 508s; these were originally used on the Southern Region as four-car sets in the 1970s before moving north. Today, sets have all been heavily refurbished with revised front ends and are operated as a core fleet with the '507s' Painted in Merseyrail silver/grey colours, set No. 508131 is seen at Hamilton Square on part of the central Liverpool underground network.* **Tim Easter**

Passenger Train Operating Companies - Merseyrail

Northern Rail

Address:	✉ Northern House, 9 Rougier Street, York, YO1 6HZ
	✒ customer.relations@northernrail.org
	✆ 0845 000125 ⓘ www.northernrail.org
Managing Director:	Alex Hynes
Franchise Dates:	12 December 2004 - March 2025
Principal Routes:	Regional services in Merseyside, Greater Manchester, South/North Yorkshire, Lancashire, Cumbria and the North East
Depots:	Newton Heath (NH), Heaton (HT), Longsight (LG), Neville Hill (NL), Allerton (AN)

The Northern franchise was taken over by Arriva from 1 April 2016. The new franchise will withdraw 'Pacer' units by the end of 2019 and introduce a fleet of new vehicles, 43 three- and 12 four-car EMUs of Class 331/0 and 331/1, and 25 two- and 30 three-car DMUs of Class 195/0 and 195/1.

Class 142
Pacer

Vehicle Length: 51ft 0½in (15.55m)
Height: 12ft 8in (3.86m)
Width: 9ft 2¼in (2.80m)
Engine: 1 x Cummins LTA10-R per vehicle
Horsepower: 460hp (343kW)
Seats (total/car): 106S, 56S/50S

Number	Formation DMS+DMSL	Depot	Livery	Owner	Operator
142001	55542+55592	NH	NOU	ANG	NOR
142003	55544+55594	NH	NOR	ANG	NOR
142004	55545+55595	NH	NOR	ANG	NOR
142005	55546+55596	NH	NOR	ANG	NOR
142007	55548+55598	NH	NOR	ANG	NOR
142009	55550+55600	NH	NOU	ANG	NOR
142011	55552+55602	NH	NOR	ANG	NOR
142012	55553+55603	NH	NOR	ANG	NOR
142013	55554+55604	NH	NOR	ANG	NOR
142014	55555+55605	NH	NOR	ANG	NOR
142015	55556+55606	HT	NOR	ANG	NOR
142016	55557+55607	HT	NOR	ANG	NOR
142017	55558+55608	HT	NOR	ANG	NOR
142018	55559+55609	HT	NOR	ANG	NOR
142019	55560+55610	HT	NOR	ANG	NOR
142020	55561+55611	HT	NOR	ANG	NOR
142021	55562+55612	HT	NOR	ANG	NOR
142022	55563+55613	HT	NOR	ANG	NOR
142023	55564+55614	NH	NOR	ANG	NOR
142024	55565+55615	HT	NOR	ANG	NOR
142025	55566+55616	HT	NOR	ANG	NOR
142026	55567+55617	HT	NOR	ANG	NOR
142027	55568+55618	NH	NOR	ANG	NOR
142028	55569+55619	NH	NOR	ANG	NOR
142029	55570+55620	NH	NOU	ANG	NOR
142030	55571+55621	NH	NOU	ANG	NOR
142031	55572+55622	NH	NOR	ANG	NOR
142032	55573+55623	NH	NOR	ANG	NOR
142033	55574+55624	NH	NOR	ANG	NOR
142034	55575+55625	HT	NOR	ANG	NOR
142035	55576+55626	NH	NOR	ANG	NOR
142036	55577+55627	NH	NOR	ANG	NOR
142037	55578+55628	NH	NOR	ANG	NOR
142038	55579+55629	NH	NOR	ANG	NOR
142039	55580+55630	NH	NOR	ANG	NOR
142040	55581+55631	NH	NOR	ANG	NOR
142041	55582+55632	NH	NOR	ANG	NOR
142042	55583+55633	NH	NOR	ANG	NOR
142043	55584+55634	NH	NOR	ANG	NOR
142044	55585+55635	NH	NOR	ANG	NOR
142045	55586+55636	NH	NOR	ANG	NOR
142046	55587+55637	NH	NOR	ANG	NOR
142047	55588+55638	NH	NOR	ANG	NOR
142048	55589+55639	NH	NOR	ANG	NOR
142049	55590+55640	NH	NOR	ANG	NOR
142050	55591+55641	HT	NOR	ANG	NOR
142051	55701+55747	NH	NOR	ANG	NOR
142052	55702+55748	NH	NOR	ANG	NOR
142053	55703+55749	NH	NOR	ANG	NOR
142054	55704+55750	NH	NOR	ANG	NOR
142055	55705+55751	NH	NOR	ANG	NOR
142056	55706+55752	NH	NOR	ANG	NOR
142057	55707+55753	NH	NOR	ANG	NOR
142058	55708+55754	NH	NOR	ANG	NOR
142060	55710+55756	NH	NOR	ANG	NOR
142061	55711+55757	NH	NOR	ANG	NOR
142062	55712+55758	NH	NOR	ANG	NOR
142063	55713+55759	NH	NOU	ANG	NOR
142064	55714+55760	NH	NOU	ANG	NOR
142065	55715+55761	HT	NOR	ANG	NOR
142066	55716+55762	HT	NOR	ANG	NOR
142067	55717+55763	NH	NOR	ANG	NOR
142068	55718+55764	NH	NOU	ANG	NOR
142070	55720+55766	HT	NOR	ANG	NOR
142071	55721+55767	HT	NOR	ANG	NOR
142078	55728+55768	HT	NOR	ANG	NOR
142079	55729+55769	HT	NOR	ANG	NOR
142084	55764+55780	HT	NOR	ANG	NOR
142086	55736+55782	HT	NOR	ANG	NOR
142087	55737+55783	HT	NOR	ANG	NOR
142088	55738+55784	HT	NOR	ANG	NOR
142089	55739+55785	HT	NOR	ANG	NOR
142090	55740+55786	HT	NOR	ANG	NOR
142091	55741+55787	HT	NOR	ANG	NOR
142092	55742+55788	HT	NOR	ANG	NOR
142093	55743+55789	HT	NOR	ANG	NOR
142094	55744+55790	HT	NOR	ANG	NOR
142095	55745+55791	HT	NOR	ANG	NOR
142096	55746+55792	HT	NOR	ANG	NOR

Train Operating Companies

Northern Rail

Due to size of network only principal stations shown

© TRC.Com Ltd 2013

Chathill, Newcastle, Hexham, Carlisle, Whitehaven, Ravenglass, Barrow-in-Furness, Heysham Port, Morecambe, Bishop Auckland, Durham, Darlington, Sunderland, Stockton, Middlesbrough, Battersby, Saltburn, Whitby, Scarborough, Redcar Central, Hull, Barton-on-Humber, Ulceby, Scunthorpe, Grimsby Town, Cleethorpes, Lincoln, Gilberdyke, Goole, Doncaster, Retford, Selby, York, Harrogate, Knottingley, Pontefract Baghill, Castleford, South Elmsall, Wakefield, Swinton, Rotherham, Sheffield, Leeds, Shipley, Bradford Forster Square, Bradford Interchange, Ilkley, Huddersfield, Penistone, Barnsley, Hadfield, Glossop, Chinley, Buxton, Romiley, Rose Hill, Stalybridge, Guide Bridge, Stockport, Cheadle Hulme, Hebden Bridge, Oldham, Colne, Skipton, Dent, Settle, Blackburn, Manchester Victoria, Manchester Piccadilly, Heald Green, Wilmslow, Stoke-on-Trent, Styal, Manchester Airport, Hale, Crewe, Lancaster, Preston, Blackpool North, Blackpool South, Ormskirk, Southport, Kirkby, Wigan Wallgate, Wigan North Western, Bolton, Trafford Park, Earlstown, Warrington Central, Warrington Bank Quay, Runcorn, Ellesmere Port, Chester, Liverpool Lime Street

Right: *The 79-strong Class 142 'Pacer' fleet operating with Northern from Newton Heath (Manchester) and Heaton (Newcastle) depots is scheduled for early withdrawal. All sets carry Northern livery. Viewed from its DMSL vehicle, set No. 142092 is seen stabled in the north bay at Doncaster.* **CJM**

Class 144
Pacer

Vehicle Length: 50ft 2in (15.25m)
Height: 12ft 2½in (3.73m)
Width: 8ft 10½in (2.70m)

Engine: 1 x Cummins LTA10-R per vehicle
Horsepower: 460hp (343kW)
Seats (total/car): 87S, 45S/42S

Number	Formation DMS+DMSL	Depot	Livery	Owner	Operator
144001	55801+55824	NL	NOR	PTR	NOR
144002	55802+55825	NL	NOR	PTR	NOR
144003	55803+55826	NL	NOR	PTR	NOR
144004	55804+55827	NL	NOR	PTR	NOR
144005	55805+55828	NL	NOR	PTR	NOR
144006	55806+55829	NL	NOR	PTR	NOR
144007	55807+55830	NL	NOR	PTR	NOR
144008	55808+55831	NL	NOR	PTR	NOR
144009	55809+55832	NL	NOR	PTR	NOR
144010	55810+55833	NL	NOR	PTR	NOR
144011	55811+55834	NL	NOR	PTR	NOR
144012§	55812+55835	NL	NOA	PTR	NOR
144013	55813+55836	NL	NOR	PTR	NOR

§ Set 144012 modified as '144evolution' train with new-style interior, seating and toilet. DMS seats 43S and DMSL 35S.

Name applied
144001   The Penistone Line Partnership

Vehicle Length: 50ft 2in (15.25m)
Height: 12ft 2½in (3.73m)
Width: 8ft 10½in (2.70m)

Engine: 1 x Cummins LTA10-R per vehicle
Horsepower: 690hp (515kW)
Seats (total/car): 145S, 45S/58S/42S

Number	Formation DMS+MS+DMSL	Depot	Livery	Owner	Operator
144014	55814+55850+55837	NL	NOR	PTR	NOR
144015	55815+55851+55838	NL	NOR	PTR	NOR
144016	55816+55852+55839	NL	NOR	PTR	NOR
144017	55817+55853+55840	NL	NOR	PTR	NOR
144018	55818+55854+55841	NL	NOR	PTR	NOR
144019	55819+55855+55842	NL	NOR	PTR	NOR
144020	55820+55856+55843	NL	NOR	PTR	NOR
144021	55821+55857+55844	NL	NOR	PTR	NOR
144022	55822+55858+55845	NL	NOR	PTR	NOR
144023	55823+(55859)+55846	NL	NOR	PTR	NOR

Right: *A total of 23 Class 144 'Pacer' sets formed as two- and three-car sets are allocated to Leeds Neville Hill. Again, these are scheduled for an early withdrawal. In 2017 sets were painted in Northern blue, mauve and grey. The pioneer of the fleet, No. 144001 The Penistone Line Partnership, is illustrated at Doncaster.* **CJM**

Passenger Train Operating Companies - Northern Rail

Northern Rail

Class 150/1
Sprinter

Vehicle Length: 64ft 9¾in (19.74m)
Height: 12ft 4½in (3.77m)
Width: 9ft 3⅛in (2.82m)

Engine: 1 x NT855R5 of 285hp per vehicle
Horsepower: 570hp (425kW)
Seats (total/car): 124S, 59S/65S

Number	Formation DMSL+DMS	Depot	Livery	Owner	Operator
150103	52103+57103	NH	NOR	ANG	NOR
150110	52110+57110	NH	NOR	ANG	NOR
150111	52111+57111	NH	NOR	ANG	NOR
150112	52112+57112	NH	NOR	ANG	NOR
150113	52113+57113	NH	NOR	ANG	NOR
150114	52114+57114	NH	NOR	ANG	NOR
150115	52115+57115	NH	NOR	ANG	NOR
150116	52116+57116	NH	NOR	ANG	NOR
150117	52117+57117	NH	NOR	ANG	NOR
150118	52118+57118	NH	NOR	ANG	NOR
150119	52119+57119	NH	NOR	ANG	NOR
150132	52132+57132	NH	NOR	ANG	NOR
150133	52133+57133	NH	NOR	ANG	NOR
150134	52134+57134	NH	NOR	ANG	NOR
150135	52135+57135	NH	NOR	ANG	NOR
150136	52136+57136	NH	NOR	ANG	NOR
150137	52137+57137	NH	NOR	ANG	NOR
150138	52138+57138	NH	NOR	ANG	NOR
150139	52139+57139	NH	NOR	ANG	NOR
150140	52140+57140	NH	NOR	ANG	NOR
150141	52141+57141	NH	NOR	ANG	NOR
150142	52142+57142	NH	NOR	ANG	NOR
150143	52143+57143	NH	NOR	ANG	NOR
150144	52144+57144	NH	NOR	ANG	NOR
150145	52145+57145	NH	NOR	ANG	NOR
150146	52146+57146	NH	NOR	ANG	NOR
150147	52147+57147	NH	NOR	ANG	NOR
150148	52148+57148	NH	NOR	ANG	NOR
150149	52149+57149	NH	NOR	ANG	NOR
150150	52150+57150	NH	NOR	ANG	NOR

Left: *A fleet of 30 Class 150/1 'Sprinter' sets is based at Newton Heath, and is used on local and medium-distance services. Sets are currently painted in unbranded Northern-style blue, mauve and grey livery. Set No. 150145 is seen approaching Manchester Oxford Road.* **Richard Tuplin**

Class 150/2
Sprinter

Vehicle Length: 64ft 9¾in (19.74m)
Height: 12ft 4½in (3.77m)
Width: 9ft 3⅛in (2.82m)

Engine: 1 x NT855R5 of 285hp per vehicle
Horsepower: 570hp (425kW)
Seats (total/car): 132S, 62S/70S

Number	Formation DMSL+DMS	Depot	Livery	Owner	Operator
150201	52201+57201	NH	NOR	ANG	NOR
150203	52203+57203	NH	NOR ¤	ANG	NOR
150204	52204+57204	NH	NOR	ANG	NOR
150205	52205+57205	NH	NOR ¤	ANG	NOR
150206	52206+57206	NH	NOR	ANG	NOR
150207	52207+57207	NH	NOR ¤	ANG	NOR
150210	52210+57210	NH	NOR	ANG	NOR
150211	52211+57211	NH	NOR ¤	ANG	NOR
150214	52214+57214	NH	NOR	ANG	NOR
150215	52215+57215	NH	NOR ¤	ANG	NOR
150218	52218+57218	NH	NOR ¤	ANG	NOR
150220	52220+57220	NH	NOR	ANG	NOR
150222	52222+57222	NH	NOR ¤	ANG	NOR
150223	52223+57223	NH	NOR	ANG	NOR
150224	52224+57224	NH	NOR	ANG	NOR
150225	52225+57225	NH	NOR ¤	ANG	NOR
150226	52226+57226	NH	NOR	ANG	NOR
150228	52228+57228	NH	NOR ¤	PTR	NOR
150268	52268+57268	NH	NOR ¤	PTR	NOR
150269	52269+57269	NH	NOR ¤	PTR	NOR
150270	52270+57270	NH	NOR ¤	PTR	NOR
150271	52271+57271	NH	NOR ¤	PTR	NOR
150272	52272+57272	NH	NOR ¤	PTR	NOR
150273	52273+57273	NH	NOR ¤	PTR	NOR
150274	52274+57274	NH	NOR ¤	PTR	NOR
150275	52275+57275	NH	NNR	PTR	NOR
150276	52276+57276	NH	NOR ¤	PTR	NOR
150277	52277+57277	NH	NOR ¤	PTR	NOR

¤ Advertising liveries
150203 - Yorkshire
150205 - Yorkshire
150207 - Yorkshire
150211 - Yorkshire
150215 - Yorkshire
150218 - Yorkshire
150222 - Yorkshire
150225 - Yorkshire
150228 - Heritage
150268 - Heritage
150269 - Yorkshire
150270 - City Life
150271 - Arts
150272 - Colne Festival
150273 - Yorkshire
150274 - Events
150275 - Yorkshire
150276 - Sport
150277 - Yorkshire

Right: *A fleet of 28 gangway-fitted Class 150/2 sets is also allocated to Newton Heath and tends to be deployed on the longer-distance services. In 2017, 19 members of the fleet carried pictogram branding on their sides depicting Northern-served locations and routes, the images being carefully applied to the mauve swirl of the bodywork. Set No. 150274 is seen at Blackrod, carrying Yorkshire Events branding.* **John Binch**

Passenger Train Operating Companies - Northern Rail

Class 153

Vehicle Length: 76ft 5in (23.29m)		Engine: 1 x NT855R5 of 285hp		
Height: 12ft 3⅛in (3.75m)		Horsepower: 285hp (213kW)		
Width: 8ft 10in (2.70m)		Seats (total/car): 70S		

Number	Formation DMSL	Depot	Livery	Owner	Operator
153301	52301	NL	NOR	ANG	NOR
153304	52304	NL	NOR	ANG	NOR
153307	52307	NL	NOR	ANG	NOR
153315	52315	NL	NOR	ANG	NOR
153316	52316	NL	NOR	PTR	NOR
153317	52317	NL	NOR	ANG	NOR
153324	52324	NL	NOR	PTR	NOR
153328	52328	NL	NOR	ANG	NOR
153330	52330	NL	NOR	PTR	NOR
153331	52331	NL	NOR	ANG	NOR
153332	52332	NL	NOR	ANG	NOR
153351	57351	NL	NOR	ANG	NOR
153352	57352	NL	NOR	ANG	NOR
153358	57358	NL	NOR	PTR	NOR
153359	57359	NL	NOR	PTR	NOR
153360	57360	NL	NOR	PTR	NOR
153363	57363	NL	NOR	PTR	NOR
153378	57378	NL	NOR	ANG	NOR

Name applied
153316 *John 'Longitude' Harrison*
Inventor of the Marine Chronometer

Below: *Neville Hill depot has an allocation of 18 single-car Class 153s for rural and secondary line use where low patronage exists. The vehicles are painted in unbranded Northern blue, mauve and grey. No. 153304 is shown on the Cumbrian Coast route.* **Nathan Williamson**

Class 155
Super Sprinter

Vehicle Length: 76ft 5in (23.29m)		Engine: 1 x NT855R5 of 285hp per vehicle		
Height: 12ft 3⅛in (3.75m)		Horsepower: 570hp (425kW)		
Width: 8ft 10in (2.70m)		Seats (total/car): 156S, 76S/80S		

Number	Formation DMSL+DMS	Depot	Livery	Owner	Operator
155341	52341+57341	NL	NOR	PTR	NOR
155342	52342+57342	NL	NOR	PTR	NOR
155343	52343+57343	NL	NOR	PTR	NOR
155344	52344+57344	NL	NOR	PTR	NOR
155345	52345+57345	NL	NOR	PTR	NOR
155346	52346+57346	NL	NOR	PTR	NOR
155347	52347+57347	NL	NOR	PTR	NOR

Northern Rail

Left: *Just seven of the once large Class 155 Leyland 'Super Sprinter' design remain in traffic, with sets Nos. 155341-155347 allocated to Leeds Neville Hill. The sets carry Northern pictogram advertising livery. Set No. 155343 is seen at Leeds.* **Ron Cover**

Class 156
Super Sprinter

Vehicle Length: 75ft 6in (23.03m)		Engine: 1 x Cummins NT855R5 of 285hp per car
Height: 12ft 6in (3.81m)		Horsepower: 570hp (425kW)
Width: 8ft 11in (2.73m)		Seats (total/car): 146S, 70/76S

Number	Formation DMSL+DMS	Depot	Livery	Owner	Operator
156420	52420+57420	AN	NOR	PTR	NOR
156421	52421+57421	AN	NOR	PTR	NOR
156423	52423+57423	AN	NOR	PTR	NOR
156424	52424+57424	AN	NOR	PTR	NOR
156425	52425+57425	AN	NOR	PTR	NOR
156426	52426+57426	AN	NOR	PTR	NOR
156427	52427+57427	AN	NOR	PTR	NOR
156428	52428+57428	AN	NOR	PTR	NOR
156429	52429+57429	AN	NOR	PTR	NOR
156438	52438+57438	HT	NOR	ANG	NOR
156440	52440+57440	AN	NOR	PTR	NOR
156441	52441+57441	AN	§	PTR	NOR
156443	52443+57443	HT	NOR	ANG	NOR
156444	52444+57444	HT	NOR	ANG	NOR
156448	52448+57448	HT	NOR	ANG	NOR
156451	52451+57451	HT	NOR	ANG	NOR
156452	52452+57452	AN	NOR	PTR	NOR
156454	52454+57454	HT	NOR	ANG	NOR
156455	52455+57455	AN	NOR	PTR	NOR
156459	52459+57459	AN	NOR	PTR	NOR
156460	52460+57460	AN	NOR	PTR	NOR
156461	52461+57461	AN	NOR	PTR	NOR
156463	52463+57463	HT	NOR	ANG	NOR
156464	52464+57464	AN	SPL	PTR	NOR
156466	52466+57466	AN	NOR	PTR	NOR
156468	52468+57468	AN	NOR	ANG	NOR
156469	52469+57469	HT	NOR	ANG	NOR
156471	52471+57471	AN	NOR	ANG	NOR
156472	52472+57472	AN	NOR	ANG	NOR
156475	52475+57475	HT	NOR	ANG	NOR
156479	52479+57479	AN	NOR	ANG	NOR
156480	52480+57480	AN	NOR	ANG	NOR
156481	52481+57481	AN	NOR	ANG	NOR
156482	52482+57482	AN	NOR	ANG	NOR
156483	52483+57483	AN	NOR	ANG	NOR
156484	52484+57484	AN	NOR	ANG	NOR
156486	52486+57486	AN	NOR	ANG	NOR
156487	52487+57487	AN	NOR	ANG	NOR
156488	52488+57488	AN	NOR	ANG	NOR
156489	52489+57489	AN	NOR	ANG	NOR
156490	52490+57490	HT	NOR	ANG	NOR
156491	52491+57491	AN	NOR	ANG	NOR

§ - Liverpool & Manchester Railway livery

Names applied
156438 *Timothy Hackworth*
156440 *George Bradshaw*
156441 *William Huskisson MP*
156444 *Councillor Bill Cameron*

156448 *Bram Stoker*
    Creator of Dracula
156459 *Benny Rothman -*
    The Manchester Rambler
156460 *Driver John Axon GC*

156466 *Gracie Fields*
156464 *Lancashire DalesRail*
156469 *The Royal Northumberland*
    Fusiliers (The Fighting Fifth)
156482 *Elizabeth Gaskell*
156490 *Captain James Cook*

Left: *Northern's largest fleet of 'Super Sprinter' stock is represented by a fleet of 42 Metro-Cammell-built Class 156s. These are deployed on longer-distance services and are based at Allerton near Liverpool and Heaton near Newcastle. A handful of sets carry 'stick-on'-style nameplates, while others carry Northern pictogram route advertising liveries. Plain Northern-liveried set No. 156488 is seen at Manchester Piccadilly.* **Ron Cover**

Class 158/0

Vehicle Length: 76ft 1¾in (23.21m)
Height: 12ft 6in (3.81m)
Width: 9ft 3¼in (2.82m)
Engine: 1 x Cummins NTA855R of 350hp per vehicle
Horsepower: 1,050hp (783kW)
Seats (total/car): 208S, 68S/70S/70S

Number	Formation DMSL+MSL+DMSL	Depot	Livery	Owner	Op'r
158752	52752+58716+57752	NL	NNR	PTR	NOR
158753	52753+58710+57753	NL	NOR	PTR	NOR
158754	52754+58708+57754	NL	NOR	PTR	NOR
158755	52755+58702+57755	NL	NOR	PTR	NOR
158756	52756+58712+57756	NL	NNR	PTR	NOR
158757	52757+58706+57757	NL	NOR	PTR	NOR
158758	52758+58714+57758	NL	NNR	PTR	NOR
158759	52759+58713+57759	NL	NOR	PTR	NOR

Names applied

158784	Barbara Castle
158791	County of Nottinghamshire
158796	Fred Trueman - Cricketing Legend
158797	Jane Tomlinson
158860	Ian Dewhirst
158861	Magna Carta 800 - Lincoln 800
158910	William Wilberforce

Leeds Neville Hill has a fleet of eight three-car Class 158s, with a passenger capacity of 208 per train. These sets are used on the longer-distance routes. Three-car set No. 158753 is recorded at Church Fenton. **Antony Christie**

Vehicle Length: 76ft 1¾in (23.21m)
Height: 12ft 6in (3.81m)
Width: 9ft 3¼in (2.82m)
Engine: 1 x Cummins NTA855R of 350hp per vehicle
Horsepower: 700hp (522kW)
Seats (total/car): 138S, 68S/70S

Number	Formation DMSL+DMSL	Depot	Livery	Owner	Operator
158784	52784+57784	NH	NOR	ANG	NOR
158787	52787+57787	NH	NOR	ANG	NOR
158790	52790+57790	NH	NOR	ANG	NOR
158791	52791+57791	NH	NOR	ANG	NOR
158792	52792+57792	NH	NOR	ANG	NOR
158793	52793+57793	NH	NOR	ANG	NOR
158794	52794+57794	NH	NOR	ANG	NOR
158795	52795+57795	NH	NOR	ANG	NOR
158796	52796+57796	NH	NOR	ANG	NOR
158797	52797+57797	NH	NOR	ANG	NOR
158815	52815+57815	NL	NOR	ANG	NOR
158816	52816+57816	NL	NOR	ANG	NOR
158817	52817+57817	NL	NOR	ANG	NOR
158842	52842+57842	NL	NOR	ANG	NOR
158843	52843+57843	NL	NOR	ANG	NOR
158844	52844+57844	NL	NOR	ANG	NOR
158845	52845+57845	NL	NOR	ANG	NOR
158848	52848+57848	NL	NOR	ANG	NOR
158849	52849+57849	NL	NOR	ANG	NOR
158850	52850+57850	NL	NOR	ANG	NOR
158851	52851+57851	NL	NOR	ANG	NOR
158853	52853+57853	NL	NOR	ANG	NOR
158855	52855+57855	NL	NOR	ANG	NOR
158859	52859+57859	NL	NOR	ANG	NOR
158860	52860+57860	NL	NOR	ANG	NOR
158861	52861+57861	NL	NOR	ANG	NOR
158872	52872+57872	NL	NOR	ANG	NOR

Class 158/9

Vehicle Length: 76ft 1¾in (23.21m)
Height: 12ft 6in (3.81m)
Width: 9ft 3¼in (2.82m)
Engine: 1 x Cummins NTA855R of 350hp per vehicle
Horsepower: 700hp (522kW)
Seats (total/car): 142S, 70S/72S

Number	Formation DMSL+DMS	Depot	Livery	Owner	Operator
158901	52901+57901	NL	NOR	EVL	NOR
158902	52902+57902	NL	NOR	EVL	NOR
158903	52903+57903	NL	NOR	EVL	NOR
158904	52904+57904	NL	NOR	EVL	NOR
158905	52905+57905	NL	NOR	EVL	NOR
158906	52906+57906	NL	NOR	EVL	NOR
158907	52907+57907	NL	NOR	EVL	NOR
158908	52908+57908	NL	NOR	EVL	NOR
158909	52909+57909	NL	NOR	EVL	NOR
158910	52910+57910	NL	NOR	EVL	NOR

Passenger Train Operating Companies - Northern Rail

Left: *The 10 Class 158/9s, originally built for West Yorkshire PTE, are now part of the Eversholt Leasing Class 158 Northern fleet, based at Neville Hill, these sets, now in route pictogram livery, are usually found working in the Leeds, Sheffield and Doncaster area. Set No. 158901 is seen at Doncaster.* **CJM**

Class 319

Vehicle Length: (Driving) 65ft 0¾in (19.83m)   Width: 9ft 3in (2.82m)
(Inter) 65ft 4¼in (19.92m)   Horsepower: 1,326hp (990kW)
Height: 11ft 9in (3.58m)   Seats (total/car): 300S, 70S/78S/74S/78S

Number	Formation DTCO+MSO+TSO+DTSO	Depot	Livery	Owner	Operator	Name
319004	77297+62894+71775+77296	AN	NOE	PTR	NOR	
319005	77299+62895+71776+77298	AN	NOE	PTR	NOR	
319218	77325+62908+71789+77324	AN	NOE	PTR	NOR	
319219	77327+62909+71790+77326	AN	NOE	PTR	NOR	
319361	77459+63043+71929+77458	AN	NOE	PTR	NOR	
319362	77461+63044+71930+77460	AN	NOE	PTR	NOR	*Northern Powerhouse*
319363	77463+63045+71931+77462	AN	NOE	PTR	NOR	
319364	77465+63046+71932+77464	AN	NOE	PTR	NOR	
319365	77467+63047+71933+77466	AN	NOE	PTR	NOR	
319366	77469+63048+71934+77468	AN	NOE	PTR	NOR	
319367	77471+63049+71935+77470	AN	NOE	PTR	NOR	
319368	77473+63050+71936+77472	AN	NOE	PTR	NOR	
319369	77475+63051+71937+77474	AN	NOE	PTR	NOR	
319371	77479+63053+71939+77478	AN	NOE	PTR	NOR	
319374	77485+63056+71942+77484	AN	NOE	PTR	NOR	
319375	77487+63057+71943+77486	AN	NOE	PTR	NOR	
319376	77489+63058+71944+77488	AN	NOE	PTR	NOR	
319377	77491+63059+71945+77490	AN	NOE	PTR	NOR	
319378	77493+63060+71946+77492	AN	NOE	PTR	NOR	
319379	77495+63061+71947+77494	AN	NOE	PTR	NOR	
319380	77497+63062+71948+77496	AN	NOE	PTR	NOR	
319382	77975+63094+71980+77976	AN	NOE	PTR	NOR	
319383	77977+63096+71981+77978	AN	NOE	PTR	NOR	
319386	77983+63098+71984+77984	AN	NOE	PTR	NOR	
319431	77351+62921+71802+77350	AN	NOE	PTR	NOR	
319442	77373+62932+71813+77372	AN	NOE	PTR	NOR	
319448	77433+62962+71867+77432	AN	NOE	PTR	NOR	
319456	77449+62970+71875+77448	AN	NOE	PTR	NOR	

Left: *A number of the Class 319s made redundant from the Thameslink line in London have now been transferred to the Northern franchise and are based at Allerton for electric local service operation on the Liverpool to Manchester route. Sets now sport a purple and blue version on the Northern livery. While not new, the refurbishment carried out by Wolverton had made these sets very impressive and well liked by passengers and staff. No. 319369 is shown at Manchester Piccadilly.* **Ron Cover**

Class 321/9

	Vehicle Length: (Driving) 65ft 0¾in (19.83m)	Width: 9ft 3in (2.82m)
	(Inter) 65ft 4¼in (19.92m)	Horsepower: 1,328hp (996kW)
	Height: 12ft 4¾in (3.78m)	Seats (total/car): 288S, 52/79S/78S/79S

Number	Formation DTSOL+MSO+TSO+DTSO	Depot	Livery	Owner	Operator
321901	77990+63153+72128+77993	NL	NOE	EVL	NOR
321902	77991+63154+72129+77994	NL	NOE	EVL	NOR
321903	77992+63155+72130+77995	NL	NOE	EVL	NOR

Right: *The original Class 321/9 sets introduced in 1991 to replace much older stock on the then recently electrified route between Doncaster and Leeds are still to be found on their intended route, now much refurbished and sporting Northern blue livery, offset by grey doors. Based at Leeds Neville Hill, set No. 321903 is shown at Doncaster, with its DTSOL nearest the camera.* **CJM**

Class 322

	Vehicle Length: (Driving) 65ft 0¾in (19.83m)	Width: 9ft 3in (2.82m)
	(Inter) 65ft 4¼in (19.92m)	Horsepower: 1,328hp (996kW)
	Height: 12ft 4¾in (3.78m)	Seats (total/car): 291S, 74S/83S/76S/58S

Number	Formation DTSOL+MSO+TSO+DTSO	Depot	Livery	Owner	Operator
322481	78163+63137+72023+77985	NL	NOR	EVL	NOR
322482	78164+63138+72024+77986	NL	NOR	EVL	NOR
322483	78165+63139+72025+77987	NL	NOR	EVL	NOR
322484	78166+63140+72026+77988	NL	NOR	EVL	NOR
322485	78167+63141+72027+77989	NL	NOR	EVL	NOR

Right: *When the five Class 322s became available, they were taken on by Northern to supplement its Class 321 fleet, being almost identical units. Now based at Leeds Neville Hill, the sets have been refurbished on a par with the Class 321/9s and operate on the Leeds to Doncaster route. Now sporting Northern blue livery, set No. 322483 is seen at Doncaster.* **CJM**

Right: *During the latest round of refurbishment of the Class 321/9 and 322 fleets a disabled access toilet has been fitted at the inner end of one of the driving vehicles, occupying most of the space between the inner set of bi-parting passenger doors and the inner end of the vehicle. Disabled passenger seating is also provided in this area. The modification to set No. 322483 is shown.* **CJM**

Northern Rail

Class 323

Vehicle Length: (Driving) 76ft 8¼in (23.37m)
(Inter) 76ft 10¾in (23.44m)
Height: 12ft 4¾in (3.78m)
Width: 9ft 2¼in (2.80m)
Horsepower: 1,565hp (1,168kW)
Seats (total/car): 323223-225: 244S, 82S/80S/82S
323226-239: 284S, 98S/88S/98S

Number	Formation	Depot	Livery	Owner	Op'r
	DMSO(A)+PTSO+DMSO(B)				
323223	64023+72223+65023	LG	NOR	PTR	NOR
323224	64024+72224+65024	LG	NOR	PTR	NOR
323225	64025+72225+65025	LG	NOR	PTR	NOR
323226	64026+72226+65026	LG	NOR	PTR	NOR
323227	64027+72227+65027	LG	NOR	PTR	NOR
323228	64028+72228+65028	LG	NOR	PTR	NOR
323229	64029+72229+65029	LG	NOR	PTR	NOR
323230	64030+72230+65030	LG	NOR	PTR	NOR
323231	64031+72231+65031	LG	NOR	PTR	NOR
323232	64032+72232+65032	LG	NOR	PTR	NOR
323233	64033+72233+65033	LG	NOR	PTR	NOR
323234	64034+72234+65034	LG	NOR	PTR	NOR
323235	64035+72235+65035	LG	NOR	PTR	NOR
323236	64036+72236+65036	LG	NOR	PTR	NOR
323237	64037+72237+65037	LG	NOR	PTR	NOR
323238	64038+72238+65038	LG	NOR	PTR	NOR
323239	64039+72239+65039	LG	NOR	PTR	NOR

Left: *South Manchester electric local services are operated by a fleet of 17 three-car Class 323 units based at Longsight depot. In the long term these sets will be replaced by new stock and will be transferred to London Midland to work alongside the sets based in the Birmingham area. Sporting unbranded Northern livery, set No. 323229 is seen at Godley.* **John Binch**

Class 333

Vehicle Length: (Driving) 77ft 10¾in (23.74m)
(Inter) 75ft 11in (23.14m)
Height: 12ft 1½in (3.79m)
Width: 9ft 0¼in (2.75m)
Horsepower: 1,877hp (1,400kW)
Seats (total/car): 353S, 90S/73S/100S/90S

Number	Formation	Depot	Livery	Owner	Op'r
	DMSO(A)+PTSO+TSO+DMSO(B)				
333001	78451+74461+74477+78452	NL	NOM	ANG	NOR
333002	78453+74462+74478+78454	NL	NOM	ANG	NOR
333003	78455+74463+74479+78456	NL	NOM	ANG	NOR
333004	78457+74464+74480+78458	NL	NOM	ANG	NOR
333005	78459+74465+74481+78460	NL	NOM	ANG	NOR
333006	78461+74466+74482+78462	NL	NOM	ANG	NOR
333007	78463+74467+74483+78464	NL	NOM	ANG	NOR
333008	78465+74468+74484+78466	NL	NOM	ANG	NOR
333009	78467+74469+74485+78468	NL	NOM	ANG	NOR
333010	78469+74470+74486+78470	NL	NOM	ANG	NOR
333011	78471+74471+74487+78472	NL	NOM	ANG	NOR
333012	78473+74472+74488+78474	NL	NOM	ANG	NOR
333013	78475+74473+74489+78476	NL	NOM	ANG	NOR
333014	78477+74474+74490+78478	NL	NOM	ANG	NOR
333015	78479+74475+74491+78480	NL	NOM	ANG	NOR
333016	78481+74476+74492+78482	NL	NOM	ANG	NOR

Names applied
333007 *Alderman J Arthur Godwin - First Lord Mayor of Bradford 1907*
333011 *Olicana Ilkley's Roman Fort*

Left: *When the Aire Valley route was electrified a fleet of 16 Class 323 sets was introduced, having the same body profile as the Class 332s used on the Heathrow Express services. Now painted in a distinctive blue and deep red livery, the Class 333s based at Leeds Neville Hill have seating for 353 standard class passengers. Set No. 333009 is seen at Leeds.* **Ron Cover**

Above: *When the Class 333s were introduced they were three-car sets, being upgraded to four-car formation in 2002-03 by inserting a TSO vehicle, increasing seating by 100 per train. With its TSO second from rear, set No. 333001 is seen passing Armley Junction, Leeds.* **Tim Easter**

Class 399
CityLink

Train Length: 122ft 0¾in (37.2m)			Power equipment: 6 x 145kW VEM traction motors			
Width: 8ft 8½in (2.65m)			Seats (total/car): 353S, 90S/73S/100S/90S			
Power supply: 25kV ac, 750V dc overhead			Seats (total/car): 90S, 23S/44S/23S			

Number		Formation	Depot	Livery	Owner	Operator
		DMSO(A)+PTSO+TSO+DMSO(B)				
399201	(201)	999001+999101+999201	§	SST	SST	SST
399202	(202)	999002+999102+999202	§	SST	SST	SST
399203	(203)	999003+999103+999203	§	SST	SST	SST
399204	(204)	999004+999104+999204	§	SST	SST	SST
399205	(205)	999005+999105+999205	§	SST	SST	SST
399206	(206)	999006+999106+999206	§	SST	SST	SST
399207	(207)	999007+999107+999207	§	SST	SST	SST

§ - Sheffield Nunnery
SST - Sheffield Super Tram

In 2016 the first of seven 'Tram-Train' Class 399 sets were delivered to the Leeds Super Tram depot. These will operate between Sheffield and Rotherham over the Sheffield Super Tram network and on Network Rail metals towards Rotherham. The first of the sets, No. 399201 or 201 in Super Tram numbering, is seen at Sheffield Nunnery depot. At first these sets will operate on the Super Tram network until Network Rail infrastructure is complete. **Richard Tuplin**

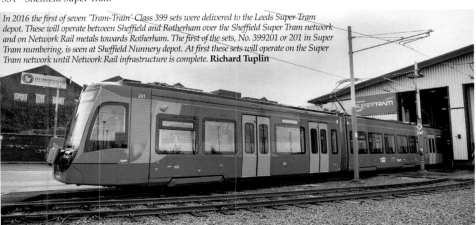

ScotRail

Address:	✉ Atrium Court, 50 Waterloo Street, Glasgow, G2 6HQ
	✆ customer.relations@scotrail.com, ✆ 0344 811 0141
	ⓘ www.scotrail.com
Managing Director:	Phil Verster
Franchise Dates:	1 April 2015 - March 2030
Principal Routes:	All Scottish services
Depots:	Corkerhill (CK), Glasgow Shields Road (GW), Haymarket (HA), Inverness (IS)
Parent Company:	Abellio

Class 156
Super Sprinter

Vehicle Length: 75ft 6in (23.03m)
Height: 12ft 6in (3.81m)
Width: 8ft 11in (2.73m)
Engine: 1 x Cummins NT855R5 of 285hp per car
Horsepower: 570hp (425kW)
Seats (total/car): 142S, 70 or 72S

Number	Formation DMSL+DMS	Depot	Livery	Owner	Operator
156430	52430+57430	CK	SCR	ANG	ASR
156431	52431+57431	CK	SCR	ANG	ASR
156432	52432+57432	CK	SCR	ANG	ASR
156433	52433+57433	CK	SCR	ANG	ASR
156434	52434+57434	CK	SCR	ANG	ASR
156435	52435+57435	CK	SCR	ANG	ASR
156436	52436+57436	CK	SCR	ANG	ASR
156437	52437+57437	CK	SCR	ANG	ASR
156439	52439+57439	CK	SCR	ANG	ASR
156442	52442+57442	CK	SCR	ANG	ASR
156445	52445+57445	CK	SCR	ANG	ASR
156446	52446+57446	CK	SRB	ANG	ASR
156447	52447+57447	CK	SRB	ANG	ASR
156449	52449+57449	CK	SRB	ANG	ASR
156450	52450+57450	CK	SRB	ANG	ASR
156453	52453+57453	CK	SRB	ANG	ASR
156456	52456+57456	CK	SRB	ANG	ASR
156457	52457+57457	CK	SRB	ANG	ASR
156458	52458+57458	CK	SRB	ANG	ASR
156462	52462+57462	CK	SRB	ANG	ASR
156465	52465+57465	CK	SRB	ANG	ASR
156467	52467+57467	CK	SRB	ANG	ASR
156474	52474+57474	CK	SRB	ANG	ASR
156476	52476+57476	CK	SRB	ANG	ASR
156477	52477+57477	CK	SRB	ANG	ASR
156478§	52478+57478	CK	SCR	BRO	ASR
156485	52485+57485	CK	SRB	ANG	ASR
156492	52492+57492	CK	SCR	ANG	ASR
156493	52493+57493	CK	SRB	ANG	ASR
156494	52494+57494	CK	SCR	ANG	ASR
156495	52495+57495	CK	SCR	ANG	ASR
156496	52496+57496	CK	SCR	ANG	ASR
156499	52499+57499	CK	SRB	ANG	ASR
156500	52500+57500	CK	SCR	ANG	ASR
156501	52501+57501	CK	SCR	ANG	ASR
156502	52502+57502	CK	SCR	ANG	ASR
156503	52503+57503	CK	SCR	ANG	ASR
156504	52504+57504	CK	SCR	ANG	ASR
156505	52505+57505	CK	SCR	ANG	ASR
156506	52506+57506	CK	SCR	ANG	ASR
156507	52507+57507	CK	SCR	ANG	ASR
156508	52508+57508	CK	SCR	ANG	ASR
156509	52509+57509	CK	SCR	ANG	ASR
156510	52510+57510	CK	SCR	ANG	ASR
156511	52511+57511	CK	SCR	ANG	ASR
156512	52512+57512	CK	SCR	ANG	ASR
156513	52513+57513	CK	SCR	ANG	ASR
156514	52514+57514	CK	SCR	ANG	ASR

§ Owned by Brodie Engineering, prototype refurbishment

Left: The largest allocation of the high-quality Metro-Cammell-built Class 156 'Super Sprinter' two-car sets is with ScotRail based at Corkerhill depot near Glasgow. Sets are currently in the process of being repainted into the latest Scottish Railways Saltire blue colours, as shown on set No. 156512 at Glasgow Central. **CJM**

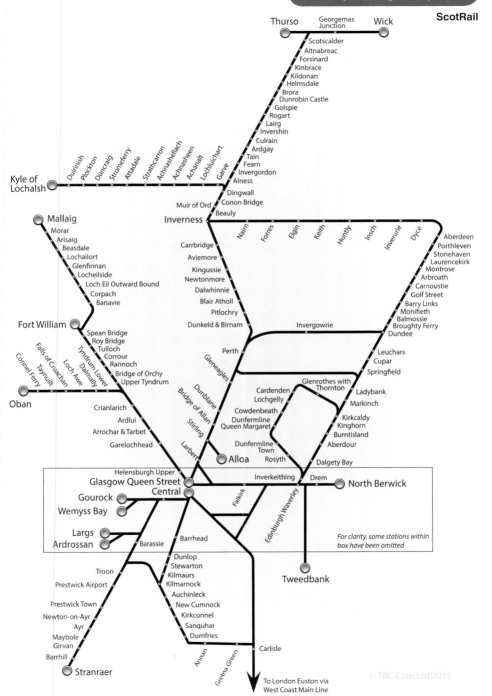

For clarity, some stations within box have been omitted

To London Euston via West Coast Main Line

© TRC.Com Ltd 2015

ScotRail

Class 158

Vehicle Length: 76ft 1¾in (23.21m)
Height: 12ft 6in (3.81m)
Width: 9ft 3¼in (2.82m)
Engine: 1 x Cummins NTA855R of 350hp per vehicle
Horsepower: 700hp (522kW)
Seats (total/car): 14F/116S, 14F-46S/70S, * 138S, 68S/70S

Number	Formation DMCL/DMSL *+DMS	Depot	Livery	Owner	Operator
158701	52701+57701	IS	SCR	PTR	ASR
158702	52702+57702	IS	SCR	PTR	ASR
158703	52703+57703	IS	SCR	PTR	ASR
158704	52704+57704	IS	SCR	PTR	ASR
158705	52705+57705	IS	SRB	PTR	ASR
158706	52706+57706	IS	SRB	PTR	ASR
158707	52707+57707	IS	SRB	PTR	ASR
158708	52708+57708	IS	SRB	PTR	ASR
158709	52709+57709	IS	SCR	PTR	ASR
158710	52710+57710	IS	SRB	PTR	ASR
158711	52711+57711	IS	SCR	PTR	ASR
158712	52712+57712	IS	SCR	PTR	ASR
158713	52713+57713	IS	SCR	PTR	ASR
158714	52714+57714	IS	SCR	PTR	ASR
158715	52715+57715	IS	SCR	PTR	ASR
158716	52716+57716	IS	SCR	PTR	ASR
158717	52717+57717	IS	SCR	PTR	ASR
158718	52718+57718	IS	SRB	PTR	ASR
158719	52719+57719	IS	SCR	PTR	ASR
158720	52720+57720	IS	SRB	PTR	ASR
158721	52721+57721	IS	SCR	PTR	ASR
158722	52722+57722	IS	SCR	PTR	ASR
158723	52723+57723	IS	SCR	PTR	ASR
158724	52724+57724	IS	SCR	PTR	ASR
158725	52725+57725	IS	SRB	PTR	ASR
158726	52726+57726	HA	SRB	PTR	ASR
158727	52727+57727	IS	SRB	PTR	ASR
158728	52728+57728	IS	SRB	PTR	ASR
158729	52729+57729	HA	SRB	PTR	ASR
158730	52730+57730	HA	SRB	PTR	ASR
158731	52731+57731	HA	SRB	PTR	ASR
158732	52732+57732	HA	SRB	PTR	ASR
158733	52733+57733	HA	SRB	PTR	ASR
158734	52734+57734	HA	SRB	PTR	ASR
158735	52735+57735	HA	SRB	PTR	ASR
158736	52736+57736	HA	SRB	PTR	ASR
158737	52737+57737	IS	SRB	PTR	ASR
158738	52738+57738	HA	SRB	PTR	ASR
158739	52739+57739	HA	SRB	PTR	ASR
158740	52740+57740	HA	SRB	PTR	ASR
158741	52741+57741	HA	SRB	PTR	ASR
158782	52782*+57782	HA	SCR	ANG	ASR
158786	52786*+57786	HA	SCR	ANG	ASR
158789	52789*+57789	HA	SCR	ANG	ASR
158867	52867*+57867	HA	SCR	ANG	ASR
158868	52868*+57868	HA	SCR	ANG	ASR
158869	52869*+57869	HA	SCR	ANG	ASR
158870	52870*+57870	HA	SCR	ANG	ASR
158871	52871*+57871	HA	SCR	ANG	ASR

Names applied
158707 *Far North Line*
158715 *Haymarket*

Left: *Inverness and Edinburgh Haymarket depots are home for the 49-strong Class 158 two-car fleet. These sets operate on medium and long-distance outer-suburban routes. In 2017 sets were in the process of being repainted into the latest Scottish Railways blue livery. Painted in former First colours, set No. 158721 is illustrated at Glasgow Central.* **CJM**

Class 170/3
Turbostar

Vehicle Length: 77ft 6in (23.62m)
Height: 12ft 4½in (3.77m)
Width: 8ft 10in (2.69m)
Engine: 1 x MTU 6R 183TD13H of 422hp per vehicle
Horsepower: 1,266hp (944kW)
Seats (total/car): 164S, 57S/43S/64S

Number	Formation DMSL+MS+DMSL	Depot	Livery	Owner	Operator
170393	50393+56393+79393	HA	SCR	PTR	ASR
170394+	50394+56394+79394	HA	SCR	PTR	ASR
170395+	50395+56395+79395	HA	SCR	PTR	ASR
170396	50396+56396+79396	HA	SRB	PTR	ASR

+ Standard class only

Class 170/4
Turbostar

Vehicle Length: 77ft 6in (23.62m)
Height: 12ft 4½in (3.77m)
Width: 8ft 10in (2.69m)
Engine: 1 x MTU 6R 183TD13H of 422hp per vehicle
Horsepower: 1,266hp (944kW)
(170431/432 have 3 x 483hp engines giving 1,449hp)
Seats (total/car): 18F/168S 9F-43S/76S/9F-49S

Number	Formation DMCL+MS+DMCL	Depot	Livery	Owner	Operator
170401	50401+56401+79401	HA	SCR	PTR	ASR
170402	50402+56402+79402	HA	SCR	PTR	ASR
170403	50403+56403+79403	HA	SCR	PTR	ASR
170404	50404+56404+79404	HA	SCR	PTR	ASR

170405	50405+56405+79405	HA	SCR	PTR	ASR
170406	50406+56406+79406	HA	SCR	PTR	ASR
170407	50407+56407+79407	HA	ADV	PTR	ASR
170408	50408+56408+79408	HA	SCR	PTR	ASR
170409	50409+56409+79409	HA	SCR	PTR	ASR
170410	50410+56410+79410	HA	SCR	PTR	ASR
170411	50411+56411+79411	HA	SCR	PTR	ASR
170412	50412+56412+79412	HA	SCR	PTR	ASR
170413	50413+56413+79413	HA	SRB	PTR	ASR
170414	50414+56414+79414	HA	ADV§	PTR	ASR
170415	50415+56415+79415	HA	SCR	PTR	ASR
170425	50425+56425+79425	HA	SCR	PTR	ASR
170426	50426+56426+79426	HA	SCR	PTR	ASR
170427	50427+56427+79427	HA	SCR	PTR	ASR
170428	50428+56428+79428	HA	SCR	PTR	ASR
170429	50429+56429+79429	HA	SCR	PTR	ASR
170430	50430+56430+79430	HA	SCR	PTR	ASR
170431	50431+56431+79431	HA	SCR	PTR	ASR
170432	50432+56432+79432	HA	SCR	PTR	ASR
170433	50433+56433+79433	HA	SCR	PTR	ASR
170434	50434+56434+79434	HA	SCR	PTR	ASR

Class 170/4
Turbostar

Vehicle Length: 77ft 6in (23.62m)	Engine: 1 x MTU 6R 183TD13H of 422hp per vehicle
Height: 12ft 4½in (3.77m)	Horsepower: 1,266hp (944kW)
Width: 8ft 10in (2.69m)	Seats: 170450-170457 (total/car) 9F/180S, 55S/76S/9F,49S
	170458-170478 (total/car) 200S, 57S/76S/67S

Number Formation   Depot Livery Owner Op'r
DMSL+MS+DMSL/DMCL§

170450	50450+56450+79450§	HA	SCR	PTR	ASR	170460	50460+56460+79460	HA	SCR	PTR	ASR
170451	50451+56451+79451§	HA	SCR	PTR	ASR	170461	50461+56461+79461	HA	SCR	PTR	ASR
170452	50452+56452+79452§	HA	SCR	PTR	ASR	170470	50470+56470+79470	HA	SCR	PTR	ASR
170453	50453+56453+79453§	HA	SCR	PTR	ASR	170471	50471+56471+79471	HA	SCR	PTR	ASR
170454	50454+56454+79454§	HA	SCR	PTR	ASR	170472	50472+56472+79472	HA	SCR	PTR	ASR
170455	50455+56455+79455§	HA	SCR	PTR	ASR	170473	50473+56473+79473	HA	SCR	PTR	ASR
170456	50456+56456+79456§	HA	SCR	PTR	ASR	170474	50474+56474+79474	HA	SCR	PTR	ASR
170457	50457+56457+79457§	HA	SCR	PTR	ASR	170475	50475+56475+79475	HA	SCR	PTR	ASR
170458	50458+56458+79458	HA	SCR	PTR	ASR	170476	50476+56476+79476	HA	SCR	PTR	ASR
170459	50459+56459+79459	HA	SCR	PTR	ASR	170477	50477+56477+79477	HA	SCR	PTR	ASR
						170478	50478+56478+79478	HA	SCR	PTR	ASR

Below: *The core Scottish Railways DMU fleet is the Class 170 three-car 'Turbostar' stock based at Edinburgh Haymarket. In common with other fleets, the '170s' are currently being repainted in the new Scottish Railways blue livery. Class 170/4 No. 170458, a standard-class-only set, is seen in the bay at Dundee.* **CJM**

Passenger Train Operating Companies - ScotRail

ScotRail

Class 314

	Vehicle Length: (Driving) 64ft 11½in (19.80m)	Width: 9ft 3in (2.82m)
	(Inter) 65ft 4¼in (19.92m)	Horsepower: 880hp (656kW)
	Height: 11ft 6½in (3.58m)	Seats (total/car): 212S, 68S/76S/68S

| Number | Formation | Depot | Livery | Owner | Operator |
	DMSO(A)+PTSO+DMSO(B)				
314201	64583+71450+64584	GW	SCC	ANG	ASR
314202	64585+71451+64586	GW	SCC	ANG	ASR
314203	64587+71452+64588*	GW	SCR	ANG	ASR
314204	64589+71453+64590	GW	SCR	ANG	ASR
314205	64591+71454+64592	GW	SCR	ANG	ASR
314206	64593+71455+64594	GW	SCC	ANG	ASR
314207	64595+71456+64596	GW	SCC	ANG	ASR
314208	64597+71457+64598	GW	SCR	ANG	ASR
314209	64599+71458+64600	GW	SCC	ANG	ASR
314210	64601+71459+64602	GW	SCC	ANG	ASR
314211	64603+71460+64604	GW	SCR	ANG	ASR
314212	64604+71461+64606	GW	SCR	ANG	ASR
314213	64607+71462+64608	GW	SCC	ANG	ASR
314214	64609+71463+64610	GW	SCR	ANG	ASR
314215	64611+71464+64612	GW	SCC	ANG	ASR
314216	64613+71465+64614	GW	SCC	ANG	ASR

* 64588 was rebuilt from Class 507 car No. 64426 and seats 74S

Left: *The oldest fleet of EMUs in traffic in Scotland is the 1972-design Class 314, introduced in 1979. Allocated to Glasgow Shields Road depot, the 16 units operate the suburban electric routes radiating from Glasgow Central. Painted in the latest Scottish Railways colours, set No. 314212 is seen at Glasgow Central.* **CJM**

Class 318

	Vehicle Length: (Driving) 65ft 0¾in (19.83m)	Width: 9ft 3in (2.82m)
	(Inter) 65ft 4¼in (19.92m)	Horsepower: 1,328hp (996kW)
	Height: 12ft 1½in (3.70m)	Seats (total/car): 216S, 66S/79S/71S

| Number | Formation | Depot | Livery | Owner | Operator |
	DTSO(A)+MSO+DTSO(B)				
318250	77240+62866+77260	GW	SCC	EVL	ASR
318251	77241+62867+77261	GW	SCR	EVL	ASR
318252	77242+62868+77262	GW	SCR	EVL	ASR
318253	77243+62869+77263	GW	SCR	EVL	ASR
318254	77244+62870+77264	GW	SCR	EVL	ASR
318255	77245+62871+77265	GW	SCC	EVL	ASR
318256	77246+62872+77266	GW	SCR	EVL	ASR
318257	77247+62873+77267	GW	SCR	EVL	ASR
318258	77248+62874+77268	GW	SCR	EVL	ASR
318259	77249+62875+77269	GW	SCR	EVL	ASR
318260	77250+62876+77270	GW	SCC	EVL	ASR
318261	77251+62877+77271	GW	SCC	EVL	ASR
318262	77252+62878+77272	GW	SCR	EVL	ASR
318263	77253+62879+77273	GW	SCC	EVL	ASR
318264	77254+62880+77274	GW	SCR	EVL	ASR
318265	77255+62881+77275	GW	SCR	EVL	ASR
318266	77256+62882+77276	GW	SCR	EVL	ASR
318267	77257+62883+77277	GW	SCC	EVL	ASR
318268	77258+62884+77278	GW	SCC	EVL	ASR
318269	77259+62885+77279	GW	SCR	EVL	ASR
318270	77288+62890+77289	GW	SCR	EVL	ASR

Right: *Used for outer-suburban services in the Glasgow area are the 21 Class 318s. These sets were originally fitted with end gangways but these were removed several years ago during refurbishment. Showing Scottish Railways blue livery, set No. 318259 is illustrated at Glasgow Central.* **CJM**

Class 320

Vehicle Length: (Driving) 65ft 0¾in (19.83m)		Width: 9ft 3in (2.82m)
(Inter) 65ft 4¼in (19.92m)		Horsepower: 1,328hp (996kW)
Height: 12ft 4¾in (3.78m)		Seats (total/car): 206S, 51S/78S/77S

Number	Formation DTSO(A)+MSO+DTSO(B)	Depot	Livery	Owner	Operator
320301	77899+63021+77921	GW	SCR	EVL	ASR
320302	77900+63022+77922	GW	SCR	EVL	ASR
320303	77901+63023+77923	GW	SCR	EVL	ASR
320304	77902+63024+77924	GW	SCR	EVL	ASR
320305	77903+63025+77925	GW	SCR	EVL	ASR
320306	77904+63026+77926	GW	SCR	EVL	ASR
320307	77905+63027+77927	GW	SCR	EVL	ASR
320308	77906+63028+77928	GW	SCR	EVL	ASR
320309	77907+63029+77929	GW	SCR	EVL	ASR
320310	77908+63030+77930	GW	SCR	EVL	ASR
320311	77909+63031+77931	GW	SCR	EVL	ASR
320312	77910+63032+77932	GW	SCR	EVL	ASR
320313	77911+63033+77933	GW	SCR	EVL	ASR
320314	77912+63034+77934	GW	SCR	EVL	ASR
320315	77913+63035+77935	GW	SCR	EVL	ASR
320316	77914+63036+77936	GW	SCR	EVL	ASR
320317	77915+63037+77937	GW	SCR	EVL	ASR
320318	77916+63038+77938	GW	SCR	EVL	ASR
320319	77917+63039+77939	GW	SCR	EVL	ASR
320320	77918+63040+77940	GW	SCR	EVL	ASR
320321	77919+63041+77941	GW	SCR	EVL	ASR
320322	77920+63042+77942	GW	SCR	EVL	ASR

Right: *The 22 Class 320 three-car sets based at Glasgow Shields Road depot operate cross-city Glasgow services. Each set seats 206 in the 2+2 layout. All sets now carry Scottish Railways blue livery. Set No. 320303 is seen at Motherwell.* **CJM**

Train Operating Companies

ScotRail

Class 320/4

		Vehicle Length: (Driving) 65ft 0¾in (19.83m)			Width: 9ft 3in (2.82m)	
		(Inter) 65ft 4¼in (19.92m)			Horsepower: 1,328hp (996kW)	
		Height: 12ft 4¾in (3.78m)			Seats (total/car): 28F/197S, 28F-40S//79S//78S	

Number	Formation DMCO+MSO+DMSO	Depot	Livery	Owner	Operator	
320411 (321411)	78105+63073+77953	GW	SCR	EVL	ASR	
320412 (321412)	78106+63074+77954	GW	SCR	EVL	ASR	■ Sets Nos. 321401/403/
320413 (321413)	78107+63075+77955	GW	SCR	EVL	ASR	404 from GTR are
320414 (321414)	78108+63076+77956	GW	SCR	EVL	ASR	scheduled to transfer to
320415 (321415)	78109+63077+77957	GW	SCR	EVL	ASR	Scotland in early 2017 and
320416 (321416)	78110+63078+77958	GW	SCR	EVL	ASR	be reduced to three-car
320417 (321417)	78111+63079+77959	GW	SCR	EVL	ASR	formation.

Class 334
Juniper

		Vehicle Length: (Driving) 69ft 0¾in (21.04m)			Width: 9ft 2¾in (2.80m)	
		(Inter) 65ft 4½in (19.93m)			Horsepower: 1,448hp (1,080kW)	
		Height: 12ft 3in (3.77m)			Seats (total/car): 183S, 64S/55S/64S	

Number	Formation DMSO(A)+PTSO+DMSO(B)	Depot	Livery	Owner	Operator
334001	64101+74301+65101	GW	SCR	EVL	ASR
334002	64102+74302+65102	GW	SCR	EVL	ASR
334003	64103+74303+65103	GW	SCR	EVL	ASR
334004	64104+74304+65104	GW	SCR	EVL	ASR
334005	64105+74305+65105	GW	SCR	EVL	ASR
334006	64106+74306+65106	GW	SCR	EVL	ASR
334007	64107+74307+65107	GW	SCR	EVL	ASR
334008	64108+74308+65108	GW	SCR	EVL	ASR
334009	64109+74309+65109	GW	SCR	EVL	ASR
334010	64110+74310+65110	GW	SCR	EVL	ASR
334011	64111+74311+65111	GW	SCR	EVL	ASR
334012	64112+74312+65112	GW	SCR	EVL	ASR
334013	64113+74313+65113	GW	SCR	EVL	ASR
334014	64114+74314+65114	GW	SCR	EVL	ASR
334015	64115+74315+65115	GW	SCR	EVL	ASR
334016	64116+74316+65116	GW	SCR	EVL	ASR
334017	64117+74317+65117	GW	SCR	EVL	ASR
334018	64118+74318+65118	GW	SCR	EVL	ASR
334019	64119+74319+65119	GW	SCR	EVL	ASR
334020	64120+74320+65120	GW	SCR	EVL	ASR
334021	64121+74321+65121	GW	SCR	EVL	ASR
334022	64122+74322+65122	GW	SCR	EVL	ASR
334023	64123+74323+65123	GW	SCR	EVL	ASR
334024	64124+74324+65124	GW	SCR	EVL	ASR
334025	64125+74325+65125	GW	SCR	EVL	ASR
334026	64126+74326+65126	GW	SCR	EVL	ASR
334027	64127+74327+65127	GW	SCR	EVL	ASR
334028	64128+74328+65128	GW	SCR	EVL	ASR
334029	64129+74329+65129	GW	SCR	EVL	ASR

Sets now all fitted with Dellner couplers.

Left: *The 40-strong 'Juniper' fleet of three-car units with accommodation for 183 in the low-density 2+2 style is based at Glasgow Shields depot and operates in the Edinburgh and Glasgow suburban areas. Owned by Eversholt Leasing, all sets now sport Scottish Railways blue livery. Set No. 334007 leads a six-car formation into Edinburgh Waverley.* **CJM**

334030	64130+74330+65130	GW	SCR	EVL	ASR
334031	64131+74331+65131	GW	SCR	EVL	ASR
334032	64132+74332+65132	GW	SCR	EVL	ASR
334033	64133+74333+65133	GW	SCR	EVL	ASR
334034	64134+74334+65134	GW	SCR	EVL	ASR
334035	64135+74335+65135	GW	SCR	EVL	ASR
334036	64136+74336+65136	GW	SCR	EVL	ASR
334037	64137+74337+65137	GW	SCR	EVL	ASR
334038	64138+74338+65138	GW	SCR	EVL	ASR
334039	64139+74339+65139	GW	SCR	EVL	ASR
334040	64140+74340+65140	GW	SCR	EVL	ASR

Class 380/0
Desiro

Vehicle Length: 77ft 3in (23.57m)	Horsepower: 1,341hp (1,000kW)	
Height: 12ft 1½in (3.7m)	Seats (total/car): 191S, 70S/57S/64S	
Width: 9ft 2in (2.7m)		

Number	Formation DMSO(A)+PTSO+DMSO(B)	Depot	Livery	Owner	Operator
380001	38501+38601+38701	GW	SCR	EVL	ASR
380002	38502+38602+38702	GW	SCR	EVL	ASR
380003	38503+38603+38703	GW	SCR	EVL	ASR
380004	38504+38604+38704	GW	SCR	EVL	ASR
380005	38505+38605+38705	GW	SCR	EVL	ASR
380006	38506+38606+38706	GW	SCR	EVL	ASR
380007	38507+38607+38707	GW	SCR	EVL	ASR
380008	38508+38608+38708	GW	SCR	EVL	ASR
380009	38509+38609+38709	GW	SCR	EVL	ASR
380010	38510+38610+38710	GW	SCR	EVL	ASR
380011	38511+38611+38711	GW	SCR	EVL	ASR
380012	38512+38612+38712	GW	SCR	EVL	ASR
380013	38513+38613+38713	GW	SCR	EVL	ASR
380014	38514+38614+38714	GW	SCR	EVL	ASR
380015	38515+38615+38715	GW	SCR	EVL	ASR
380016	38516+38616+38716	GW	SCR	EVL	ASR
380017	38517+38617+38717	GW	SCR	EVL	ASR
380018	38518+38618+38718	GW	SCR	EVL	ASR
380019	38519+38619+38719	GW	SCR	EVL	ASR
380020	38520+38620+38720	GW	SCR	EVL	ASR
380021	38521+38621+38721	GW	SCR	EVL	ASR
380022	38522+38622+38722	GW	SCR	EVL	ASR

Below: *A fleet of 22 three-car Siemens 'Desiro' Class 380/0 sets was introduced in 2009-2010 to operate in both the Edinburgh and Glasgow areas. These high-specification sets are fitted with a unique retractable front end gangway connection, which gives a very cluttered appearance to the front end. Set No. 380017 is shown at Motherwell.* **CJM**

Class 380/1
Desiro

Vehicle Length: 77ft 3in (23.57m)		Horsepower: 1,341hp (1,000kW)	
Height: 12ft 1½in (3.7m)		Seats (total/car): 265S, 70S/57S/74S/64S	
Width: 9ft 2in (2.7m)			

Number	Formation	Depot	Livery	Owner	Operator
	DMSO(A)+PTSO+MSO+DMSO(B)				
380101	38551+38651+38851+38751	GW	SCR	EVL	ASR
380102	38552+38652+38852+38752	GW	SCR	EVL	ASR
380103	38553+38653+38853+38753	GW	SCR	EVL	ASR
380104	38554+38654+38854+38754	GW	SCR	EVL	ASR
380105	38555+38655+38855+38755	GW	SCR	EVL	ASR
380106	38556+38656+38856+38756	GW	SCR	EVL	ASR
380107	38557+38657+38857+38757	GW	SCR	EVL	ASR
380108	38558+38658+38858+38758	GW	SCR	EVL	ASR
380109	38559+38659+38859+38759	GW	SCR	EVL	ASR
380110	38560+38660+38860+38760	GW	SCR	EVL	ASR
380111	38561+38661+38861+38761	GW	SCR	EVL	ASR
380112	38562+38662+38862+38762	GW	SCR	EVL	ASR
380113	38563+38663+38863+38763	GW	SCR	EVL	ASR
380114	38564+38664+38864+38764	GW	SCR	EVL	ASR
380115	38565+38665+38865+38765	GW	SCR	EVL	ASR
380116	38566+38666+38866+38766	GW	SCR	EVL	ASR

Class 385 (AT200)

With the new Scottish Railway franchise let in 2015 came the announcement that a new fleet of Hitachi AT200 suburban electric multiple units was to be built. Funded by Sumitomo Mitsui Banking Corporation (SMBC) Leasing, 46 three-car and 24 four-car sets will be built. The 23m-long vehicles will be introduced in 2017-18; the first seven complete sets will be assembled in Japan, with the remaining 63 assembled at the Hitachi plant in Newton Aycliffe. An option exists for a further 10 Class 385/0s if the franchise is extended.

Class 385/0 3-car sets

Number	Formation	Depot	Livery	Owner	Operator
	DMSO(A)+PTSO+DMSO(B)				
385001	441001+442001+443001	GW	SCR	SMB	ASR
385002	441002+442002+443002	GW	SCR	SMB	ASR
385003	441003+442003+443003	GW	SCR	SMB	ASR
385004	441004+442004+443004	GW	SCR	SMB	ASR
385005	441005+442005+443005	GW	SCR	SMB	ASR

Below: *The first of the Class 385 Hitachi AT200 emu sets to arrive in the UK was No. 385102 and after formation at Newton Aycliffe was transferred to Scotland for commissioning. It is seen here at Gourock during dynamic testing.* **Ian Lothian**

385006	441006+442006+443006	GW	SCR	SMB	ASR
385007	441007+442007+443007	GW	SCR	SMB	ASR
385008	441008+442008+443008	GW	SCR	SMB	ASR
385009	441009+442009+443009	GW	SCR	SMB	ASR
385010	441010+442010+443010	GW	SCR	SMB	ASR
385011	441011+442011+443011	GW	SCR	SMB	ASR
385012	441012+442012+443012	GW	SCR	SMB	ASR
385013	441013+442013+443013	GW	SCR	SMB	ASR
385014	441014+442014+443014	GW	SCR	SMB	ASR
385015	441015+442015+443015	GW	SCR	SMB	ASR
385016	441016+442016+443016	GW	SCR	SMB	ASR
385017	441017+442017+443017	GW	SCR	SMB	ASR
385018	441018+442018+443018	GW	SCR	SMB	ASR
385019	441019+442019+443019	GW	SCR	SMB	ASR
385020	441020+442020+443020	GW	SCR	SMB	ASR
385021	441021+442021+443021	GW	SCR	SMB	ASR
385022	441022+442022+443022	GW	SCR	SMB	ASR
385023	441023+442023+443023	GW	SCR	SMB	ASR
385024	441024+442024+443024	GW	SCR	SMB	ASR
385025	441025+442025+443025	GW	SCR	SMB	ASR
385026	441026+442026+443026	GW	SCR	SMB	ASR
385027	441027+442027+443027	GW	SCR	SMB	ASR
385028	441028+442028+443028	GW	SCR	SMB	ASR
385029	441029+442029+443029	GW	SCR	SMB	ASR
385030	441030+442030+443030	GW	SCR	SMB	ASR
385031	441031+442031+443031	GW	SCR	SMB	ASR
385032	441032+442032+443032	GW	SCR	SMB	ASR
385033	441033+442033+443033	GW	SCR	SMB	ASR
385034	441034+442034+443034	GW	SCR	SMB	ASR
385035	441035+442035+443035	GW	SCR	SMB	ASR
385036	441036+442036+443036	GW	SCR	SMB	ASR
385037	441037+442037+443037	GW	SCR	SMB	ASR
385038	441038+442038+443038	GW	SCR	SMB	ASR
385039	441039+442039+443039	GW	SCR	SMB	ASR
385040	441040+442040+443040	GW	SCR	SMB	ASR
385041	441041+442041+443041	GW	SCR	SMB	ASR
385042	441042+442042+443042	GW	SCR	SMB	ASR
385043	441043+442043+443043	GW	SCR	SMB	ASR
385044	441044+442044+443044	GW	SCR	SMB	ASR
385045	441045+442045+443045	GW	SCR	SMB	ASR
385046	441046+442046+443046	GW	SCR	SMB	ASR

Class 385/1 4-car sets

385101	441101442101+443101+444101	GW	SCR	SMB	ASR
385102*	441102+442102+443102+444102	GW	SCR	SMB	ASR
385103	441103+442103+443103+444103	GW	SCR	SMB	ASR
385104	441104+442104+443104+444104	GW	SCR	SMB	ASR
385105	441105+442105+443105+444105	GW	SCR	SMB	ASR
385106	441106+442106+443106+444106	GW	SCR	SMB	ASR
385107	441107+442107+443107+444107	GW	SCR	SMB	ASR
385108	441108+442108+443108+444108	GW	SCR	SMB	ASR
385109	441109+442109+443109+444109	GW	SCR	SMB	ASR
385110	441110+442110+443110+444110	GW	SCR	SMB	ASR
385111	441111+442111+443111+444111	GW	SCR	SMB	ASR
385112	441112+442112+443112+444112	GW	SCR	SMB	ASR
385113	441113+442113+443113+444113	GW	SCR	SMB	ASR
385114	441114+442114+443114+444114	GW	SCR	SMB	ASR
385115	441115+442115+443115+444115	GW	SCR	SMB	ASR
385116	441116+442116+443116+444116	GW	SCR	SMB	ASR
385117	441117+442117+443117+444117	GW	SCR	SMB	ASR
385118	441118+442118+443118+444118	GW	SCR	SMB	ASR
385119	441119+442119+443119+444119	GW	SCR	SMB	ASR
385120	441120+442120+443120+44120	GW	SCR	SMB	ASR
385121	441121+442121+443121+444121	GW	SCR	SMB	ASR
385122	441122+442122+443121+444122	GW	SCR	SMB	ASR
385123	441123+442123+443123+444123	GW	SCR	SMB	ASR
385124	441124+442124+443124+444124	GW	SCR	SMB	ASR

Passenger Train Operating Companies - ScotRail

Class 68 'UK Light'

Vehicle Length: 67ft 3in (20.5m)
Height: 12ft 6½in (3.82m)
Speed: 100mph (161km/h)

Engine: Caterpillar C175-16
Horsepower: 3,750hp (2,800kW)
Electrical Equipment: ABB

Number	Depot	Pool	Livery	Owner	Operator	Name
68006	CR	XHVE	SCR	BEA	DRS	*Daring*
68007	CR	XHVE	SCR	BEA	DRS	*Valiant*

Left: *Carlisle-based Direct Rail Services provides two Class 68s each day to ScotRail for peak-hour loco-hauled services in the Edinburgh area. Two locos, Nos. 68006 and 68007, have been repainted into full Scottish Railways colours, and these locos are usually used on the duties, but other DRS locos can also be seen. ScotRail-liveried No. 68007 is seen at Edinburgh Waverley with a matching rake of Mk2 stock.* **Ron Cover**

Mk2 Hauled Stock

Vehicle Length: 66ft 0in (20.11m)
Height: 12ft 9½in (3.89m)

Width: 9ft 3in (2.81m)
Seats (total/car): 60S

AC2F - TSO *Seating 60S*

Number	Depot	Livery	Op'r
5945	ML	SCR	ASR
5952	ML	SCR	ASR
5955	ML	SCR	ASR
5965	ML	SCR	ASR
5976	ML	SCR	ASR
5987	ML	SCR	ASR
6027	ML	SCR	ASR
6137	ML	SCR	ASR
6176	ML	SCR	ASR
6177	ML	SCR	ASR
6183	ML	SCR	ASR

AE2F - BSO *Seating 32S*

Number	Depot	Livery	Op'r
9521	ML	SCR	ASR
9539	ML	SCR	ASR

Left: *To operate the Scottish Railways loco-hauled peak-hour trains in Edinburgh, a fleet of 13 Mk2s, fully refurbished and owned by Direct Rail Services is in service. TSO No. 6183, attached to No. 6177 is seen passing through Princes Street Gardens, Edinburgh.* **Antony Christie**

ScotRail HST introduction

As part of the new Scottish Railways franchise, it was announced that following replacement of the Great Western HST fleet with Class 800, 801 and 802 'IEP' stock, 26 reduced HST sets are to be introduced in Scotland to operate an enhanced service between Edinburgh, Glasgow, Dundee, Perth, Aberdeen and Inverness.

Nine four-car and 17 five-car sets are to be formed; four-car sets will be formed Trailer First Catering (TFC), Trailer Standard Disabled (TSD), Trailer Standard Bike (TSB) and a Trailer Standard (TS). The five-car sets will have an extra TS coach. A nine-car set will seat 32 first and 206 standard, while a five-car set will seat 32 first and 278 standard. A total of 54 Class 43s will be transferred to Scotland to be based at a new facility at Dundee.

Before transfer to Scotland, chemical retention toilets will be fitted as well as power-operated passenger doors, the latter provided by Vapour Stone. Overhaul work to power cars will be undertaken at Wabtec, Loughborough, and work on coaching stock will be undertaken at Wabtec, Doncaster.

Serco Caledonian Sleepers

Address: ✉ 1 Union Street, Inverness, IV1 1PP
✎ enquiry@Sleeper.scot ✆ 0330 060 0500
ⓘ www.sleeper.scot

Managing Director: Peter Strachan
Franchise Dates: 1 April 2015 - 1 April 2030
Principal Routes: Inverness, Aberdeen, Fort William, Edinburgh, Glasgow
to London Euston
Depots: Inverness (IS)
Parent Company: Serco

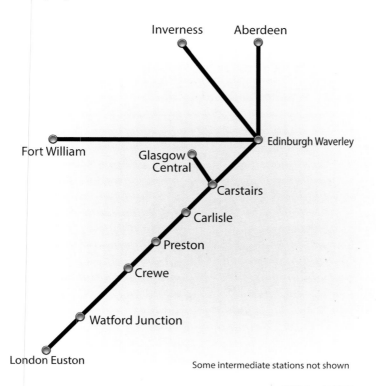

Some intermediate stations not shown

© TRC.Com Ltd 2015

New stock for Caledonian Sleeper Services

With the award of a separate Caledonian Sleeper franchise awarded to Serco in 2015 came a commitment to invest in new rolling stock. A fleet of 75 new Mk5 vehicles are currently on order from CAF for delivery in 2018, consisting of four 16-car sets plus 11 spare vehicles. All will be based at Inverness. When this stock is introduced all existing Mk2 and Mk3 vehicles will be returned to their lease owner.

A new numbering range will be introduced with this stock. The Seating vehicles will be numbered 15001-15011. Club Cars will be 15101-15110, Fully Accessible Sleepers will be 15201-15214, while all-Sleeper Carriages will be 15301-15340.

Serco Caledonian

Class 73/9

Vehicle Length: 53ft 8in (16.35m)				Power: MTU 8V4000R43L		
Height: 12ft 5⁵⁄₁₆in (3.79m)				Horsepower: diesel - 1,550hp (1,119kW)		
Width: 8ft 8in (2.64m)				ETH index: 96		
Electrical Equipment: English Electric						

Number		Depot	Pool	Livery	Owner	Operator
73966	(73005)	EC	GBCS	SCS	GBR	SCS
73967	(73006)	EC	GBCS	SCS	GBR	SCS
73968	(73117)	EC	GBCS	SCS	GBR	SCS
73969	(73105)	EC	GBCS	SCS	GBR	SCS
73970	(73103)	EC	GBCS	SCS	GBR	SCS
73971	(73207/122)	EC	GBCS	SCS	GBR	SCS

To be fitted with Dellner auto couplers and other modifications for attachment to new Mk5 CAF sleeper stock under construction.

Left: The Serco Caledonian Sleeper operation is currently introducing rebuilt Class 73/9s to operate sleeper services to Fort William, Aberdeen and Inverness. Introduction has been protracted with many problems encountered. Painted in SCS livery with branding, Nos. 73967 and 73966 pose with the sleeper train at Fort William. **Richard Tuplin**

Class 86

Vehicle Length: 58ft 6in (17.83m)			Power Collection: 25kV ac overhead			
Height: 13ft 0⁵⁄₈in (3.97m)			Horsepower: 5,900hp (4,400kW)			
Width: 8ft 8¼in (2.64m)			Electrical Equipment: GEC			

Number	Depot	Pool	Livery	Owner	Operator	Name
86101	WA	GBCH	SCS	ETL	GBR	*Sir William Stanier FRS*
86401	WA	GBCH	SCS	ETL	GBR	*Mons Meg*

Left: To assist with empty stock movements in the London and Glasgow/Edinburgh areas Electric Traction Ltd has supplied three locos, two Class 86s and one Class 87s which have been repainted in full Caledonian Sleeper livery. It is not unknown for these locos to power the sleeper service if there is a shortage of traction. Class 86/4 No. 86401 Mons Meg is shown. **Antony Christie**

Class 87

Vehicle Length: 58ft 6in (17.83m)		Power Collection: 25kV ac overhead	
Height: 13ft 1¼in (3.99m)		Horsepower: 7,860hp (5,680kW)	
Width: 8ft 8¼in (2.64m)		Electrical Equipment: GEC	

Left: The Class 87 No. 87002, owned by Electric Traction Ltd, has been known to operate charter services if not required for sleeper duties. It is seen here powering a charter at York. **Antony Christie**

Number	Depot	Pool	Livery	Owner	Operator	Name
87002	WN	GBCH	SCS	ETL	GBR	*Royal Sovereign*

Class 92

Vehicle Length: 70ft 1in (21.34m)	Power Collection: 25kV ac overhead / 750V dc third rail
Height: 13ft 0in (3.95m)	Horsepower: ac - 6,700hp (5,000kW) / dc - 5,360hp (4,000kW)
Width: 8ft 8in (2.66m)	Electrical Equipment: Brush

Number	Depot	Pool	Livery	Owner	Operator		Number	Depot	Pool	Livery	Owner	Operator
92014	CO	GBSL	SCS	GBR	SCS		92033	CO	GBSL	SCS	GBR	SCS
92018	CO	GBSL	SCS	GBR	SCS		92038	CO	GBCT	SCS	GBR	SCS
92023	CO	GBSL	SCS	GBR	SCS							

Right: *Core traction for the Caledonian Sleeper duty between Edinburgh/ Glasgow and London Euston is booked for GBRf Class 92s, but considerable trouble has been experienced with the electronics on these locos, which have now received a major upgrade by Brush/ Wabtec at Loughborough. Painted in full Caledonian Sleeper livery, No. 92038 is seen in the south bay at Edinburgh Waverley.* **CJM**

Mk2 and Mk3 Hauled Stock

Mk2
Vehicle Length: 66ft 0in (20.11m)   Width: 9ft 3in (2.81m)
Height: 12ft 9½in (3.89m)   Seats (total/car): 60S

Mk3
Vehicle Length: 75ft 0in (22.86m)   Width: 8ft 11in (2.71m)
Height: 12ft 9in (3.88m)   Bogie Type: BT10

AN1F (Mk2) - RLO *Seating 28-30F*

Number	Depot	Livery	Owner
6700 (3347)	PO	SCR	EVL
6701 (3346)	PO	CAS	EVL
6702 (3421)	PO	SRB	EVL
6703 (3308)	PO	SRB	EVL
6704 (3341)	PO	SRB	EVL
6705 (3310)	PO	SRB	EVL
6706 (3283)	PO	SRB	EVL
6707 (3276)	PO	SRB	EVL
6708 (3370)	PO	SRB	EVL

AN1F (Mk2) - BUO *Seating 31U*

Number	Depot	Livery	Owner
9800 (5751)	PO	SRB	EVL
9801 (5760)	PO	CAS	EVL
9802 (5772)	PO	CAS	EVL
9803 (5799)	PO	SRB	EVL
9804 (5826)	PO	SRB	EVL
9805 (5833)	PO	SRB	EVL
9806 (5840)	PO	SRB	EVL
9807 (5851)	PO	SCR	EVL
9808 (5871)	PO	SCR	EVL
9809 (5890)	PO	SRB	EVL
9810 (5892)	PO	SRB	EVL

AU4G (Mk3) - SLEP *Comps 12*

Number	Depot	Livery	Owner
10501	PO	SRB	PTR
10502	PO	SRB	PTR

Number	Depot	Livery	Owner
10504	PO	SRB	PTR
10506	PO	SRB	PTR
10507	PO	SRB	PTR
10508	PO	SRB	PTR
10513	PO	SRB	PTR
10516	PO	SCR	PTR
10519	PO	SRB	PTR
10520	PO	SRB	PTR
10522	PO	SRB	PTR
10523	PO	SRB	PTR
10526	PO	SRB	PTR
10527	PO	SRB	PTR
10529	PO	SRB	PTR
10531	PO	SRB	PTR
10542	PO	SRB	PTR
10543	PO	SRB	PTR
10544	PO	SRB	PTR
10548	PO	SRB	PTR
10551	PO	SRB	PTR
10553	PO	SRB	PTR
10561	PO	SRB	PTR
10562	PO	SCR	PTR
10565	PO	SRB	PTR
10580	PO	CAS	PTR
10597	PO	SRB	PTR
10598	PO	SRB	PTR
10600	PO	SRB	PTR
10605	PO	SRB	PTR
10607	PO	SRB	PTR
10610	PO	SRB	PTR

Number	Depot	Livery	Owner
10613	PO	SRB	PTR
10614	PO	SRB	PTR
10617	PO	SRB	PTR

AS4G (MK3) - SLE *Comps 13*

Number	Depot	Livery	Owner
10675	PO	SRB	PTR
10683	PO	SRB	PTR
10688	PO	SRB	PTR
10690	PO	SRB	PTR
10693	PO	CAS	PTR
10703	PO	SRB	PTR

AQ4G (Mk3) - SLED *Comps 11*

Number	Depot	Livery	Owner
10648	PO	SRB	PTR
10650	PO	SRB	PTR
10666	PO	SRB	PTR
10680	PO	SRB	PTR
10689	PO	SRB	PTR
10699	PO	SRB	PTR
10706	PO	SRB	PTR
10714	PO	SRB	PTR
10718	PO	SRB	PTR
10719	PO	SRB	PTR
10722	PO	SRB	PTR
10723	PO	SRB	PTR

South Eastern

Address:	✉ Friars Bridge Court, 41-45 Blackfriars Road, London, SE1 8NZ
	✍ info@southeasternrailway.co.uk
	✆ 08700 000 2222
	① www.southeasternrailway.co.uk
Managing Director:	David Stratham
Franchise Dates:	1 April 2006 - 24 June 2018
Principal Routes:	London to Kent and parts of East Sussex, domestic services on HS1
Depots:	Slade Green (SG), Ramsgate (RM), Ashford* (AD) * Operated by Hitachi
Parent Company:	Govia

Class 375/3
Electrostar

Vehicle Length: (Driving) 66ft 9in (20.3m)   *Width: 9ft 2in (2.79m)*
(Inter) 65ft 6in (19.96m)   *Horsepower: 1,341hp (1,000kW)*
Height: 12ft 4in (3.75m)   *Seats (total/car): 16F-170S,60S/16F-50S/60S*

Number	Formation DMSO+MCO+DMSO	Depot	Livery	Owner	Operator	Name
375301	67921+74351+67931	RM	SEB	EVL	SET	
375302	67922+74352+67932	RM	SEB	EVL	SET	
375303	67923+74353+67933	RM	SEB	EVL	SET	
375304	67924+74354+67934	RM	SEB	EVL	SET	
375305	67925+74355+67935	RM	SEB	EVL	SET	
375306	67926+74356+67936	RM	SEB	EVL	SET	
375307	67927+74357+67937	RM	SEB	EVL	SET	
375308	67928+74358+67938	RM	SEB	EVL	SET	
375309	67929+74359+67939	RM	SEB	EVL	SET	
375310	67930+74360+67940	RM	SEB	EVL	SET	

Class 375/6
Electrostar

Vehicle Length: (Driving) 66ft 9in (20.3m)   *Width: 9ft 2in (2.79m)*
(Inter) 65ft 6in (19.96m)   *Horsepower: 2,012hp (1,500kW)*
Height: 12ft 4in (3.75m)   *Seats (total/car): 16F-226S, 60S/16F-50S/56S/60S*

Number	Formation DMSO(A)+MCO+TSO+DMSO(B)	Depot	Livery	Owner	Operator	Name
375601	67801+74251+74201+67851	RM	SEB	EVL	SET	
375602	67802+74252+74202+67852	RM	SEB	EVL	SET	
375603	67803+74253+74203+67853	RM	SEB	EVL	SET	
375604	67804+74254+74204+67854	RM	SEB	EVL	SET	
375605	67805+74255+74205+67855	RM	SEB	EVL	SET	
375606	67806+74256+74206+67856	RM	SEB	EVL	SET	
375607	67807+74257+74207+67857	RM	SEB	EVL	SET	
375608	67808+74258+74208+67858	RM	SEB	EVL	SET	
375609	67809+74259+74209+67859	RM	SEB	EVL	SET	
375610	67810+74260+74210+67860	RM	SEB	EVL	SET	
375611	67811+74261+74211+67861	RM	SEB	EVL	SET	
375612	67812+74262+74212+67862	RM	SEB	EVL	SET	
375613	67813+74263+74213+67863	RM	SEB	EVL	SET	
375614	67814+74264+74214+67864	RM	SEB	EVL	SET	
375615	67815+74265+74215+67865	RM	SEB	EVL	SET	
375616	67816+74266+74216+67866	RM	SEB	EVL	SET	
375617	67817+74267+74217+67867	RM	SEB	EVL	SET	
375618	67818+74268+74218+67868	RM	SEB	EVL	SET	
375619	67819+74269+74219+67869	RM	SEB	EVL	SET	*Driver John Neve*

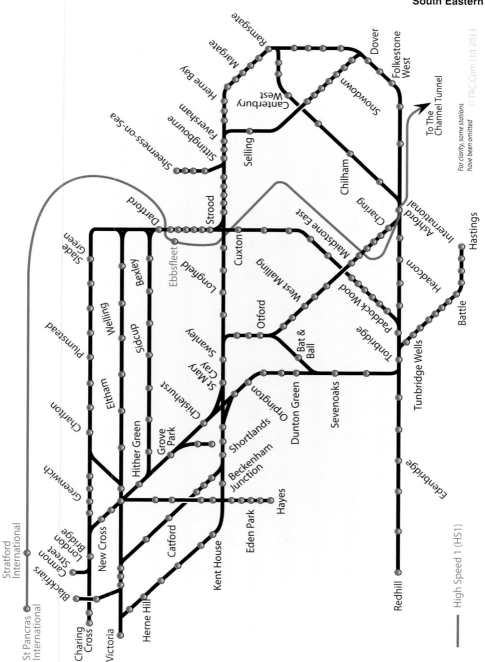

Train Operating Companies

South Eastern

Passenger Train Operating Companies - South Eastern

© TRC.Com Ltd 2013

For clarity, some stations have been omitted

— High Speed 1 (HS1)

South Eastern

Number	Formation	Depot	Livery	Owner	Operator	Name
375620	67820+74270+74220+67870	RM	SEB	EVL	SET	
375621	67821+74271+74221+67871	RM	SEB	EVL	SET	
375622	67822+74272+74222+67872	RM	SEB	EVL	SET	
375623	67823+74273+74223+67873	RM	SEB	EVL	SET	
375624	67824+74274+74224+67874	RM	SEB	EVL	SET	*Hospice in the Weald*
375625	67825+74275+74225+67875	RM	SEB	EVL	SET	
375626	67826+74276+74226+67876	RM	SEB	EVL	SET	
375627	67827+74277+74227+67877	RM	SEB	EVL	SET	
375628	67828+74278+74228+67878	RM	SEB	EVL	SET	
375629	67829+74279+74229+67879	RM	SEB	EVL	SET	
375630	67830+74280+74230+67880	RM	SEB	EVL	SET	

Class 375/7
Electrostar

Vehicle Length: (Driving) 66ft 9in (20.3m) / (Inter) 65ft 6in (19.96m) Width: 9ft 2in (2.79m) Height: 12ft 4in (3.75m) Horsepower: 2,012hp (1,500kW) Seats (total/car): 16S-226S, 60S/16F-50S/56S/60S

Number	Formation DMSO(A)+MCO+TSO+DMSO(B)	Depot	Livery	Owner	Operator	Name
375701	67831+74281+74231+67881	RM	SEB	EVL	SET	*Kent Air Ambulance Explorer*
375702	67832+74282+74232+67882	RM	SEB	EVL	SET	
375703	67833+74283+74233+67883	RM	SEB	EVL	SET	
375704	67834+74284+74234+67884	RM	SEB	EVL	SET	
375705	67835+74285+74235+67885	RM	SEB	EVL	SET	
375706	67836+74286+74236+67886	RM	SEB	EVL	SET	
375707	67837+74287+74237+67887	RM	SEB	EVL	SET	
375708	67838+74288+74238+67888	RM	SEB	EVL	SET	
375709	67839+74289+74239+67889	RM	SEB	EVL	SET	
375710	67840+74290+74240+67890	RM	SEB	EVL	SET	*Rochester Castle*
375711	67841+74291+74241+67891	RM	SEB	EVL	SET	
375712	67842+74292+74242+67892	RM	SEB	EVL	SET	
375713	67843+74293+74243+67893	RM	SEB	EVL	SET	*Rochester Cathedral*
375714	67844+74294+74244+67894	RM	SEB	EVL	SET	
375715	67845+74295+74245+67895	RM	SEB	EVL	SET	

Class 375/8
Electrostar

Vehicle Length: (Driving) 66ft 9in (20.3m) / (Inter) 65ft 6in (19.96m) Width: 9ft 2in (2.79m) Height: 12ft 4in (3.75m) Horsepower: 2,012hp (1,500kW) Seats (total/car): 16S-226S, 60S/16F-50S/56S/60S

Number	Formation DMSO(A)+MCO+TSO+DMSO(B)	Depot	Livery	Owner	Operator	Name
375801	73301+79001+78201+73701	RM	SEB	EVL	SET	
375802	73302+79002+78202+73702	RM	SEB	EVL	SET	
375803	73303+79003+78203+73703	RM	SEB	EVL	SET	
375804	73304+79004+78204+73704	RM	SEB	EVL	SET	
375805	73305+79005+78205+73705	RM	SEB	EVL	SET	
375806	73306+79006+78206+73706	RM	SEB	EVL	SET	
375807	73307+79007+78207+73707	RM	SEB	EVL	SET	
375808	73308+79008+78208+73708	RM	SET	EVL	SET	
375809	73309+79009+78209+73709	RM	SET	EVL	SET	
375810	73310+79010+78210+73710	RM	SET	EVL	SET	
375811	73311+79011+78211+73711	RM	SET	EVL	SET	
375812	73312+79012+78212+73712	RM	SET	EVL	SET	
375813	73313+79013+78213+73713	RM	SET	EVL	SET	
375814	73314+79014+78214+73714	RM	SET	EVL	SET	
375815	73315+79015+78215+73715	RM	SET	EVL	SET	
375816	73316+79016+78216+73716	RM	SET	EVL	SET	
375817	73317+79017+78217+73717	RM	SET	EVL	SET	
375818	73318+79018+78218+73718	RM	SET	EVL	SET	
375819	73319+79019+78219+73719	RM	SET	EVL	SET	
375820	73320+79020+78220+73720	RM	SET	EVL	SET	
375821	73321+79021+78221+73721	RM	SET	EVL	SET	
375822	73322+79022+78222+73722	RM	SET	EVL	SET	
375823	73323+79023+78223+73723	RM	SET	EVL	SET	
375824	73324+79024+78224+73724	RM	SET	EVL	SET	
375825	73325+79025+78225+73725	RM	SET	EVL	SET	

375826	73326+79026+78226+73726	RM	SET	EVL	SET	
375827	73327+79027+78227+73727	RM	SET	EVL	SET	
375828	73328+79028+78228+73728	RM	SET	EVL	SET	
375829	73329+79029+78229+73729	RM	SET	EVL	SET	
375830	73330+79030+78230+73730	RM	SET	EVL	SET	*City of London*

Above: *The backbone of South Eastern main-line services is a fleet of 112 Bombardier-built 'Electrostar' sets in five sub-classes. All are four-car sets except for a fleet of 10 Class 375/3s. In 2017 the project is ongoing to refurbish and repaint sets in the latest SET two-tone blue livery. An eight-car set led by No. 375606 is illustrated. Note that the first class accommodation has now been repositioned into an intermediate vehicle.* **Jamie Squibbs**

Class 375/9
Electrostar

Vehicle Length: (Driving) 66ft 9in (20.3m)	Width: 9ft 2in (2.79m)
(Inter) 65ft 6in (19.96m)	Horsepower: 2,012hp (1,500kW)
Height: 12ft 4in (3.75m)	Seats (total/car): 16F-226S, 60S/16F-50S/56S/60S

Number	Formation	Depot	Livery	Owner	Operator
	DMSO(A)+MCO+TSO+DMSO(B)				
375901	73331+79031+79061+73731	RM	SET	EVL	SET
375902	73332+79032+79062+73732	RM	SET	EVL	SET
375903	73333+79033+79063+73733	RM	SET	EVL	SET
375904	73334+79034+79064+73734	RM	SET	EVL	SET
375905	73335+79035+79065+73735	RM	SET	EVL	SET
375906	73336+79036+79066+73736	RM	SEB	EVL	SET
375907	73337+79037+79067+73737	RM	SEB	EVL	SET
375908	73338+79038+79068+73738	RM	SEB	EVL	SET
375909	73339+79039+79069+73739	RM	SEB	EVL	SET
375910	73340+79040+79070+73740	RM	SET	EVL	SET
375911	73341+79041+79071+73741	RM	SET	EVL	SET
375912	73342+79042+79072+73742	RM	SET	EVL	SET
375913	73343+79043+79073+73743	RM	SET	EVL	SET
375914	73344+79044+79074+73744	RM	SET	EVL	SET
375915	73345+79045+79075+73745	RM	SET	EVL	SET
375916	73346+79046+79076+73746	RM	SET	EVL	SET
375917	73347+79047+79077+73747	RM	SET	EVL	SET
375918	73348+79048+79078+73748	RM	SEB	EVL	SET
375919	73349+79049+79079+73749	RM	SET	EVL	SET
375920	73350+79050+79080+73750	RM	SET	EVL	SET
375921	73351+79051+79081+73751	RM	SET	EVL	SET
375922	73352+79052+79082+73752	RM	SET	EVL	SET
375923	73353+79053+79083+73753	RM	SET	EVL	SET
375924	73354+79054+79084+73754	RM	SEB	EVL	SET
375925	73355+79055+79085+73755	RM	SET	EVL	SET
375926	73356+79056+79086+73756	RM	SET	EVL	SET
375927	73357+79057+79087+73757	RM	SET	EVL	SET

South Eastern

Class 376
Electrostar

Vehicle Length: (Driving) 66ft 9in (20.3m)	Width: 9ft 2in (2.79m)
(Inter) 65ft 6in (19.96m)	Horsepower: 2,682hp (2,000kW)
Height: 12ft 4in (3.75m)	Seats (total/car): 216S, 36S/48S/48S/48S/36S + 116 perch

Number	Formation DMSO(A)+MSO+TSO+MSO+DMSO(B)	Depot	Livery	Owner	Operator
376001	61101+63301+64301+63501+61601	SG	SET	EVL	SET
376002	61102+63302+64302+63502+61602	SG	SET	EVL	SET
376003	61103+63303+64303+63503+61603	SG	SET	EVL	SET
376004	61104+63304+64304+63504+61604	SG	SET	EVL	SET
376005	61105+63305+64305+63505+61605	SG	SET	EVL	SET
376006	61106+63306+64306+63506+61606	SG	SET	EVL	SET
376007	61107+63307+64307+63507+61607	SG	SET	EVL	SET
376008	61108+63308+64308+63508+61608	SG	SET	EVL	SET
376009	61109+63309+64309+63509+61609	SG	SET	EVL	SET
376010	61110+63310+64310+63510+61610	SG	SET	EVL	SET
376011	61111+63311+64311+63511+61611	SG	SET	EVL	SET
376012	61112+63312+64312+63512+61612	SG	SET	EVL	SET
376013	61113+63313+64313+63513+61613	SG	SET	EVL	SET
376014	61114+63314+64314+63514+61614	SG	SET	EVL	SET
376015	61115+63315+64315+63515+61615	SG	SET	EVL	SET
376016	61116+63316+64316+63516+61616	SG	SET	EVL	SET
376017	61117+63317+64317+63517+61617	SG	SET	EVL	SET
376018	61118+63318+64318+63518+61618	SG	SET	EVL	SET
376019	61119+63319+64319+63519+61619	SG	SET	EVL	SET
376020	61120+63320+64320+63520+61620	SG	SET	EVL	SET
376021	61121+63321+64321+63521+61621	SG	SET	EVL	SET
376022	61122+63322+64322+63522+61622	SG	SET	EVL	SET
376023	61123+63323+64323+63523+61623	SG	SET	EVL	SET
376024	61124+63324+64324+63524+61624	SG	SET	EVL	SET
376025	61125+63325+64325+63525+61625	SG	SET	EVL	SET
376026	61126+63326+64326+63526+61626	SG	SET	EVL	SET
376027	61127+63327+64327+63527+61627	SG	SET	EVL	SET
376028	61128+63328+64328+63528+61628	SG	SET	EVL	SET
376029	61129+63329+64329+63529+61629	SG	SET	EVL	SET
376030	61130+63330+64330+63530+61630	SG	SET	EVL	SET
376031	61131+63331+64331+63531+61631	SG	SET	EVL	SET
376032	61132+63332+64332+63532+61632	SG	SET	EVL	SET
376033	61133+63333+64333+63533+61633	SG	SET	EVL	SET
376034	61134+63334+64334+63534+61634	SG	SET	EVL	SET
376035	61135+63335+64335+63535+61635	SG	SET	EVL	SET
376036	61136+63336+64336+63536+61636	SG	SET	EVL	SET

Below left: *A fleet of 36 high-capacity five-car suburban 'Electrostar' sets of Class 376 is based at Slade Green, owned by Eversholt Leasing and used on heavily loaded commuter services in 10-car formations. These sets have Metro-style seating with huge amounts of standing room, especially in door pocket positions. Sets Nos. 376006 and 376003 are seen at Grove Park.* **Antony Christie**

Right: *Domestic services that operate over High Speed 1 between London and Ashford and feed Kent coast towns are formed of a fleet of 29 Hitachi-built Class 395 'Javelin' sets. Based at Ashford, these sets are basic in terms of facilities but adequate for journeys of around an hour or less travelling to and from the capital at speeds up to 140mph. Set No. 395015 is seen on the classic tracks of South Eastern at Sevington; it will cross to the high-speed tracks at Ashford.* **Antony Christie**

Class 395
Javelin

	Vehicle Length: (Driving) 67ft 7in (20.6m)		Width: 9ft 2in (2.79m)	
	(Inter) 67ft 6in (20.5m)		Horsepower: 4,504hp (3,360kW)	
	Height: 12ft 6in (3.81m)		Seats (total/car): 340S, 28S/66S/66S/66S/66S/48S	

Number	Formation DMSO(A)+MSO(A)+MSO(B)+ MSO(C)+MSO(D)+DMSO(B)	Depot	Livery	Owner	Operator	Name
395001	39011+39012+39013+39014+39015+39016	AD	HS1	EVL	SET	Dame Kelly Holmes
395002	39021+39022+39023+39024+39025+39026	AD	HS1	EVL	SET	Sebastian Coe
395003	39031+39032+39033+39034+39035+39036	AD	HS1	EVL	SET	Sir Steve Redgrave
395004	39041+39042+39043+39044+39045+39046	AD	HS1	EVL	SET	Sir Chris Hoy
395005	39051+39052+39053+39054+39055+39056	AD	HS1	EVL	SET	Dame Tanni Grey-Thompson
395006	39061+39062+39063+39064+39065+39066	AD	HS1	EVL	SET	Daley Thompson
395007	39071+39072+39073+39074+39075+39076	AD	HS1	EVL	SET	Steve Backley
395008	39081+39082+39083+39084+39085+39086	AD	HS1	EVL	SET	Ben Ainslie
395009	39091+39092+39093+39094+39095+39096	AD	HS1	EVL	SET	Rebecca Adlington
395010	39101+39102+39103+39104+39105+39106	AD	HS1	EVL	SET	Duncan Goodhew
395011	39111+39112+39113+39114+39115+39116	AD	HS1	EVL	SET	Katherine Grainger
395012	39121+39122+39123+39124+39125+39126	AD	HS1	EVL	SET	
395013	39131+39132+39133+39134+39135+39136	AD	HS1	EVL	SET	
395014	39141+39142+39143+39144+39145+39146	AD	HS1	EVL	SET	The Victoria Cross
395015	39151+39152+39153+39154+39155+39156	AD	HS1	EVL	SET	
395016	39161+39162+39163+39164+39165+39166	AD	HS1	EVL	SET	Jamie Staff / Somme 100
395017	39171+39172+39173+39174+39175+39176	AD	HS1	EVL	SET	Dame Sarah Storey
395018	39181+39182+39183+39184+39185+39186	AD	HS1	EVL	SET	Mo Farah
395019	39191+39192+39193+39194+39195+39196	AD	HS1	EVL	SET	Jessica Ennis
395020	39201+39202+39203+39204+39205+39206	AD	HS1	EVL	SET	Jason Kenny
395021	39211+39212+39213+39214+39215+39216	AD	HS1	EVL	SET	Ed Clancy MBE
395022	39221+39222+39223+39224+39225+39226	AD	HS1	EVL	SET	Alistair Brownlee
395023	39231+39232+39233+39234+39235+39236	AD	HS1	EVL	SET	Ellie Simmonds
395024	39241+39242+39243+39244+39245+39246	AD	HS1	EVL	SET	Jonnie Peacock
395025	39251+39252+39253+39254+39255+39256	AD	HS1	EVL	SET	Victoria Pendleton
395026	39261+39262+39263+39264+39265+39266	AD	HS1	EVL	SET	Marc Woods
395027	39271+39272+39273+39274+39275+39276	AD	HS1	EVL	SET	Hannah Cockcroft
395028	39281+39282+39283+39284+39285+39286	AD	HS1	EVL	SET	Laura Trott
395029	39291+39292+39293+39294+39295+39296	AD	HS1	EVL	SET	David Weir

South Eastern

Class 465/0
Networker

	Vehicle Length: (Driving) 68ft 6½in (20.89m)	Width: 9ft 3in (2.81m)
	(Inter) 65ft 9¾in (20.05m)	Horsepower: 2,252hp (1,680kW)
	Height: 12ft 4½in (3.77m)	Seats (total/car): 348S, 86S/90S/86S/86S

Number	Formation	Depot	Livery	Owner	Operator
	DMSO(A)+TSO+TSO+DMSO(B)				
465001	64759+72028+72029+64809	SG	SET	EVL	SET
465002	64760+72030+72031+64810	SG	SET	EVL	SET
465003	64761+72032+72033+64811	SG	SET	EVL	SET
465004	64762+72034+72035+64812	SG	SET	EVL	SET
465005	64763+72036+72037+64813	SG	SET	EVL	SET
465006	64764+72038+72039+64814	SG	SET	EVL	SET
465007	64765+72040+72041+64815	SG	SET	EVL	SET
465008	64766+72042+72043+64816	SG	SET	EVL	SET
465009	64767+72044+72045+64817	SG	SET	EVL	SET
465010	64768+72046+72047+64818	SG	SET	EVL	SET
465011	64769+72048+72049+64819	SG	SET	EVL	SET
465012	64770+72050+72051+64820	SG	SET	EVL	SET
465013	64771+72052+72053+64821	SG	SET	EVL	SET
465014	64772+72054+72055+64822	SG	SET	EVL	SET
465015	64773+72056+72057+64823	SG	SET	EVL	SET
465016	64774+72058+72059+64824	SG	SET	EVL	SET
465017	64775+72060+72061+64825	SG	SET	EVL	SET
465018	64776+72062+72063+64826	SG	SET	EVL	SET
465019	64777+72064+72065+64827	SG	SET	EVL	SET
465020	64778+72066+72067+64828	SG	SET	EVL	SET
465021	64779+72068+72069+64829	SG	SET	EVL	SET
465022	64780+72070+72071+64830	SG	SET	EVL	SET
465023	64781+72072+72073+64831	SG	SET	EVL	SET
465024	64782+72074+72075+64832	SG	SET	EVL	SET
465025	64783+72076+72077+64833	SG	SET	EVL	SET
465026	64784+72078+72079+64834	SG	SET	EVL	SET
465027	64785+72080+72081+64835	SG	SET	EVL	SET
465028	64786+72082+72083+64836	SG	SET	EVL	SET
465029	64787+72084+72085+64837	SG	SET	EVL	SET
465030	64788+72086+72087+64838	SG	SET	EVL	SET
465031	64789+72088+72089+64839	SG	SET	EVL	SET
465032	64790+72090+72091+64840	SG	SET	EVL	SET
465033	64791+72092+72093+64841	SG	SET	EVL	SET
465034	64792+72094+72095+64842	SG	SET	EVL	SET
465035	64793+72096+72097+64843	SG	SET	EVL	SET
465036	64794+72098+72099+64844	SG	SET	EVL	SET
465037	64795+72100+72101+64845	SG	SET	EVL	SET
465038	64796+72102+72103+64846	SG	SET	EVL	SET
465039	64797+72104+72105+64847	SG	SET	EVL	SET
465040	64798+72106+72107+64848	SG	SET	EVL	SET
465041	64799+72108+72109+64849	SG	SET	EVL	SET
465042	64800+72110+72111+64850	SG	SET	EVL	SET
465043	64801+72112+72113+64851	SG	SET	EVL	SET
465044	64802+72114+72115+64852	SG	SET	EVL	SET
465045	64803+72116+72117+64853	SG	SET	EVL	SET
465046	64804+72118+72119+64854	SG	SET	EVL	SET
465047	64805+72120+72121+64855	SG	SET	EVL	SET
465048	64806+72122+72123+64856	SG	SET	EVL	SET
465049	64807+72124+72125+64857	SG	SET	EVL	SET
465050	64808+72126+72127+64858	SG	SET	EVL	SET

Class 465/1
Networker

	Vehicle Length: (Driving) 68ft 6½in (20.89m)	Width: 9ft 3in (2.81m)
	(Inter) 65ft 9¾in (20.05m)	Horsepower: 2,252hp (1,680kW)
	Height: 12ft 4½in (3.77m)	Seats (total/car): 348S, 86S/90S/86S/86S

Number	Formation	Depot	Livery	Owner	Operator
	DMSO(A)+TSO+TSO+DMSO(B)				
465151	65800+72900+72901+65847	SG	SET	EVL	SET
465152	65801+72902+72903+65848	SG	SET	EVL	SET
465153	65802+72904+72905+65849	SG	SET	EVL	SET

465154	65803+72906+72907+65850	SG	SET	EVL	SET
465155	65804+72908+72909+65851	SG	SET	EVL	SET
465156	65805+72910+72911+65852	SG	SET	EVL	SET
465157	65806+72912+72913+65853	SG	SET	EVL	SET
465158	65807+72914+72915+65854	SG	SET	EVL	SET
465159	65808+72916+72917+65855	SG	SET	EVL	SET
465160	65809+72918+72919+65856	SG	SET	EVL	SET
465161	65810+72920+72921+65857	SG	SET	EVL	SET
465162	65811+72922+72923+65858	SG	SET	EVL	SET
465163	65812+72924+72925+65859	SG	SET	EVL	SET
465164	65813+72926+72927+65860	SG	SET	EVL	SET
465165	65814+72928+72929+65861	SG	SET	EVL	SET
465166	65815+72930+72931+65862	SG	SET	EVL	SET
465167	65816+72932+72933+65863	SG	SET	EVL	SET
465168	65817+72934+72935+65864	SG	SET	EVL	SET
465169	65818+72936+72937+65865	SG	SET	EVL	SET
465170	65819+72938+72939+65866	SG	SET	EVL	SET
465171	65820+72940+72941+65867	SG	SET	EVL	SET
465172	65821+72942+72943+65868	SG	SET	EVL	SET
465173	65822+72944+72945+65869	SG	SET	EVL	SET
465174	65823+72946+72947+65870	SG	SET	EVL	SET
465175	65824+72948+72949+65871	SG	SET	EVL	SET
465176	65825+72950+72951+65872	SG	SET	EVL	SET
465177	65826+72952+72952+65873	SG	SET	EVL	SET
465178	65827+72954+72955+65874	SG	SET	EVL	SET
465179	65828+72956+72957+65875	SG	SET	EVL	SET
465180	65829+72958+72959+65876	SG	SET	EVL	SET
465181	65830+72960+72961+65877	SG	SET	EVL	SET
465182	65831+72962+72963+65878	SG	SET	EVL	SET
465183	65832+72964+72965+65879	SG	SET	EVL	SET
465184	65833+72966+72967+65880	SG	SET	EVL	SET
465185	65834+72968+72969+65881	SG	SET	EVL	SET
465186	65835+72970+72971+65882	SG	SET	EVL	SET
465187	65836+72972+72973+65883	SG	SET	EVL	SET
465188	65837+72974+72975+65884	SG	SET	EVL	SET
465189	65838+72976+72977+65885	SG	SET	EVL	SET
465190	65839+72978+72979+65886	SG	SET	EVL	SET
465191	65840+72980+72981+65887	SG	SET	EVL	SET
465192	65841+72982+72983+65888	SG	SET	EVL	SET
465193	65842+72984+72985+65889	SG	SET	EVL	SET
465194	65843+72986+72987+65890	SG	SET	EVL	SET
465195	65844+72988+72989+65891	SG	SET	EVL	SET
465196	65845+72990+72991+65892	SG	SET	EVL	SET
465197	65846+72992+72993+65893	SG	SET	EVL	SET

Below: *The suburban South Eastern services are in the hands of pre-privatisation Class 465 'Networker' sets, introduced as modernisation of the 'Kent Link' lines by Network SouthEast. Four sub-classes of four-car sets are in service. ABB-built Class 465/1 No. 465170 is seen at Charing Cross alongside a later-built Bombardier 'Electrostar' Class 375/8 set, showing how the front end design has changed with products from the same manufacturing group.* **Antony Christie**

Passenger Train Operating Companies - South Eastern

Passenger Train Operating Companies - South Eastern

South Eastern

Class 465/2
Networker

		Vehicle Length: (Driving) 68ft 6½in (20.89m)	Width: 9ft 3in (2.81m)
		(Inter) 65ft 9¾in (20.05m)	Horsepower: 2,252hp (1,680kW)
		Height: 12ft 4½in (3.77m)	Seats (total/car): 348S, 86S/90S/86S/86S

Number	Formation	Depot	Livery	Owner	Operator
	DMSO(A)+TSO+TSO+DMSO(B)				
465235	65734+72787+72788+65784	SG	SET	ANG	SET
465236	65735+72789+72790+65785	SG	SET	ANG	SET
465237	65736+72791+72792+65786	SG	SET	ANG	SET
465238	65737+72793+72794+65787	SG	SET	ANG	SET
465239	65738+72795+72796+65788	SG	SET	ANG	SET
465240	65739+72797+72798+65789	SG	SET	ANG	SET
465241	65740+72799+72800+65790	SG	SET	ANG	SET
465242	65741+72801+72802+65791	SG	SET	ANG	SET
465243	65742+72803+72804+65792	SG	SET	ANG	SET
465244	65743+72805+72806+65793	SG	SET	ANG	SET
465245	65744+72807+72808+65794	SG	SET	ANG	SET
465246	65745+72809+72810+65795	SG	SET	ANG	SET
465247	65746+72811+72812+65796	SG	SET	ANG	SET
465248	65747+72813+72814+65797	SG	SET	ANG	SET
465249	65748+72815+72816+65798	SG	SET	ANG	SET
465250	65749+72817+72818+65799	SG	SET	ANG	SET

Class 465/9
Networker

		Vehicle Length: (Driving) 68ft 6½in (20.89m)	Width: 9ft 3in (2.81m)
		(Inter) 65ft 9¾in (20.05m)	Horsepower: 2,252hp (1,680kW)
		Height: 12ft 4½in (3.77m)	Seats (total/car): 24F-302S, 12F-68S/76S/90S/12F-68S

Number	Formation	Depot	Livery	Owner	Operator
	DMCO(A)+TSO+TSO+DMCO(B)				
465901 (465201)	65700+72719+72720+65750	SG	SET	ANG	SET
465902 (465202)	65701+72721+72722+65751	SG	SET	ANG	SET
465903 (465203)	65702+72723+72724+65752	SG	SET	ANG	SET
465904 (465204)	65703+72725+72726+65753	SG	SET	ANG	SET
465905 (465205)	65704+72727+72728+65754	SG	SET	ANG	SET
465906 (465206)	65705+72729+72730+65755	SG	SET	ANG	SET
465907 (465207)	65706+72731+72732+65756	SG	SET	ANG	SET
465908 (465208)	65707+72733+72734+65757	SG	SET	ANG	SET
465909 (465209)	65708+72735+72736+65758	SG	SET	ANG	SET
465910 (465210)	65709+72737+72738+65759	SG	SET	ANG	SET
465911 (465211)	65710+72739+72740+65760	SG	SET	ANG	SET
465912 (465212)	65711+72741+72742+65761	SG	SET	ANG	SET
465913 (465213)	65712+72743+72744+65762	SG	SET	ANG	SET
465914 (465214)	65713+72745+72746+65763	SG	SET	ANG	SET
465915 (465215)	65714+72747+72748+65764	SG	SET	ANG	SET
465916 (465216)	65715+72749+72750+65765	SG	SET	ANG	SET
465917 (465217)	65716+72751+72752+65766	SG	SET	ANG	SET
465918 (465218)	65717+72753+72754+65767	SG	SET	ANG	SET
465919 (465219)	65718+72755+72756+65768	SG	SET	ANG	SET
465920 (465220)	65719+72757+72758+65769	SG	SET	ANG	SET
465921 (465221)	65720+72759+72760+65770	SG	SET	ANG	SET
465922 (465222)	65721+72761+72762+65771	SG	SET	ANG	SET
465923 (465223)	65722+72763+72764+65772	SG	SET	ANG	SET
465924 (465224)	65723+72765+72766+65773	SG	SET	ANG	SET
465925 (465225)	65724+72767+72768+65774	SG	SET	ANG	SET
465926 (465226)	65725+72769+72770+65775	SG	SET	ANG	SET
465927 (465227)	65726+72771+72772+65776	SG	SET	ANG	SET
465928 (465228)	65727+72773+72774+65777	SG	SET	ANG	SET
465929 (465229)	65728+72775+72776+65778	SG	SET	ANG	SET
465930 (465230)	65729+72777+72778+65779	SG	SET	ANG	SET
465931 (465231)	65730+72779+72780+65780	SG	SET	ANG	SET
465932 (465232)	65731+72781+72782+65781	SG	SET	ANG	SET
465933 (465233)	65732+72783+72784+65782	SG	SET	ANG	SET
465934 (465234)	65733+72785+72786+65783	SG	SET	ANG	SET

Right: *All allocated to Slade Green, the Class 465s usually operate suburban services in eight-car formations. All sets have been refurbished from their NSE days and now sport South Eastern Trains white and grey livery, offset by lilac passenger doors. The 34 members of Class 465/9 are rebuilds of the original Class 465/2 design, having first class accommodation fitted in the driving cars, and are deployed on longer-distance outer-suburban services. Set No. 465248 is illustrated at Lewisham.* **Antony Christie**

Class 466
Networker

Vehicle Length: (Driving) 68ft 6½in (20.89m)
Height: 12ft 4½in (3.77m)
Width: 9ft 3in (2.81m)
Horsepower: 1,126hp (840kW)
Seats (total/car): 168S, 86S/82S

Number	Formation DMSO+DTSO	Depot	Livery	Owner	Operator
466001	64860+78312	SG	SET	ANG	SET
466002	64861+78313	SG	SET	ANG	SET
466003	64862+78314	SG	SET	ANG	SET
466004	64863+78315	SG	SET	ANG	SET
466005	64864+78316	SG	SET	ANG	SET
466006	64865+78317	SG	SET	ANG	SET
466007	64866+78318	SG	SET	ANG	SET
466008	64867+78319	SG	SET	ANG	SET
466009	64868+78320	SG	SET	ANG	SET
466010	64869+78321	SG	SET	ANG	SET
466011	64870+78322	SG	SET	ANG	SET
466012	64871+78323	SG	SET	ANG	SET
466013	64872+78324	SG	SET	ANG	SET
466014	64873+78325	SG	SET	ANG	SET
466015	64874+78326	SG	SET	ANG	SET
466016	64875+78327	SG	SET	ANG	SET
466017	64876+78328	SG	SET	ANG	SET
466018	64877+78329	SG	SET	ANG	SET
466019	64878+78330	SG	SET	ANG	SET
466020	64879+78331	SG	SET	ANG	SET
466021	64880+78332	SG	SET	ANG	SET
466022	64881+78333	SG	SET	ANG	SET
466023	64882+78334	SG	SET	ANG	SET
466024	64883+78335	SG	SET	ANG	SET
466025	64884+78336	SG	SET	ANG	SET
466026	64885+78337	SG	SET	ANG	SET
466027	64886+78338	SG	SET	ANG	SET
466028	64887+78339	SG	SET	ANG	SET
466029	64888+78340	SG	SET	ANG	SET
466030	64889+78341	SG	SET	ANG	SET
466031	64890+78342	SG	SET	ANG	SET
466032	64891+78343	SG	SET	ANG	SET
466033	64892+78344	SG	SET	ANG	SET
466034	64893+78345	SG	SET	ANG	SET
466035	64894+78346	SG	SET	ANG	SET
466036	64895+78347	SG	SET	ANG	SET
466037	64896+78348	SG	SET	ANG	SET
466038	64897+78349	SG	SET	ANG	SET
466039	64898+78350	SG	SET	ANG	SET
466040	64899+78351	SG	SET	ANG	SET
466041	64900+78352	SG	SET	ANG	SET
466042	64901+78353	SG	SET	ANG	SET
466043	64902+78354	SG	SET	ANG	SET

Right: *Under the NSE banner, South Eastern had a need to operate two-car sets, either on branch lines of low patronage or to strengthen eight-car sets to 10-car formations. To satisfy this need a fleet of 43 two-car Class 466 sets was built by GEC-Alstom, classified as 466. These sets, based at Slade Green, have been through the same refurbishment programme as the Class 465s. Set No. 466013 is shown.* **Richard Tuplin**

South West Trains

Address: Friars Bridge Court, 41-45 Blackfriars Road, London, SE1 8NZ
　　　　　　　✍ customerrelations@swtrains.co.uk
　　　　　　　✆ 08700 00 5151　　ⓘ www.southwesttrains.co.uk

Managing Director:　Tim Shoveller
Franchise Dates:　4 December 1996 - June 2017
Principal Routes:　London Waterloo - Weymouth, Exeter, Portsmouth and
　　　　　　　　　　suburban services in Surrey, Berkshire, Hampshire
Depots:　Wimbledon Park (WD), Bournemouth (BM), Clapham
　　　　　　Junction (CJ) [Stabling point], Salisbury (SA),
　　　　　　Northam (Siemens Transportation) (NT)
Parent Company:　Stagecoach Group

Class 158

Vehicle Length: 76ft 1¾in (23.21m)	Engine: 1 x Cummins NTA855R of 350hp per vehicle
Height: 12ft 6in (3.81m)	Horsepower: 700hp (522kW)
Width: 9ft 3¼in (2.82m)	Seats (total/car): 13F-114S, 13F-44S/70S

Number	Formation DMCL+DMSL	Depot	Livery	Owner	Operator
158880 (158737)	52737+57737	SA	SWR	PTR	SWT
158881 (158742)	52742+57742	SA	SWM	PTR	SWT
158882 (158743)	52743+57743	SA	SWM	PTR	SWT
158883 (158744)	52744+57744	SA	SWM	PTR	SWT
158884 (158772)	52772+57772	SA	SWM	PTR	SWT
158885 (158775)	52775+57775	SA	SWM	PTR	SWT
158886 (158779)	52779+57779	SA	SWM	PTR	SWT
158887 (158781)	52781+57781	SA	SWM	PTR	SWT
158888 (158802)	52802+57802	SA	SWM	PTR	SWT
158889 (158808)	52808+57808	NM	SWM	PTR	EMT Long-term hire to East Midland Trains
158890 (158814)	52814+57814	SA	SWM	PTR	SWT

Above: *With one of its allocation of Class 158s on franchise-long sub-hire to East Midlands Trains, SWT operates a fleet of 10 two-car Class 158 sets. Refurbished with both first and standard class seating, these sets operate the few non-electrified routes radiating from Salisbury, as well as working on the core Waterloo-Salisbury to Exeter route. On Bank Holidays SWT hires a '158' to Great Western and here we see set No. 158882 in the West Country on a Riviera Line service.* **CJM**

Train Operating Companies

South West Trains

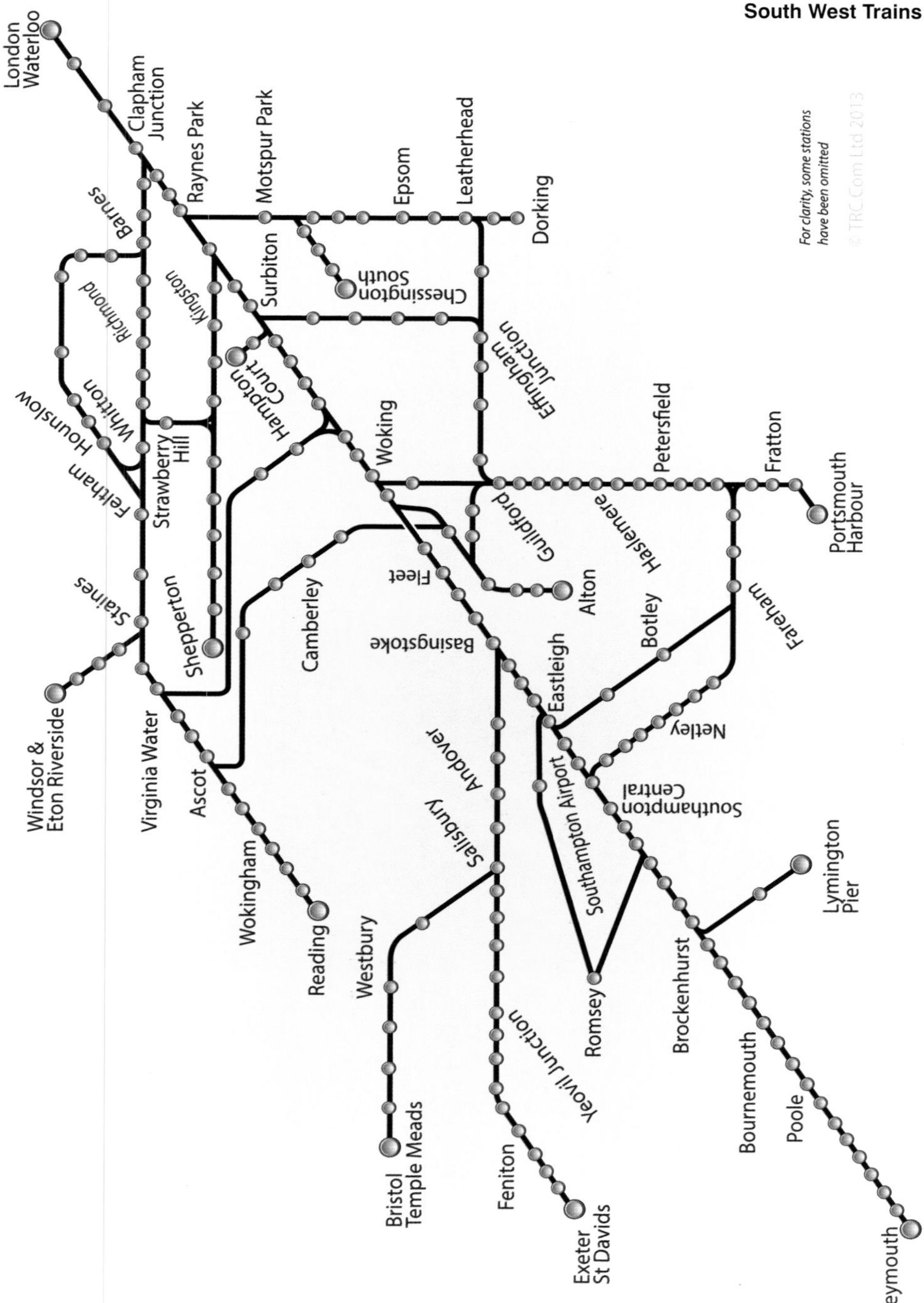

For clarity, some stations have been omitted

© TRC.Com Ltd 2013

Stations shown on the map:

London Waterloo, Clapham Junction, Raynes Park, Motspur Park, Epsom, Leatherhead, Dorking, Barnes, Richmond, Kingston, Surbiton, Chessington South, Effingham Junction, Whitton, Hounslow, Feltham, Strawberry Hill, Hampton Court, Woking, Petersfield, Fratton, Portsmouth Harbour, Staines, Shepperton, Guildford, Haslemere, Camberley, Fleet, Basingstoke, Alton, Botley, Fareham, Windsor & Eton Riverside, Virginia Water, Ascot, Eastleigh, Netley, Southampton Central, Wokingham, Andover, Salisbury, Southampton Airport, Lymington Pier, Reading, Westbury, Romsey, Brockenhurst, Bournemouth, Poole, Bristol Temple Meads, Feniton, Yeovil Junction, Exeter St Davids, Weymouth

South West Trains

Class 159/0

Vehicle Length: 76ft 1¾in (23.21m)	Engine: 1 x Cummins NTA855R of 400hp per vehicle		
Height: 12ft 6in (3.81m)	Horsepower: 1,200hp (895kW)		
Width: 9ft 3¼in (2.82m)	Seats (total/car): 24F-172S, 24F-28S/72S/72S		

Number	Formation DMCL+MSL+DMS	Depot	Livery	Owner	Operator	Name
159001	52873+58718+57873	SA	SWM	PTR	SWT	*City of Exeter*
159002	52874+58719+57874	SA	SWM	PTR	SWT	*City of Salisbury*
159003	52875+58720+57875	SA	SWM	PTR	SWT	*Templecombe*
159004	52876+58721+57876	SA	SWM	PTR	SWT	*Basingstoke and Deane*
159005	52877+58722+57877	SA	SWM	PTR	SWT	*West of England Line*
159006	52878+58723+57878	SA	SWM	PTR	SWT	*Seaton Tramway, Seaton-Colyford-Colyton*
159007	52879+58724+57879	SA	SWM	PTR	SWT	
159008	52880+58725+57880	SA	SWM	PTR	SWT	
159009	52881+58726+57881	SA	SWM	PTR	SWT	
159010	52882+58727+57882	SA	SWM	PTR	SWT	
159011	52883+58728+57883	SA	SWM	PTR	SWT	
159012	52884+58729+57884	SA	SWM	PTR	SWT	
159013	52885+58730+57885	SA	SWM	PTR	SWT	
159014	52886+58731+57886	SA	SWM	PTR	SWT	
159015	52887+58732+57887	SA	SWM	PTR	SWT	
159016	52888+58733+57888	SA	SWM	PTR	SWT	
159017	52889+58734+57889	SA	SWM	PTR	SWT	
159018	52890+58735+57890	SA	SWM	PTR	SWT	
159019	52891+58736+57891	SA	SWM	PTR	SWT	
159020	52892+58737+57892	SA	SWM	PTR	SWT	
159021	52893+58738+57893	SA	SWM	PTR	SWT	
159022	52894+58739+57894	SA	SWM	PTR	SWT	

Above: *A fleet of 30 Class 159s, of two sub-classes, is the mainstay of Waterloo-Exeter/Bristol services. All sets are based at Salisbury depot and sport the Stagecoach/SWT main-line white livery; refurbished sets sport a revised graduation between the white and orange. Set No. 159018 is seen at Westbury on a Bristol to Waterloo service.* **CJM**

Class 159/1

Vehicle Length: 76ft 1¾in (23.21m)	Engine: 1 x Cummins NTA855R of 350hp per vehicle		
Height: 12ft 6in (3.81m)	Horsepower: 1,050hp (782kW)		
Width: 9ft 3¼in (2.82m)	Seats (total/car): 24F-170S, 24F-28S/70S/72S		

Number	Formation DMCL+MSL+DMSL	Depot	Livery	Owner	Operator
159101 (158800)	52800+58717+57800	SA	SWR	PTR	SWT
159102 (158803)	52803+58703+57803	SA	SWR	PTR	SWT
159103 (158804)	52804+58704+57804	SA	SWR	PTR	SWT
159104 (158805)	52805+58705+57805	SA	SWR	PTR	SWT
159105 (158807)	52807+58707+57807	SA	SWR	PTR	SWT
159106 (158809)	52809+58709+57809	SA	SWR	PTR	SWT
159107 (158811)	52811+58711+57811	SA	SWR	PTR	SWT
159108 (158801)	52801+58701+57801	SA	SWR	PTR	SWT

Right: *The eight Class 159/1 sets were obtained to strengthen SWT services and are refurbished and modified Class 158s. However, the interior layout closely follows that of the purpose-designed '159/0s'. Units of this sub-class are currently being refurbished and sport a slightly revised livery. Painted in original SWT colours, set No. 159108 is seen near Winchfield with a Salisbury to Waterloo service.*
CJM

Class 444
Desiro

Vehicle Length: 77ft 3in (23.57m)	Horsepower: 2,682hp (2,000kW)
Height: 12ft 1½in (3.7m)	Seats (total/car): 35F-299S, 35F-24S/47S/76S/76S/76S
Width: 9ft 2in (2.7m)	

Number	Formation DMCO+TSO+TSO+TSRMB+DMSO	Depot	Livery	Owner	Operator	Name
444001	63801+67101+67151+67201+63851	NT	SWM	ANG	SWT	*Naomi House*
444002	63802+67102+67152+67202+63852	NT	SWM	ANG	SWT	
444003	63803+67103+67153+67203+63853	NT	SWM	ANG	SWT	
444004	63804+67104+67154+67204+63854	NT	SWM	ANG	SWT	
444005	63805+67105+67155+67205+63855	NT	SWM	ANG	SWT	
444006	63806+67106+67156+67206+63856	NT	SWM	ANG	SWT	
444007	63807+67107+67157+67207+63857	NT	SWM	ANG	SWT	
444008	63808+67108+67158+67208+63858	NT	SWM	ANG	SWT	
444009	63809+67109+67159+67209+63859	NT	SWM	ANG	SWT	
444010	63810+67110+67160+67210+63860	NT	SWM	ANG	SWT	
444011	63811+67111+67161+67211+63861	NT	SWM	ANG	SWT	
444012	63812+67112+67162+67212+63862	NT	SWM	ANG	SWT	*Destination Weymouth*
444013	63813+67113+67163+67213+63863	NT	SWM	ANG	SWT	
444014	63814+67114+67164+67214+63864	NT	SWM	ANG	SWT	
444015	63815+67115+67165+67215+63865	NT	SWM	ANG	SWT	
444016	63816+67116+67166+67216+63866	NT	SWM	ANG	SWT	
444017	63817+67117+67167+67217+63867	NT	SWM	ANG	SWT	
444018	63818+67118+67168+67218+63868	NT	SWM	ANG	SWT	*The FAB 444*
444019	63819+67119+67169+67219+63869	NT	SWM	ANG	SWT	
444020	63820+67120+67170+67220+63870	NT	SWM	ANG	SWT	
444021	63821+67121+67171+67221+63871	NT	SWM	ANG	SWT	
444022	63822+67122+67172+67222+63872	NT	SWM	ANG	SWT	
444023	63823+67123+67173+67223+63873	NT	SWM	ANG	SWT	
444024	63824+67124+67174+67224+63874	NT	SWM	ANG	SWT	
444025	63825+67125+67175+67225+63875	NT	SWM	ANG	SWT	
444026	63826+67126+67176+67226+63876	NT	SWM	ANG	SWT	
444027	63827+67127+67177+67227+63877	NT	SWM	ANG	SWT	
444028	63828+67128+67178+67228+63878	NT	SWM	ANG	SWT	
444029	63829+67129+67179+67229+63879	NT	SWM	ANG	SWT	
444030	63830+67130+67180+67230+63880	NT	SWM	ANG	SWT	
444031	63831+67131+67181+67231+63881	NT	SWM	ANG	SWT	
444032	63832+67132+67182+67232+63882	NT	SWM	ANG	SWT	
444033	63833+67133+67183+67233+63883	NT	SWM	ANG	SWT	
444034	63834+67134+67184+67234+63884	NT	SWM	ANG	SWT	
444035	63835+67135+67185+67235+63885	NT	SWM	ANG	SWT	
444036	63836+67136+67186+67236+63886	NT	SWM	ANG	SWT	
444037	63837+67137+67187+67237+63887	NT	SWM	ANG	SWT	
444038	63838+67138+67188+67238+63888	NT	SWM	ANG	SWT	*South Western Railway*
444039	63839+67139+67189+67239+63889	NT	SWM	ANG	SWT	
444040	63840+67140+67190+67240+63890	NT	SWM	ANG	SWT	

South West Trains

444041	63841+67141+67191+67241+63891	NT	SWM	ANG	SWT
444042	63842+67142+67192+67242+63892	NT	SWM	ANG	SWT
444043	63843+67143+67193+67243+63893	NT	SWM	ANG	SWT
444044	63844+67144+67194+67244+63894	NT	SWM	ANG	SWT
444045	63845+67145+67195+67245+63895	NT	SWM	ANG	SWT

Left: *When slam-door replacement stock was ordered for South West Trains, a contract was won by Siemens for its 'Desiro' product platform, and 45 five-car Class 444 main-line sets were ordered. Built in Austria and Germany, these sets operate main line services on the Waterloo-Bournemouth/ Weymouth and Waterloo to Portsmouth routes. With its first class end leading, identified by the blue dots at cantrail height and a yellow cover to the coupling drum, set No. 444011 passes through Raynes Park heading to Waterloo.* **CJM**

Class 450/0
Desiro

Vehicle Length: 66ft 9in (20.4m)
Height: 12ft 1½in (3.7m)
Width: 9ft 2in (2.7m)
Horsepower: 2,682hp (2,000kW)
Seats (total/car): 24F-237S, 70S/24F-36S/61S/70S

Number	Formation DMSO+TCO+TSO+DMSO	Depot	Livery	Owner	Operator	Name
450001	63201+64201+68101+63601	NT	SWO	ANG	SWT	
450002	63202+64202+68102+63602	NT	SWO	ANG	SWT	
450003	63203+64203+68103+63603	NT	SWO	ANG	SWT	
450004	63204+64204+68104+63604	NT	SWO	ANG	SWT	
450005	63205+64205+68205+63605	NT	SWO	ANG	SWT	
450006	63206+64206+68206+63606	NT	SWO	ANG	SWT	
450007	63207+64207+68207+63607	NT	SWO	ANG	SWT	
450008	63208+64208+68108+63608	NT	SWO	ANG	SWT	
450009	63209+64209+68109+63609	NT	SWO	ANG	SWT	
450010	63210+64210+68110+63610	NT	SWO	ANG	SWT	
450011	63211+64211+68111+63611	NT	SWO	ANG	SWT	
450012	63212+64212+68112+63612	NT	SWO	ANG	SWT	
450013	63213+64213+68113+63613	NT	SWO	ANG	SWT	
450014	63214+64214+68114+63614	NT	SWO	ANG	SWT	
450015	63215+64215+68115+63615	NT	SWO	ANG	SWT	*Desiro*
450016	63216+64216+68116+63616	NT	SWO	ANG	SWT	
450017	63217+64217+68117+63617	NT	SWO	ANG	SWT	
450018	63218+64218+68118+63618	NT	SWO	ANG	SWT	
450019	63219+64219+68119+63619	NT	SWO	ANG	SWT	
450020	63220+64220+68120+63620	NT	SWO	ANG	SWT	
450021	63221+64221+68121+63621	NT	SWO	ANG	SWT	
450022	63222+64222+68122+63622	NT	SWO	ANG	SWT	
450023	63223+64223+68123+63623	NT	SWO	ANG	SWT	
450024	63224+64224+68124+63624	NT	SWO	ANG	SWT	
450025	63225+64225+68125+63625	NT	SWO	ANG	SWT	
450026	63226+64226+68126+63626	NT	SWO	ANG	SWT	
450027	63227+64227+68127+63627	NT	SWO	ANG	SWT	
450028	63228+64228+68128+63628	NT	SWO	ANG	SWT	
450029	63229+64229+68129+63629	NT	SWO	ANG	SWT	
450030	63230+64230+68130+63630	NT	SWO	ANG	SWT	
450031	63231+64231+68131+63631	NT	SWO	ANG	SWT	
450032	63232+64232+68132+63632	NT	SWO	ANG	SWT	
450033	63233+64233+68133+63633	NT	SWO	ANG	SWT	
450034	63234+64234+68134+63634	NT	SWO	ANG	SWT	
450035	63235+64235+68135+63635	NT	SWO	ANG	SWT	
450036	63236+64236+68136+63636	NT	SWO	ANG	SWT	

450037	63237+64237+68137+63637	NT	SWO	ANG	SWT	
450038	63238+64238+68138+63638	NT	SWO	ANG	SWT	
450039	63239+64239+68139+63639	NT	SWO	ANG	SWT	
450040	63240+64240+68140+63640	NT	SWO	ANG	SWT	
450041	63241+64241+68141+63641	NT	SWO	ANG	SWT	
450042	63242+64242+68142+63642	NT	SWO	ANG	SWT	*Treloar College*
450071	63271+64271+68171+63671	NT	SWO	ANG	SWT	
450072	63272+64272+68172+63672	NT	SWO	ANG	SWT	
450073	63273+64273+68173+63673	NT	SWO	ANG	SWT	
450074	63274+64274+68174+63674	NT	SWO	ANG	SWT	
450075	63275+64275+68175+63675	NT	SWO	ANG	SWT	
450076	63276+64276+68176+63676	NT	SWO	ANG	SWT	
450077	63277+64277+68177+63677	NT	SWO	ANG	SWT	
450078	63278+64278+68178+63678	NT	SWO	ANG	SWT	
450079	63279+64279+68179+63679	NT	SWO	ANG	SWT	
450080	63280+64280+68180+63680	NT	SWO	ANG	SWT	
450081	63281+64281+68181+63681	NT	SWO	ANG	SWT	
450082	63282+64282+68182+63682	NT	SWO	ANG	SWT	
450083	63283+64283+68183+63683	NT	SWO	ANG	SWT	
450084	63284+64284+68184+63684	NT	SWO	ANG	SWT	
450085	63285+64285+68185+63685	NT	SWO	ANG	SWT	
450086	63286+64286+68186+63686	NT	SWO	ANG	SWT	
450087	63287+64287+68187+63687	NT	SWO	ANG	SWT	
450088	63288+64288+68188+63688	NT	SWO	ANG	SWT	
450089	63289+64289+68189+63689	NT	SWO	ANG	SWT	
450090	63290+64290+68190+63690	NT	SWO	ANG	SWT	
450091	63291+64291+68191+63691	NT	SWO	ANG	SWT	
450092	63292+64292+68192+63692	NT	SWO	ANG	SWT	
450093	63293+64293+68193+63693	NT	SWO	ANG	SWT	
450094	63294+64294+68194+63694	NT	SWO	ANG	SWT	
450095	63295+64295+68195+63695	NT	SWO	ANG	SWT	
450096	63296+64296+68196+63696	NT	SWO	ANG	SWT	
450097	63297+64297+68197+63697	NT	SWO	ANG	SWT	
450098	63298+64298+68198+63698	NT	SWO	ANG	SWT	
450099	63299+64299+68199+63699	NT	SWO	ANG	SWT	
450100	63300+64300+68200+63700	NT	SWO	ANG	SWT	
450101	63701+66851+66801+63751	NT	SWO	ANG	SWT	
450102	63702+66852+66802+63752	NT	SWO	ANG	SWT	
450103	63703+66853+66803+63753	NT	SWO	ANG	SWT	
450104	63704+66854+66804+63754	NT	SWO	ANG	SWT	
450105	63705+66855+66805+63755	NT	SWO	ANG	SWT	
450106	63706+66856+66806+63756	NT	SWO	ANG	SWT	
450107	63707+66857+66807+63757	NT	SWO	ANG	SWT	
450108	63708+66858+66808+63758	NT	SWO	ANG	SWT	
450109	63709+66859+66809+63759	NT	SWO	ANG	SWT	
450110	63710+66860+66810+63750	NT	SWO	ANG	SWT	
450111	63901+66921+66901+63921	NT	SWO	ANG	SWT	
450112	63902+66922+66902+63922	NT	ADV	ANG	SWT	
450113	63903+66923+66903+63923	NT	SWO	ANG	SWT	
450114	63904+66924+66904+63924	NT	SWO	ANG	SWT	*Fairbridge - investing in the Future*
450115	63905+66925+66905+63925	NT	SWO	ANG	SWT	
450116	63906+66926+66906+63926	NT	SWO	ANG	SWT	
450117	63907+66927+66907+63927	NT	SWO	ANG	SWT	
450118	63908+66928+66908+63928	NT	ADV	ANG	SWT	
450119	63909+66929+66909+63929	NT	SWO	ANG	SWT	
450120	63910+66930+66910+63930	NT	SWO	ANG	SWT	
450121	63911+66931+66911+63931	NT	SWO	ANG	SWT	
450122	63912+66932+66912+63932	NT	SWO	ANG	SWT	
450123	63913+66933+66913+63933	NT	SWO	ANG	SWT	
450124	63914+66934+66914+63934	NT	SWO	ANG	SWT	
450125	63915+66935+66915+63935	NT	SWO	ANG	SWT	
450126	63916+66936+66916+63936	NT	SWO	ANG	SWT	
450127	63917+66937+66917+63937	NT	SWO	ANG	SWT	

Above: *The outer-suburban slam-door replacement stock came from Siemens in a fleet of 127 four-car Class 450s 'Desiro' sets. Currently 99 Class 450/0s are in traffic, allocated to Northam, and are the backbone of most core SWT services. Set No. 450028 is seen forming a Basingstoke to Waterloo semi-fast service through Raynes Park.* **CJM**

Class 450/5
Desiro

Vehicle Length: 66ft 9in (20.4m)			Horsepower: 2,682hp (2,000kW)		
Height: 12ft 1½in (3.7m)			Seats (total/car):		
Width: 9ft 2in (2.7m)			24F/206S, 64S-24F/32S/56S/54S		

Number		Formation DMSO+TCO+TSO+DMSO	Depot	Livery	Owner	Operator
450543	(450043)	63243+64243+68143+63643	NT	SWO	ANG	SWT
450544	(450044)	63244+64244+68144+63644	NT	SWO	ANG	SWT
450545	(450045)	63245+64245+68145+63645	NT	SWO	ANG	SWT
450546	(450046)	63246+64246+68146+63646	NT	SWO	ANG	SWT
450547	(450047)	63247+64247+68147+63647	NT	SWO	ANG	SWT
450548	(450048)	63248+64248+68148+63648	NT	SWO	ANG	SWT
450549	(450049)	63249+64249+68149+63649	NT	SWO	ANG	SWT
450550	(450050)	63250+64250+68150+63650	NT	SWO	ANG	SWT
450551	(450051)	63251+64251+68151+63651	NT	SWO	ANG	SWT
450552	(450052)	63252+64252+68152+63652	NT	SWO	ANG	SWT
450553	(450053)	63253+64253+68153+63653	NT	SWO	ANG	SWT
450554	(450054)	63254+64254+68154+63654	NT	SWO	ANG	SWT
450555	(450055)	63255+64255+68155+63655	NT	SWO	ANG	SWT
450556	(450056)	63256+64256+68156+63656	NT	SWO	ANG	SWT
450557	(450057)	63257+64257+68157+63657	NT	SWO	ANG	SWT
450558	(450058)	63258+64258+68158+63658	NT	SWO	ANG	SWT
450559	(450059)	63259+64259+68159+63659	NT	SWO	ANG	SWT
450560	(450060)	63260+64260+68160+63660	NT	SWO	ANG	SWT
450561	(450061)	63261+64261+68161+63661	NT	SWO	ANG	SWT
450562	(450062)	63262+64262+68162+63662	NT	SWO	ANG	SWT
450563	(450063)	63263+64263+68163+63663	NT	SWO	ANG	SWT
450564	(450064)	63264+64264+68164+63664	NT	SWO	ANG	SWT
450565	(450065)	63265+64265+68165+63665	NT	SWO	ANG	SWT
450566	(450066)	63266+64266+68166+63666	NT	SWO	ANG	SWT
450567	(450067)	63267+64267+68167+63667	NT	SWO	ANG	SWT
450568	(450068)	63268+64268+68168+63668	NT	SWO	ANG	SWT
450569	(450069)	63269+64269+68169+63669	NT	SWO	ANG	SWT
450570	(450070)	63270+64270+68170+63670	NT	SWO	ANG	SWT

Right: *To deal with passenger overcrowding, mainly on the 'Windsor' lines into Waterloo, a batch of 28 Class 450s was modified with high-capacity interiors and altered to all-standard-class seating, being reclassified as 450/5s. In more recent years, following the delivery of extra stock, the first class area has been returned but the seating remains in the high-capacity style. Modified Class 450/5 No. 450553 (the original 450053) is captured leading an eight-car formation towards Wimbledon.* **Antony Christie**

Class 455/7

	Vehicle Length: (Driving) 65ft 0½in (19.83m)				Width: 9ft 3¼in (2.82m)		
	(Inter) 65ft 4½in (19.92m)				Horsepower: 1,000hp (746kW)		
	Height: 12ft 1½in (3.79m) [TSO- 11ft 6½in (3.58m)]				Seats (total/car): 244S, 54S/68S/68S/54S		

Number	Formation DMSO(A)+MSO+TSO+DTSO(B)	Depot	Livery	Owner	Operator	Note
(45)5701	77727+62783+71545+77728	WD	SWS	PTR	SWT	
(45)5702	77729+62784+71547+77730	WD	SWS	PTR	SWT	
(45)5703	77731+62785+71540+77732	WD	SWS	PTR	SWT	
(45)5704	77733+62786+71548+77734	WD	SWS	PTR	SWT	
(45)5705*	77735+62787+71565+77736	WD	SWS	PTR	SWT	
(45)5706	77737+62788+71534+77738	WD	SWS	PTR	SWT	
(45)5707*	77739+62789+71536+77740	WD	SWS	PTR	SWT	
(45)5708	77741+62790+71560+77742	WD	SWS	PTR	SWT	
(45)5709*	77743+62791+71532+77744	WD	SWS	PTR	SWT	
(45)5710*	77745+62792+71566+77746	WD	SWS	PTR	SWT	
(45)5711*	77747+62793+71542+77748	WD	SWS	PTR	SWT	
(45)5712	77749+62794+71546+77750	WD	SWS	PTR	SWT	
(45)5713*	77751+62795+71567+77752	WD	SWS	PTR	SWT	
(45)5714*	77753+62796+71539+77754	WD	SWS	PTR	SWT	
(45)5715*	77755+62796+71535+77756	WD	SWS	PTR	SWT	
(45)5716*	77757+62798+71564+77758	WD	SWS	PTR	SWT	
(45)5717	77759+62799+71528+77760	WD	SWS	PTR	SWT	
(45)5718	77761+62800+71557+77762	WD	SWS	PTR	SWT	
(45)5719*	77763+62801+71558+77764	WD	SWS	PTR	SWT	
(45)5720*	77765+62802+71568+77766	WD	SWS	PTR	SWT	
(45)5721*	77767+62803+71553+77768	WD	SWS	PTR	SWT	
(45)5722*	77769+62804+71533+77770	WD	SWS	PTR	SWT	
(45)5723*	77771+62805+71526+77772	WD	SWS	PTR	SWT	
(45)5724	77773+62806+71561+77774	WD	SWS	PTR	SWT	
(45)5725*	77775+62807+71541+77776	WD	SWS	PTR	SWT	
(45)5726*	77777+62608+71556+77778	WD	SWS	PTR	SWT	
(45)5727	77779+62809+71562+77780	WD	SWS	PTR	SWT	
(45)5728	77781+62810+71527+77782	WD	SWS	PTR	SWT	
(45)5729*	77783+62811+71550+77784	WD	SWS	PTR	SWT	
(45)5730*	77785+62812+71551+77786	WD	SWS	PTR	SWT	
(45)5731*	77787+62813+71555+77788	WD	SWS	PTR	SWT	
(45)5732*	77789+62814+71552+77790	WD	SWS	PTR	SWT	
(45)5733*	77791+62815+71549+77792	WD	SWS	PTR	SWT	
(45)5734*	77793+62816+71531+77794	WD	SWS	PTR	SWT	
(45)5735*	77795+62817+71563+77796	WD	SWS	PTR	SWT	
(45)5736*	77797+62818+71554+77798	WD	SWS	PTR	SWT	
(45)5737	77799+62819+71544+77800	WD	SWS	PTR	SWT	
(45)5738*	77801+62820+71529+77802	WD	SWS	PTR	SWT	
(45)5739	77803+62821+71537+77804	WD	SWS	PTR	SWT	
(45)5740	77805+62822+71530+77806	WD	SWS	PTR	SWT	
(45)5741*	77807+62823+71559+77808	WD	SWS	PTR	SWT	
(45)5742*	77809+62824+71543+77810	WD	SWS	PTR	SWT	
(45)5750§	77811+62825+71538+77812	WD	SWS	PTR	SWT	§ Originally numbered (45)5743

South West Trains

* Fitted with AC traction package

Left: *South West Trains' suburban services are in the hands of three sub-classes of Class 455 and two-car Class 456s. All sets are based at Wimbledon and sport SWT suburban red livery. Two different body profiles exist within the main class. The Class 455/7s and 455/9s have the rounded cab roof design, with the 455/7s having one 'odd' coach, a TS transferred to the sets from a Class 508. Set No. (45)5710 is seen near Wimbledon.* **Antony Christie**

Class 455/8

Vehicle Length: (Driving) 65ft 0½in (19.83m)	Width: 9ft 3¼in (2.82m)
(Inter) 65ft 4½in (19.92m)	Horsepower: 1,000hp (746kW)
Height: 12ft 1½in (3.79m)	Seats (total/car): 268S, 50S/84S/84S/50S

Number	Formation DMSO(A)+MSO+TSO+DTSO(B)	Depot	Livery	Owner	Operator
(45)5847	77671+62755+71683+77672	WD	SWS	PTR	SWT
(45)5848	77673+62756+71684+77674	WD	SWS	PTR	SWT
(45)5849	77675+62757+71685+77676	WD	SWS	PTR	SWT
(45)5850	77677+62758+71686+77678	WD	SWS	PTR	SWT
(45)5851	77679+62759+71687+77680	WD	SWS	PTR	SWT
(45)5852	77681+62760+71688+77682	WD	SWS	PTR	SWT
(45)5853	77683+62761+71689+77684	WD	SWS	PTR	SWT
(45)5854	77685+62762+71690+77686	WD	SWS	PTR	SWT
(45)5855	77687+62763+71691+77688	WD	SWS	PTR	SWT
(45)5856	77689+62764+71692+77690	WD	SWS	PTR	SWT
(45)5857	77691+62765+71693+77692	WD	SWS	PTR	SWT
(45)5858	77693+62766+71694+77694	WD	SWS	PTR	SWT
(45)5859	77695+62767+71695+77696	WD	SWS	PTR	SWT
(45)5860	77697+62768+71696+77698	WD	SWS	PTR	SWT
(45)5861	77699+62769+71697+77700	WD	SWS	PTR	SWT
(45)5862	77701+62770+71698+77702	WD	SWS	PTR	SWT
(45)5863	77703+62771+71699+77704	WD	SWS	PTR	SWT
(45)5864	77705+62772+71700+77706	WD	SWS	PTR	SWT
(45)5865	77707+62773+71701+77708	WD	SWS	PTR	SWT
(45)5866	77709+62774+71702+77710	WD	SWS	PTR	SWT
(45)5867	77711+62775+71703+77712	WD	SWS	PTR	SWT
(45)5868	77713+62776+71704+77714	WD	SWS	PTR	SWT
(45)5869	77715+62777+71705+77716	WD	SWS	PTR	SWT
(45)5870*	77717+62778+71706+77718	WD	SWS	PTR	SWT
(45)5871	77719+62779+71707+77720	WD	SWS	PTR	SWT
(45)5872	77721+62780+71708+77722	WD	SWS	PTR	SWT
(45)5873	77723+62781+71709+77724	WD	SWS	PTR	SWT
(45)5874	77725+62782+71710+77726	WD	SWS	PTR	SWT

* Fitted with AC traction package

Left: *The batch of 28 Class 455/8 sets was the original '455' and has the older-style cab front design. Interior styling is identical throughout the fleet and all have been heavily refurbished since their original introduction. Seating is currently for 268 with room for more than that figure standing. Large stand-back door openings are now provided. Set No. 5849 is illustrated.* **CJM**

Class 455/9

			Vehicle Length: (Driving) 65ft 0½in (19.83m)		Width: 9ft 3¼in (2.82m)	
			(Inter) 65ft 4½in (19.92m)		Horsepower: 1,000hp (746kW)	
			Height: 12ft 1½in (3.79m)		Seats (total/car): 236S, 50S/68S/68S/50S	

Number	Formation DMSO(A)+MSO+TSO+DTSO(B)	Depot	Livery	Owner	Operator
(45)5901	77813+62826+71714+77814	WD	SWS	PTR	SWT
(45)5902	77815+62827+71715+77816	WD	SWS	PTR	SWT
(45)5903	77817+62828+71716+77818	WD	SWS	PTR	SWT
(45)5904*	77819+62829+71717+77820	WD	SWS	PTR	SWT
(45)5905	77821+62830+71725+77822	WD	SWS	PTR	SWT
(45)5906	77823+62831+71719+77824	WD	SWS	PTR	SWT
(45)5907	77825+62832+71720+77826	WD	SWS	PTR	SWT
(45)5908	77827+62833+71721+77828	WD	SWS	PTR	SWT
(45)5909	77829+62834+71722+77830	WD	SWS	PTR	SWT
(45)5910	77831+62835+71723+77832	WD	SWS	PTR	SWT
(45)5911	77833+62836+71724+77834	WD	SWS	PTR	SWT
(45)5912	77835+62837+67400+77836	WD	SWS	PTR	SWT
(45)5913	77837+62838+71726+77838	WD	SWS	PTR	SWT
(45)5914	77839+62839+71727+77840	WD	SWS	PTR	SWT
(45)5915	77841+62840+71728+77842	WD	SWS	PTR	SWT
(45)5916*	77843+62841+71729+77844	WD	SWS	PTR	SWT
(45)5917	77845+62842+71730+77846	WD	SWS	PTR	SWT
(45)5918	77847+62843+71732+77848	WD	SWS	PTR	SWT
(45)5919	77849+62844+71718+77850	WD	SWS	PTR	SWT
(45)5920	77851+62845+71733+77852	WD	SWS	PTR	SWT

* Fitted with AC traction package

Right: *The 20 members of Class 455/9 were the final sets introduced and naturally have the later smooth front end style. These sets also have a slightly different roof profile and can thus be recognised from a distance On the left we see a Class 455/7, while on the right is Class 455/9 No. 5902. The pair of suburban sets are passing near Wimbledon West Junction.* **Antony Christie**

Class 456

	Vehicle Length: (Driving) 65ft 3¼in (19.89m)	Horsepower: 500hp (370kW)
	Height: 12ft 4½in (3.77m)	Seats (total/car): 152S, 79S/73S
	Width: 9ft 3in (2.81m)	

Right: *Until 2014, the two-car Class 456 sets were operated by Southern, being taken over by SWT to allow the operation of 10-car trains on suburban routes. Based at Wimbledon, the sets sport SWT suburban red livery and have an interior much in keeping with the Class 455. Set No. 456020 is illustrated 'on shed' at its home depot.* **CJM**

Number	Formation DMSO+DTSO	Depot	Livery	Owner	Operator						
456001	64735+78250	WD	SWS	PTR	SWT	456005	64739+78254	WD	SWS	PTR	SWT
456002	64736+78251	WD	SWS	PTR	SWT	456006	64740+78255	WD	SWS	PTR	SWT
456003	64737+78252	WD	SWS	PTR	SWT	456007	64741+78256	WD	SWS	PTR	SWT
456004	64738+78253	WD	SWS	PTR	SWT	456008	64742+78257	WD	SWS	PTR	SWT
						456009	64743+78258	WD	SWS	PTR	SWT
						456010	64744+78259	WD	SWS	PTR	SWT

South West Trains

456011	64745+78260	WD	SWS	PTR	SWT		456018	64752+78267	WD	SWS	PTR	SWT
456012	64746+78261	WD	SWS	PTR	SWT		456019	64753+78268	WD	SWS	PTR	SWT
456013	64747+78262	WD	SWS	PTR	SWT		456020	64754+78269	WD	SWS	PTR	SWT
456014	64748+78263	WD	SWS	PTR	SWT		456021	64755+78270	WD	SWS	PTR	SWT
456015	64749+78264	WD	SWS	PTR	SWT		456022	64756+78271	WD	SWS	PTR	SWT
456016	64750+78265	WD	SWS	PTR	SWT		456023	64757+78272	WD	SWS	PTR	SWT
456017	64751+78266	WD	SWS	PTR	SWT		456024	64758+78273	WD	SWS	PTR	SWT

Class 458
Juniper

Vehicle Length: (Driving) 69ft 6in (21.16m)
(Inter) 65ft 4in (19.91m)
Height: 12ft 3in (3.73m)
Width: 9ft 2in (2.79m)
Horsepower: 2,172hp (1,620kW)
Seats (total/car): 266S, 60S/52S/42S/52S/60S

Number	Original Number	Formation DMSO(A)+TSO+TSO+MSO+DMSO(B)	Depot	Livery	Owner	Operator
458501	(458001)	67601+74431+74001+74101+67701	WD	SWO	PTR	SWT
458502	(458002)	67602+74421+74002+74102+67702	WD	SWO	PTR	SWT
458503	(458003)	67603+74441+74003+74103+67703	WD	SWO	PTR	SWT
458504	(458004)	67604+74451+74004+74104+67704	WD	SWO	PTR	SWT
458505	(458005)	67605+74425+74005+74105+67705	WD	SWO	PTR	SWT
458506	(458006)	67606+74436+74006+74106+67706	WD	SWO	PTR	SWT
458507	(458007)	67607+74428+74007+74107+67707	WD	SWO	PTR	SWT
458508	(458008)	67608+74433+74008+74108+67708	WD	SWO	PTR	SWT
458509	(458009)	67609+74452+74009+74109+67709	WD	SWO	PTR	SWT
458510	(458010)	67610+74405+74010+74110+67710	WD	SWO	PTR	SWT
458511	(458011)	67611+74435+74011+74111+67711	WD	SWO	PTR	SWT
458512	(458012)	67612+74427+74012+74112+67712	WD	SWO	PTR	SWT
458513	(458013)	67613+74437+74013+74113+67713	WD	SWO	PTR	SWT
458514	(458014)	67614+74407+74014+74114+67714	WD	SWO	PTR	SWT
458515	(458015)	67615+74404+74015+74115+67715	WD	SWO	PTR	SWT
458516	(458016)	67616+74406+74016+74116+67716	WD	SWO	PTR	SWT
458517	(458017)	67617+74426+74017+74117+67717	WD	SWO	PTR	SWT
458518	(458018)	67618+74432+74018+74118+67718	WD	SWO	PTR	SWT
458519	(458019)	67619+74403+74019+74119+67719	WD	SWO	PTR	SWT
458520	(458020)	67620+74401+74020+74120+67720	WD	SWO	PTR	SWT
458521	(458021)	67621+74438+74021+74121+67721	WD	SWO	PTR	SWT
458522	(458022)	67622+74424+74022+74122+67722	WD	SWO	PTR	SWT
458523	(458023)	67623+74434+74023+74123+67723	WD	SWO	PTR	SWT
458524	(458024)	67624+74402+74024+74124+67724	WD	SWO	PTR	SWT
458525	(458025)	67625+74422+74025+74125+67725	WD	SWO	PTR	SWT
458526	(458026)	67626+74442+74026+74126+67726	WD	SWO	PTR	SWT
458527	(458027)	67627+74412+74027+74127+67727	WD	SWO	PTR	SWT
458528	(458028)	67628+74408+74028+74128+67728	WD	SWO	PTR	SWT
458529	(458029)	67629+74423+74029+74129+67729	WD	SWO	PTR	SWT
458530	(458030)	67630+74411+74030+74130+67730	WD	SWO	PTR	SWT
458531		67913+74418+74446+74458+67912	WD	SWO	PTR	SWT
458532		67904+74417+74447+74457+67905	WD	SWO	PTR	SWT
458533		67917+74413+74443+74453+67916	WD	SWO	PTR	SWT
458534		67914+74414+74444+74454+67918	WD	SWO	PTR	SWT
458535		67915+74415+74445+74455+67911	WD	SWO	PTR	SWT
458536		67906+74416+74448+74456+67902	WD	SWO	PTR	SWT

Left: *Now all strengthened to five-car formations with the addition of a former Class 460 vehicle, the fleet of 36 Class 458 'Juniper' sets is based at Wimbledon and mainly used on the 'Windsor' lines into Waterloo. Sporting a totally new front end design from the original, set No. 458510 is captured at Putney with a Waterloo-bound train.* **Antony Christie**

Class 707
Desiro City

		Vehicle Length: (Driving) 20m	Weight: tba
		(Inter) 20.16m	Power output: 3.3MW
		Height: 3.73m	Seats (total/car): -271S, 46/64/53/62/46S

Number	Formation DMSO(A)+PTSO+TSO+TSO+DMSO(B)	Depot	Livery	Owner	Operator	
707001*	421001+422001+423001+424001+425001	WD	SWS	ANG	SWT	* Delivered to the UK
707002	421001+422002+423002+424002+425002	WD	SWS	ANG	SWT	
707003*	421001+422003+423003+424003+425003	WD	SWS	ANG	SWT	
707004*	421001+422004+423004+424004+425004	WD	SWS	ANG	SWT	
707005	421001+422005+423005+424005+425005	WD	SWS	ANG	SWT	
707006	421001+422006+423006+424006+425006	WD	SWS	ANG	SWT	
707007	421001+422007+423007+424007+425007	WD	SWS	ANG	SWT	
707008	421001+422008+423008+424008+425008	WD	SWS	ANG	SWT	
707009	421001+422009+423009+424009+425009	WD	SWS	ANG	SWT	
707010	421001+422010+423010+424010+425010	WD	SWS	ANG	SWT	
707011	421001+422011+423011+424011+425011	WD	SWS	ANG	SWT	
707012	421001+422012+423012+424012+425012	WD	SWS	ANG	SWT	
707013	421001+422013+423013+424013+425013	WD	SWS	ANG	SWT	
707014	421001+422014+423014+424014+425014	WD	SWS	ANG	SWT	
707015	421001+422015+423015+424015+425015	WD	SWS	ANG	SWT	
707016	421001+422016+423016+424016+425016	WD	SWS	ANG	SWT	
707017	421001+422017+423017+424017+425017	WD	SWS	ANG	SWT	
707018	421001+422018+423018+424018+425018	WD	SWS	ANG	SWT	
707019	421001+422019+423019+424019+425019	WD	SWS	ANG	SWT	
707020	421001+422020+423020+424020+425020	WD	SWS	ANG	SWT	
707021	421001+422021+423021+424021+425021	WD	SWS	ANG	SWT	
707022	421001+422022+423022+424022+425022	WD	SWS	ANG	SWT	
707023	421001+422023+423023+424023+425023	WD	SWS	ANG	SWT	
707024	421001+422024+423024+424024+425024	WD	SWS	ANG	SWT	
707025	421001+422025+423025+424025+425025	WD	SWS	ANG	SWT	
707026	421001+422026+423026+424026+425026	WD	SWS	ANG	SWT	
707027	421001+422027+423027+424027+425027	WD	SWS	ANG	SWT	
707028	421001+422028+423028+424028+425028	WD	SWS	ANG	SWT	
707029	421001+422029+423029+424029+425029	WD	SWS	ANG	SWT	
707030	421001+422030+423030+424030+425030	WD	SWS	ANG	SWT	

Below: *The 30-strong Siemens-built 'Desiro City' five-car sets are now under construction and will enter service in 2017-2018 on suburban lines from Waterloo. Finished in the SWT red livery with an interior set out in the 2+2 style, these sets will be based at Wimbledon. Set No. 707006 is seen on display at the 2016 Innotrans exhibition in Berlin, Germany.* **CJM**

Govia Thameslink Railway

Address: Thameslink, Hertford House, 1 Cranwood Street, London, EC1V 9QS
✉ icustomer service@thameslinkrailway.com ✆ 0345 0264700
ⓘ www.thameslinkrailway.com

Managing Director: Charles Horton
Franchise Dates: September 2014 - September 2021
Principal Routes: London Victoria/London Bridge to Brighton, 'Coastway' route, Uckfield/East Grinstead. Services to Surrey/Sussex, London King's Cross - King's Lynn, Peterborough/Cambridge, Moorgate - Hertford Loop/Letchworth, Bedford - Brighton/Sutton/Wimbledon
Depots: Bedford Cauldwell Walk (BF), Brighton (BI), Hornsey (HE), Selhurst (SU), Stewarts Lane (SL)
Parent Company: Govia

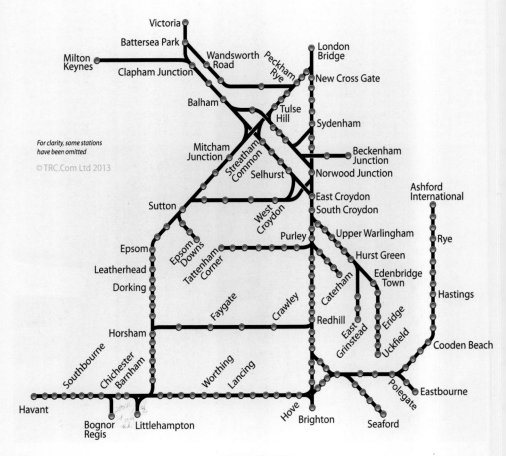

For clarity, some stations have been omitted

© TRC.Com Ltd 2013

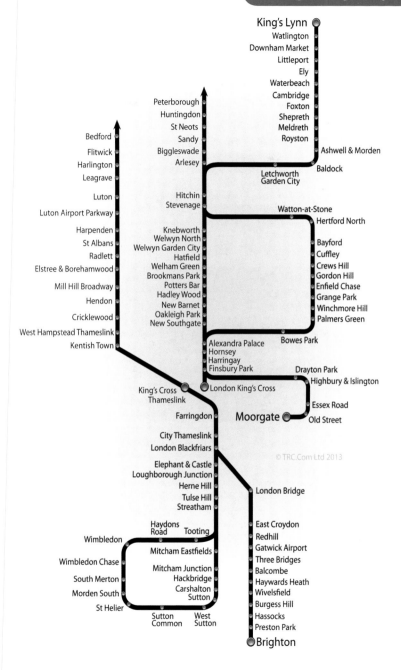

© TRC.Com Ltd 2013

Govia Thameslink Railway

Class 73/2

Vehicle Length: 53ft 8in (16.35m)				Power: 750V dc third rail or English Electric 6K		
Height: 12ft 5⅝in (3.79m)				Horsepower: E/D - 1,600hp (1,193kW) / 600hp (447kW)		
Width: 8ft 8in (2.64m)				Electrical Equipment: English Electric		

Number	Depot	Pool	Livery	Owner	Operator	Name
73202 (73137)	SL	MBED	SOU	PTR	GTR	*Graham Stenning*

Class 171/2
Turbostar

Vehicle Length: 77ft 6in (23.62m)			Engine: 1 x MTU 6R 183TD13H of 422hp per vehicle	
Height: 12ft 4½in (3.77m)			Horsepower: 844hp (629kW)	
Width: 8ft 10in (2.69m)			Seats (total/car): 9F-107S 9F-43S/64S	

Number	Former Number	Formation DMCL+DMSL	Depot	Livery	Owner	Operator
171201	(170421)	50421+79421	SU	SOU	EVL	GTR
171202	(170423)	50423+79423	SU	SOU	EVL	GTR

Class 171/4
Turbostar

Vehicle Length: 77ft 6in (23.62m)			Engine: 1 x MTU 6R 183TD13H of 422hp per vehicle	
Height: 12ft 4½in (3.77m)			Horsepower: 1,688hp (1,259kW)	
Width: 8ft 10in (2.69m)			Seats (total/car): 9F-259S 9F-43S/76S/76S/64S	

Number	Former Number	Formation DMCL+MS+MS+DMSL	Depot	Livery	Owner	Operator
171401	(171422)	50422+56421+56422+79422	SU	SOU	EVL	GTR
171402	(170424)	50424+56423+56424+79424	SU	SOU	EVL	GTR

Left: *In the summer of 2016 the first of the former Scottish Railways ex-Class 170/4 sets transferred to GTR entered traffic. Sets have been totally reformed with two two-car and two four-car sets currently in service. These are being used to strengthen Southern-operated diesel services. Four-car set No. 171401 is seen approaching East Croydon with a London Bridge to Uckfield service.* **CJM**

Class 171/7
Turbostar

Vehicle Length: 77ft 6in (23.62m)			Engine: 1 x MTU 6R 183TD13H of 422hp per vehicle	
Height: 12ft 4½in (3.77m)			Horsepower: 844hp (629kW)	
Width: 8ft 10in (2.69m)			Seats (total/car): 9F-107S 9F-43S/64S	

Number	Formation DMCL+DMSL	Depot	Livery	Owner	Operator	Number	Formation	Depot	Livery	Owner	Operator
171721	50721+79721	SU	SOU	PTR	GTR	171726	50726+79726	SU	SOU	PTR	GTR
171722	50722+79722	SU	SOU	PTR	GTR	171727	50727+79727	SU	SOU	PTR	GTR
171723	50723+79723	SU	SOU	PTR	GTR	171728	50728+79728	SU	SOU	PTR	GTR
171724	50724+79724	SU	SOU	PTR	GTR	171729	50729+79729	SU	SOU	PTR	GTR
171725	50725+79725	SU	SOU	PTR	GTR	171730	50392+79392	SU	SOU	PTR	GTR

171730 previously numbered 170392

Left: *The original Southern allocation of Class 171s have the later-designed 'Turbostar' front end with larger headlight and a combined marker/tail light, when compared with the recently introduced 171/2 and 171/4 sets. No. 171727 is seen departing from Brighton.* **Antony Christie**

Class 171/8
Turbostar

Vehicle Length: 77ft 6in (23.62m)
Height: 12ft 4½in (3.77m)
Width: 8ft 10in (2.69m)
Engine: 1 x MTU 6R 183TD13H of 422hp per vehicle
Horsepower: 1,688hp (1,259kW)
Seats (total/car): 18F-241S 9F-43S/74S/74S/9F-50S

Number	Formation DMCL(A)+MS+MS+DMCL(B)	Depot	Livery	Owner	Operator
171801	50801+54801+56801+79801	SU	SOU	PTR	GTR
171802	50802+54802+56802+79802	SU	SOU	PTR	GTR
171803	50803+54803+56803+79803	SU	SOU	PTR	GTR
171804	50804+54804+56804+79804	SU	SOU	PTR	GTR
171805	50805+54805+56805+79805	SU	SOU	PTR	GTR
171806	50806+54806+56806+79806	SU	SOU	PTR	GTR

Class 170/4

These sets are to be reclassified
as Class 171 and renumbered

Vehicle Length: 77ft 6in (23.62m)
Height: 12ft 4½in (3.77m)
Width: 8ft 10in (2.69m)
Engine: 1 x MTU 6R 183TD13H of 422hp per vehicle
Horsepower: 1,266hp (944kW)
Seats (total/car): 18F-168S 9F-43S/76S/9F-49S

Number	Formation DMCL(A)+MS+DMCL(B)	Depot	Livery	Owner	Operator
170416	50416+56416+79416	HA	SRB	EVL	ASR - Sub-lease to ScotRail
170417	50417+56417+79417	HA	SRB	EVL	ASR - Sub-lease to ScotRail
170418	50418+56418+79418	HA	SCR	EVL	ASR - Sub-lease to ScotRail
170419	50419+56419+79419	HA	SRB	EVL	ASR - Sub-lease to ScotRail
170420	50420+56420+79420	HA	SRB	EVL	ASR - Sub-lease to ScotRail

Class 313/0 & 313/1

Vehicle Length: (Driving) 64ft 11½in (20.75m)
(Inter) 65ft 4¼in (19.92m)
Height: 11ft 9in (3.58m)
Width: 9ft 3in (2.82m)
Horsepower: 880hp (656kW)
Seats (total/car): 231S, 74S/83S/74S

Number	Formation DMSO+PTSO+BDMSO	Depot	Livery	Owner	Operator	Name
313018	62546+71230+62160	HE	FCC	EVL	GTR	
313024	62552+71236+62616	HE	FCC	EVL	GTR	
313025	62553+71237+62617	HE	FCC	EVL	GTR	
313026	62554+71238+62618	HE	FCC	EVL	GTR	
313027	62555+71239+62619	HE	FCC	EVL	GTR	
313028	62556+71240+62620	HE	FCC	EVL	GTR	
313029	62557+71241+62621	HE	FCC	EVL	GTR	
313030	62558+71242+62622	HE	FCC	EVL	GTR	
313031	62559+71243+62623	HE	FCC	EVL	GTR	
313032	62560+71244+62643	HE	FCC	EVL	GTR	
313033	62561+71245+62625	HE	FCC	EVL	GTR	
313035	62563+71247+62627	HE	FCC	EVL	GTR	
313036	62564+71248+62628	HE	FCC	EVL	GTR	
313037	62565+71249+62629	HE	FCC	EVL	GTR	
313038	62566+71250+62630	HE	FCC	EVL	GTR	
313039	62567+71251+62631	HE	FCC	EVL	GTR	
313040	62568+71252+62632	HE	FCC	EVL	GTR	
313041	62569+71253+62633	HE	FCC	EVL	GTR	
313042	62570+71254+62634	HE	FCC	EVL	GTR	
313043	62571+71255+62635	HE	FCC	EVL	GTR	
313044	62572+71256+62636	HE	FCC	EVL	GTR	
313045	62573+71257+62637	HE	FCC	EVL	GTR	
313046	62574+71258+62638	HE	FCC	EVL	GTR	
313047	62575+71259+62639	HE	FCC	EVL	GTR	
313048	62576+71260+62640	HE	FCC	EVL	GTR	
313049	62577+71261+62641	HE	FCC	EVL	GTR	
313050	62578+71262+62649	HE	FCC	EVL	GTR	
313051	62579+71263+62624	HE	FCC	EVL	GTR	
313052	62580+71264+62644	HE	FCC	EVL	GTR	
313053	62581+71265+62645	HE	FCC	EVL	GTR	
313054	62582+71266+62646	HE	FCC	EVL	GTR	Captain William Leefe Robinson VC
313055	62583+71267+62647	HE	FCC	EVL	GTR	
313056	62584+71268+62648	HE	FCC	EVL	GTR	
313057	62585+71269+62642	HE	FCC	EVL	GTR	

Govia Thameslink Railway

313058	62586+71270+62650	HE	FCC	EVL	GTR	
313059	62587+71271+62651	HE	FCC	EVL	GTR	
313060	62588+71272+62652	HE	FCC	EVL	GTR	
313061	62589+71273+62653	HE	FCC	EVL	GTR	
313062	62590+71274+62654	HE	FCC	EVL	GTR	
313063	62591+71275+62655	HE	FCC	EVL	GTR	
313064	62592+71276+62656	HE	FCC	EVL	GTR	
313122	62550+71234+62614	HE	FCC	EVL	GTR	*Eric Roberts 1946-2012 'The Flying Nottsman'*
313123	62551+71235+62615	HE	FCC	EVL	GTR	
313134	62562+71246+62626	HE	FCC	EVL	GTR	*City of London*

Left: *Scheduled for early withdrawal and replacement by 25 Class 717 'Desiro City' sets, the 1972-design Class 313s still operate the Great Northern suburban electric services from London Moorgate and King's Cross. Set No. 313134 is illustrated. These sets carry the former First Group colours with Great Northern bodyside branding.* **John Binch**

Class 313/2

Vehicle Length: (Driving) 64ft 11½in (20.75m)		Width: 9ft 3in (2.82m)	
(Inter) 65ft 4½in (19.92m)		Horsepower: 880hp (656kW)	
Height: 11ft 9in (3.58m)		Seats (total/car): 202S, 66S/70S/66S	

Number	Formation DMSO+PTSO+BDMSO	Depot	Livery	Owner	Operator
313201 (313101)	62529+71213+62593	BI	SOU	BEA	GTR
313202 (313102)	62530+71214+62594	BI	SOU	BEA	GTR
313203 (313103)	62531+71215+62595	BI	SOU	BEA	GTR
313204 (313104)	62532+71216+62596	BI	SOU	BEA	GTR
313205 (313105)	62533+71217+62597	BI	SOU	BEA	GTR
313206 (313106)	62534+71218+62598	BI	SOU	BEA	GTR
313207 (313107)	62535+71219+62599	BI	SOU	BEA	GTR
313208 (313108)	62536+71220+62600	BI	SOU	BEA	GTR
313209 (313109)	62537+71221+62601	BI	SOU	BEA	GTR
313210 (313110)	62538+71222+62602	BI	SOU	BEA	GTR
313211 (313111)	62539+71223+62603	BI	SOU	BEA	GTR
313212 (313112)	62540+71224+62604	BI	SOU	BEA	GTR
313213 (313113)	62541+71225+62605	BI	SOU	BEA	GTR
313214 (313114)	62542+71226+62606	BI	SOU	BEA	GTR
313215 (313115)	62543+71227+62607	BI	SOU	BEA	GTR
313216 (313116)	62544+71228+62608	BI	SOU	BEA	GTR
313217 (313117)	62545+71229+61609	BI	SOU	BEA	GTR
313219 (313119)	62547+71231+61611	BI	SOU	BEA	GTR
313220 (313120)	62548+71232+61612	BI	SOU	BEA	GTR

Left: *The Southern operation of the GTR franchise uses a fleet of 19 three-car Class 313/2s sets based at Brighton for 'Coastway' services. These are rebuilds of the original Class 313 GN sets but now have their ac power equipment isolated, operating only from dc third rail supply. Sets are painted in a route-specific pictogram livery based on the Southern green and white style. Set No. 313204 is seen at Brighton.* **CJM**

Class 317/3

Vehicle Length: (Driving) 65ft 0¾in (19.83m)		Width: 9ft 3in (2.82m)		
(Inter) 65ft 4¼in (19.92m)		Horsepower: 1,000hp (746kW)		
Height: 12ft 1½in (3.58m)		Seats (total/car): 22F/269S, 74S/79S/22F-46S/70S		

Number	Formation DTSO+MSO+TCO+DTSO	Depot	Livery	Owner	Operator	Name
317337	77036+62671+71613+77084	HE	TLK	ANG	GTR	
317338	77037+62698+71614+77085	HE	TLK	ANG	GTR	
317339	77038+62699+71615+77086	HE	TLK	ANG	GTR	
317340	77039+62700+71616+77087	HE	TLK	ANG	GTR	
317341	77040+62701+71617+77088	HE	TLK	ANG	GTR	
317342	77041+62702+71618+77089	HE	TLK	ANG	GTR	
317343	77042+62703+71619+77090	HE	TLK	ANG	GTR	
317344	77029+62690+71620+77091	HE	FCC	ANG	GTR	
317345	77044+62705+71621+77092	HE	FCC	ANG	GTR	Driver John Webb
317346	77045+62706+71622+77093	HE	FCC	ANG	GTR	
317347	77046+62707+71623+77094	HE	FCC	ANG	GTR	
317348	77047+62708+71624+77095	HE	FCC	ANG	GTR	Richard A. Jenner

Right: *Still carrying a mix of former First Capital Connect and GTR liveries, the 12 Class 317/3 sets based at Hornsey for GN operation are likely to be candidates for early withdrawal when new stock is commissioned. Carrying GTR white and grey livery, offset by blue passenger doors, set No. 317340 is seen at London King's Cross.* **Antony Christie**

Class 319/0

Vehicle Length: (Driving) 65ft 0¾in (19.83m)		Width: 9ft 3in (2.82m)		
(Inter) 65ft 4¼in (19.92m)		Horsepower: 1,326hp (990kW)		
Height: 11ft 9in (3.58m)		Seats (total/car): 319S, 82S/82S/77S/78S		

Number	Formation DTSO(A)+MSO+TSO+DTSO(B)	Depot	Livery	Owner	Operator	Name
319001	77291+62891+71772+77290	SU	TLK	PTR	GTR	Driver Mick Winnett
319002	77293+62892+71773+77292	SU	TLK	PTR	GTR	
319003	77295+62893+71774+77294	SU	TLK	PTR	GTR	
319006	77301+62896+71777+77300	SU	TLK	PTR	GTR	
319007	77303+62897+71778+77302	SU	TLK	PTR	GTR	
319008	77305+62898+71779+77304	SU	TLK	PTR	GTR	Cheriton
319009	77307+62899+71780+77306	SU	TLK	PTR	GTR	Coquelles
319010	77309+62900+71781+77308	SU	TLK	PTR	GTR	
319011	77311+62901+71782+77310	SU	TLK	PTR	GTR	John Ruskin College
319012	77313+62902+71783+77312	SU	TLK	PTR	GTR	

Right: *The full introduction of the new Siemens Class 700 stock onto the Thameslink operation of GTR will see the entire fleet of Class 319s removed from the GTR roster, with many sets passing to new operators via refurbishment. The numbers of operational '319s' on GTR reduces weekly. Set No. 319002 is seen operating south of the Thames on the dc third rail system.* **Antony Christie**

Govia Thameslink Railway

Class 319/2

		Vehicle Length: (Driving) 65ft 0¾in (19.83m)	Width: 9ft 3in (2.82m)
		(Inter) 65ft 4¼in (19.92m)	Horsepower: 1,326hp (990kW)
		Height: 11ft 9in (3.58m)	Seats (total/car): 18F/212S, 64S/60S/52S/18F-36S

Number	Formation DTSO+MSO+TSO+DTCO	Depot	Livery	Owner	Operator	Name
319214	77317+62904+71785+77316	SU	TLK	PTR	GTR	
319215	77319+62905+71786+77318	SU	TLK	PTR	GTR	
319217	77323+62907+71788+77322	BF	TLK	PTR	GTR	Brighton
319220	77329+62910+71791+77328	BF	TLK	PTR	GTR	

Class 319/3

		Vehicle Length: (Driving) 65ft 0¾in (19.83m)	Width: 9ft 3in (2.82m)
		(Inter) 65ft 4¼in (19.92m)	Horsepower: 1,326hp (990kW)
		Height: 11ft 9in (3.58m)	Seats (total/car): 300S, 70S/78S/74S/78S

Number	Formation DTSO(A)+MSO+TSO+DTSO(B)	Depot	Livery	Owner	Operator
319370	77477+63052+71938+77476	BF	FCC	PTR	GTR
319372	77481+63054+71940+77480	BF	TLK	PTR	GTR
319373	77483+63055+71941+77482	BF	TLK	PTR	GTR
319381	77973+63093+71979+77974	BF	FCC	PTR	GTR
319384	77979+63096+71982+77980	BF	FCC	PTR	GTR
319385	77981+63097+71983+77982	BF	FCC	PTR	GTR

Class 319/4

		Vehicle Length: (Driving) 65ft 0¾in (19.83m)	Width: 9ft 3in (2.82m)
		(Inter) 65ft 4¼in (19.92m)	Horsepower: 1,326hp (990kW)
		Height: 11ft 9in (3.58m)	Seats (total/car): 12F/277S, 12F-54S/77S/72S/74S

Number	Formation DTCO+MSO+TSO+DTSO	Depot	Livery	Owner	Operator	Name
319421	77331+62911+71792+77330	BF	TLK	PTR	GTR	
319422	77333+62912+71793+77332	BF	TLK	PTR	GTR	
319423	77335+62913+71794+77334	BF	TLK	PTR	GTR	
319424	77337+62914+71795+77336	ZN	TLK	PTR	-	
319425	77339+62915+71796+77338	BF	TLK	PTR	GTR	
319426	77341+62916+71797+77340	BF	TLK	PTR	GTR	
319427§	77343+62917+71798+77342	LB	TLK	PTR	-	
319428	77345+62918+71799+77344	BF	TLK	PTR	GTR	
319430	77349+62920+71801+77348	BF	TLK	PTR	GTR	
319432	77353+62922+71803+77352	BF	TLK	PTR	GTR	
319433	77355+62923+71804+77354	BF	TLK	PTR	GTR	
319434	77357+62924+71805+77356	ZN	TLK	PTR	-	
319435	77359+62925+71806+77358	BF	TLK	PTR	GTR	Adrian Jackson-Robbins Chairman 1987-2007 Association of Public Transport Users
319436	77361+62926+71807+77360	BF	TLK	PTR	GTR	
319437	77363+62927+71808+77362	BF	TLK	PTR	GTR	
319438	77365+62928+71809+77364	BF	TLK	PTR	GTR	
319439	77367+62929+71810+77366	BF	TLK	PTR	GTR	
319440	77369+62930+71811+77368	BF	TLK	PTR	GTR	
319443	77375+62933+71814+77374	BF	TLK	PTR	GTR	
319444	77377+62934+71815+77376	BF	TLK	PTR	GTR	City of St Albans

§ 319427 at Brush Traction, Loughborough as part of a project to fit a diesel raft to eight members of the 319/4 fleet to form the Class 319 'Flex' fleet for Northern.

Left: Operating on the 25kV ac overhead system, Class 319/4 No. 319427 is seen passing Millbrook in Bedfordshire, leading another unit of the same class. Soon all these services will be in the hands of Class 700 stock. **Antony Christie**

319445	77379+62935+71816+77378	BF	TLK	PTR	GTR
319446	77381+62936+71817+77380	BF	TLK	PTR	GTR
319447	77431+62961+71866+77430	BF	TLK	PTR	GTR
319449	77435+62963+71868+77434	BF	TLK	PTR	GTR
319450	77437+62964+71869+77436	BF	TLK	PTR	GTR
319451	77439+62965+71870+77438	BF	FCC	PTR	GTR
319452	77441+62966+71871+77440	BF	FCC	PTR	GTR
319453	77443+62967+71872+77442	BF	FCC	PTR	GTR
319454	77445+62968+71873+77444	BF	FCC	PTR	GTR
319458	77453+62972+71877+77452	ZN	TLK	PTR	-
319459	77455+62973+71878+77454	BF	TLK	PTR	GTR

Class 321/4

Vehicle Length: (Driving) 65ft 0¾in (19.83m)
(Inter) 65ft 4¼in (19.92m)
Height: 12ft 4¾in (3.78m)
Width: 9ft 3in (2.82m)
Horsepower: 1,328hp (996kW)
Seats (total/car): 28F/271S, 28F-40S/79S/74S/78S

Number	Formation DMCO+MSO+TSO+DMSO	Depot	Livery	Owner	Operator	Name
321401±	78095+63063+71949+77943	HE	FCC	EVL	GTR	
321402	78096+63064+71950+77944	HE	FCC	EVL	GTR	
321403±	78097+63065+71951+77945	HE	FCC	EVL	GTR	*Stewart Fleming Signalman King's Cross*
321404±	78098+63066+71952+77946	HE	FCC	EVL	GTR	
321405	78099+63067+71953+77947	HE	FCC	EVL	GTR	
321406	78100+63068+71954+77948	HE	FCC	EVL	GTR	
321407	78101+63069+71955+77949	HE	FCC	EVL	GTR	
321408	78102+63070+71956+77959	HE	FCC	EVL	GTR	
321409	78103+63071+71957+77960	HE	FCC	EVL	GTR	*Dame Alice Owen's School 400 years of Learning*
321410	78104+63072+71958+77961	HE	FCC	EVL	GTR	
321418	78112+63080+71968+77962	HE	FCC	EVL	GTR	
321419	78113+63081+71969+77963	HE	FCC	EVL	GTR	
321420	78114+63082+71970+77964	HE	FCC	EVL	GTR	*We are proud supporters of Movember*

± Sets Nos. 321401/403/404 are scheduled to move to Scotland for conversion to Class 320/4 units.

Right: *Other units set for early withdrawal from Great Northern/ Anglia operations are the 13 Class 321/4 sets. Due to their imminent withdrawal from service in the area GTR has not funded repainting with sets retaining the livery of the previous operator (First Group), with just Great Northern branding. Set No. 321408 is viewed arriving at London King's Cross.*
Antony Christie

Class 365
Networker Express

Vehicle Length: (Driving) 68ft 6½in (20.89m)
(Inter) 65ft 9¼in (20.89m)
Height: 12ft 4½in (3.77m)
Width: 9ft 2½in (2.81m)
Horsepower: 1,684hp (1,256kW)
Seats (total/car): 24F/239S, 12F-56S/59S/68S/12F-56S

Number	Formation DMCO(A)+TSO+PTSO+DMCO(B)	Depot	Livery	Owner	Operator	Name
365501	65894+72241+72240+65935	HE	TLK	EVL	GTR	
365502	65895+72243+72242+65936	HE	TLK	EVL	GTR	
365503	65896+72245+72244+65937	HE	TLK	EVL	GTR	
365504	65897+72247+72246+65938	HE	TLK	EVL	GTR	
365505	65898+72249+72248+65939	HE	TLK	EVL	GTR	
365506	65899+72251+72250+65940	HE	TLK	EVL	GTR	
365507	65900+72253+72252+65941	HE	TLK	EVL	GTR	
365508	65901+72255+72254+65942	HE	TLK	EVL	GTR	
365509	65902+72257+72256+65943	HE	TLK	EVL	GTR	
365510	65903+72259+72258+65944	HE	TLK	EVL	GTR	

Govia Thameslink Railway

365511	65904+72261+72260+65945	HE	TLK	EVL	GTR
365512	65905+72263+72262+65946	HE	TLK	EVL	GTR
365513	65906+72265+72264+65947	HE	TLK	EVL	GTR
365514	65907+72267+72266+65948	HE	TLK	EVL	GTR
365515	65908+72269+72268+65949	HE	TLK	EVL	GTR
365516	65909+72271+72270+65950	HE	TLK	EVL	GTR
365517	65910+72273+72272+65951	HE	TLK	EVL	GTR
365518	65911+72275+72274+65952	HE	TLK	EVL	GTR
365519	65912+72277+72276+65953	HE	TLK	EVL	GTR
365520	65913+72279+72278+65954	HE	TLK	EVL	GTR
365521	65914+72281+72280+65955	HE	TLK	EVL	GTR
365522	65915+72283+72282+65956	HE	TLK	EVL	GTR
365523	65916+72285+72284+65957	HE	TLK	EVL	GTR
365524	65917+72287+72286+65958	HE	TLK	EVL	GTR
365525	65918+72289+72288+65959	HE	TLK	EVL	GTR
365527	65920+72293+72292+65961	HE	TLK	EVL	GTR
365528	65921+72296+72294+65962	HE	TLK	EVL	GTR
365529	65922+72297+72296+65963	HE	TLK	EVL	GTR
365530	65923+72299+72298+65964	HE	TLK	EVL	GTR
365531	65924+72301+72300+65965	HE	TLK	EVL	GTR
365532	65925+72303+72302+65966	HE	TLK	EVL	GTR
365533	65926+72305+72304+65967	HE	TLK	EVL	GTR	*Max Appeal*
365534	65927+72307+72306+65968	HE	TLK	EVL	GTR
365535	65928+72309+72308+65969	HE	TLK	EVL	GTR
365536	65929+72311+72310+65970	HE	TLK	EVL	GTR
365537	65930+72313+72312+65971	HE	TLK	EVL	GTR	*Daniel Edwards (1974-2010) Cambridge Driver*
365538	65931+72315+72314+65972	HE	TLK	EVL	GTR
365539	65932+72317+72316+65973	HE	TLK	EVL	GTR
365540	65933+72319+72318+65974	HE	TLK	EVL	GTR
365541	65934+72321+72320+65975	HE	TLK	EVL	GTR

Left: *The long-term future of the 40-strong Class 365 'Networker Express' fleet has yet to be finally announced. These sets will soon with replaced on Great Northern medium-distance routes by new Class 387 'Electrostar' stock. At one time the '365s' were scheduled to move to Great Western, but this will now not happen as GWR has a fleet of new Class 387 stock. Painted in GTR grey and white, set No. 365515 is pictured at London King's Cross.* **Antony Christie**

Class 377/1
Electrostar

Vehicle Length: (Driving) 66ft 9in (20.3m) Width: 9ft 2in (2.79m)
(Inter) 65ft 6in (19.96m) Horsepower: 2,012hp (1,500kW)
Height: 12ft 4in (3.75m) Seats (total/car): 24F-210S or 244S 12F-48S(56S)/62S(70S)/52S(62S)/12F-48S(56S)

Number	Formation DMCO(A)+MSO+TSO+DMCO(B)	Depot	Livery	Owner	Operator
377101	78501+77101+78901+78701	BI	SOU	PTR	GTR
377102	78502+77102+78902+78702	BI	SOU	PTR	GTR
377103	78503+77103+78903+78703	BI	SOU	PTR	GTR
377104	78504+77104+78904+78704	BI	SOU	PTR	GTR
377105	78505+77105+78905+78705	BI	SOU	PTR	GTR
377106	78506+77106+78906+78706	BI	SOU	PTR	GTR
377107	78507+77107+78907+78707	BI	SOU	PTR	GTR
377108	78508+77108+78908+78708	BI	SOU	PTR	GTR
377109	78509+77109+78909+78709	BI	SOU	PTR	GTR
377110	78510+77110+78910+78710	BI	SOU	PTR	GTR

Right: *The Southern operation of GTR uses a sizeable fleet of Class 377 'Electrostar' stock on its outer-suburban and main-line services, with units formed into five different sub-classes. A fleet of 64 Class 377/1 dc-only sets is in operation, based at Brighton. Set No. 377158 is seen arriving at East Croydon with a service bound for the South Coast.* **CJM**

■ Thirty-six Class 377/1 sets are scheduled to transfer to South Eastern in 2017.

377111	78511+77111+78911+78711	BI	SOU	PTR	GTR
377112	78512+77112+78912+78712	BI	SOU	PTR	GTR
377113	78513+77113+78913+78713	BI	SOU	PTR	GTR
377114	78514+77114+78914+78714	BI	SOU	PTR	GTR
377115	78515+77115+78915+78715	BI	SOU	PTR	GTR
377116	78516+77116+78916+78716	BI	SOU	PTR	GTR
377117	78517+77117+78917+78717	BI	SOU	PTR	GTR
377118	78518+77118+78918+78718	BI	SOU	PTR	GTR
377119	78519+77119+78919+78719	BI	SOU	PTR	GTR
377120	78520+77120+78920+78720	BI	SOU	PTR	GTR
377121	78521+77121+78921+78721	BI	SOU	PTR	GTR
377122	78522+77122+78922+78722	BI	SOU	PTR	GTR
377123	78523+77123+78923+78723	BI	SOU	PTR	GTR
377124	78524+77124+78924+78724	BI	SOU	PTR	GTR
377125	78525+77125+78925+78725	BI	SOU	PTR	GTR
377126	78526+77126+78926+78726	BI	SOU	PTR	GTR
377127	78527+77127+78927+78727	BI	SOU	PTR	GTR
377128	78528+77128+78928+78728	BI	SOU	PTR	GTR
377129	78529+77129+78929+78729	BI	SOU	PTR	GTR
377130	78530+77130+78930+78730	BI	SOU	PTR	GTR
377131	78531+77131+78931+78731	BI	SOU	PTR	GTR
377132	78532+77132+78932+78732	BI	SOU	PTR	GTR
377133	78533+77133+78933+78733	BI	SOU	PTR	GTR
377134	78534+77134+78934+78734	BI	SOU	PTR	GTR
377135	78535+77135+78935+78735	BI	SOU	PTR	GTR
377136	78536+77136+78936+78736	BI	SOU	PTR	GTR
377137	78537+77137+78937+78737	BI	SOU	PTR	GTR
377138	78538+77138+78938+78738	BI	SOU	PTR	GTR
377139	78539+77139+78939+78739	BI	SOU	PTR	GTR
377140	78540+77140+78940+78740	BI	SOU	PTR	GTR
377141	78541+77141+78941+78741	BI	SOU	PTR	GTR
377142	78542+77142+78942+78742	BI	SOU	PTR	GTR
377143	78543+77143+78943+78743	BI	SOU	PTR	GTR
377144	78544+77144+78944+78744	BI	SOU	PTR	GTR
377145	78545+77145+78945+78745	BI	SOU	PTR	GTR
377146	78546+77146+78946+78746	BI	SOU	PTR	GTR
377147	78547+77147+78947+78747	BI	SOU	PTR	GTR
377148	78548+77148+78948+78748	BI	SOU	PTR	GTR
377149	78549+77149+78949+78749	BI	SOU	PTR	GTR
377150	78550+77150+78950+78750	BI	SOU	PTR	GTR
377151	78551+77151+78951+78751	BI	SOU	PTR	GTR
377152	78552+77152+78952+78752	BI	SOU	PTR	GTR
377153	78553+77153+78953+78753	BI	SOU	PTR	GTR
377154	78554+77154+78954+78754	BI	SOU	PTR	GTR

Govia Thameslink Railway

377155	78555+77155+78955+78755	BI	SOU	PTR	GTR
377156	78556+77156+78956+78756	BI	SOU	PTR	GTR
377157	78557+77157+78957+78757	BI	SOU	PTR	GTR
377158	78558+77158+78958+78758	BI	SOU	PTR	GTR
377159	78559+77159+78959+78759	BI	SOU	PTR	GTR
377160	78560+77160+78960+78760	BI	SOU	PTR	GTR
377161	78561+77161+78961+78761	BI	SOU	PTR	GTR
377162	78562+77162+78962+78762	BI	SOU	PTR	GTR
377163	78563+77163+78963+78763	BI	SOU	PTR	GTR
377164	78564+77164+78964+78764	BI	SOU	PTR	GTR

Class 377/2
Electrostar

Vehicle Length: (Driving) 66ft 9in (20.3m) Width: 9ft 2in (2.79m)
(Inter) 65ft 6in (19.96m) Horsepower: 2,012hp (1,500kW)
Height: 12ft 4in (3.75m) Seats (total/car): 24F-222S, 12F-48S/69S/57S/12F-48S

Number	Formation	Depot	Livery	Owner	Operator
	DMCO(A)+MSO+PTSO+DMCO(B)				
377201	78571+77171+78971+78771	SU	SOU	PTR	GTR
377202	78572+77172+78972+78772	SU	SOU	PTR	GTR
377203	78573+77173+78973+78773	SU	SOU	PTR	GTR
377204	78574+77174+78974+78774	SU	SOU	PTR	GTR
377205	78575+77175+78975+78775	SU	SOU	PTR	GTR
377206	78576+77176+78976+78776	SU	SOU	PTR	GTR
377207	78577+77177+78977+78777	BF	FGB	PTR	GTR
377208	78578+77178+78978+78778	BF	SOU	PTR	GTR
377209	78579+77179+78979+78779	BF	SOU	PTR	GTR
377210	78580+77180+78980+78780	BF	SOU	PTR	GTR
377211	78581+77181+78981+78781	BF	SOU	PTR	GTR
377212	78582+77182+78982+78782	BF	SOU	PTR	GTR
377213	78583+77183+78983+78783	BF	SOU	PTR	GTR
377214	78584+77184+78984+78784	BF	SOU	PTR	GTR
377215	78585+77185+78985+78785	BF	SOU	PTR	GTR

Left: *The 15 members of Class 377/2 are four-car dual ac/dc sets and able to operate on through south-north London services via either the 'Thameslink' or West London line. Painted in First Group blue with Thameslink branding, set No. 377207 is pictured at Bedford.* **Nathan Williamson**

Class 377/3
Electrostar

Vehicle Length: (Driving) 66ft 9in (20.3m) Width: 9ft 2in (2.79m)
(Inter) 65ft 6in (19.96m) Horsepower: 2,012hp (1,500kW)
Height: 12ft 4in (3.75m) Seats (total/car): 24F-152S, 12F-48S/56S/12F-48S

Number		Formation	Depot	Livery	Owner	Operator
		DMCO(A)+TSO+DMCO(B)				
377301	(375311)	68201+74801+68401	SU	SOU	PTR	GTR
377302	(375312)	68202+74802+68402	SU	SOU	PTR	GTR
377303	(375313)	68203+74803+68403	SU	SOU	PTR	GTR
377304	(375314)	68204+74804+68404	SU	SOU	PTR	GTR
377305	(375315)	68205+74805+68405	SU	SOU	PTR	GTR
377306	(375316)	68206+74806+68406	SU	SOU	PTR	GTR
377307	(375317)	68207+74807+68407	SU	SOU	PTR	GTR
377308	(375318)	68208+74808+68408	SU	SOU	PTR	GTR
377309	(375319)	68209+74809+68409	SU	SOU	PTR	GTR
377310	(375320)	68210+74810+68410	SU	SOU	PTR	GTR
377311	(375321)	68211+74811+68411	SU	SOU	PTR	GTR
377312	(375322)	68212+74812+68412	SU	SOU	PTR	GTR

377313 (375323)	68213+74813+68413	SU	SOU	PTR	GTR
377314 (375324)	68214+74814+68414	SU	SOU	PTR	GTR
377315 (375325)	68215+74815+68415	SU	SOU	PTR	GTR
377316 (375326)	68216+74816+68416	SU	SOU	PTR	GTR
377317 (375327)	68217+74817+68417	SU	SOU	PTR	GTR
377318 (375328)	68218+74818+68418	SU	SOU	PTR	GTR
377319 (375329)	68219+74819+68419	SU	SOU	PTR	GTR
377320 (375330)	68220+74820+68420	SU	SOU	PTR	GTR
377321 (375331)	68221+74821+68421	SU	SOU	PTR	GTR
377322 (375332)	68222+74822+68422	SU	SOU	PTR	GTR
377323 (375333)	68223+74823+68423	SU	SOU	PTR	GTR
377324 (375334)	68224+74824+68424	SU	SOU	PTR	GTR
377325 (375335)	68225+74825+68425	SU	SOU	PTR	GTR
377326 (375336)	68226+74826+68426	SU	SOU	PTR	GTR
377327 (375337)	68227+74827+68427	SU	SOU	PTR	GTR
377328 (375338)	68228+74828+68428	SU	SOU	PTR	GTR

Class 377/4
Electrostar

Vehicle Length: (Driving) 66ft 9in (20.3m) Width: 9ft 2in (2.79m)
(Inter) 65ft 6in (19.96m) Horsepower: 2,012hp (1,500kW)
Height: 12ft 4in (3.75m) Seats (total/car): 20F-221S, 10F-48S/69S/56S/10F-48S

Number	Formation DMCO(A)+MSO+TSO+DMCO(B)	Depot	Livery	Owner	Operator
377401	73401+78801+78601+73801	BI	SOU	PTR	GTR
377402	73402+78802+78602+73802	BI	SOU	PTR	GTR
377403	73403+78803+78603+73803	BI	SOU	PTR	GTR
377404	73404+78804+78604+73804	BI	SOU	PTR	GTR
377405	73405+78805+78605+73805	BI	SOU	PTR	GTR
377406	73406+78806+78606+73806	BI	SOU	PTR	GTR
377407	73407+78807+78607+73807	BI	SOU	PTR	GTR
377408	73408+78808+78608+73808	BI	SOU	PTR	GTR
377409	73409+78809+78609+73809	BI	SOU	PTR	GTR
377410	73410+78810+78610+73810	BI	SOU	PTR	GTR
377411	73411+78811+78611+73811	BI	SOU	PTR	GTR
377412	73412+78812+78612+73812	BI	SOU	PTR	GTR
377413	73413+78813+78613+73813	BI	SOU	PTR	GTR
377414	73414+78814+78614+73814	BI	SOU	PTR	GTR
377415	73415+78815+78615+73815	BI	SOU	PTR	GTR
377416	73416+78816+78616+73816	BI	SOU	PTR	GTR
377417	73417+78817+78617+73817	BI	SOU	PTR	GTR
377418	73418+78818+78618+73818	BI	SOU	PTR	GTR
377419	73419+78819+78619+73819	BI	SOU	PTR	GTR
377420	73420+78820+78620+73820	BI	SOU	PTR	GTR
377421	73421+78821+78621+73821	BI	SOU	PTR	GTR
377422	73422+78822+78622+73822	BI	SOU	PTR	GTR
377423	73423+78823+78623+73823	BI	SOU	PTR	GTR
377424	73424+78824+78624+73824	BI	SOU	PTR	GTR
377425	73425+78825+78625+73825	BI	SOU	PTR	GTR
377426	73426+78826+78626+73826	BI	SOU	PTR	GTR
377427	73427+78827+78627+73827	BI	SOU	PTR	GTR
377428	73428+78828+78628+73828	BI	SOU	PTR	GTR
377429	73429+78829+78629+73829	BI	SOU	PTR	GTR
377430	73430+78830+78630+73830	BI	SOU	PTR	GTR
377431	73431+78831+78631+73831	BI	SOU	PTR	GTR
377432	73432+78832+78632+73832	BI	SOU	PTR	GTR
377433	73433+78833+78633+73833	BI	SOU	PTR	GTR
377434	73434+78834+78634+73834	BI	SOU	PTR	GTR
377435	73435+78835+78635+73835	BI	SOU	PTR	GTR
377436	73436+78836+78636+73836	BI	SOU	PTR	GTR
377437	73437+78837+78637+73837	BI	SOU	PTR	GTR
377438	73438+78838+78638+73838	BI	SOU	PTR	GTR
377439	73439+78839+78639+73839	BI	SOU	PTR	GTR
377440	73440+78840+78640+73840	BI	SOU	PTR	GTR
377441	73441+78841+78641+73841	BI	SOU	PTR	GTR
377442	73442+78842+78642+73842	BI	SOU	PTR	GTR

Passenger Train Operating Companies - Govia Thameslink Railway

Govia Thameslink Railway

377443	73443+78843+78643+73843	BI	SOU	PTR	GTR
377444	73444+78844+78644+73844	BI	SOU	PTR	GTR
377445	73445+78845+78645+73845	BI	SOU	PTR	GTR
377446	73446+78846+78646+73846	BI	SOU	PTR	GTR
377447	73447+78847+78647+73847	BI	SOU	PTR	GTR
377448	73448+78848+78648+73848	BI	SOU	PTR	GTR
377449	73449+78849+78649+73849	BI	SOU	PTR	GTR
377450	73450+78850+78650+73850	BI	SOU	PTR	GTR
377451	73451+78851+78651+73851	BI	SOU	PTR	GTR
377452	73452+78852+78652+73852	BI	SOU	PTR	GTR
377453	73453+78853+78653+73853	BI	SOU	PTR	GTR
377454	73454+78854+78654+73854	BI	SOU	PTR	GTR
377455	73455+78855+78655+73855	BI	SOU	PTR	GTR
377456	73456+78856+78656+73856	BI	SOU	PTR	GTR
377457	73457+78857+78657+73857	BI	SOU	PTR	GTR
377458	73458+78858+78658+73858	BI	SOU	PTR	GTR
377459	73459+78859+78659+73859	BI	SOU	PTR	GTR
377460	73460+78860+78660+73860	BI	SOU	PTR	GTR
377461	73461+78861+78661+73861	BI	SOU	PTR	GTR
377462	73462+78862+78662+73862	BI	SOU	PTR	GTR
377463	73463+78863+78663+73863	BI	SOU	PTR	GTR
377464	73464+78864+78664+73864	BI	SOU	PTR	GTR
377465	73465+78865+78665+73865	BI	SOU	PTR	GTR
377466	73466+78866+78666+73866	BI	SOU	PTR	GTR
377467	73467+78867+78667+73867	BI	SOU	PTR	GTR
377468	73468+78868+78668+73868	BI	SOU	PTR	GTR
377469	73469+78869+78669+73869	BI	SOU	PTR	GTR
377470	73470+78870+78670+73870	BI	SOU	PTR	GTR
377471	73471+78871+78671+73871	BI	SOU	PTR	GTR
377472	73472+78872+78672+73872	BI	SOU	PTR	GTR
377473	73473+78873+78673+73873	BI	SOU	PTR	GTR
377474	73474+78874+78674+73874	BI	SOU	PTR	GTR
377475	73475+78875+78675+73875	BI	SOU	PTR	GTR

Left: *The largest sub-class of Class 377 stock is 75 units forming Class 377/4. Owned by Porterbrook, these sets carry Southern white and green livery and can be seen throughout the South Thames operating area. These sets are dc power only. Set No. 377425 is seen arriving on the down main track at East Croydon. All Class 377s have first class accommodation in the driving cars, directly to the rear of the driving cab.* **CJM**

Class 377/5
Electrostar

Vehicle Length: (Driving) 66ft 9in (20.40m)
(Inter) 65ft 6in (19.99m)
Height: 12ft 4in (3.77m)
Width: 9ft 2in (2.79m)
Horsepower: 2,012hp (1,500kW) (ac), dual-voltage sets
Seats (total/car): 20F-221S, 10F-48S/69S/56S/10F-48S

Number	Formation DMCO(A)+MSO+PTSO+DMCO(B)	Depot	Livery	Owner	Operator
377501	73501+75901+74901+73601	SU	FGB	PTR	**Transferred to SouthEastern 12/16**
377502	73502+75902+74902+73602	SU	FGB	PTR	**Transferred to SouthEastern 12/16**

377503	73503+75903+74903+73603	SU	FGB	PTR	Transferred to SouthEastern 12/16
377504	73504+75904+74904+73604	SU	FGB	PTR	Transferred to SouthEastern 12/16
377505	73505+75905+74905+73605	SU	FGB	PTR	Transferred to SouthEastern 12/16
377506	73506+75906+74906+73606	SU	FGB	PTR	Transferred to SouthEastern 12/16
377507	73507+75907+74907+73607	SU	FGB	PTR	Transferred to SouthEastern 12/16
377508	73508+75908+74908+73608	SU	FGB	PTR	Transferred to SouthEastern 12/16
377509	73509+75909+74909+73609	BF	FGB	PTR	GTR
377510	73510+75910+74910+73610	BF	FGB	PTR	GTR
377511	73511+75911+74911+73611	BF	FGB	PTR	GTR
377512	73512+75912+74912+73612	BF	FGB	PTR	GTR
377513	73513+75913+74913+73613	BF	FGB	PTR	GTR
377514	73514+75914+74914+73614	BF	FGB	PTR	GTR
377515	73515+75915+74915+73615	BF	FGB	PTR	GTR
377516	73516+75916+74916+73616	BF	FGB	PTR	GTR
377517	73517+75917+74917+73617	BF	FGB	PTR	GTR
377518	73518+75918+74918+73618	BF	FGB	PTR	GTR
377519	73519+75919+74919+73619	BF	FGB	PTR	GTR
377520	73520+75920+74920+73620	BF	FGB	PTR	GTR
377521	73521+75921+74921+73621	BF	FGB	PTR	GTR
377522	73522+75922+74922+73622	BF	FGB	PTR	GTR
377523	73523+75923+74923+73623	BF	FGB	PTR	GTR

Right: Ordered and delivered to Southern, the 23 members of Class 377/5 were sub-leased on delivery to Thameslink and allocated to Bedford for cross-London services. Now the Class 700s have been introduced, the Class 377/5s are transferring to 'Southern' operations and joining the core pool. Set No. 377517 is illustrated at East Croydon. **Antony Christie**

Class 377/6
Electrostar

Vehicle Length: (Driving) 66ft 9in (20.3m) Width: 9ft 2in (2.79m)
(Inter) 65ft 6in (19.96m) Horsepower: 2,012hp (1,500kW)
Height: 12ft 4in (3.75m) Seats (total/car): 298S-60S/64S/46S/66S/62S

Number	Formation DMSO(A)+MSO+TSO+MSO+DMSO(B)	Depot	Livery	Owner	Operator
377601	70101+70201+70301+70401+70501	SU	SOU	PTR	GTR
377602	70102+70202+70302+70402+70502	SU	SOU	PTR	GTR
377603	70103+70203+70303+70403+70503	SU	SOU	PTR	GTR
377604	70104+70204+70304+70404+70504	SU	SOU	PTR	GTR
377605	70105+70205+70305+70405+70505	SU	SOU	PTR	GTR
377606	70106+70206+70306+70406+70506	SU	SOU	PTR	GTR
377607	70107+70207+70307+70407+70507	SU	SOU	PTR	GTR
377608	70108+70208+70308+70408+70508	SU	SOU	PTR	GTR
377609	70109+70209+70309+70409+70509	SU	SOU	PTR	GTR
377610	70110+70210+70310+70410+70510	SU	SOU	PTR	GTR
377611	70111+70211+70311+70411+70511	SU	SOU	PTR	GTR
377612	70112+70212+70312+70412+70512	SU	SOU	PTR	GTR
377613	70113+70213+70313+70413+70513	SU	SOU	PTR	GTR
377614	70114+70214+70314+70414+70514	SU	SOU	PTR	GTR
377615	70115+70215+70315+70415+70515	SU	SOU	PTR	GTR
377616	70116+70216+70316+70416+70516	SU	SOU	PTR	GTR
377617	70117+70217+70317+70417+70517	SU	SOU	PTR	GTR
377618	70118+70218+70318+70418+70518	SU	SOU	PTR	GTR
377619	70119+70219+70319+70419+70519	SU	SOU	PTR	GTR

Govia Thameslink Railway

377620	70120+70220+70320+70420+70520	SU	SOU	PTR	GTR
377621	70121+70221+70321+70421+70521	SU	SOU	PTR	GTR
377622	70122+70222+70322+70422+70522	SU	SOU	PTR	GTR
377623	70123+70223+70323+70423+70523	SU	SOU	PTR	GTR
377624	70124+70224+70324+70424+70524	SU	SOU	PTR	GTR
377625	70125+70225+70325+70425+70525	SU	SOU	PTR	GTR
377626	70126+70226+70326+70426+70526	SU	SOU	PTR	GTR

Left: The 26 members of Class 377/6 were designed for Southern 'Metro' services, where high numbers of people are needed to be shifted. These sets also sport a downward-facing track light in the front valance and were the first of the 'Electrostar' builds not to have ribbon glazing, instead using individual window frames. Set No. 377601 is seen at Mitcham. **Antony Christie**

Class 377/7
Electrostar

Vehicle Length: (Driving) 66ft 9in (20.3m)	Width: 9ft 2in (2.79m)
(Inter) 65ft 6in (19.96m)	Horsepower: 2,012hp (1,500kW)
Height: 12ft 4in (3.75m)	Seats (total/car): 298S-60S/64S/46S/66S/62S
Dual-voltage sets	

Number	Formation DMSO(A)+MSO+TSO+MSO+DMSO(B)	Depot	Livery	Owner	Op'r
377701	65201+70601+65601+70701+65401	SU	SOU	PTR	TSG
377702	65202+70602+65602+70702+65402	SU	SOU	PTR	TSG
377703	65203+70603+65603+70703+65403	SU	SOU	PTR	TSG
377704	65204+70604+65604+70704+65404	SU	SOU	PTR	TSG
377705	65205+70605+65605+70705+65405	SU	SOU	PTR	TSG
377706	65206+70606+65606+70706+65406	SU	SOU	PTR	TSG
377707	65207+70607+65607+70707+65407	SU	SOU	PTR	TSG
377708	65208+70608+65608+70708+65408	SU	SOU	PTR	TSG

Below: A fleet of eight five-car dual-voltage Class 377/7s is in traffic with Southern. These are a Class 377/6 equipped for dual-voltage operation. When introduced they were used on the Croydon to Milton Keynes route, but in 2015 this was suspended. The sets then worked with the core Southern '377' fleet. No. 377708 is seen at Kensington Olympia. **Nathan Williamson**

Class 387/1
Electrostar

Vehicle Length: (Driving) 66ft 9in (20.3m) Width: 9ft 2in (2.79m)
            (Inter) 65ft 6in (19.96m) Horsepower: 2,012hp (1,500kW)
Height: 12ft 4in (3.75m)   Seats (total/car): 223S, 56S/62S/45S/60S

Number	Formation DMSO(A)+MSO+TSO+DMSO(B)	Depot	Livery	Owner	Operator
387101	421101+422101+423101+424101	BI	TMK	PTR	GTR
387102	421102+422102+423102+424102	BI	TMK	PTR	GTR
387103	421103+422103+423103+424103	BI	TMK	PTR	GTR
387104	421104+422104+423104+424104	HE	TMK	PTR	GTR
387105	421105+422105+423105+424105	BI	TMK	PTR	GTR
387106	421106+422106+423106+424106	HE	TMK	PTR	GTR
387107	421107+422107+423107+424107	BI	TMK	PTR	GTR
387108	421108+422108+423108+424108	BI	TMK	PTR	GTR
387109	421109+422109+423109+424109	HE	TMK	PTR	GTR
387110	421110+422110+423110+424110	HE	TMK	PTR	GTR
387111	421111+422111+423111+424111	HE	TMK	PTR	GTR
387112	421112+422112+423112+424112	HE	TMK	PTR	GTR
387113	421113+422113+423113+424113	BI	TMK	PTR	GTR
387114	421114+422114+423114+424114	HE	TMK	PTR	GTR
387115	421115+422115+423115+424115	BI	TMK	PTR	GTR
387116	421116+422116+423116+424116	BI	TMK	PTR	GTR
387117	421117+422117+423117+424117	BI	TMK	PTR	GTR
387118	421118+422118+423118+424118	BI	TMK	PTR	GTR
387119	421119+422119+423119+424119	HE	TMK	PTR	GTR
387120	421120+422120+423120+424120	HE	TMK	PTR	GTR
387121	421121+422121+423121+424121	BI	TMK	PTR	GTR
387122	421122+422122+423122+424122	BI	TMK	PTR	GTR
387123	421123+422123+423123+424123	BI	TMK	PTR	GTR
387124	421124+422124+423124+424124	BI	TMK	PTR	GTR
387125	421125+422125+423125+424125	BI	TMK	PTR	GTR
387126	421126+422126+423126+424126	BI	TMK	PTR	GTR
387127	421127+422127+423127+424127	BI	TMK	PTR	GTR
387128	421128+422128+423128+424128	BI	TMK	PTR	GTR
387129	421129+422129+423129+424129	BI	TMK	PTR	GTR

Right: GTR has a fleet of 29 four-car Class 387/1 'Electrostar' sets, based at Hornsey and Brighton for use on Thameslink and Great Northern/Anglia services. Sets are finished in GTR white with dark green passenger doors and a grey window band. Set No. 387116 is viewed at East Croydon forming a Thameslink Bedford to Brighton service, a route that is being quickly taken over by new Class 700 sets. **CJM**

Class 387/2
Electrostar

Vehicle Length: (Driving) 66ft 9in (20.3m) Width: 9ft 2in (2.79m)
            (Inter) 65ft 6in (19.96m) Horsepower: 2,012hp (1,500kW)
Height: 12ft 4in (3.75m)   Seats (total/car): 201S/22F

Number	Formation DMCO+MSO+PTSO+DMSO	Depot	Livery	Owner	Operator
387201	421201+422201+423201+424201	SL	GAT	PTR	GTR
387202	421202+422202+423202+424202	SL	GAT	PTR	GTR
387203	421203+422203+423203+424203	SL	GAT	PTR	GTR
387204	421204+422204+423204+424204	SL	GAT	PTR	GTR
387205	421205+422205+423205+424205	SL	GAT	PTR	GTR

Govia Thameslink Railway

387206	421206+422206+423206+424206	SL	GAT	PTR	GTR
387207	421207+422207+423207+424207	SL	GAT	PTR	GTR
387208	421208+422208+423208+424208	SL	GAT	PTR	GTR
387209	421209+422209+423209+424209	SL	GAT	PTR	GTR
387210	421210+422210+423210+424210	SL	GAT	PTR	GTR
387211	421211+422211+423211+424211	SL	GAT	PTR	GTR
387212	421212+422212+423212+424212	SL	GAT	PTR	GTR
387213	421213+422213+423213+424213	SL	GAT	PTR	GTR
387214	421214+422214+423214+424214	SL	GAT	PTR	GTR
387215	421215+422215+423215+424215	SL	GAT	PTR	GTR
387216	421216+422216+423216+424216	SL	GAT	PTR	GTR
387217	421217+422217+423217+424217	SL	GAT	PTR	GTR
387218	421218+422218+423218+424218	SL	GAT	PTR	GTR
387219	421219+422219+423219+424219	SL	GAT	PTR	GTR
387220	421220+422220+423220+424220	SL	GAT	PTR	GTR
387221	421221+422221+423221+424221	SL	GAT	PTR	GTR
387222	421222+422222+423222+424222	SL	GAT	PTR	GTR
387223	421223+422223+423223+424223	SL	GAT	PTR	GTR
387224	421224+422224+423224+424224	SL	GAT	PTR	GTR
387225	421225+422225+423225+424225	SL	GAT	PTR	GTR
387226	421226+422226+423226+424226	SL	GAT	PTR	GTR
387227	421227+422227+423227+424227	SL	GAT	PTR	GTR

In 2016 a fleet of 27 Class 387/2s was introduced for Gatwick Express operations between London Victoria and Gatwick Airport, as well as services on the Brighton main line. These sets have reduced seating and extra luggage space and are finished in a bright red livery, offset by silver passenger doors. Set No. 378211 is seen approaching East Croydon. **CJM**

Passenger Train Operating Companies - Govia Thameslink Railway

Class 442

Vehicle Length: (Driving) 75ft 11½in (23.15m) Width: 8ft 11½in (2.73m)
(Inter) 75ft 5½in (22.99m) Horsepower: 1,608hp (1,200kW)
Height: 12ft 4in (3.81m) Seats (total/car): 24F-318S, 74S/76S/24F-28S/66S/74S

Number	Formation DTSO(A)+TSO+MBC+TSO+DTSO(B)	Depot	Livery	Owner	Operator
442401	77382+71818+62937+71841+77414	-	SGX	ANG	- Off lease stored Eastleigh Works
442402	77383+71819+62938+71842+77407	-	SGX	ANG	- Off lease stored
442403	77384+71820+62941+71843+77408	-	SGX	ANG	- Off lease stored Ely Papworth Sdg
442404	77385+71821+62939+71844+77409	-	SGX	ANG	- Off lease stored Ely Papworth Sdg
442405	77386+71822+62944+71845+77410	-	SGX	ANG	- Off lease stored Eastleigh Works
442406	77389+71823+62942+71846+77411	-	SGX	ANG	- Off lease stored
442407	77388+71824+62943+71847+77412	-	SGX	ANG	- Off lease stored Ely Papworth Sdg

442408	77387+71825+62945+71848+77413	-	SGX	ANG	- Off lease stored	
442409	77390+71826+62946+71849+77406	-	SGX	ANG	- Off lease stored Ely Papworth Sdg	
442410	77391+71827+62948+71850+77415	-	SGX	ANG	- Off lease stored	
442411	77392+71828+62940+71851+77422	-	SGX	ANG	- Off lease stored Ely Papworth Sdg	
442412	77393+71829+62947+71858+77417	-	SGX	ANG	- Off lease stored Ely Papworth Sdg	
442413	77394+71830+62949+71853+77418	-	SGX	ANG	- Off lease stored	
442414	77395+71831+62950+71854+77419	-	SGX	ANG	- Off lease stored Eastleigh Works	
442415	77396+71832+62951+71855+77420	-	SGX	ANG	- Off lease stored Ely Papworth Sdg	
442416	77397+71833+62952+71856+77421	-	SGX	ANG	- Off lease stored Ely Papworth Sdg	
442417	77398+71834+62953+71857+77416	-	SGX	ANG	- Off lease stored Eastleigh Works	
442418	77399+71835+62954+71852+77423	-	SGX	ANG	- Off lease stored Ely Papworth Sdg	
442419	77400+71836+62955+71859+77424	-	SGX	ANG	- Off lease stored	
442420	77401+71837+62956+71860+77425	-	SGX	ANG	- Off lease stored Ely Papworth Sdg	
442421	77402+71838+62957+71861+77426	-	SGX	ANG	- Off lease stored Ely Papworth Sdg	
442422	77403+71839+62958+71862+77427	-	SGX	ANG	- Off lease stored Ely Papworth Sdg	
442423	77404+71840+62959+71863+77428	-	SGX	ANG	- Off lease stored Ely Papworth Sdg	
442424	77405+71841+62960+71864+77429	-	SGX	ANG	- Off lease stored Eastleigh Works	

Right: *As new Class 387/2s were introduced on Gatwick Express operations, the Class 442 sets were taken off lease and stored for re-hire by another operator. In the days of GTR operations, set No. 442408, is seen at East Croydon.* **CJM**

Class 455/8

Vehicle Length: (Driving) 65ft 0½in (19.83m) (Inter) 65ft 4½in (19.92m)
Height: 12ft 1½in (3.79m)
Width: 9ft 3¼in (2.82m)
Horsepower: 1,000hp (746kW)
Seats (total/car): 310S, 74S/78S/84S/74S

Number	Formation DTSO(A)+MSO+TSO+DTSO(B)	Depot	Livery	Owner	Operator
455801	77627+62709+71657+77580	SL	SOU	EVL	GTR
455802	77581+62710+71664+77582	SL	SOU	EVL	GTR
455803	77583+62711+71639+77584	SL	SOU	EVL	GTR
455804	77585+62712+71640+77586	SL	SOU	EVL	GTR
455805	77587+62713+71641+77588	SL	SOU	EVL	GTR
455806	77589+62714+71642+77590	SL	SOU	EVL	GTR
455807	77591+62715+71643+77592	SL	SOU	EVL	GTR
455808	77637+62716+71644+77594	SL	SOU	EVL	GTR
455809	77623+62717+71648+77602	SL	SOU	EVL	GTR
455810	77597+62718+71646+77598	SL	SOU	EVL	GTR
455811	77599+62719+71647+77600	SL	SOU	EVL	GTR
455812	77595+62720+71645+77626	SL	SOU	EVL	GTR
455813	77603+62721+71649+77604	SL	SOU	EVL	GTR
455814	77605+62722+71650+77606	SL	SOU	EVL	GTR
455815	77607+62723+71651+77608	SL	SOU	EVL	GTR
455816	77609+62724+71652+77633	SL	SOU	EVL	GTR
455817	77611+62725+71653+77612	SL	SOU	EVL	GTR
455818	77613+62726+71654+77632	SL	SOU	EVL	GTR
455819	77615+62727+71637+77616	SL	SOU	EVL	GTR
455820	77617+62728+71656+77618	SL	SOU	EVL	GTR
455821	77619+62729+71655+77620	SL	SOU	EVL	GTR
455822	77621+62730+71658+77622	SL	SOU	EVL	GTR
455823	77601+62731+71659+77596	SL	SOU	EVL	GTR
455824	77593+62732+71660+77624	SL	SOU	EVL	GTR

Govia Thameslink Railway

455825	77579+62733+71661+77628	SL	SOU	EVL	GTR
455826	77630+62734+71662+77629	SL	SOU	EVL	GTR
455827	77610+62735+71663+77614	SL	SOU	EVL	GTR
455828	77631+62736+71638+77634	SL	SOU	EVL	GTR
455829	77635+62737+71665+77636	SL	SOU	EVL	GTR
455830	77625+62743+71666+77638	SL	SOU	EVL	GTR
455831	77639+62739+71667+77640	SL	SOU	EVL	GTR
455832	77641+62740+71668+77642	SL	SOU	EVL	GTR
455833	77643+62741+71669+77644	SL	SOU	EVL	GTR
455834	77645+62742+71670+77646	SL	SOU	EVL	GTR
455835	77647+62738+71671+77648	SL	SOU	EVL	GTR
455836	77649+62744+71672+77650	SL	SOU	EVL	GTR
455837	77651+62745+71673+77652	SL	SOU	EVL	GTR
455838	77653+62746+71674+77654	SL	SOU	EVL	GTR
455839	77655+62747+71675+77656	SL	SOU	EVL	GTR
455840	77657+62748+71676+77658	SL	SOU	EVL	GTR
455841	77659+62749+71677+77660	SL	SOU	EVL	GTR
455842	77661+62750+71678+77662	SL	SOU	EVL	GTR
455843	77663+62751+71679+77664	SL	SOU	EVL	GTR
455844	77665+62752+71680+77666	SL	SOU	EVL	GTR
455845	77667+62753+71681+77668	SL	SOU	EVL	GTR
455846	77669+62754+71682+77670	SL	SOU	EVL	GTR

Left: *A fleet of 46 four-car Class 455 suburban or Metro units operates on the busy 'Southern' south London services, based at Stewarts Lane. These four-car sets each seat 310 standard class passengers with room for more than an equal number to stand. From their original design when introduced in the 1980s, the Southern sets have had their front end gangways removed and revised light clusters fitted. Set No. 455827 is illustrated at Purley.*
Antony Christie

Class 700
Desiro City

Vehicle Length: (Driving) 20m	Weight: 278tonne/410 tonne
(Inter) 20m	Power output: 3.3/5.0MW
Height: tba	Seats (total/car): 8-car - 427 52F/375S,
	12-car 666 52F/614S

The proposed delivery order for the Class 700 stock is:
11 x 12-car Class 700/1
6 x 8-car Class 700/0
4 x 12-car Class 700/1
40 x 8-car Class 700/0
30 x 12-car Class 700/1
12 x 8-car Class 700/0
10 x 12-car Class 700/1
2 x 80-car Class 700/0
Sets marked * have been delivered to the UK

Number	Formation	Depot	Livery	Owner	Operator
	DMCO+PTSO+MSO+TSO+TSO+MSO+PTSO+DMCO				
700001	401001+402001+403001+406001+407001+410001+411001+412001	TB	TMK		GTR
700002*	401002+402002+403002+406002+407002+410002+411002+412002	TB	TMK		GTR
700003*	401003+402003+403003+406003+407003+410003+411003+412003	TB	TMK		GTR
700004*	401004+402004+403004+406004+407004+410004+411004+412004	TB	TMK		GTR
700005*	401005+402005+403005+406005+407005+410005+411005+412005	TB	TMK		GTR
700006*	401006+402006+403006+406006+407006+410006+411006+412006	TB	TMK		GTR
700007*	401007+402007+403007+406007+407007+410007+411007+412007	TB	TMK		GTR
700008*	401008+402008+403008+406008+407008+410008+411008+412008	TB	TMK		GTR
700009*	401009+402009+403009+406009+407009+410009+411009+412009	TB	TMK		GTR
700010*	401010+402010+403010+406010+407010+410010+411010+412010	TB	TMK		GTR
700011	401011+402011+403011+406011+407011+410011+411011+412011	TB	TMK		GTR

Passenger Train Operating Companies – Govia Thameslink Railway

Number	Formation	Depot	Livery	Owner	Operator
700012*	401012+402012+403012+406012+407012+410012+411012+412012	TB	TMK		GTR
700013	401013+402013+403013+406013+407013+410013+411013+412013	TB	TMK		GTR
700014*	401014+402014+403014+406014+407014+410014+411014+412014	TB	TMK		GTR
700015*	401015+402015+403015+406015+407015+410015+411015+412015	TB	TMK		GTR
700016*	401016+402016+403016+406016+407016+410016+411016+412016	TB	TMK		GTR
700017*	401017+402017+403017+406017+407017+410017+411017+412016	TB	TMK		GTR
700018*	401018+402018+403018+406018+407018+410018+411018+412018	TB	TMK		GTR
700019*	401019+402019+403019+406019+407019+410019+411019+412019	TB	TMK		GTR
700020*	401020+402020+403020+406020+407020+410020+411020+412020	TB	TMK		GTR
700021*	401021+402021+403021+406021+407021+410021+411021+412021	TB	TMK		GTR
700022	401022+402022+403022+406022+407022+410022+411022+412022	TB	TMK		GTR
700023*	401023+402023+403023+406023+407023+410023+411023+412023	TB	TMK		GTR
700024*	401024+402024+403024+406024+407024+410024+411024+412024	TB	TMK		GTR
700025	401025+402025+403025+406025+407025+410025+411025+412025	TB	TMK		GTR
700026	401026+402026+403026+406026+407026+410026+411026+412026	TB	TMK		GTR
700027	401027+402027+403027+406027+407027+410027+411027+412027	TB	TMK		GTR
700028	401028+402028+403028+406028+407028+410028+411028+412028	TB	TMK		GTR
700029*	401029+402029+403029+406029+407029+410029+411029+412029	TB	TMK		GTR
700030	410030+402030+403030+406030+407030+410030+411030+412030	TB	TMK		GTR
700031*	401031+402031+403031+406031+407031+410031+411031+412031	TB	TMK		GTR
700032	401032+402032+403032+406032+407032+410032+411032+412032	TB	TMK		GTR
700033	401033+402033+403033+406033+407033+410033+411033+412033	TB	TMK		GTR
700034	401034+402034+403034+406034+407034+410034+411034+412034	TB	TMK		GTR
700035*	401035+402035+403035+406035+407035+410035+411035+412035	TB	TMK		GTR
700036	401036+402036+403036+406036+407036+410036+411036+412036	TB	TMK		GTR
700037	401037+402037+403037+406037+407037+410037+411037+412037	TB	TMK		GTR
700038	401038+402038+403038+406038+407038+410038+411038+412038	TB	TMK		GTR
700039	401039+402039+403039+406039+407039+410039+411039+412039	TB	TMK		GTR
700040	401040+402040+403040+406040+407040+410040+411040+412040	TB	TMK		GTR
700041	401041+402041+403041+406041+407041+410041+411041+412041	TB	TMK		GTR
700042	401042+402042+403042+406042+407042+410042+411042+412042	TB	TMK		GTR
700043	401043+402043+403043+406043+407043+410043+411043+412043	TB	TMK		GTR
700044	401044+402044+403044+406044+407044+410044+411044+412044	TB	TMK		GTR
700045	401045+402045+403045+406045+407045+410045+411045+412045	TB	TMK		GTR
700046	401046+402046+403046+406046+407046+410046+411046+412046	TB	TMK		GTR
700047	401047+402047+403047+406047+407047+410047+411047+412047	TB	TMK		GTR
700048	401048+402048+403048+406048+407048+410048+411048+412048	TB	TMK		GTR
700049	401049+402049+403049+406049+407049+410049+411049+412049	TB	TMK		GTR
700050	401050+402050+403050+406050+407050+410050+411050+412050	TB	TMK		GTR
700051	401051+402051+403051+406051+407051+410051+411051+412051	TB	TMK		GTR
700052	401052+402052+403052+406052+407052+410052+411052+412052	TB	TMK		GTR
700053	401053+402053+403053+406053+407053+410053+411053+412053	TB	TMK		GTR
700054	401054+402054+403054+406054+407054+410054+411054+412054	TB	TMK		GTR
700055	401055+402055+403055+406055+407055+410055+411055+412055	TB	TMK		GTR
700056	401056+402056+403056+406056+407056+410056+411056+412056	TB	TMK		GTR
700057	401057+402057+403057+406057+407057+410057+411057+412057	TB	TMK		GTR
700058	401058+402058+403058+406058+407058+410058+411058+412058	TB	TMK		GTR
700059	401059+402059+403059+406059+407059+410059+411059+412059	TB	TMK		GTR
700060	410060+402060+406030+406060+407060+410060+411060+412060	TB	TMK		GTR

Number	Formation DMCO+PTSO+MSO+MSO+TSO+TSO+ TSO+TSO+MSO+MSO+PTSO+DMCO	Depot	Livery	Owner	Operator
700101*	401101+402101+403101+404101+405101+406101+ 407101+408101+409101+410101+411101+412101	TB	TMK		GTR
700102*	401102+402102+403102+404102+405102+406102+ 407102+408102+409102+410102+411102+412102	TB	TMK		GTR
700103*	401103+402103+403103+404103+405103+406103+ 407103+408103+409103+410103+411103+412103	TB	TMK		GTR
700104*	401104+402104+403104+404104+405104+406104+ 407104+408104+409104+410104+411104+412104	TB	TMK		GTR
700105*	401105+402105+403105+404105+405105+406105+ 407105+408105+409105+410105+411105+412105	TB	TMK		GTR
700106*	401106+402106+403106+404106+405106+406106+ 407106+408106+409106+410106+411106+412106	TB	TMK		GTR

Govia Thameslink Railway

700107*	401107+402107+403107+404107+405107+406107+ 407107+408107+409107+410107+411107+412107	TB	TMK	GTR
700108*	401108+402108+403108+404108+405108+406108+ 407108+408108+409108+410108+411108+412108	TB	TMK	GTR
700109*	401109+402109+403109+404109+405109+406109+ 407109+408109+409109+410109+411109+412109	TB	TMK	GTR
700110*	401110+402110+403110+404110+405110+406110+ 407110+408110+409110+410110+411110+412110	TB	TMK	GTR
700111*	401111+402111+403111+404111+405111+406111+ 407111+408111+409111+411101+411111+412111	TB	TMK	GTR
700112*	401112+402112+403112+404112+405112+406112+ 407112+408112+409112+410112+411112+412102	TB	TMK	GTR
700113*	401113+402113+403113+404113+405113+406113+ 407113+408113+409113 410113+411113+412113	TB	TMK	GTR
700114*	401114+402114+403114+404114+405114+406114+ 407114+408114+409114+410114+411114+412114	TB	TMK	GTR
700115*	401115+402115+403115+404115+405115+406115+ 407115+408115+409115+410115+411105+412115	TB	TMK	GTR
700116	401116+402116+403116+404116+405116+406116+ 407116+408116+409116+410116+411116+412116	TB	TMK	GTR
700117	401117+402117+403117+404117+405117+406117+ 407117+408117+409117+410117+411107+412117	TB	TMK	GTR
700118	401118+402118+403118+404118+405118+406118+ 407118+408118+409118+410118+411108+412118	TB	TMK	GTR
700119	401119+402119+403119+404119+405119+406119+ 407119+408119+409119+410119+411109+412119	TB	TMK	GTR
700120	401120+402120+403120+404120+405120+406120+ 407120+408120+409120+410120+411120+412120	TB	TMK	GTR
700121	401121+402121+403121+404121+405121+406121+ 407121+408121+409121+410121+411121+412121	TB	TMK	GTR
700122	401122+402122+403122+404122+405122+406122+ 407122+408122+409122+410122+411122+412122	TB	TMK	GTR
700123	401123+402123+403123+404123+405123+406123+ 407123+408123+409123+410123+411123+412123	TB	TMK	GTR
700124	401124+402124+403124+404124+405124+406124+ 407124+408124+409124+410124+411124+412124	TB	TMK	GTR
700125	401125+402125+403125+404125+405125+406125+ 407125+408125+409125+410125+411125+412125	TB	TMK	GTR
700126	401126+402126+403126+404126+405126+406126+ 407126+408126+409126+410126+411126+412126	TB	TMK	GTR
700127	401127+402127+403127+404127+405127+406127+ 407127+408127+409127+410127+411127+412127	TB	TMK	GTR
700128	401128+402128+403128+404128+405128+406128+ 407128+408128+409128+410128+411128+412128	TB	TMK	GTR
700129	401129+402129+403129+404129+405129+406129+ 407129+408129+409129+410129+411129+412129	TB	TMK	GTR
700130	401130+402130+403130+404130+405130+406130+ 40713+408130+409130+410130+411130+412130	TB	TMK	GTR
700131	401131+402131+403131+404131+405131+406131+ 407131+408131+409131+410131+411131+412131	TB	TMK	GTR
700132	400132+402132+403132+404132+405132+406132+ 407132+408132+409132+410132+411132+412132	TB	TMK	GTR
700133	400133+402133+403133+404133+405133+406133+ 407133+408133+409133+410133+411133+412133	TB	TMK	GTR
700134	400134+402134+403134+404134+405134+406134+ 407134+408134+409134+410134+411134+412134	TB	TMK	GTR
700135	400135+402135+403135+404135+405135+406135+ 407135+408135+409135+410135+411135+412135	TB	TMK	GTR
700136	400136+402136+403136+404136+405136+406136+ 407136+408136+409136+410136+411136+412136	TB	TMK	GTR
700137	400137+402137+403137+404137+405137+406137+ 407137+408137+409137+410137+411137+412137	TB	TMK	GTR
700138	400138+402138+403138+404138+405138+406138+ 407138+408138+409138+410138+411138+412138	TB	TMK	GTR
700139	400139+402139+403139+404139+405139+406139+ 407139+408139+409139+410139+411139+412139	TB	TMK	GTR

Number	Depot	Livery	Owner
41097	EC	VEC	ANG
41098	EC	VEC	ANG
41099	EC	VEC	ANG
41100	EC	VEC	ANG
41112	EC	VEC	PTR
41115	EC	VEC	PTR
41118	EC	VEC	ANG
41120	EC	VEC	ANG
41150	EC	VEC	ANG
41151	EC	VEC	ANG
41152	EC	VEC	ANG
41154	EC	VEC	PTR
41159	EC	VEC	PTR
41164	EC	VEC	ANG
41165	EC	VEC	PTR
41170(41001)	EC	VEC	ANG
41185(42313	EC	VEC	PTR
41190(42088)	EC	VEC	PTR

GH2G - TS (*TSD) *Seating 76/62*S*

Number	Depot	Livery	Owner
42057	EC	VEC	ANG
42058	EC	VEC	ANG
42059	EC	VEC	ANG
42063	EC	VEC	ANG
42064	EC	VEC	ANG
42065	EC	VEC	ANG
42091*	EC	VEC	ANG
42106	EC	VEC	ANG
42109	EC	VEC	PTR
42110	EC	VEC	PTR
42116*	EC	VEC	ANG
42117	EC	VEC	PTR
42122	EC	VEC	ANG
42123	EC	VEC	PTR
42125	EC	VEC	PTR
42127*	EC	VEC	ANG
42128*	EC	VEC	ANG
42130	EC	VEC	PTR
42134	EC	VEC	ANG

Number	Depot	Livery	Owner
42146	EC	VEC	ANG
42147	EC	NXE	PTR
42150	EC	VEC	ANG
42154	EC	VEC	ANG
42158	EC	VEC	ANG
42159*	EC	VEC	PTR
42160	EC	VEC	PTR
42161*	EC	VEC	PTR
42163	EC	VEC	PTR
42171	EC	VEC	ANG
42172	EC	VEC	ANG
42179	EC	VEC	ANG
42180	EC	VEC	ANG
42181	EC	VEC	ANG
42182	EC	VEC	ANG
42186	EC	VEC	ANG
42188*	EC	VEC	ANG
42189*	EC	VEC	ANG
42190	EC	VEC	ANG
42191	EC	VEC	ANG
42192	EC	VEC	ANG
42193	EC	VEC	ANG
42194	EC	VEC	PTR
42198	EC	VEC	ANG
42199	EC	VEC	ANG
42205	EC	VEC	PTR
42210	EC	VEC	PTR
42215	EC	VEC	ANG
42219	EC	VEC	ANG
42225	EC	VEC	PTR
42226	EC	VEC	ANG
42227	EC	VEC	PTR
42228	EC	VEC	PTR
42229	EC	VEC	PTR
42235	EC	VEC	ANG
42237	EC	VEC	PTR
42238*	EC	VEC	ANG
42239*	EC	VEC	ANG
42240	EC	VEC	ANG
42241	EC	VEC	ANG

Number	Depot	Livery	Owner
42242	EC	VEC	ANG
42243	EC	VEC	ANG
42244	EC	VEC	ANG
42286	EC	VEC	PTR
42306	EC	VEC	PTR
42307	EC	VEC	PTR
42322	EC	VEC	PTR
42323	EC	VEC	ANG
42326	EC	VEC	PTR
42330	EC	VEC	PTR
42335	EC	VEC	PTR
42340	EC	VEC	ANG
42352(41176)	EC	NXE	PTR
42354(41175)	EC	VEC	ANG
42355(41172)	EC	VEC	ANG
42357(41174)	EC	VEC	ANG
42363(41082)	EC	VEC	ANG

GJ2G - TGS *Seating 65S*

Number	Depot	Livery	Owner
44019	EC	VEC	ANG
44027	EC	VEC	PTR
44031	EC	VEC	ANG
44045	EC	VEC	PTR
44050	EC	VEC	PTR
44056	EC	VEC	ANG
44057	EC	VEC	PTR
44058	EC	VEC	ANG
44061	EC	VEC	ANG
44063	EC	VEC	ANG
44073	EC	VEC	PTR
44075	EC	VEC	PTR
44077	EC	VEC	ANG
44080	EC	VEC	ANG
44094	EC	VEC	ANG
44098	EC	VEC	ANG

Right: *The entire Virgin Trains East Coast HST fleet of passenger stock is finished in Virgin red and white swirl livery. The buffet/kitchen vehicles have a larger proportion of red on the bodyside covering the non-passenger area. Vehicles with first class seating have blue lines below the passenger windows in place of the time-honoured yellow cantrail band. In the upper of these two illustrations TRFB No. 40706 is seen from the passenger seating end, while in the lower picture TGS No. 44056 is seen from the seating end. Both:* **Antony Christie**

Passenger Train Operating Companies - Virgin Trains East Coast

Virgin Trains East Coast

Mk4 Stock

Vehicle Length: 75ft 5in (23m) Width: 8ft 11in (2.73m)
Height: 12ft 5in (3.79m) Bogie Type: BT41

AJ2J - RSB Seating 30S

Number	Depot	Livery	Owner
10300	BN	VEC	EVL
10301	BN	VEC	EVL
10302	BN	VEC	EVL
10303	BN	VEC	EVL
10304	BN	VEC	EVL
10305	BN	VEC	EVL
10306	BN	VEC	EVL
10307	BN	VEC	EVL
10308	BN	VEC	EVL
10309	BN	VEC	EVL
10310	BN	VEC	EVL
10311	BN	VEC	EVL
10312	BN	VEC	EVL
10313	BN	VEC	EVL
10315	BN	VEC	EVL
10317	BN	VEC	EVL
10318	BN	VEC	EVL
10319	BN	VEC	EVL
10320	BN	VEC	EVL
10321	BN	VEC	EVL
10323	BN	VEC	EVL
10324	BN	VEC	EVL
10325	BN	VEC	EVL
10326	BN	VEC	EVL
10328	BN	VEC	EVL
10329	BN	VEC	EVL
10330	BN	VEC	EVL
10331	BN	VEC	EVL
10332	BN	VEC	EVL
10333	BN	VEC	EVL

AD1J - FO Seating 46F

Number	Depot	Livery	Owner
11201	BN	VEC	EVL
11219	BN	VEC	EVL
11229	BN	VEC	EVL
11237	BN	VEC	EVL
11241	BN	VEC	EVL
11244	BN	VEC	EVL
11273	BN	VEC	EVL
11277(12408)	BN	VEC	EVL
11278(12479)	BN	VEC	EVL
11279(12521)	BN	VEC	EVL
11280(12523)	BN	VEC	EVL
11281(12418)	BN	VEC	EVL
11282(12524)	BN	VEC	EVL
11283(12435)	BN	VEC	EVL
11284(12487)	BN	VEC	EVL
11285(12537)	BN	VEC	EVL
11286(12482)	BN	VEC	EVL
11287(12527)	BN	VEC	EVL
11288(12517)	BN	VEC	EVL
11289(12528)	BN	VEC	EVL
11290(12530)	BN	VEC	EVL
11291(12535)	BN	VEC	EVL
11292(12451)	BN	VEC	EVL
11293(12536)	BN	VEC	EVL
11294(12529)	BN	VEC	EVL
11295(12475)	BN	VEC	EVL
11298(12416)	BN	VEC	EVL
11299(12532)	BN	VEC	EVL

AL1J - FOD Seating 42F

Number	Depot	Livery	Owner
11301(11215)	BN	VEC	EVL
11302(11203)	BN	VEC	EVL
11303(11211)	BN	VEC	EVL
11304(11257)	BN	VEC	EVL
11305(11261)	BN	VEC	EVL
11306(11276)	BN	VEC	EVL
11307(11217)	BN	VEC	EVL
11308(11263)	BN	VEC	EVL
11309(11262)	BN	VEC	EVL
11310(11272)	BN	VEC	EVL
11311(11221)	BN	VEC	EVL
11312(11225)	BN	VEC	EVL
11313(11210)	BN	VEC	EVL
11314(11207)	BN	VEC	EVL
11315(11238)	BN	VEC	EVL
11316(11227)	BN	VEC	EVL
11317(11223)	BN	VEC	EVL
11318(11251)	BN	VEC	EVL
11319(11247)	BN	VEC	EVL
11320(11255)	BN	VEC	EVL
11321(11245)	BN	VEC	EVL
11322(11228)	BN	VEC	EVL
11323(11235)	BN	VEC	EVL
11324(11253)	BN	VEC	EVL
11325(11231)	BN	VEC	EVL
11326(11206)	BN	ECG	EVL
11327(11236)	BN	VEC	EVL
11328(11274)	BN	VEC	EVL
11329(11243)	BN	VEC	EVL
11330(11249)	BN	VEC	EVL

AD1J - FO Seating 46F (55F*)

Number	Depot	Livery	Owner
11401(11214)	BN	VEC	EVL*
11402(11216)	BN	VEC	EVL
11403(11258)	BN	VEC	EVL
11404(11202)	BN	VEC	EVL
11405(11204)	BN	VEC	EVL
11406(11205)	BN	VEC	EVL
11407(11256)	BN	VEC	EVL
11408(11218)	BN	VEC	EVL
11409(11259)	BN	VEC	EVL
11410(11260)	BN	VEC	EVL
11411(11240)	BN	VEC	EVL
11412(11209)	BN	VEC	EVL
11413(11212)	BN	VEC	EVL
11414(11246)	BN	VEC	EVL
11415(11208)	BN	VEC	EVL
11416(11254)	BN	VEC	EVL
11417(11226)	BN	VEC	EVL
11418(11222)	BN	VEC	EVL
11419(11250)	BN	VEC	EVL
11420(11242)	BN	VEC	EVL
11421(11220)	BN	VEC	EVL
11422(11232)	BN	VEC	EVL
11423(11230)	BN	VEC	EVL
11424(11239)	BN	VEC	EVL
11425(11234)	BN	VEC	EVL
11426(11252)	BN	VEC	EVL
11427(11200)	BN	VEC	EVL
11428(11233)	BN	VEC	EVL

Number	Depot	Livery	Owner
11429(11275)	BN	VEC	EVL
11430(11248)	BN	VEC	EVL
11998(10314)	BN	VEC	EVL
11999(10316)	BN	VEC	EVL

AI2J - TSOE Seating 76S

Number	Depot	Livery	Owner
12200	BN	VEC	EVL
12201	BN	VEC	EVL
12202	BN	VEC	EVL
12203	BN	VEC	EVL
12204	BN	VEC	EVL
12205	BN	VEC	EVL
12207	BN	VEC	EVL
12208	BN	VEC	EVL
12209	BN	VEC	EVL
12210	BN	VEC	EVL
12211	BN	VEC	EVL
12212	BN	VEC	EVL
12213	BN	VEC	EVL
12214	BN	VEC	EVL
12215	BN	VEC	EVL
12216	BN	VEC	EVL
12217	BN	VEC	EVL
12218	BN	VEC	EVL
12219	BN	VEC	EVL
12220	BN	VEC	EVL
12222	BN	VEC	EVL
12223	BN	VEC	EVL
12224	BN	VEC	EVL
12225	BN	VEC	EVL
12226	BN	VEC	EVL
12227	BN	VEC	EVL
12228	BN	VEC	EVL
12229	BN	VEC	EVL
12230	BN	VEC	EVL
12231	BN	VEC	EVL
12232	BN	VEC	EVL

AL2J - TSOD Seating 68S

Number	Depot	Livery	Owner
12300	BN	VEC	EVL
12301	BN	VEC	EVL
12302	BN	VEC	EVL
12303	BN	VEC	EVL
12304	BN	VEC	EVL
12305	BN	VEC	EVL
12307	BN	VEC	EVL
12308	BN	VEC	EVL
12309	BN	VEC	EVL
12310	BN	VEC	EVL
12311	BN	VEC	EVL
12312	BN	VEC	EVL
12313	BN	VEC	EVL
12315	BN	VEC	EVL
12316	BN	VEC	EVL
12317	BN	VEC	EVL
12318	BN	VEC	EVL
12319	BN	VEC	EVL
12320	BN	VEC	EVL
12321	BN	VEC	EVL
12322	BN	VEC	EVL
12323	BN	VEC	EVL

Virgin Trains East Coast

Number	Depot	Livery	Owner
12324	BN	VEC	EVL
12325	BN	VEC	EVL
12326	BN	VEC	EVL
12327	BN	VEC	EVL
12328	BN	VEC	EVL
12329	BN	VEC	EVL
12330	BN	VEC	EVL
12331(12531)	BN	VEC	EVL

AC2J - TSO *Seating 76S*

Number	Depot	Livery	Owner
12400	BN	VEC	EVL
12401	BN	VEC	EVL
12402	BN	VEC	EVL
12403	BN	VEC	EVL
12404	BN	VEC	EVL
12405	BN	VEC	EVL
12406	BN	VEC	EVL
12407	BN	VEC	EVL
12409	BN	VEC	EVL
12410	BN	VEC	EVL
12411	BN	VEC	EVL
12414	BN	VEC	EVL
12415	BN	VEC	EVL
12417	BN	VEC	EVL
12419	BN	VEC	EVL
12420	BN	VEC	EVL
12421	BN	VEC	EVL
12422	BN	VEC	EVL
12423	BN	VEC	EVL
12424	BN	VEC	EVL
12425	BN	VEC	EVL
12426	BN	VEC	EVL
12427	BN	VEC	EVL
12428	BN	VEC	EVL
12429	BN	VEC	EVL
12430	BN	VEC	EVL
12431	BN	VEC	EVL
12432	BN	VEC	EVL
12433	BN	VEC	EVL
12434	BN	VEC	EVL
12436	BN	VEC	EVL
12437	BN	VEC	EVL
12438	BN	VEC	EVL
12439	BN	VEC	EVL
12440	BN	VEC	EVL
12441	BN	VEC	EVL
12442	BN	VEC	EVL
12443	BN	VEC	EVL
12444	BN	VEC	EVL
12445	BN	VEC	EVL
12446	BN	VEC	EVL
12447	BN	VEC	EVL
12448	BN	VEC	EVL
12449	BN	VEC	EVL
12450	BN	VEC	EVL
12452	BN	VEC	EVL
12453	BN	VEC	EVL
12454	BN	VEC	EVL
12455	BN	VEC	EVL
12456	BN	ECG	EVL
12457	BN	VEC	EVL
12458	BN	VEC	EVL
12459	BN	VEC	EVL
12460	BN	VEC	EVL
12461	BN	VEC	EVL
12462	BN	VEC	EVL
12463	BN	VEC	EVL
12464	BN	VEC	EVL
12465	BN	ECG	EVL
12466	BN	VEC	EVL
12467	BN	VEC	EVL
12468	BN	VEC	EVL
12469	BN	VEC	EVL
12470	BN	VEC	EVL
12471	BN	VEC	EVL
12472	BN	VEC	EVL
12473	BN	VEC	EVL
12474	BN	VEC	EVL
12476	BN	VEC	EVL
12477	BN	VEC	EVL
12478	BN	VEC	EVL
12480	BN	VEC	EVL
12481	BN	VEC	EVL
12483	BN	VEC	EVL
12484	BN	VEC	EVL
12485	BN	VEC	EVL
12486	BN	VEC	EVL
12488	BN	VEC	EVL
12489	BN	VEC	EVL
12513	BN	VEC	EVL
12514	BN	VEC	EVL
12515	BN	VEC	EVL
12518	BN	VEC	EVL
12519	BN	VEC	EVL
12520	BN	VEC	EVL
12522	BN	VEC	EVL
12526	BN	VEC	EVL
12533	BN	VEC	EVL
12534	BN	ECG	EVL
12538	BN	ECG	EVL

NZAJ - DVT

Number	Depot	Livery	Owner
82200	BN	VEC	EVL
82201	BN	VEC	EVL
82202	BN	VEC	EVL
82203	BN	VEC	EVL
82204	BN	VEC	EVL
82205	BN	VEC	EVL
82206	BN	ECG	EVL
82207	BN	VEC	EVL
82208	BN	VEC	EVL
82209	BN	VEC	EVL
82210	BN	VEC	EVL
82211	BN	VEC	EVL
82212	BN	VEC	EVL
82213	BN	VEC	EVL
82214	BN	VEC	EVL
82215	BN	VEC	EVL
82216	BN	VEC	EVL
82217	BN	VEC	EVL
82218	BN	VEC	EVL
82219	BN	VEC	EVL
82220	BN	VEC	EVL
82222	BN	VEC	EVL
82223	BN	VEC	EVL
82224	BN	VEC	EVL
82225	BN	VEC	EVL
82226	BN	VEC	EVL
82227	BN	VEC	EVL
82228	BN	VEC	EVL
82229	BN	VEC	EVL
82230	BN	VEC	EVL
82231	BN	VEC	EVL

Below: *The backbone of East Coast services currently is the fleet of Mk4 stock allocated to Bounds Green. All vehicles are currently painted in Virgin red and grey livery, passenger seating vehicles have a predominately grey body with red end bands, while non-passenger areas including the DVTs are predominately red. A Mk4 set is seen at Doncaster with DVT No. 82211 nearest the camera.* **CJM**

Passenger Train Operating Companies - Virgin Trains East Coast

Virgin Trains East Coast

Service Stock

HST and Mk4 Barrier Vehicles

Number	Depot	Livery	Owner	Former Identity
6340	EC	NEG	ANG	BCK - 21251
6344	EC	NEG	ANG	BG - 92080
6346	EC	NEG	ANG	BSO - 9422
6352	BN	HSB	HSB	SK - 19465

6353	BN	HSB	HSB	SK - 19478
9393	EC	PTR	PTR	BG - 92196
9394	EC	PTR	PTR	BG - 92906

Class 800/1 Bi-Mode 'Azuma' stock

9-car sets

Vehicle Length: (Driving) 85ft 4in (26m)
Height: 12ft 4in (3.75m)
Engine: MTU 12V 1600R80L of 750hp (560kW) x 5

Width: 8ft 10in (2.7m)
Horsepower: Electric 6,061hp (4,520kW)
Seats (total/car): 93F/534S - 56S, 88S, 88S, 88S, 88S, 88S,30F/38S, 48F, 15F

Number	Formation	Depot	Livery	Owner	Operator
800101 (T58)*	811101+812101+813101+814101+815101+816101+817101+818101+819101	VEC	EVL		HIT
800102	811102+812102+813102+814102+815102+816102+817102+818102+819102	VEC	EVL		VEC
800103	811103+812103+813103+814103+815103+816103+817103+818103+819103	VEC	EVL		VEC
800104	811104+812104+813104+814104+815104+816104+817104+818104+819104	VEC	EVL		VEC
800105	811105+812105+813105+814105+815105+816105+817105+818105+819105	VEC	EVL		VEC
800106	811106+812106+813106+814106+815106+816106+817106+818106+819106	VEC	EVL		VEC
800107	811107+812107+813107+814107+815107+816107+817107+818107+819107	VEC	EVL		VEC
800108	811108+812108+813108+814108+815108+816108+817108+818108+819108	VEC	EVL		VEC
800109	811109+812109+813109+814109+815109+816109+817109+818109+819109	VEC	EVL		VEC
800110	811110+812110+813110+814110+815110+816110+817110+818110+819110	VEC	EVL		VEC
800111	811111+812111+813111+814111+815111+816111+817111+818111+819111	VEC	EVL		VEC
800112	811112+812112+813112+814112+815112+816112+817112+818112+819112	VEC	EVL		VEC
800113	811113+812113+813113+814113+815113+816113+817113+818113+819113	VEC	EVL		VEC

Class 800/2 Bi-Mode 'Azuma' stock

5-car sets

Vehicle Length: (Driving) 85ft 4in (26m)
Height: 12ft 4in (3.75m)
Engine: MTU 12V 1600R80L of 750hp (560kW) x 3

Width: 8ft 10in (2.7m)
Horsepower: Electric 3,636hp (2,712kW)
Seats (total/car): 45F/270S - 56S, 88S,88S,30F/38S,15F

Number	Formation	Depot	Livery	Owner	Operator
800201	811201+812201+813201+814201+815201		VEC	EVL	VEC
800202	811202+812202+813202+814202+815202		VEC	EVL	VEC
800203	811203+812203+813203+814203+815203		VEC	EVL	VEC
800204	811204+812204+813204+814204+815204		VEC	EVL	VEC
800205	811205+812205+813205+814205+815205		VEC	EVL	VEC
800206	811206+812206+813206+814206+815206		VEC	EVL	VEC
800207	811207+812207+813207+814207+815207		VEC	EVL	VEC
800208	811208+812208+813208+814208+815208		VEC	EVL	VEC
800209	811209+812209+813209+814209+815209		VEC	EVL	VEC
800210	811210+812210+813210+814210+815210		VEC	EVL	VEC

Class 801/1 Electric 'Azuma' stock

5-car sets

Vehicle Length: (Driving) 85ft 4in (26m)
Height: 12ft 4in (3.75m)
Engine: MTU 12V 1600R80L of 750hp (560kW) x 1

Width: 8ft 10in (2.7m)
Horsepower: 3,636hp (2,712kW)
Seats (total/car): 45F/270S - 56S, 88S,88S,30F/38S,15F

Number	Formation	Depot	Livery	Owner	Operator
801101	821101+822101+823101+824101+825101		VEC	EVL	VEC
801102	821102+822102+823102+824102+825102		VEC	EVL	VEC
801103	821103+822103+823103+824103+825103		VEC	EVL	VEC
801104	821104+822104+823104+824104+825104		VEC	EVL	VEC
801105	821105+822105+823105+824105+825105		VEC	EVL	VEC
801106	821106+822106+823106+824106+825106		VEC	EVL	VEC
801107	821107+822107+823107+824107+825107		VEC	EVL	VEC

801108	821108+822108+823108+824108+825108	VEC	EVL	VEC
801109	821109+822109+823109+824109+825109	VEC	EVL	VEC
801110	821110+822110+823110+824110+825110	VEC	EVL	VEC
801111	821111+822111+823111+824111+825111	VEC	EVL	VEC
801112	821112+822112+823112+824112+825112	VEC	EVL	VEC

Class 801/2 Electric 'Azuma' stock

9-car sets

Vehicle Length: (Driving) 85ft 4in (26m)
Height: 12ft 4in (3.75m)
Engine: MTU 12V 1600R80L of 750hp (560kW) x 1

Width: 8ft 10in (2.7m)
Horsepower: 6,061hp (4,520kW)
Seats (total/car): 93F/534S -
56S, 88S, 88S, 88S, 88S, 88S,30F/38S, 48F, 15F

Number	Formation	Depot	Livery	Owner	Operator
801201	821201+822201+823201+824201+825201+826201+827201+828201+829201		VEC	EVL	VEC
801202	821202+822202+823202+824202+825202+826202+827202+828202+829202		VEC	EVL	VEC
801203	821203+822203+823203+824203+825203+826203+827203+828203+829203		VEC	EVL	VEC
801204	821204+822204+823204+824204+825204+826204+827204+828204+829204		VEC	EVL	VEC
801205	821205+822205+823205+824205+825205+826205+827205+828205+829205		VEC	EVL	VEC
801206	821206+822206+823206+824206+825206+826206+827206+828206+829206		VEC	EVL	VEC
801207	821207+822207+823207+824207+825207+826207+827207+828207+829207		VEC	EVL	VEC
801208	821208+822208+823208+824208+825208+826208+827208+828208+829208		VEC	EVL	VEC
801209	821209+822209+823209+824209+825209+826209+827209+828209+829209		VEC	EVL	VEC
801210	821210+822210+823210+824210+825210+826210+827210+828210+829210		VEC	EVL	VEC
801211	821211+822211+823211+824211+825211+826211+827211+828211+829211		VEC	EVL	VEC
801212	821212+822212+823212+824212+825212+826212+827212+828212+829212		VEC	EVL	VEC
801213	821213+822213+823213+824213+825213+826213+827213+828213+829213		VEC	EVL	VEC
801214	821214+822214+823214+824214+825214+826214+827214+828214+829214		VEC	EVL	VEC
801215	821215+822215+823215+824215+825215+826215+827215+828215+829215		VEC	EVL	VEC
801216	821216+822216+823216+824216+825216+826216+827216+828216+829216		VEC	EVL	VEC
801217	821217+822217+823217+824217+825217+826217+827217+828217+829217		VEC	EVL	VEC
801218	821218+822218+823218+824218+825218+826218+827218+828218+829218		VEC	EVL	VEC
801219	821219+822219+823219+824219+825219+826219+827219+828219+829219		VEC	EVL	VEC
801220	821220+822220+823220+824220+825220+826220+827220+828220+829220		VEC	EVL	VEC
801221	821221+822221+823221+824221+825221+826221+827221+828221+829221		VEC	EVL	VEC
801222	821222+822222+823222+824222+825222+826222+827222+828222+829222		VEC	EVL	VEC
801223	821223+822223+823223+824223+825223+826223+827223+828223+829223		VEC	EVL	VEC
801224	821224+822224+823224+824224+825224+826224+827224+828224+829224		VEC	EVL	VEC
801225	821225+822225+823225+824225+825225+826225+827225+828225+829225		VEC	EVL	VEC
801226	821226+822226+823226+824226+825226+826226+827226+828226+829226		VEC	EVL	VEC
801227	821227+822227+823227+824227+825227+826227+827227+828227+829227		VEC	EVL	VEC
801228	821228+822228+823228+824228+825228+826228+827228+828228+829228		VEC	EVL	VEC
801229	821229+822229+823229+824229+825229+826229+827229+828229+829229		VEC	EVL	VEC
801230	821230+822230+823230+824230+825230+826230+827230+828230+829230		VEC	EVL	VEC

* Built in Japan, currently in the UK

Right: *The pre-production Class 800 and 801 sets built in Japan arrived in the UK in 2016-2017, with production from the UK factory at Newton Aycliffe commencing in very late 2016 and continuing for some three years. In 2016 main-line testing was undertaken by sets carrying Great Western and Virgin East Coast colours. In this illustration one of the eventual East Coast sets, No. 800101 in full Virgin livery, is seen at Acton Main Line on the Great Western during part of the test period.* **Antony Christie**

Virgin West Coast

Address: 85 Smallbrook Queensway,
Birmingham, B5 4HA
✆ info@virgintrains.co.uk
✆ 0845 000 8000
ⓘ www.virgintrains.co.uk

Lead Executive: Phil Whittingham

Franchise Dates: 12 December 2006 - Sept 2017

Principal Routes: London Euston - Birmingham,
Holyhead, Manchester
Liverpool, Glasgow and
Edinburgh

Depots: Edge Hill** (LL), Longsight**
(MA), Oxley** (OY),
Wembley** (WB), Central
Rivers (CZ)
** Operated by Alstom

Parent Company: Virgin Group

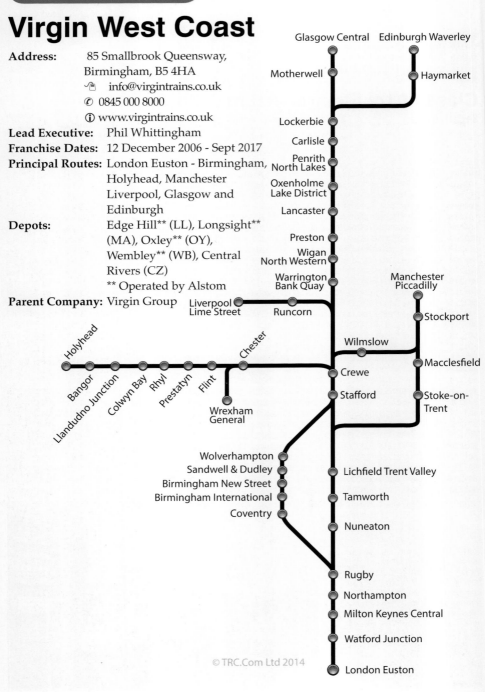

© TRC.Com Ltd 2014

Class 221
Super Voyager

Vehicle Length: 77ft 6in (23.62m)
Height: 12ft 4in (3.75m)
Width: 8ft 11in (2.73m)
Engine: 1 x Cummins 750hp per vehicle
Horsepower: 5-car - 3,750hp (2,796kW). 4-car - 3,000hp (2,237kW)
Seats (total/car): 26F/214S 42S/60S/60S/52S*/26F (*not in 4-car set)

Number	Formation DMS+MS+MS+MSRMB+DMF	Depot	Livery	Owner	Operator	Name
221101	60351+60951+60851+60751+60451	CZ	VWC	HBS	VWC	Louis Bleriot
221102	60352+60952+60852+60752+60452	CZ	VWC	HBS	VWC	John Cabot
221103	60353+60953+60853+60753+60453	CZ	VWC	HBS	VWC	Christopher Columbus
221104	60354+60954+60854+60754+60454	CZ	VWC	HBS	VWC	Sir John Franklin
221105	60355+60955+60855+60755+60455	CZ	VWC	HBS	VWC	William Baffin
221106	60356+60956+60856+60756+60456	CZ	VWC	HBS	VWC	Willem Barents
221107	60357+60957+60857+60757+60457	CZ	VWC	HBS	VWC	Sir Martin Frobisher
221108	60358+60958+60858+60758+60458	CZ	VWC	HBS	VWC	Sir Ernest Shackleton
221109	60359+60959+60859+60759+60459	CZ	VWC	HBS	VWC	Marco Polo
221110	60360+60960+60860+60760+60460	CZ	VWC	HBS	VWC	James Cook
221111	60361+60961+60861+60761+60461	CZ	VWC	HBS	VWC	Roald Amundsen
221112	60362+60962+60862+60762+60462	CZ	VWC	HBS	VWC	Ferdinand Magellan
221113	60363+60963+60863+60763+60463	CZ	VWC	HBS	VWC	Sir Walter Raleigh
221114	60364+60964+60864+60764+60464	CZ	VWC	HBS	VWC	
221115	60365+60965+60865+60765+60465	CZ	VWC¤	HBS	VWC	Polmadie Depot
221116	60366+60966+60866+60766+60466	CZ	VWC	HBS	VWC	
221117	60367+60967+60867+60767+60467	CZ	VWC	HBS	VWC	The Wrekin Giant
221118	60368+60968+60868+60768+60468	CZ	VWC	HBS	VWC	
221142	60392+60992+60994ø+60792+60492	CZ	VWC	HBS	VWC	Bombardier Voyager
221143	60393+60993+60794+60793+60493	CZ	VWC	HBS	VWC	Auguste Picard

¤ One driving car carries Bombardier branding. ø MRSMB vehicle

Below: *A fleet of 20 Class 221 'Super Voyager' sets is operated by Virgin West Coast, based at Central Rivers (between Birmingham and Burton), and operating non-electrified services over the North Wales coast route as well as working 'under the wires' trains on the Birmingham-London corridor to supplement the 'Pendolino' service. With its first class end nearest the camera, set No. 221114 approaches South Kenton with a Chester to London Euston service.* **CJM**

Class 390
Pendolino

Vehicle Length (Driving): 75ft 6in (23.01m)
Height: 11ft 6in (3.50m)
Width: 8ft 11in (2.71m)

Horsepower: 6,840hp (5,100kW)
Seats (total/car): 147F/300S, 18F/39F/44F/46F/74S/76S/76S/66S/48S/64S/46S
35 sets are now formed of 11 vehicles 147F/450S

Number	Formation DMRFO+MFO+PTFO+MFO[MSO]*+(TSO+MSO)+TSO+MSO+PTSRMB+MSO+DMSO	Depot	Livery	Owner	Operator	Name
390001	69101+69401+69501+69601*+68801+69701+69801+69901+69201	MA	VWC	ANG	VWC	Virgin Pioneer
390002	69102+69402+69502+69602*+68802+69702+69802+69902+69202	MA	VWC	ANG	VWC	Stephen Sutton
390103	69103+69403+69503+69603+68803+69703+69803+69903+69203	MA	VWC	ANG	VWC	Virgin Hero
390104	69104+69404+69504+65304+68904+69704+69804+69904+69204	MA	VWC	ANG	VWC	Alstom Pendolino
390005	69105+69405+69505+69605+68805+69705+69805+69905+69205	MA	VWC	ANG	VWC	City of Wolverhampton
390006	69106+69406+69506+69606+68806+69706+69806+69906+69206	MA	VWC	ANG	VWC	Tate Liverpool
390107	69107+69407+69507+69607+65307+68907+69707+69807+69907+69207	MA	VWC	ANG	VWC	Independence Day Resurgence
390008	69108+69408+69508+69608+68808+69708+69808+69908+69208	MA	VWC	ANG	VWC	Virgin King
390009	69109+69409+69509+69609+68809+69709+69809+69909+69209	MA	VWC	ANG	VWC	Treaty of Union
390010	69110+69410+69510+69610*+68810+69710+69810+69910+69210	MA	VWC	ANG	VWC	Cumbrian Progress
390011	69111+69411+69511+69611*+68811+69711+69811+69911+69211	MA	VWC	ANG	VWC	City of Lichfield
390112	69112+69412+69512+65312+68812+69712+69812+69912+69212	MA	VWC	ANG	VWC	Virgin Star
390013	69113+69413+69513+69613*+68813+69713+69813+69913+69213	MA	VWC	ANG	VWC	Virgin Spirit
390114	69114+69414+69514+65314+68914+69714+69814+69914+69214	MA	VWC	ANG	VWC	City of Manchester
390115	69115+69415+69515+69615+68815+69715+69815+69915+69215	MA	VWC	ANG	VWC	Virgin Crusader
390016	69116+69416+69516+69616*+68816+69716+69816+69916+69216	MA	VWC	ANG	VWC	Virgin Champion
390117§	69117+69417+69517+69617*+68817+69717+69817+69917+69217	MA	VWC	ANG	VWC	Virgin Prince
390018	69118+69418+69518+69618+68818+69718+69818+69918+69218	MA	VWC	ANG	VWC	Virgin Princess
390019	69119+69419+69519+69619+68819+69719+69819+69919+69219	MA	VWC	ANG	VWC	Virgin Warrior
390020	69120+69420+69520+69620*+68820+69720+69820+69920+69220	MA	VWC	ANG	VWC	Virgin Cavalier
390021	69121+69421+69521+69621+68821+69721+69821+69921+69221	MA	VWC	ANG	VWC	Virgin Dream
390022	69122+69422+69522+69622+68822+69722+69822+69922+69222	MA	VWC	ANG	VWC	Penny the Pendolino
390023	69123+69423+69523+69623+68823+69723+69823+69923+69223	MA	VWC	ANG	VWC	Virgin Glory
390024	69124+69424+69524+69624+68824+69724+69824+69924+69224	MA	VWC	ANG	VWC	Virgin Venturer
390025	69125+69425+69525+69625+68825+69725+69825+69925+69225	MA	VWC	ANG	VWC	Virgin Stagecoach
390026	69126+69426+69526+69626+68826+69726+69826+69926+69226	MA	VWC	ANG	VWC	Virgin Enterprise
390127§	69127+69427+69527+69627+68827+69727+69827+69927+69227	MA	VWC	ANG	VWC	Virgin Buccaneer
390028	69128+69428+69528+69628+68828+69728+69828+69928+69228	MA	VWC	ANG	VWC	City of Preston
390029	69129+69429+69529+69629+68829+69729+69829+69929+69229	MA	VWC	ANG	VWC	City of Stoke-on-Trent
390030	69130+69430+69530+69630+68830+69730+69830+69930+69230	MA	VWC	ANG	VWC	City of Edinburgh
390131§	69131+69431+69531+69631+68831+69731+69831+69931+69231	MA	VWC	ANG	VWC	City of Liverpool
390132	69132+69432+69532+69632+68832+69732+69832+69932+69232	MA	VWC	ANG	VWC	City of Birmingham
390134	69134+69434+69534+69634+68834+69734+69834+69934+69234	MA	VWC	ANG	VWC	City of Carlisle
390135	69135+69435+69535+69635+68835+69735+69835+69935+69235	MA	VWC	ANG	VWC	City of Lancaster
390136	69136+69436+69536+69636+68836+69736+69836+69936+69236	MA	VWC	ANG	VWC	City of Coventry
390137	69137+69437+69537+69637+68837+69737+69837+69937+69237	MA	VWC	ANG	VWC	Virgin Difference
390138	69138+69438+69538+69638+68838+69738+69838+69938+69238	MA	VWC	ANG	VWC	City of London
390039	69139+69439+69539+69639*+68839+69739+69839+69939+69239	MA	VWC	ANG	VWC	Virgin Quest
390040	69140+69440+69540+69640*+68840+69740+69840+69940+69240	MA	VWC	ANG	VWC	Virgin Radio Star

Set	Vehicle numbers				Name
390141	69141+69441+69541+69641+65341+69841+68841+69741+69841+69941+69241	MA	VWC	ANG	City of Chester
390142	69142+69442+69542+69642*+68842+69742+69842+69942+69242	MA	VWC	ANG	City of Bangor / Dinas Bangor
390143	69143+69443+69543+69643*+68843+69743+69943+69243	MA	VWC	ANG	Virgin Explorer
390144	69144+69444+69544+69644*+68844+69744+69844+69944+69244	MA	VWC	ANG	Virgin Lionheart
390145	69145+69445+69545+69645*+68845+69745+69845+69945+69245	MA	VWC	ANG	101 Squadron
390146	69146+69446+69546+69646*+68846+69746+69846+69946+69246	MA	VWC	ANG	Virgin Soldiers
390147	69147+69447+69547+69647+69847+69947+69247	MA	VWC	ANG	Clic Sargent
390148	69148+69448+69548+69648+65348+68848+68948+69748+69848+69948+69248	MA	VWC	ANG	Virgin Harrier
390149	69149+69449+69549+69649+69749+69849+69949+69249	MA	VWC	ANG	Virgin Express
390150	69150+69450+69550+69650*+68850+69750+69850+69950-69250	MA	VWC	ANG	Virgin Invader
390151	69151+69451+69551+69651+65351+68851+69751+69851+69951+69251	MA	VWC	ANG	Virgin Ambassador
390152	69152+69452+69552+69652+65352+68852+69752+69852+69952+69252	MA	VWC	ANG	Alison Waters
390153	69153+69453+69553+69653+65353+68853+69753+69853+69953+69253	MA	VWC	ANG	Mission Accomplished
390154	69154+69454+69554+69654+65354+68854+69754+69854+69954+69254	MA	VWC	ANG	Matthew Flinders
390155	69155+69455+69555+69655+68855+69755+69855+69955+69255	MA	VWC	ANG	X-Men Days of Future Past
390156	69156+69456+69556+69656+68856+68956+69756+69856+69956+69256	MA	VWC	ANG	Stockport 170
390157	69157+69457+69557+69657+68857+69757+69857+69957+69257	MA	VWC	ANG	Chad Varah

■ Vehicles 69133 and 69833 have been rebuilt as static training vehicles for use at the Virgin Trains training school in Crewe. Nos. 69933 and 69733 are in use at the fire training school in Moreton-in-Marsh. These coaches came from collision-damaged and withdrawn set No. 390033.

§ 'Fly the Flag' branding.

Left: *The core West Coast passenger service is operated by a fleet of 56 nine- or 11-car Class 390 tilting 'Pendolino' sets. Nominally based at Manchester Longsight, the sets operate throughout the West Coast electrified network. Set No. 390154, one of the longer 11-car sets, is seen heading south through Motherwell.* **CJM**

Colas Rail Freight

Address: ✉ Dacre House, 19 Dacre Street, London, SW1H 0DJ
📠 enquiries@colasrail.co.uk, ✆ 0207 593 5353, ⓘ www.colasrail.co.uk
Chairman: Charles-Albert Giral
Depots: Washwood Heath (AW), Rugby (RU), Eastleigh Works (ZG)

Class 37

Vehicle Length: 61ft 6in (18.74m)
Height: 13ft 0¼in (3.96m)
Width: 8ft 11⅝in (2.73m)
Class 37/4 - Electric Train Heat fitted

Engine: English Electric 12CSVT
Horsepower: 1,750hp (1,304kW)
Electrical Equipment: English Electric

Number	Depot	Pool	Livery	Owner	Operator	Name
37025		COTS	BLL	STS	COL	*Inverness TMD*
37057 (D6757)	RU	COTS	GRN	PRI	COL	
37099 (37324)	RU	COTS	COL	COL	COL	*Merl Evans 1947 - 2016*
37116	RU	COTS	COL	COL	COL	
37146(S)	RU	COTS	-	-	-	
37175	RU	COTS	COL	COL	COL	
37188	RU	COTS	-	-	-	
37207(S)	RU	COTS	-	-	-	
37219	RU	COTS	COL	COL	COL	
37254	RU	COTS	ICS	COL	COL	
37421 (37267)	RU	COTS	BLL	COL	COL	
37901 (37150)	SE	COLS	-	COL	COL	

Left: *Colas Rail freight is a keen Class 37 user, mainly for Network Rail test trains. Restored to large logo blue, Class 37/0 No. 37025 Inverness TMD is seen light loco in Devon.* **CJM**

Below: *Most of the Colas Rail freight Class 37s carry company orange and lime livery, as shown on Class 37/0 No. 37175 powering a Network Rail test train.* **John Tuffs**

Class 47/7

Vehicle Length: 63ft 6in (19.35m)
Height: 12ft 10⅜in (3.91m)
Width: 9ft 2in (2.79m)
Electric Train Heat fitted

Engine: Sulzer 12LDA28C
Horsepower: 2,580hp (1,922kW)
Electrical Equipment: Brush

Number	Depot	Pool	Livery	Owner	Operator	Name
47727 (47569)	WH	COLS	COL	COL	COL	*Rebecca*
47739 (47594)	WH	COFS	COL	COL	COL	*Robin of Templecombe 1938-2013*
47749 (47625)	WH	COFS	COL	COL	COL	*City of Truro*

Right: *Although today not seen in front-line action a lot, Colas Rail Freight has three Class 47/7s on its roster, which can be used for general freight and engineering train operations. All three carry full Colas livery in either the early or more recent style. No. 47739 Robin of Templecombe 1938-2013 is illustrated coupled to one of the Swedish rail cleaning vacuum vehicles.* **CJM**

Class 56

Vehicle Length: 63ft 6in (19.35m)			Engine: Ruston Paxman 16RK3CT			
Height: 13ft 0in (3.96m)			Horsepower: 3,250hp (2,420kW)			
Width: 9ft 2in (2.79m)			Electrical Equipment: Brush			

Number	Depot	Pool	Livery	Owner	Operator	Name
56049	WH	COLS	COL	COL	COL	
56051(S)	WH	COLS	?	COL	-	
56078	WH	COFS	COL	COL	COL	
56087	WH	COFS	COL	COL	COL	
56090(S)	WH	COLS	COL	COL	-	
56094	WH	COFS	COL	COL	COL	
56096	WH	COLS	COL	COL	COL	
56105	WH	COFS	COL	COL	COL	
56113	WH	COFS	COL	COL	COL	
56302 (56124)	WH	COFS	COL	COL	COL	*Peco The Railway Modeller 2016 70 Years*

Right: *The heavy-duty and powerful Class 56s locos are used to power some of the heavier trains operated by Colas. Locos of this fleet are still under restoration with four locos operational when we closed for press in early 2017. Operational locos are painted in Colas Rail Freight colours. Two examples, Nos. 56105 and 56078, are illustrated working in multiple. The red diamond multiple control facility has been retained on this fleet.* **Mark V. Pike**

Class 60

Vehicle Length: 70ft 0½in (21.34m)			Engine: Mirrlees MB275T			
Height: 12ft 10⅝in (3.92m)			Horsepower: 3,100hp (2,240kW)			
Width: 8ft 8in (2.64m)			Electrical Equipment: Brush			

Number	Depot	Pool	Livery	Owner	Operator	Name
60002	RU	COLO	COL	COL	COL	
60021	RU	COLO	COL	COL	COL	
60026	RU	COLO	COL	COL	COL	
60047	RU	COLO	COL	COL	COL	
60056	RU	COLO	COL	COL	COL	
60076	RU	COLO	COL	COL	COL	*Dunbar*
60085	RU	COLO	COL	COL	COL	
60087	RU	COLO	COL	COL	COL	*CLIC Sargent*
60095	RU	COLO	COL	COL	COL	
60096	RU	COLO	COL	COL	COL	

Colas Rail Freight

Left: *In 2014 Colas Rail Freight purchased 10 Class 60s from DB-Schenker and returned these to main-line operations through a refurbishment contract undertaken by DB-S at Toton. The 10 locos, finished in Colas Rail freight livery, operate general freight and infrastructure trains and have a superior pulling power to other locos classes operated by the company. Here No. 60047 is seen with just one RailVac track machine.* **CJM**

Class 66/8

Vehicle Length: 70ft 0½in (21.34m)
Height: 12ft 10in (3.91m)
Width: 8ft 8¼in (2.65m)

Engine: EMD 12N-710G3B-EC
Horsepower: 3,300hp (2,462kW)
Electrical Equipment: EMD

Number		Depot	Pool	Livery	Owner	Operator	Name
66846	(66573)	RU	COLO	COL	COL	COL	
66847	(66574)	RU	COLO	COL	COL	COL	
66848	(66575)	RU	COLO	COL	COL	COL	
66849	(66576)	RU	COLO	COL	COL	COL	Wylam Dilly
66850	(66577)	RU	COLO	COL	COL	COL	David Maidment OBE
							www.railwaychildren.org.uk

Left: *Five former Freightliner-owned Class 66s (Nos. 66573-66577) are now on the books of Colas Rail Freight as Nos. 66846-66850. These Colas Rail Freight-liveried locos are used on general engineering and infrastructure traffic and are frequently to be found working in the Westbury, Eastleigh and Tonbridge areaa. No. 66850 is seen at Westbury.* **Antony Christie**

Class 70 - PH37ACmi

Vehicle Length: 71ft 2½in (21.71m)
Height: 12ft 10in (3.91m)
Width: 8ft 8in (2.64m)

Engine: GE V16-cylinder PowerHaul 616
Horsepower: 3,700hp (2,750kW)
Electrical Equipment: General Electric

Number	Depot	Pool	Livery	Owner	Operator
70801 (70099)	RU	COLO	COL	COL	COL
70802	RU	COLO	COL	COL	COL
70803(S)	RU(LA)	COLS	COL	COL	-
70804	RU	COLO	COL	COL	COL
70805	RU	COLO	COL	COL	COL
70806	RU	COLO	COL	COL	COL
70807	RU	COLO	COL	COL	COL
70808	RU	COLO	COL	COL	COL
70809	RU	COLO	COL	COL	COL
70810	RU	COLO	COL	COL	COL
70811	RU	COLO	COL	COL	COL
70812	RU	COLO	COL	COL	COL
70813	RU	COLO	COL	COL	COL
70814	RU	COLO	COL	COL	COL
70815	RU	COLO	COL	COL	COL
70816	RU	COLO	COL	COL	COL
70817	RU	COLO	COL	COL	COL

70099 was built as a demonstrator at the GE plant in Turkey, tested in mainland Europe then the UK, and sold to Colas Rail Freight.

Above: *The fleet of 17 General Electric designed-and-built Class 70s are usually out-based in the Westbury area, where frequently 80% of them can be seen in one day. The locos are used on revenue-earning freight, engineers and infrastructure trains. No. 70805 is seen with a weekend engineering train traversing the Dawlish sea wall.* **CJM**

Hauled Stock (NPCCS)

Barrier Vans

Mk1		Height: 12ft 9½in (3.89m)
Vehicle Length: 64ft 6in (19.65m)		Width: 9ft 3in (2.81m)

AW51

Number	Depot	Livery	Owner
6376 (ADB975973, 1021)	Barry	BLU	PTR
6377 (ADB975975, 1042)	Barry	BLU	PTR
6378 (ADB975971, 1054)	Barry	BLU	PTR
6379 (ADB975972, 1039)	Barry	BLU	PTR

Motorail Vans (to be used by Network Rail as brake runners)

96602 (96150) NV	COL	RU	
96603 (96155) NV	COL	RU	
96604 (96156) NV	COL	RU	
96605 (96157) NV	COL	RU	
96606 (96213) NV	COL	RU	
96607 (96215) NV	COL	RU	
96608 (96216) NV	COL	RU*	
96609 (96217) NV	COL	RU*	

* In yellow NR livery as brake force runner

Right: *The eight former First Great Western side-loading Motorail vans are on the Colas Rail Freight roster and used as brake force runners. The vehicles are not maintained as road vehicle carrying vans. Two are painted in all-over Network Rail yellow. Green-liveried No. 96606 is illustrated.* **CJM**

Colas Rail Freight currently holds the contract to operate the Network Rail test trains throughout the UK network, including the provision of drivers and traction units.

Freight Operating Companies

DB-Cargo - (EWS)

Address (UK): ✉ Lakeside Business Park, Caroline Way, Doncaster, DN4 5PN
✎ info@uk.dbcargo.com
☎ 0870 140 5000   ⓘ https://uk.dbcargo.com

Chief Executive: Hans-Georg Werner

Class 08 & 09

Vehicle Length: 29ft 3in (8.91m)
Height: 12ft 8⅜in (3.87m)
Width: 8ft 6in (2.59m)

Engine: English Electric 6K
Horsepower: 400hp (298kW)
Electrical Equipment: English Electric

Number	Depot	Pool	Livery	Owner	Operator
08480(S)	TO	WQBA	EWS	DBC	-
08495¤(S)	EH	WSSK	EWS	DBC	-
08499	WQ	WSXX	BLU	DBC	PUL
08605¤	TO	WQAA	DBS	DBC	DBC
08623(S)	TO	WSSC	DBS	DBC	DBC
08632(S)	TO	WSRC	EWS	DBC	DBC
08706¤(S)	TO	WNYX	EWS	DBC	-
08735¤(S)	EH	WNYX	EWS	DBC	-
08757¤(S)	TO	WNYX	RES	DBC	-

Number	Depot	Pool	Livery	Owner	Operator
08784¤(S)	TO	WNTS	EWS	DBC	-
08799	TO	WQBA	EWS	DBC	DBC
08804¤(S)	TO	WNYX	EWS	DBC	-
08879	TO	WQBA	EWS	DBC	DBC
08922(S)	TO	WNTS	BRD	DBC	-
08994+(S)	DR	WNTS	EWS	DBC	-
08995+(S)	TO	WSSK	EWS	DBC	-
09106	TO	WSSC	DBS	DBC	DBC

Names applied
08495 *Noel Kirton OBE*

08799 *Andy Bower / Fred*

+ 08994/995 were previously Nos. 08562, 08687.

¤ Remote control fitted.

◼ In summer 2016 DB-Cargo announced that it was in the process of disposing of all remaining Class 08 and 09 shunting locos and that in future all shunting operations would either be undertaken by train locomotives or shunting power would be hired-in as required. The handful of locos listed above are all awaiting sale and disposal.

Left: Painted in EWS maroon and gold livery, No. 08799 is shown shunting high-capacity Network Rail ballast box wagons at Westbury. Locations such as this are likely to see the use of a privately owned shunting loco on hire to DB-C in the future.
Nathan Williamson

Class 58

Vehicle Length: 62ft 9½in (19.13m)
Height: 12ft 10in (3.91m)
Width: 9ft 1in (2.72m)

Engine: Ruston Paxman 12RK3ACT
Horsepower: 3,300hp (2,460kW)
Electrical Equipment: Brush

Number	Hire No.	Depot	Pool	Livery	Owner	Location	Operator	Name
58001		-	WNTS	ETF	DBC	France	ETF	
58004§		-	WNTS	TSO	DBC	France	TSO	
58005		-	WNTS	ETF	DBC	France	ETF	
58006§		-	WNTS	ETF	DBC	France	ETF	
58007		-	WNTS	TSO	DBC	France	TSO	
58009		-	WNTS	TSO	DBC	France	TSO	
58010		-	WNTS	FER	DBC	France	TSO	
58011§		-	WNTS	TSO	DBC	France	TSO	
58013		-	WNTS	ETF	DBC	France	ETF	
58015	L54	CON/SS	-	CON	DBC/T	Spain	TRN	
58017(S)		EH	WNTS	MLG	DBC	UK	-	
58018		EH	WNTS	TSO	DBC	France	TSO	
58020	L43	CON/SS	-	CON	DBC/T	Spain	TRN	
58021		-	WNTS	TSO	DBC	France	TSO	
58024	L42	CON/SS	-	CON	DBC/T	Spain	TRN	

58025	L41	CON/SS	-	CON	DBC	Spain	CON	
58026§		-	WNTS	TSO	DBC	France	TSO	
58027	L52	CON/SS	-	CON	DBC	Spain	CON	
58029	L44	CON/SS	-	CON	DBC/T	Spain	TRN	
58030	L46	CON/SS	-	CON	DBC/T	Spain	TRN	
58031	L45	CON/SS	-	CON	DBC/T	Spain	TRN	*Cabellero Ferroviaro*
58032		-	WNTS	ETF	DBC	France	ETF	
58033		-	WNTS	TSO	DBC	France	TSO	
58034		-	WNTS	TSO	DBC	France	TSO	
58035		-	WNTS	TSO	DBC	France	TSO	
58036		-	WNTS	ETF	DBC	France	ETF	
58038	58-038	-	WNTS	ETF	DBC	France	ETF	
58039	58-039	-	WNTS	ETF	DBC	France	ETF	
58040§		-	WNTS	TSO	DBC	France	TSO	
58041	L36	CON/SS	-	CON	DBC/T	Spain	TRN	
58042		-	WNTS	TSO	DBC	France	TSO	
58043	L37	CON/SS	-	CON	DBC/T	Spain	TRN	
58044	58-044	-	WZFF	ETF	DBC	France	ETF	
58046		-	WNTS	TSO	DBC	France	TSO	
58047	L51	CON/SS	-	CON	DBC/T	Spain	TRN	
50049§		-	WNTS	TSO	DBC	France	ETF	
58050	L53	CON/SS	-	CON	DBC	Spain	CON	

§ Stored at Alizay (Rouen)

Class 59/2

Vehicle Length: 70ft 0½in (21.34m)	Engine: EMD 16-645 E3C	
Height: 12ft 10in (3.91m)	Horsepower: 3,000hp (2,462kW)	
Width: 8ft 8¼in (2.65m)	Electrical Equipment: EMD	

Number	Depot	Pool	Livery	Owner	Operator	Name
59201	MD	WDAM	DBS	DBC	DBC	
59202	MD	WDAM	DBS	DBC	DBC	*Alan Meddows Taylor MD, Mendip Rail Limited*
59203	MD	WDAM	DBS	DBC	DBC	
59204	MD	WDAM	DBS	DBC	DBC	
59205	MD	WDAM	DBS	DBC	DBC	
59206	MD	WDAM	DBS	DBC	DBC	*John F. Yeoman Rail Pioneer*

Right: *The six DB-C-owned Class 59/2s are used in a pool with the privately owned Mendip Rail locos, based at Merehead for Mendip aggregate traffic. These locos were the original National Power locomotives. No. 59203 is seen departing from Westbury with a rake of high-capacity Foster Yeoman hoppers.* **CJM**

Class 60

Vehicle Length: 70ft 0½in (21.34m)	Engine: Mirrlees MB275T	
Height: 12ft 10⅝in (3.92m)	Horsepower: 3,100hp (2,240kW)	
Width: 8ft 8in (2.64m)	Electrical Equipment: Brush	

Number	Depot	Pool	Livery	Owner	Operator	Name
60001‡	TO	WCAT	DBS	DBC	DBC	
60003 ■	TO	WNWX	EWS	DBC	-	*Freight Transport Association*
60004 ■	TO	WNTS	EWS	DBC	-	
60005 ■	TO	WNTS	EWS	DBC	-	
60007‡	TO	WCBT	DBS	DBC	-	*The Spirit of Tom Kendell*
60009(S)	TO	WNTS	EWS	DBC	-	

DB-Cargo

60010‡	TO	WCBT	DBS	DBC	DBC	
60011	TO	WCAT	DBS	DBC	DBC	
60012(S)	TO	WNWX	EWS	DBC	-	
60015‡	TO	WCBT	DBS	DBC	DBC	
60017‡	TO	WCBT	DBS	DBC	DBC	
60018 ■	TO	WNTS	EWS	DBC	-	
60019‡	TO	WCAT	DBS	DBC	DBC	Port of Grimsby & Immingham
60020‡	TO	WCBT	DBS	DBC	DBC	The Willows
60022 ■	TO	WNTS	EWS	DBC	-	
60024‡	TO	WCAT	DBS	DBC	DBC	Clitheroe Castle
60025 ■	TO	WNTS	EWS	DBC	-	
60027 ■	TO	WNTS	EWS	DBC	-	
60030 ■	TO	WNTS	EWS	DBC	-	
60032 ■	TO	WNWX	EWS	DBC	-	
60034(S)	TO	WNTS	RFE	DBC	-	Carnedd Llewelyn
60035	TO	WCAT	EWS	DBC	DBC	
60036(S)	TO	WNTS	EWS	DBC	-	GEFCO
60037 ■	TO	WNWX	EWS	DBC	-	
60039‡	TO	WCAT	DBS	DBC	DBC	Dove Holes
60040‡	TO	WCAT	DBS	DBC	DBC	The Territorial Army Centenary
60043(S)	TO	WNWX	EWS	DBC	-	
60044‡	TO	WCAT	DBS	DBC	-	Dowlow
60045(S)	TO	WQAA	EWS	DBC	-	The Permanent Way Institution
60049	TO	WQAA	EWS	DBC	DBC	
60051 ■	TO	WNTS	EWS	DBC	-	
60052 ■	TO	WNTS	EWS	DBC	-	Glofa Twr - The last deep mine in Wales - Tower Colliery
60053(S)	TO	WNTS	EWS	DBC	-	
60054‡	TO	WCBT	DBS	DBC	DBC	
60057(S)	TO	WNWX	RFE	DBC	-	Adam Smith
60059‡	TO	WCBT	DBS	DBC	DBC	Swinden Dalesman
60060(S)	TO	WNWX	RFE	DBC	-	
60062‡	TO	WQAA	DBS	DBC	DBC	Stainless Pioneer
60063‡	TO	WCAT	DBS	DBC	DBC	
60064(S)	TO	WNWX	RFE	DBC	-	Back Tor
60065	TO	WCAT	EWS	DBC	DBC	Spirit of Jaguar

Below: *The numbers of fully operational Class 60s owned by DB-Cargo is very fluid, with locos frequently passing from operational to stored status. Displaying DB-Schenker red livery, No. 60059* Swinden Dalesman *is seen passing through Yate station with a heavy but empty fuel train from the nearby Westerleigh Oil Terminal.* **CJM**

60066‡(S)	TO	WCAT	ADV	DBC	-	
60067(S)	TO	WNWX	RFE	DBC	-	
60069(S)	TO	WNWX	EWS	DBC	-	Slioch
60071(S)	TO	WQAA	DBS	DBC	-	Ribblehead Viaduct
60072(S)	TO	WNWX	RFE	DBC	-	Cairn Toul
60073(S)	TO	WNTS	RFE	DBC	-	Cairn Gorm
60074‡	TO	WCAT	DBS	DBC	DBC	
60077(S)	TO	WNWX	RFE	DBC	-	
60079‡	TO	WQAA	DBS	DBC	DBC	
60083(S)	TO	WNTS	EWS	DBC	-	
60084(S)	TO	WNTS	RFE	DBC	-	Cross Fell
60086(S)	TO	WNWX	RFE	DBC	-	
60088(S)	TO	WNWX	MLG	DBC	-	
60090(S)	TO	WNTS	RFE	DBC	-	Quinag
60091‡	TO	WCBT	DBS	DBC	DBC	Barry Needham
60092‡	TO	WCBT	DBS	DBC	DBC	
60093(S)	TO	WNTS	EWS	DBC	-	
60094(S)	CD	WNTS	EWS	DBC	-	Rugby Flyer
60097(S)	TO	WNTS	EWS	DBC	-	
60099(S)	TO	WQAA	TAT	DBC	-	
60100‡	TO	WCAT	DBS	DBC	DBC	
60500(S)*	TO	WNTS	EWS	DBC	-	

* Previously numbered 60016. ‡ Refurbished 'Super 60'. ADV = Drax biomass livery.
■ Locos offered for sale in August 2016, plus Nos. 60006/08/13/14/23/31/42/50 not listed above.

Class 66

Vehicle Length: 70ft 0½in (21.34m)
Height: 12ft 10in (3.91m)
Width: 8ft 8¼in (2.65m)
Engine: EMD 12N-710G3B-EC
Horsepower: 3,300hp (2,462kW)
Electrical Equipment: EMD

Number	Depot	Pool	Livery	Owner	Operator	Number	Depot	Pool	Livery	Owner	Operator
66001‡	TO	WBAT	DBS	DBC	DBC	66036 ●	AZ	WBEN	EWS	DBC	ECR
66002‡	TO	WBAT	EWS	DBC	DBC	66037	TO	WBAE	EWS	DBC	DBC
66003	TO	WBAT	EWS	DBC	DBC	66038 ●	AZ	WBEN	EWS	DBC	ECR
66004	TO	WBAE	EWS	DBC	DBC	66039	TO	WBAE	EWS	DBC	DBC
66005	TO	WBAT	EWS	DBC	DBC	66040	TO	WBAR	EWS	DBC	DBC
66006	TO	WBAT	EWS	DBC	DBC	66041	TO	WBAT	DBC	DBC	DBC
66007	TO	WBAR	EWS	DBC	DBC	66042 ●	AZ	WFMS	EWS	DBC	ECR
66008	TO	WQAA	EWS	DBC	DBC	66043	TO	WBAE	EWS	DBC	DBC
66009	TO	WBAE	EWS	DBC	DBC	66044	TO	WBAE	EWS	DBC	DBC
66010 ●	AZ	WBEN	EWS	DBC	DBC	66045 ●	AZ	WBEN	EWS	DBC	ECR
66011	TO	WBAE	EWS	DBC	DBC	66046	TO	WQAA	EWS	DBC	DBC
66012	TO	WBAT	EWS	DBC	DBC	66047	TO	WBAT	EWS	DBC	DBC
66013 ●	TO	WBAE	EWS	DBC	DBC	66049 ●	AZ	WBEN	EWS	DBC	ECR
66014	TO	WBAE	EWS	DBC	DBC	66050	TO	WBAE	EWS	DBC	DBC
66015	TO	WBAE	EWS	DBC	DBC	66051	TO	WBAR	EWS	DBC	DBC
66016	TO	WBAE	EWS	DBC	DBC	66052 ●	AZ	WFMS	EWS	DBC	ECR
66017	TO	WBTT	EWS	DBC	DBC	66053	TO	WBAT	EWS	DBC	DBC
66018	TO	WBAE	EWS	DBC	DBC	66054	TO	WBAR	EWS	DBC	DBC
66019	TO	WBTT	EWS	DBC	DBC	66055	TO	WBAR	DBC	DBC	DBC
66020	TO	WBAT	EWS	DBC	DBC	66056	TO	WBLT	EWS	DBC	DBC
66021	TO	WBAR	EWS	DBC	DBC	66057	TO	WBLT	EWS	DBC	DBC
66022 ●	AZ	WBEN	EWS	DBC	DBC	66058	TO	WBLT ·	DBS	DBC	DBC
66023	TO	WBAT	EWS	DBC	DBC	66059	TO	WBLE	EWS	DBC	DBC
66024	TO	WBAE	EWS	DBC	DBC	66060	TO	WBAT	EWS	DBC	DBC
66025	TO	WBAE	EWS	DBC	DBC	66061	TO	WBAE	EWS	DBC	DBC
66026 ●	TO	WBEN	EWS	DBC	ECR	66062 ●	AZ	WBEN	EWS	DBC	DBC
66027	TO	WBAE	EWS	DBC	DBC	66063	TO	WBAT	EWS	DBC	DBC
66028 ●	AZ	WBEN	EWS	DBC	ECR	66064 ●	AZ	WBEN	EWS	DBC	DBC
66029 ●	TO	WGEA	EWS	DBC	DBC	66065	TO	WBAR	EWS	DBC	DBC
66030	TO	WBAR	EWS	DBC	DBC	66066	TO	WBAR	DBC	DBC	DBC
66031 ●	TO	WBAT	EWS	DBC	DBC	66067	TO	WBAR	EWS	DBC	DBC
66032 ●	AZ	WBES	EWS	DBC	ECR	66068	TO	WBAT	EWS	DBC	DBC
66033 ●	AZ	WBEN	EWS	DBC	DBC	66069	TO	WBAT	EWS	DBC	DBC
66034	TO	WBAT	EWS	DBC	DBC	66070	TO	WBAT	EWS	DBC	DBC
66035	TO	WBAT	EWS	DBC	DBC	66071 ●	AZ	WBEN	EWS	DBC	DBC
						66072 ●	AZ	WBEN	EWS	DBC	DBC

Freight Operating Companies

DB-Cargo

Above: *Although 249 Class 66s are on the roster only some 150-170 are to be found in the UK, the others have been exported to mainland Europe and operating in either France or Poland. In 2017 no great haste has been seen in repainting locos into the latest DB-C red/grey livery and a high proportion of the fleet remains in as-delivered EWS maroon, now sporting DB branding. No. 66122 is illustrated heading a container train south through Doncaster.* **CJM**

66073 ●	AZ	WBEN	EWS	DBC	ECR	66110	TO	WBBE	EWS	DBC	DBC
66074	TO	WBAE	EWS	DBC	DBC	66111	TO	WBBT	EWS	DBC	DBC
66075	TO	WBAT	EWS	DBC	DBC	66112	TO	WBBE	EWS	DBC	DBC
66076	TO	WBAT	EWS	DBC	DBC	66113	TO	WBBE	EWS	DBC	DBC
66077	TO	WBAE	EWS	DBC	DBC	66114	TO	WBBT	DBS	DBC	DBC
66078	TO	WBAT	EWS	DBC	DBC	66115	TO	WBAT	EWS	DBC	DBC
66079	TO	WBAR	EWS	DBC	DBC	66116	TO	WBAE	EWS	DBC	DBC
66080	TO	WBAE	EWS	DBC	DBC	66117	TO	WBAT	EWS	DBC	DBC
66081	TO	WBAR	EWS	DBC	DBC	66118	TO	WBAE	DBS	DBC	DBC
66082	TO	WBAT	EWS	DBC	DBC	66119	TO	WBAE	EWS	DBC	DBC
66083	TO	WBAR	EWS	DBC	DBC	66120	TO	WBAE	EWS	DBC	DBC
66084	TO	WBAT	EWS	DBC	DBC	66121	TO	WBAE	EWS	DBC	DBC
66085	TO	WBAR	EWS	DBC	DBC	66122	TO	WBAT	EWS	DBC	DBC
66086	TO	WBAT	EWS	DBC	DBC	66123 ●	TO	WGEA	EWS	DBC	DBC
66087	TO	WBAT	EWS	DBC	DBC	66124	TO	WBAT	EWS	DBC	DBC
66088	TO	WBAT	EWS	DBC	DBC	66125	TO	WBAT	EWS	DBC	DBC
66089	TO	WBAR	EWS	DBC	DBC	66126	TO	WBAE	EWS	DBC	DBC
66090	TO	WBAT	EWS	DBC	DBC	66127	TO	WBAT	EWS	DBC	DBC
66091	TO	WBAE	EWS	DBC	DBC	66128	TO	WBAT	DBC	DBC	DBC
66092	TO	WBAE	EWS	DBC	DBC	66129	TO	WBAE	EWS	DBC	DBC
66093	TO	WBAE	EWS	DBC	DBC	66130	TO	WBAT	EWS	DBC	DBC
66094	TO	WBAT	EWS	DBC	DBC	66131	TO	WBAT	EWS	DBC	DBC
66095	TO	WBAE	EWS	DBC	DBC	66132	TO	WBAE	EWS	DBC	DBC
66096	TO	WBAE	EWS	DBC	DBC	66133	TO	WBAE	EWS	DBC	DBC
66097	TO	WBAE	DBS	DBC	DBC	66134	TO	WBAE	EWS	DBC	DBC
66098	TO	WBAT	EWS	DBC	DBC	66135	TO	WBAE	EWS	DBC	DBC
66099	TO	WBBE	EWS	DBC	DBC	66136	TO	WBAT	DBC	DBC	DBC
66100	TO	WBBE	EWS	DBC	DBC	66137	TO	WBAE	EWS	DBC	DBC
66101	TO	WBBT	DBS	DBC	DBC	66138	TO	WBAE	EWS	DBC	DBC
66102	TO	WBBE	EWS	DBC	DBC	66139	TO	WBAE	EWS	DBC	DBC
66103	TO	WBBE	EWS	DBC	DBC	66140	TO	WBAT	EWS	DBC	DBC
66104	TO	WBAR	EWS	DBC	DBC	66141	TO	WQAA	EWS	DBC	DBC
66105	TO	WBBE	EWS	DBC	DBC	66142	TO	WBAR	EWS	DBC	DBC
66106	TO	WBBE	EWS	DBC	DBC	66143	TO	WBAE	EWS	DBC	DBC
66107	TO	WBAR	EWS	DBC	DBC	66144	TO	WBAE	EWS	DBC	DBC
66108	TO	WBBT	EWS	DBC	DBC	66145	TO	WBAE	EWS	DBC	DBC
66109	TO	WBAR	EWS	DBC	DBC	66146 P	PN	WBEP	EWS	DBC	DBC

66147		TO	WBAT	EWS	DBC	DBC		66200		TO	WBAE	EWS	DBC	DBC

66147	TO	WBAT	EWS	DBC	DBC	66200	TO	WBAE	EWS	DBC	DBC
66148	TO	WBAT	EWS	DBC	DBC	66201 ● AZ	WBEN	EWS	DBC	ECR
66149	TO	WBAE	DBC	DBC	DBC	66202 ● AZ	WBEN	EWS	DBC	ECR
66150	TO	WBAT	EWS	DBC	DBC	66203 ● AZ	WBEN	EWS	DBC	ECR
66151	TO	WBAE	EWS	DBC	DBC	66204 ● AZ	WBEN	EWS	DBC	ECR
66152	TO	WBAE	DBS	DBC	DBC	66205 ● AZ	WBEN	EWS	DBC	ECR
66153 P	PN	WBEP	EWS	DBC	DBC	66206	TO	WBAR	EWS	DBC	DBC
66154	TO	WBAE	EWS	DBC	DBC	66207	TO	WBAE	EWS	DBC	DBC
66155	TO	WBAT	EWS	DBC	DBC	66208 ● AZ	WBEN	EWS	DBC	ECR
66156	TO	WBAE	EWS	DBC	DBC	66209 ● AZ	WBEN	EWS	DBC	ECR
66157 P	PN	WBEP	EWS	DBC	DBC	66210 ● AZ	WBEN	EWS	DBC	ECR
66158	TO	WBAE	EWS	DBC	DBC	66211 ● TO	WBEN	EWS	DBC	ECR
66159 P	PN	WBEP	EWS	DBC	DBC	66212 ● AZ	WBEN	EWS	DBC	ECR
66160	TO	WBAE	EWS	DBC	DBC	66213 ● AZ	WBEN	EWS	DBC	ECR
66161	TO	WBAE	EWS	DBC	DBC	66214 ● AZ	WBEN	EWS	DBC	ECR
66162	TO	WBAE	EWS	DBC	DBC	66215 ● AZ	WBEN	EWS	DBC	ECR
66163 P	PN	WBEP	DBS	DBC	DBC	66216 ● AZ	WBEN	EWS	DBC	ECR
66164	TO	WBAT	EWS	DBC	DBC	66217 ● AZ	WBEN	EWS	DBC	ECR
66165	TO	WBAR	EWS	DBC	DBC	66218 ● AZ	WGEA	EWS	DBC	ECR
66166 P	PN	WBEP	EWS	DBC	DBC	66219 ● AZ	WGEA	EWS	DBC	ECR
66167	TO	WBAE	EWS	DBC	DBC	66220 P	TO	WBEP	DBS	DBC	DBC
66168	TO	WBAR	EWS	DBC	DBC	66221	TO	WBAT	EWS	DBC	DBC
66169	TO	WBAT	EWS	DBC	DBC	66222 ● AZ	WBEN	EWS	DBC	ECR
66170	TO	WBAT	EWS	DBC	DBC	66223 ● AZ	WBEN	EWS	DBC	DBC
66171	TO	WBAT	EWS	DBC	DBC	66224 ● AZ	WBEN	EWS	DBC	ECR
66172	TO	WBAT	EWS	DBC	DBC	66225 ● AZ	WBEN	EWS	DBC	ECR
66173 P	PN	WBEP	EWS	DBC	DBC	66226 ● AZ	WBEN	EWS	DBC	ECR
66174	TO	WBAE	EWS	DBC	DBC	66227 P	PN	WBEP	EWS	DBC	DBC
66175	TO	WBAE	EWS	DBC	DBC	66228 ● AZ	WBEN	EWS	DBC	ECR
66176	TO	WBAE	EWS	DBC	DBC	66229 ● AZ	WBEN	EWS	DBC	ECR
66177	TO	WBAT	EWS	DBC	DBC	66230	TO	WBAT	EWS	DBC	DBC
66178 P	PN	WBEP	EWS	DBC	DBC	66231 ● AZ	WBEN	EWS	DBC	ECR
66179 ●	TO	WBAK	EWS	DBC	ECR	66232 ● AZ	WBEN	EWS	DBC	ECR
66180 P	PN	WBEP	EWS	DBC	DBC	66233 ● AZ	WBEN	EWS	DBC	ECR
66181	TO	WBAT	EWS	DBC	DBC	66234 ● AZ	WBEN	EWS	DBC	ECR
66182	TO	WBAT	EWS	DBC	DBC	66235 ● AZ	WBEN	EWS	DBC	ECR
66183	TO	WBAE	EWS	DBC	DBC	66236 ● AZ	WBEN	EWS	DBC	ECR
66184	TO	WBAT	EWS	DBC	DBC	66237 P	PN	WBEP	EWS	DBC	DBC
66185	TO	WBAE	DBS	DBC	DBC	66238	TO	WBAR	EWS	DBC	DBC
66186	TO	WBAT	EWS	DBC	DBC	66239 ● AZ	WBEN	EWS	DBC	ECR
66187	TO	WBAE	EWS	DBC	DBC	66240 ● AZ	WBEN	EWS	DBC	ECR
66188	TO	WBAR	EWS	DBC	DBC	66241 ● AZ	WBEN	EWS	DBC	ECR
66189 P	PN	WBEP	EWS	DBC	DBC	66242 ● AZ	WGEA	EWS	DBC	ECR
66190 ●	AZ	WBEN	EWS	DBC	ECR	66243 ● TO	WBEN	EWS	DBC	ECR
66191 ●	AZ	WBEN	EWS	DBC	DBC	66244 ● AZ	WBEN	EWS	DBC	ECR
66192	TO	WBAE	EWS	DBC	DBC	66245 ● AZ	WBEN	EWS	DBC	DBC
66193 ●	AZ	WBEN	EWS	DBC	ECR	66246 ● AZ	WBEN	EWS	DBC	ECR
66194	TO	WBAR	EWS	DBC	DBC	66247 ● AZ	WBEN	EWS	DBC	ECR
66195 ●	TO	WBEN	EWS	DBC	ECR	66248 P	PN	WBEP	DBS	DBC	DBC
66196 P	PN	WBEP	EWS	DBC	DBC	66249 ● AZ	WBES	EWS	DBC	DBC
66197	TO	WBAE	EWS	DBC	DBC	66250	TO	WQAB	EWS	DBC	DBC
66198	TO	WBAR	EWS	DBC	DBC						
66199	TO	WBAE	EWS	DBC	DBC						

‡ Not fitted with combination couplers

Names applied

66002	*Lafarge Quorn*
66050	*EWS Energy*
66055	*Alain Thauvette*
66058	*Derek Clark*
66066	*Geoff Spencer*

66077	*Benjamin Gimbert GC*
66079	*James Nightall GC*
66152	*Derek Holmes Railway Operator*
66172	*Paul Melleney*
66185	*DP World London Gateway*
66250	*Robert K. Romak (not standard nameplate)*

● Modified to operate with Euro Cargo Rail in mainland Europe.

P Locomotives operated by DB-Schenker in Poland. Only locos from the series 66146-250 can be modified for this contract.

DB-Cargo

Class 67

Vehicle Length: 64ft 7in (19.68m)				Engine: EMD 12N-710G3B-EC		
Height: 12ft 9in (3.88m)				Horsepower: 2,980hp (2,223kW)		
Width: 8ft 9in (2.66m)				Electrical Equipment: EMD		

Number	Depot	Pool	Livery	Owner	Operator	Name/Notes
67001	CE	WAWC	ATW	DBC	DBC/ATW	
67002	CE	WAWC	ATW	DBC	DBC/ATW	
67003	CE	WAWC	ATW	DBC	DBC/ATW	
67004	CE	WABC	DBC	DBC	DBC	
67005	CE	WAAC	ROY	DBC	DBC	*Queen's Messenger*
67006	CE	WAAC	ROY	DBC	DBC	*Royal Sovereign*
67007	CE	WABC	EWS	DBC	-	
67008	CE	WAAC	EWS	DBC	DBC	
67009	CE	WABC	EWS	DBC	DBC	
67010	CE	WAAC	DBC	DBC	DBC	
67011	CE	WQAA	EWS	DBC	-	
67012	CE	WAAC	WSR	DBC	-	
67013	CE	WAWC	DBS	DBC	DBC	
67014	CE	WAAC	WSR	DBC	DBC	
67015	CE	WAAC	DBS	DBC	DBC	
67016	CE	WAAC	EWS	DBC	DBC	
67017	CE	WQAA	EWS	DBC	-	*Arrow*
67018	CE	WAAC	DBS	DBC	DBC	*Keith Heller*
67019	CE	WQAA	EWS	DBC	-	
67020	CE	WAAC	EWS	DBC	DBC	
67021	CE	WAAC	EWS	DBC	DBC	
67022	CE	WAWC	EWS	DBC	-	
67023(S)	-	WQAA	EWS	DBC	-	*Sold in January 2017 to Colas Rail Freight*
67024	CE	WAAC	EWS	DBC	DBC	
67025	CE	WQAA	EWS	DBC	-	*Western Star*
67026	CE	WQAA	ROJ	DBC	-	*Diamond Jubilee*
67027(S)	-	WQAA	DBS	DBC	-	*Sold in January 2017 to Colas Rail Freight*
67028	CE	WAAC	EWS	DBC	DBC	
67029	CE	WAAC	EWE	DBC	DBC	*Royal Diamond*
67030	CE	WABC	EWS	DBC	-	

Below: *Sadly the 28-strong Class 67 fleet, based at Crewe, sees little main-line work these days, apart from charter trains, 'Thunderbird' duties on the East Coast or engineering/freight trains. Displaying EWS maroon and gold livery, No. 67007 is seen near Stenson Junction hauling a Class 325 'Railnet' formation to Toton depot.* **John Tuffs**

Class 90

				Vehicle Length: 61ft 6in (18.74m)		Power Collection: 25kV ac overhead
				Height: 13ft 0¼in (3.96m)		Horsepower: 7,860hp (5,860kW)
				Width: 9ft 0in (2.74m)		Electrical Equipment: GEC

Number		Depot	Pool	Livery	Owner	Operator	Name/Notes
90017		CE	WQBA	EWS	DBC	-	
90018		CE	WEAC	DBS	DBC	-	The Pride of Bellshill
90019		CE	WEAC	DBC	DBC	DBC	Multimodal
90020		CE	WQAA	EWS	DBC	-	Collingwood
90021	(90221)	CE	WEDC	FGS	DBC	DBC	
90022(S)	(90222)	CE	WQBA	RFE	DBC	-	Freightconnection
90023(S)	(90223)	CE	WQBA	EWS	DBC	-	
90024	(90224)	CE	WEAC	ADV±	DBC	DBC	
90025	(90225)	CE	WEAC	RFD	DBC	DBC	
90026		CE	WQAA	EWS	DBC	DBC	
90027(S)	(90227)	CE	WQBA	RFD	DBC	-	Allerton T&RS Depot Quality Approved
90028		CE	WEAC	EWS	DBC	DBC	
90029		CE	WEAC	DBS	DBC	DBC	
90030(S)	(90130)	CE	WQBA	EWS	DBC	-	
90031(S)	(90131)	CE	WQBA	EWS	DBC	-	The Railway Children Partnership - Working for Street Children Worldwide
90032(S)	(90132)	CE	WQBA	EWS	DBC	-	
90033(S)	(90233)	CE	WQBA	RFI	DBC	DBC	
90034	(90134)	CE	WEAC	DRB	DBC	DBC	
90035	(90135)	CE	WEAC	EWS	DBC	DBC	
90036	(90136)	CE	WEAC	DBS	DBC	DBC	Driver Jack Mills
90037	(90137)	CE	WEAC	EWS	DBC	DBC	Spirit of Dagenham
90038(S)	(90238)	CE	WQBA	RFI	DBC	-	
90039	(90239)	CE	WEAC	EWS	DBC	DBC	
90040	(90140)	CE	WEAC	DBS	DBC	DBC	
90050(S)	(90050)	BA	DHLT	FLG	FLT	-	(Stored at Crewe Basford Hall, for scrap)

± Carries W H Malcolm livery

Below: *Carrying the latest DB-Cargo red and grey livery, No. 90019* Multimodal *is seen arriving at York with a charter service.* **Ron Cover**

DB-Cargo

Class 92

	Vehicle Length: 70ft 1in (21.34m)	Power Collection: 25kV ac overhead / 750V dc third rail
	Height: 13ft 0in (3.95m)	Horsepower: ac - 6,700hp (5,000kW) / dc - 5,360hp (4,000kW)
	Width: 8ft 8in (2.66m)	Electrical Equipment: Brush

Number	Depot	Pool	Livery	Owner	Operator	Name
92001■	-	WGEE	DBS	HBS	Exported Romania (91 53 0472 002-1)	Mircea Eliade
92002■	-	WGEE	DBS	DBC	Exported Romania (91 53 0472 003-9)	
92003±	-	WGEE	RFE	DBC	Exported Bulgaria (91 70 0092 002-x)	Beethoven
92004(S)	CE	WQBA	RFE	DBC	(for Eastern Europe)	Jane Austen
92005±	-	WGEE	DBS	DBC	Exported Bulgaria (91 70 0092 005-x)	Emil Cioran
92007(S)	CE	WQAA	RFE	DBC	-	Schubert
92008(S)	CE	WQAB	RFE	DBC	-	Jules Verne
92009§(S)	CE	WQBA	DBS	DBC	-	Marco Polo
92011	CE	WFBC	RFE	DBC	DBC	Handel
92012■	-	WGEE	DBS	HBS	Exported Romania (91 53 0472 001-3)	Mihai Eminescu
92013(S)	CE	WQBA	RFE	DBC	(for Eastern Europe)	Puccini
92015§	CE	WFBC	DBS	DBC	DBC	
92016§	CE	WFBC	DBS	DBC	DBC	
92017(S)	CE	WQAA	STO	DBC	-	Bart the Engine
92019	CE	WFBC	RFE	DBC	DBC	Wagner
92022(S)	CE	WQAB	RFE	DBC	-	Charles Dickens
92024■	-	WGEE	DBS	DBC	Exported Romania (91 53 0472 004-7)	Marin Preda
92025±	-	WGEE	RFE	HBS	Exported Bulgaria (91 70 0092 025-1)	Oscar Wilde
92026±	-	WGEE	RFE	DBC	Exported Bulgaria (91 70 0092 026-X)	Britten
92027±	-	WGEE	RFE	HBS	Exported Bulgaria (91 70 0092 027-7)	George Eliot
92029±	-	WGEE	RFE	DBC	Exported Bulgaria (91 70 0092 029-x)	Dante
92030±	-	WGEE	RFE	DBC	Exported Bulgaria (91 70 0092 030-1)	
92031§(S)	CE	WQAA	DBS	DBC	For export	
92034±	-	WGEE	RFE	HBS	Exported Bulgaria (91 70 0092 034-3)	Kipling
92035(S)	CE	WQBA	RFE	DBC	-	Mendelssohn
92036§	CE	WFBC	RFE	DBC	DBC	Bertolt Brecht
92037	CE	WQAA	RFE	DBC	DBC	Sullivan
92039■	-	WGEE	DBS	DBC	Exported Romania (91 53 0472 006-2)	Eugen Ionescu
92041(S)	CE	WQAA	RFE	DBC	-	Vaughan Williams
92042§	CE	WFBC	DBS	DBC	DBC	

§ Fitted with equipment to allow operation over HS1
± Exported to Bulgaria
■ Exported to Romania

Left: *A handful of DB-Cargo-operated Class 92s remain in traffic in the UK, while a greater number have been exported to Romania and Bulgaria for use by DB-Cargo. Sporting EWS stickers on its original Channel Tunnel grey livery, No. 92036 Bertolt Brecht is illustrated.* **Nathan Williamson**

Hauled Stock (Passenger)

Mk1		Height: 12ft 9½in (3.89m)	
Vehicle Length: 64ft 6in (19.65m)		Width: 9ft 3in (2.81m)	

Mk2		Height: 12ft 9½in (3.89m)	
Vehicle Length: 66ft 0in (20.11m)		Width: 9ft 3in (2.81m)	

Mk 3		Height: 12ft 9in (3.88m)	
Vehicle Length: 75ft 0in (22.86m)		Width: 8ft 11in (2.71m)	

AD1F - FO ‡ For sale

Number	Depot	Livery	Owner
3279	ME	MAR	DBR
3292	ME	MAR	DBR
3318	ME	MAR	DBR/FSR
3331	ME	MAR	DBR/FSR
3358	ME	MAR	DBR

3375(S) ‡	EH	MAR	DBR
3400	ME	MAR	DBR/FSR
3424	ME	MAR	DBR/FSR

AC2B - TSO

Number	Depot	Livery	Owner
5482	TO	BLG	DBR

AC2D - TSO

Number	Depot	Livery	Owner
5631	ME	DBS	DBR
5632	ME	DBS	DBR
5657	ME	DBS	DBR

AC2F - TSO ‡ For sale

Number	Depot	Livery	Owner
5922 ‡	DN	MAR	DBR
5924 ‡	DN	MAR	DBR
5954	ME	DBS	DBR
5959 ‡	DN	MAR	DBR
6036 ‡	DN	MAR	DBR
6110	ME	DBS	DBR
6139(S)	ME	MAR	DBR
6152 ‡	DN	MAR	DBR

AE2D - BSO

Number	Depot	Livery	Owner
9494	ME	MAR	DBR/SCR

AE2E - BSO

Number	Depot	Livery	Location
9506	ME	MAR	Brodie Eng

AE2F - BSO

Number	Depot	Livery	Owner
9522	ME	DBS	DBR/SCR
9529(S)	DN	MAR	DBR
9531(S)	DN	MAR	DBR

AJ1G - RFM

Number		Depot	Livery	Owner
10201(S)	(40520)	LM	VIR	DBR
10202	(40504)	LM	BLG	DBR/CRW
10211	(40510)	TO	EWE	DBS
10215	(11032)	LM	BLG	DBR/CRW
10222(S)	(11063)	BY	BLG	DBR
10226(S)	(11015)	LM	VIR	DBR
10233(S)	(10013)	LM	VIR	DBR
10235	(10015)	LM	BLG	DBR/CRW
10237(S)	(10022)	BY	DRU	DBR
10242(S)	(10002)	LM	BLG	DBR
10246	(10114)	CF	BLG	DBR/ATW
10250(S)	(10020)	LM	VIR	DBR
10257(S)	(10007)	BY	BLG	DBR

AU4G - SLEP

Number	Depot	Livery	Owner
10546	TO	EWE	DBS

AD1G - FO

Number	Depot	Livery	Owner
11005(S)	LM	VIR	DBR
11019(S)	ZB	DRU	DBR
11028(S)	ZB	VIR	DBR
11030(S)	ZB	DRU	DBR
11033(S)	LM	DRU	DBR
11039	TO	EWE	DBS
11046(S)	ZB	DRU	DBR
11054(S)	ZB	DRU	DBR
11079(S)	LM	BLG	DBR/CRW
11097(S)	LM	BLG	DBR

GK2G - TRSB

Number	Depot	Livery	Owner
40402(S) (40002)	LM	VIR	DBR
40403(S) (40003)	LM	VIR	DBR
40416(S) (40016)	LM	VIR	DBR
40419(S) (40019)	LM	VIR	DBR
40434(S) (40234)	LM	VIR	DBR

Saloon

Number	Depot	Livery	Owner
45020(S)	TO	MAR	DBR

Hauled Stock (NPCCS)

Mk 3 (DVT) — Height: 12ft 9in (3.88m)
Vehicle Length: 61ft 9in (18.83m) — Width: 8ft 11in (2.71m)

NZAG - DVT

Number	Depot	Livery	Owner
82106(S)	BRUSH	VIR	DBR
82110(S)	LM	VIR	DBR
82113(S)	BRUSH	VIR	DBR
82116(S)	LM	VIR	DBR
82120(S)	LM	VIR	DBR
82122(S)	LM	VIR	DBR
82123(S)	LM	VIR	DBR
82137(S)	LM	VIR	DBR
82138(S)	LM	VIR	DBR
82141(S)	LM	VIR	DBR
82146	TO	DBE	DBS
82148(S)	LM	VIR	DBR
82150(S)	LM	VIR	DBR

Below: *DB Management Train sleeper vehicle No. 10546 is part of the four-vehicle VIP train operated by the company. The vehicle is seen at Goodrington.* **Antony Christie**

DB-Cargo

NOA1 - H-GUV

Number	Depot	Livery	Owner
95727 (95127)	WE	RES	DBS

95761 (95161)	WE	RES	DBS
95763 (95163)	BS	RES	DBS

Euro Cargo Rail A part of DB-Cargo

Address: ✉ Immeuble la Palacio, 25-29 Place de la Madeleine, Paris, 75008
✉ info@eurocargorail.com, © +33 977 400000, ① www.eurocargorail.com

Class 21

Vehicle Length: (21/5) 48ft 2in (14.70m), (21/6) 46ft 3in (14.13m)   Engine: (21/5) Caterpillar 3512B DITA of 2,011hp
Height: (21/5) 13ft 8in (4.16m), (21/6) 13ft 9in (4.19m)   (21/6) MTU 8V 4000 R41L of 1,475hp
Width: 8ft 8¼in (2.65m)   Hydraulic Equipment: Voith

Number	Depot	Pool	Livery	Owner	Operator
21544 (FB1544)	DM	WLAN	MAR	ANG	ECR
21545 (FB1545)	DM	WLAN	MAR	ANG	ECR
21546 (FB1546)	DM	WLAN	MAR	ANG	ECR
21547 (FB1547)	DM	WLAN	MAR	ANG	ECR
21610 (FB1610)	DM	WLAN	MAR	ANG	ECR
21611 (FB1611)	DM	WLAN	MAR	ANG	ECR

Class 77
(JT42CWRM)

Vehicle Length: 70ft 0½in (21.34m)   Engine: EMD 12N-710G3B-EC
Height: 12ft 10in (3.91m)   Horsepower: 3,300hp (2,462kW)
Width: 8ft 8¼in (2.65m)   Electrical Equipment: EMD

Number	Depot	Livery	Owner	Op'r
77001	ND	ELR	DBS	ECR
77002	ND	ELR	DBS	ECR
77003‡	ND	ELR	DBS	ECR
77004	ND	ELR	DBS	ECR
77005‡	ND	ELR	DBS	ECR
77006‡	ND	ELR	DBS	ECR
77007	ND	ELR	DBS	ECR
77008	ND	ELR	DBS	ECR
77009‡	ND	ELR	DBS	ECR
77010	ND	ELR	DBS	ECR
77011	ND	ELR	DBS	ECR
77012	ND	ELR	DBS	ECR
77013‡	ND	ELR	DBS	ECR
77014	ND	ELR	DBS	ECR
77015‡	ND	ELR	DBS	ECR
77016	ND	ELR	DBS	ECR
77017‡	ND	ELR	DBS	ECR
77018	ND	ELR	DBS	ECR
77019‡	ND	ELR	DBS	ECR
77020	ND	ELR	DBS	ECR
77021‡	ND	ELR	DBS	ECR
77022	ND	ELR	DBS	ECR
77023	ND	ELR	DBS	ECR
77024	ND	ELR	DBS	ECR
77025	ND	ELR	DBS	ECR
77026	ND	ELR	DBS	ECR
77027	ND	ELR	DBS	ECR
77028	ND	ELR	DBS	ECR
77029	ND	ELR	DBS	ECR
77030	ND	ELR	DBS	ECR
77031	ND	ELR	DBS	ECR
77032	ND	ELR	DBS	ECR
77033	ND	ELR	DBS	ECR
77034	ND	ELR	DBS	ECR
77035	ND	ELR	DBS	ECR
77036	ND	ELR	DBS	ECR
77037‡	ND	ELR	DBS	ECR
77038	ND	ELR	DBS	ECR
77039	ND	ELR	DBS	ECR
77040	ND	ELR	DBS	ECR
77041	ND	ELR	DBS	ECR
77042	ND	ELR	DBS	ECR
77043	ND	ELR	DBS	ECR
77044	ND	ELR	DBS	ECR
77045	ND	ELR	DBS	ECR
77046	ND	ELR	DBS	ECR
77047	ND	ELR	DBS	ECR
77048	ND	ELR	DBS	ECR
77049	ND	ELR	DBS	ECR
77050	ND	ELR	DBS	ECR
77051	ND	ELR	DBS	ECR
77052	ND	ELR	DBS	ECR
77053	ND	ELR	DBS	ECR
77054	ND	ELR	DBS	ECR
77055	ND	ELR	DBS	ECR
77056	ND	ELR	DBS	ECR
77057	ND	ELR	DBS	ECR
77058	ND	ELR	DBS	ECR
77059	ND	ELR	DBS	ECR
77060	ND	ELR	DBS	ECR

‡ Operating in France, remainder operating in Germany

Left: *Euro Cargo Rail, a subsidiary of DB-Cargo, operates a fleet of Euro 66s in mainland Europe, classified as 77. The 60-strong fleet sports Euro Cargo Rail grey livery with maroon branding. Two locos of the fleet Nos. 247 045-7 and 77-002-9, are seen on shed at Salzburg on 13 March 2016.* **CJM**

66761	PG	GBEL	GBN	GBR	GBR	*Wensleydale Railway Association 25 Years 1990-2015*
66762	PG	GBEL	GBN	GBR	GBR	
66763	PG	GBEL	GBN	GBR	GBR	*Severn Valley Railway*
66764	PG	GBEL	GBN	GBR	GBR	
66765	PG	GBEL	GBN	GBR	GBR	
66766	PG	GBEL	GBN	GBR	GBR	
66767	PG	GBEL	GBN	GBR	GBR	
66768	PG	GBEL	GBN	GBR	GBR	
66769	PG	GBEL	GBN	GBR	GBR	
66770	PG	GBEL	GBN	GBR	GBR	
66771	PG	GBEL	GBN	GBR	GBR	
66772	PG	GBEL	GBN	GBR	GBR	
66773	PG	GBNB	GBN	GBR	GBR	
66774	PG	GBNB	GBN	GBR	GBR	
66775	PG	GBNB	GBN	GBR	GBR	
66776	PG	GBNB	GBN	GBR	GBR	
66777	PG	GBNB	GBN	GBR	GBR	
66778	PG	GBNB	GBN	GBR	GBR	
66779	PG	GBEL	GRN	GBR	GBR	*Evening Star*

§ 66751 Fitted with drophead Dellner coupling

Right: *Sporting standard GBRf Class 66 livery, No. 66704, one of the original batch of locos, is seen at Doncaster. The '66s' form the backbone of all GBRf operations and are based at Peterborough.* **CJM**

Below: *After winning the Royal Scotsman contract, two Class 66,s Nos. 66743 and 66746, were repainted into 'Royal Scotsman' maroon livery in 2016 and look stunning when coupled with the Royal Scotsman VIP train. The pair are seen with the train at Starcross, Devon, during a West Country tour.* **Antony Christie**

Freight Operating Companies - GBRf

GBRf

Class 73/1, 73/2

Vehicle Length: 53ft 8in (16.35m)
Height: 12ft 5⁵⁄₁₆in (3.79m)
Width: 8ft 8in (2.64m)

Power: 750V dc third rail or English Electric 6K
Horsepower: electric - 1,600hp (1,193kW)
Horsepower: diesel - 600hp (447kW)
Electrical Equipment: English Electric

Number		Depot	Pool	Livery	Owner	Operator	Name
73107		SE	GBED	GBN	GBR	GBR	Tracy
73109		SE	GBED	GBN	GBR	GBR	
73119		SE	GBED	GBN	GBR	GBR	
73128		SE	GBED	GBN	GBR	GBR	
73136		SE	GBED	GBU	GBR	GBR	Mhairi
73141		SE	GBED	GBU	GBR	GBR	Charlotte
73201	(73142)	SE	GBED	BLU	GBR	GBR	Broadlands
73212	(73102)	SE	GBED	GBU	GBR	GBR	Fiona
73213	(73112)	SE	GBED	GBU	GBR	GBR	Rhodalyn

Class 73/9

Vehicle Length: 53ft 8in (16.35m)
Height: 12ft 5⁵⁄₁₆in (3.79m)
Width: 8ft 8in (2.64m)
ETH Index 66 or 96 for sleeper locos

Power: 750V dc third rail or MTU 8V 4000 R43L
Horsepower: electric - 1,600hp (1,193kW)
Horsepower: diesel - 1,600hp (1,193kW)
Electrical Equipment: English Electric

Number		Depot	Pool	Livery	Owner	Operator	Name
73961	(73209/120)	SE/TG	GBNR	GBB	GBR	GBR	Alison
73962	(73204/125)	SE/TG	GBNR	GBB	GBR	GBR	Dick Mabbutt
73963	(73206/123)	SE/TG	GBNR	GBB	GBR	GBR	Janice
73964	(73205/124)	SE/TG	GBNR	GBB	GBR	GBR	Jeanette
73965	(73208/121)	SE/TG	GBNR	GBB	GBR	GBR	
73966	(73005)	EC	GBCS	SCS	GBR	SCS	
73967	(73006)	EC	GBCS	SCS	GBR	SCS	
73968	(73117)	EC	GBCS	SCS	GBR	SCS	
73969	(73105)	EC	GBCS	SCS	GBR	SCS	
73970	(73103)	EC	GBCS	SCS	GBR	SCS	
73971	(73207/122)	EC	GBCS	SCS	GBR	SCS	

Above: *The massive rebuilding project of the 11 Class 73/9s for GBRf by Brush Traction, Loughborough, has been a massive undertaking, with a new MAN diesel engine and Lechmotoren alternator installed, plus the full rebuild and upgrade of the original electric traction system. Body louvres have been changed and front connections altered, including a central AAR-style multiple control system in addition to the blue star and nose air connections, which now 'hook up' on the front to avoid hanging over the light clusters. Nos. 73963 and 73961 are seen passing Headcorn.* **Antony Christie**

Class 92

	Vehicle Length: 70ft 1in (21.34m)	Power Collection: 25kV ac overhead / 750V dc third rail
	Height: 13ft 0in (3.95m)	Horsepower: ac - 6,700hp (5,000kW) / dc - 5,360hp (4,000kW)
	Width: 8ft 8in (2.66m)	Electrical Equipment: Brush

Number	Depot	Pool	Livery	Owner	Operator	Name
92006(S)	Brush	GBET	SNF	GBR	-	Louis Armand
92010	CO	GBST	SCS	GBR	GBR	
92014	CO	GBSL	SCS	GBR	SCS	
92018	CO	GBST	SCS	GBR	SCS	
92020(S)	DM	GBET	EU2	GBR	-	Milton
92021(S)	CO	GBET	EU2	GBR	-	Purcell
92023	CO	GBST	SCS	GBR	SCS	
92028	WN	GBSL	GBN	GBR	GBR	
92032	CO	GBST	GBN	GBR	GBR	I Mech E Railway Division
92033	WN	GBSL	SCS	GBR	SCS	
92038	WN	GBST	SCS	GBR	SCS	
92040(S)	CO	GBET	EU2	GBR	-	Goethe
92043	CO	GBST	EU2	GBR	GBR	Debussy
92044	CO	GBST	SCS	GBR	GBR	Couperin
92045(S)	Brush	GBET	EU2	GBR	-	Chaucer
92046(S)	Brush	GBET	EU2	GBR	-	Sweelinck

Above: GBRf has a fleet of 16 Class 92s on its roster, but several are in long-term store and a source of spare parts to operational locos. Allocated between Willesden (London) and Coquelles (France), the locos operate international freight traffic on the Calais, Dollands Moor to the UK corridor, UK domestic freight and on contract to Caledonian Sleepers to power overnight sleeping car services between Euston and Edinburgh/Glasgow. Painted in full GBRf livery, No. 92032 is illustrated powering a Caledonian sleeper service on the West Coast Main Line. **Jamie Squibbs**

Class Di 8

	Vehicle Length: 57ft 1in (17.38m)	Engine: Caterpillar 3516 DITA
	Height: 13ft 3in (4.01m)	Horsepower: 2,100hp (1,566kW)
	Width: 9ft 8in (2.95m)	Electrical Equipment: Siemens

GBRf purchased 12 former Cargo-Net, Norway, Class Di 8 locos for use within the SSI Lackenby Steelworks in Redcar. The 2,100hp (1,566kW) locos were built in 1996-97 by Mak in Kiel, Germany, as an order for 20 locos. In the UK the fleet is classified by the UIC as 308. With closure of the complex these locos have now been transferred to Scunthorpe to replace Class 20 operations.

8.701	8.704	8.712	8.718
8.702	8.708	8.716	8.719
8.703	8.711	8.717	8.720

Industrial 0-6-0DH

DH50-1 Works No. TH278V - 0-6-0DH 50-ton design, built 1978, fitted with a Cummins engine
DH50-2 Works No. TH246V - 0-6-0DH 50-ton design, built 1973

The above two industrial locos are operated by GBRf at the Celsa steel plant in Cardiff.

Freight Operating Companies

Freightliner

Address: ✉ 3rd Floor, The Podium, 1 Eversholt Street, London, NW1 2FL
🖰 pressoffice@freightliner.co.uk
✆ 0207 200 3900
ⓘ www.freightliner.com

Chief Executive: Peter Maybury
Managing Director Intermodal: Adam Cunliffe **Heavy Haul:** Paul Smart
Depots: Freightliner Diesels (FD), Freightliner Electrics (FE), Freightliner Shunters (FS), Crewe, Ipswich* (IP), Leeds Midland Road (LD), Southampton Maritime (SZ)
* Stabling point
Parent Company: Genesee & Wyoming Incorporated

Class 08/0

Vehicle Length: 29ft 3in (8.91m)	Engine: English Electric 6K
Height: 12ft 8⅝in (3.87m)	Horsepower: 400hp (298kW)
Width: 8ft 6in (2.59m)	Electrical Equipment: English Electric

Number	Depot	Pool	Livery	Owner	Operator
08530(S)	LH	DFLS	FLR	PTR	FLR
08531	SZ	DFLS	FLP	PTR	FLR
08575	LH	DHLT	FLR	PTR	FLR
08585	LH	DFLS	FLP	PTR	FLR
08624	LH	DFLS	FLP	PTR	FLR
08691	SZ	DFLS	FLR	FLR	FLR
08785	LH	DFLS	FLR	PTR	FLR
08873	SZ	DFLS	FLR	PTR	FLR
08891	FD	DFLS	FLR	PTR	FLR

Names applied

08585	**Vicky**
08691	**Terri**
08624	**Rambo Paul Ramsey**

Class 47/4

Vehicle Length: 63ft 6in (19.35m)	Engine: Sulzer 12LDA28C
Height: 12ft 10⅗in (3.91m)	Horsepower: 2,580hp (1,922kW)
Width: 9ft 2in (2.79m)	Electrical Equipment: Brush
Electric Train Heat fitted	

Number		Depot	Pool	Livery	Owner	Operator	Name
47811(S)	(47656)	FD	DFLH	GRN	FLR	-	
47816(S)	(47661)	FD	DFLH	GRN	FLR	-	
47830	(47649)	BH	DFLH	GRN	FLR	FLR	**Beeching's Legacy**

Left: *Although not part of its core traction operation, Freightliner still has three Class 47s in its ownership. Two locos are long-term stored at Crewe, while one, No. 47830, is operational and is available for work or spot hire contracts. In the summer of 2016 it spent a short period working for the Rail Operations Group, powering empty stock movements. Here the loco, complete with ROG headboard, is seen passing Cullompton with a rake of refurbished GWR HST stock from Kilmarnock to Laira.* **CJM**

Class 66/4

Vehicle Length: 70ft 0½in (21.34m)	Engine: EMD 12N-710G3B-EC
Height: 12ft 10in (3.91m)	Horsepower: 3,300hp (2,462kW)
Width: 8ft 8¼in (2.65m)	Electrical Equipment: EMD

Number	Depot	Pool	Livery	Owner	Operator	Name
66411	Exported, working in Poland for Freightliner Poland as 66013FPL					
66412	Exported, working in Poland for Freightliner Poland as 66015FPL					

Right: *Testing of the two heavily rebuilt Class 73/9s for Network Rail by RVEL has continued through 2016. Now carrying Network Rail yellow livery and named after non-executive directors of Network Rail, Both locos are shown on the Severn Valley Railway taking part in a diesel gala event. The front ends of these RVEL rebuilds are very different from the 73/9s modified by Brush.*
Antony Christie

Class 37 & 97/3

	Vehicle Length: 61ft 6in (18.74m)	Engine: English Electric 12CSVT
	Height: 13ft 0¼in (3.96m)	Horsepower: 1,750hp (1,304kW)
	Width: 8ft 11⅝in (2.73m)	Electrical Equipment: English Electric

Number	Depot	Pool	Livery	Owner	Operator	Name
37198(S)	BU	MBDL	NRL	NRL	-	Chief Engineer
97301 (37100)§	ZA	QETS	NRL	NRL	NRL	
97302 (37170)±	ZA	QETS	NRL	NRL	NRL	
97303 (37178)±	ZA	QETS	NRL	NRL	NRL	
97304 (37217)±	ZA	QETS	NRL	NRL	NRL	John Tiley

§ Fitted with Hitachi ERTMS, ± Fitted with Ansaldo ERTMS

Right: *Network Rail operates a fleet of four Class 97/3 locomotives, rebuilt from Class 37s and now numbered in the 973xx series. The one Class 37 remaining on its books is stored at Burton. The Class 97/3s were used to develop the ERTMS equipment on the Cambrian Coast routes, with in 2017 one loco having the Hitachi system and three the earlier-design Ansaldo system. All four locos are painted in NR yellow and when not required for ERTMS work are available to Network Rail for test train power. No. 97304 John Tiley is illustrated from its No. 1 end.* **Antony Christie**

Class 950

	Vehicle Length: 64ft 9⅜in (19.74m)	Engine: 1 x NT855R5 of 285hp per vehicle
	Height: 12ft 4½in (3.77m)	Horsepower: 570hp (425kW)
	Width: 9ft 3⅛in (2.82m)	Seats (total/car): 124S, 59S/65S

Number	Formation	Depot	Livery	Owner	Operator	Note
950001	999600+999601	ZA	NRL	NRL	NRL	Track assessment train (Class 150 outline)

Right: *In 2016 new branding was applied to several of the Network Rail Derby-based test vehicles, in some cases advising the public of what these previously mysterious vehicles actually do. The Class 950 two-car Class 150-style DMU now carries Track Recording Unit bodyside branding and a 'track and magnifying glass' logo. The train, complete with many new frontal lights, is seen passing Dawlish.* **CJM**

Infrastructure Companies - Network Rail

Network Rail

Class 313/1

Vehicle Length: (Driving) 64ft 11½in (19.80m)	Width: 9ft 3in (2.82m)
(Inter) 65ft 4¼in (19.92m)	Horsepower: 880hp (656kW)
Height: 11ft 9in (3.58m)	

ERTMS development unit

Number	Formation DMSO+PTSO+BDMSO	Depot	Livery	Owner	Operator
313121	62549+71233+61613	HR	YEL	BEA	NRL

Left: Network Rail is currently leasing Beacon Rail-owned No. 313121 as a test set for the European Rail Traffic Management System (ERTMS) on the Hertford Loop in preparation for Class 700 stock. The set is seen at Camden Road, carrying its 2016-applied ERTMS pictogram branding. The set maintains the ability to operate from both dc and ac power systems.
Nathan Williamson

De-icing Cars

Vehicle Length: 66ft 4in (20.22m)	Horsepower: 500hp (370kW)
Height: 12ft 4in (3.75m)	Seats (total/car): None
Width: 9ft 2in (2.82m)	

Number	Vehicle	Depot	Livery	Owner	Operator	Notes
489102	68501	ZG	NRL	NRL	GBR	De-icing vehicle modified from Class 489 DMBS
489105	68504	ZG	NRL	NRL	GBR	De-icing vehicle modified from Class 489 DMBS
489106	68505	ZG	NRL	NRL	GBR	De-icing vehicle modified from Class 489 DMBS

Hauled Stock

Royal Train

Mk2	
Vehicle Length: 66ft 0in (20.11m)	Height: 12ft 9½in (3.89m) Width: 9ft 3in (2.81m)
Mk 3	
Vehicle Length: 75ft 0in (22.86m)	Height: 12ft 9in (3.88m) Width: 8ft 11in (2.71m)

Number		Type	Depot	Livery	Operator	Use
2903	(11001)	AT5G	ZN	ROY	NRL/DBS	HM The Queen's Saloon
2904	(12001)	AT5G	ZN	ROY	NRL/DBS	HRH The Duke of Edinburgh's Saloon
2915	(10735)	AT5G	ZN	ROY	NRL/DBS	Royal Household Sleeping Coach
2916	(40512)	AT5G	ZN	ROY	NRL/DBS	HRH The Prince of Wales's Dining Coach
2917	(40514)	AT5G	ZN	ROY	NRL/DBS	Kitchen Car and Royal Household Dining Coach
2918	(40515)	AT5G	ZN	ROY	NRL/DBS	Royal Household Coach
2919	(40518)	AT5G	ZN	ROY	NRL/DBS	Royal Household Coach
2920	(17109)	AT5B	ZN	ROY	NRL/DBS	Generator Coach and Household Sleeping Coach
2921	(17107)	AT5B	ZN	ROY	NRL/DBS	Brake, Coffin Carrier and Household Accommodation
2922		AT5G	ZN	ROY	NRL/DBS	HRH The Prince of Wales's Sleeping Coach
2923		AT5G	ZN	ROY	NRL/DBS	HRH The Prince of Wales's Saloon Coach

Left: The UK Royal Train, consisting of 11 Mk2 and Mk3 vehicles, is used by senior members of the Royal family for overnight and special journeys. It is kept at Wolverton Works when not in use and is powered and manned by DB Cargo. The specially prepared 'Royal' Class 67s are usually the chosen motive power. In this view we see Support coach No. 2921, a brake and household accommodation vehicle. It is the luggage van of this vehicle which will eventually be used to transport the body of HM The Queen from Paddington to Windsor for burial at the Royal Mausoleum on the Frogmore Estate in the Home Park at Windsor. **Antony Christie**

Hauled Stock

Number		Type	Depot	Livery	Operator	Use
1256	(3296)	AJIF/RFO	ZA	NRL	NRL	Special vehicle - PLPR3
5981		AC2F/TSO	ZA	NRL	NRL	Special vehicle
6260	(92116)	AX51/GEN	ZA	NRL	NRL/LUL	Generator (owned by DBS)
6261	(92988)	AX51/GEN	ZA	NRL	NRL	Generator (owned by DBS)
6262	(92928)	AX51/GEN	ZA	NRL	NRL	Generator (owned by DBS)
6263	(92961)	AX51/GEN	ZA	NRL	NRL	Generator (owned by DBS)
6264	(92923)	AX51/GEN	ZA	NRL	NRL	Generator (owned by DBS)
9481		AE2D/BSO	ZA	NRL	NRL	Radio Survey coach
9516		AE2D/BSO	ZA	NRL	NRL	Ultrasonic test car support
9523		AE2D/BSO	ZA	NRL	NRL	Ultrasonic test car support
9701	(9528)	AF2F/DBSO	ZA	NRL	NRL	Remote driving car (Mentor train)
9702	(9510)	AF2F/DBSO	ZA	NRL	NRL	Remote driving car
9703	(9517)	AF2F/DBSO	ZA	NRL	NRL	Remote driving car
9708	(9530)	AF2F/DBSO	ZA	NRL	NRL	Remote driving car (Structure Gauging)
9714	(9536)	AF2F/DBSO	ZA	NRL	NRL	Remote driving car
62384		MBS	ZA	NRL	NRL	Structure Gauging test car (SGT2)
72612	(6156)	Mk2f/TSO	ZA	NRL	NRL	Brake force runner
72616	(6007)	Mk2f/TSO	ZA	NRL	NRL	Brake force runner
72630	(6094)	Mk2f/TSO	ZA	NRL	NRL	Brake force runner
72631	(6096)	Mk2f/TSO	ZA	NRL	NRL	Brake force runner
72639	(6070)	Mk2f/TSO	ZA	NRL	NRL	Brake force runner
82111		MK3/DVT	CS	NRL	NRL	Driving Van Trailer
82115		MK3/DVT	ZA	VIR	NRL	Driving Van Trailer
82124		MK3/DVT	ZA	NRL	NRL	Driving Van Trailer
82129		MK3/DVT	CS	NRL	NRL	Driving Van Trailer
82145		MK3/DVT	CS	NRL	NRL	Driving Van Trailer
92114	(81443)	Mk1/BG	ZA	NRL	NRL	Special vehicle
92939	(92039)	Mk1/BG	ZA	INT	NRL	Special vehicle
99666	(3250)	Mk2e/FO	ZA	NRL	NRL	Ultrasonic Test Train
971001	(94150)	Mk1/NKA	BS	NRL	NRL	Tool Van
971002	(94190)	Mk1/NKA	±	NRL	NRL	Tool Van (± at Worksop)
971003	(94191)	Mk1/NKA	BS	NRL	NRL	Tool Van
971004	(94168)	Mk1/NKA	SP	NRL	NRL	Tool Van
975025	(60755)	6B Buffet	ZA	GRN	NRL	Control Inspection Saloon *Caroline*
975081	(35313)	Mk1/BSK	ZA	NRL	NRL	Structure Gauging Train
975087	(34289)	MK1/BSK	SP	NRL	NRL	Recovery train support coach
975091	(34615)	Mk1/BSK	ZA	NRL	NRL	Overhead line test coach *Mentor*
975280	(21263)	Mk1/BCK	ZA	NRL	NRL	Staff coach
975464	(35171)	MK1/BSK	SP	NRL	NRL	Snowblower coach *Ptarmigan*
975477	(35108)	MK1/BSK	SP	NRL	NRL	Recovery train support coach

Right: *In recent years the Network Rail test train fleet has been modernised and most trains now operate with a remote driving car at the opposite end from the powering locomotive. In 2017 five Mk2 DBSO vehicles were operated by Network Rail, each allocated to a specific train with a specified test role. In this view taken on the Derby-Trent Junction route a four-coach test train with Class 37 No. 37608 on the rear is led by DBSO No. 9714.* **Antony Christie**

Network Rail

975486	(34100)	Mk1/BSK	SP	NRL	NRL	Snowblower coach *Polar Bear*
975814	(41000)	HST/TF	EC	NRL	NRL	NMT Conference coach
975984	(40000)	HST/TRUB	EC	NRL	NRL	NMT Lecture coach
977868	(5846)	Mk2e/TSO	ZA	NRL	NRL	Radio Survey coach
977869	(5858)	Mk2e/TSO	ZA	NRL	NRL	Radio Survey coach (stored)
977969	(14112)	Mk2/BFK	ZA	NRL	NRL	Staff coach (former Royal Saloon 2906)
977974	(5854)	Mk2e/TSO	ZA	NRL	NRL	Laboratory coach (owned by Delta Rail)
977983	(3407)	Mk2f/FO	ZA	NRL	NRL	Overhead Line Inspection vehicle
977984	(40501)	HST/TRFK	EC	NRL	NRL	NMT Staff coach
977985	(6019)	Mk2f/TSO	ZA	NRL	NRL	Structure Gauging Train (SGT2)
977986	(3189)	Mk2d/FO	ZA	NRL	NRL	Track Recording coach
977993	(44053)	HST/TGS	EC	NRL	NRL	NMT Overhead Line Test coach
977994	(44087)	HST/TGS	EC	NRL	NRL	NMT Recording coach
977995	(40719)	HST/TRFM	EC	NRL	NRL	NMT Generator coach
977997	(72613)	Mk2f/TSO	ZA	NRL	NRL	Radio Survey Test Vehicle (originally TSO 6126)
999550		Mk2	ZA	NRL	NRL	Track Recording coach (purpose-built) TRC
999602	(62483)	Mk1/CIG	ZA	NRL	SEC	Ultrasonic Test coach - UTU3
999605	(62482)	Mk1/CIG	ZA	NRL	NRL	Ultrasonic Test coach - UTU2
999606	(62356)	Mk1/CIG	ZA	NRL	NRL	Ultrasonic Test coach - UTU4

Left: *A coach which has been with the test train fleet for a very long time is No. 975091, converted from Mk1 BSK No. 34615. Although now heavily rebuilt, this vehicle in the late 1960s was test car MENTOR (Mobile Electronic Test and Observation Recorder) and used extensively on the West Coast Main Line. Today it is involved in many other test and recording projects.* **Antony Christie**

Totally unrecognisable from its previous life as a MBSO from a Southern Region 4-CIG set, coach No. 62356 is now Ultrasonic Test Unit 4 (UTU4) and travels all over the main line network testing track condition. With its illuminated bogie at the near end, the coach is seen within a test formation at Exeter St Davids.
Antony Christie

Above: *Former Mk2 First Open No. 3407 is now an Overhead Line Inspection vehicle numbered 977983. It has a modified roof at one end (closest in picture) where overhead contact wire inspection is undertaken. Like all the test car fleet it will undertake more than one role, and it is seen here operating away from an overhead power supply.* **CJM**

Snowploughs
Independent Drift Ploughs – ZZA

Number	Allocation				
ADB965203	Carlisle	ADB965219	Mossend	ADB965235	Cardiff
ADB965206	Doncaster	ADB965223	Cardiff	ADB965236	Tonbridge
ADB965208	Inverness	ADB965224	Carlisle KM	ADB965237	March
ADB965209	Taunton	ADB965230	Carlisle KM	ADB965240	Inverness
ADB965210	Tonbridge	ADB965231	Taunton	ADB965242	Carlisle
ADB965211	March	ADB965232	Peterborough	ADB965243	Slateford
ADB965217	Slateford	ADB965233	Peterborough		
		ADB965234	Carlisle		

Beilhack Patrol Ploughs (ex-Class 40 bogies) – ZZA

Number	Allocation				
ADB965576	Doncaster	ADB965578	Carlisle	ADB965581	Wigan
ADB965577	Doncaster	ADB965579	Carlisle	ADB966098	Doncaster
		ADB965580	Wigan	ADB966099	Doncaster

Right: *Eight withdrawn Class 40 bogies were rebuilt to act as snowploughs, fitted with Beilhack ploughs at one end, standard draw gear at the other and weight stabilisation blocks. These plough pairs are allocated two to Doncaster and one set each to Carlisle and Springs Branch (Wigan). No. ADB965577 is illustrated at Doncaster.* **CJM**

Beilhack Snow Blowers – ZWA

Number	Allocation		
ADB968500	Rutherglen	ADB968501	Rutherglen

Network Rail

Track Machines (On-Track Plant)

Plasser & Theurer DTS-62-N – Dynamic Track Stabiliser – ZWA

| DR72211 | Balfour Beatty | DR72213 | Balfour Beatty |

Plasser & Theurer 09-16-CSM – Tamper/Liner – ZWA

| DR73105(S) | Colas |

Plasser & Theurer 09-32-RT – Tamper/Liner – ZWA

| DR73108 | *Tiger* | Colas |

Plasser & Theurer 09-3X – Tamper/Liner – ZWA

| DR73109 | | SB Rail | DR73110 | *Peter White* | SB Rail |

Plasser & Theurer 09-3X-D-RT – Tamper/Liner ZWA

DR73111		Network Rail	DR73116		Network Rail
DR73113	*Dai Evans*	Network Rail	DR73117		Network Rail
DR73114	*Ron Henderson*	Network Rail	DR73118		Network Rail
DR73115		Network Rail			

Plasser & Theurer 09-3x – Duomatic Tamper/Liner – ZWA

| DR73121 (99 70 9123 121-4) | Network Rail | DR73122 (99 70 9123 122-2) | Network Rail |

Plasser & Theurer 07-32 – Duomatic Tamper/Liner – ZWA

| DR73434(S) | Balfour Beatty |

Plasser & Theurer 08-16/90 – Tamper/Liner – ZWA

| DR73502 | Trackwork |

Plasser & Theurer 08-32U RT – Plain Line Tamper – ZWA

| DR73803 | *Alexander Graham Bell* | SBRail |

Plasser & Theurer 08-16U RT – Plain Line Tamper – ZWA

| DR73804 | *James Watt* | SBRail |

Plasser & Theurer 08-16(32)U RT – Plain Line Tamper – ZWA

| DR73805 | Colas | DR73806 | *Karine* | Colas |

Plasser & Theurer 08-4x4/4S - RT – Switch/Crossing Tamper – ZWA

DR73904	*Thomas Telford*	SB Rail	DR73908		Colas
DR73905		Colas	DR73909	*Saturn*	Colas
DR73906	*Panther*	Colas	DR73910	*Jupiter*	Colas
DR73907		Colas			

Left: *Displaying Colas orange and yellow livery, DR73907 one of the massive Plasser & Theurer 08-4x4/3S-RT switch and crossing machines. The vehicle is seen at work on a crossover near Teignmouth.* **Antony Christie**

Plasser & Theurer 08-16/4x4C - RT – Switch/Crossing Tamper – ZWA

DR73911	*Puma*	Colas	DR73913		Colas
DR73912	*Lynx*	Colas			

Plasser & Theurer 08-4x4S - RT – Switch/Crossing Tamper – ZWA

DR73914	*Robert McAlpine*	SB Rail

Plasser & Theurer 08-16/4x4C - RT – Switch/Crossing Tamper – ZWA

DR73915	*William Arrol*	SB Rail	DR73916	*First Engineering*	SBRail

Plasser & Theurer 08-4x4S - RT – Switch/Crossing Tamper – ZWA

DR73917		Balfour Beatty	DR93918	Balfour Beatty

Plasser & Theurer 08-16/4x4 C100 - RT – Tamper – ZWA

DR73919	Colas

Right: *Plasser & Theurer 08-16/4x4 C100 RT tamping machine of TOPS classification ZWA. It is owned by Colas and painted in Colas Rail orange and yellow livery.* **Antony Christie**

Plasser & Theurer 08-16/4x4C80 - RT – Tamper – ZWA

DR73920	Colas	DR73921	Colas	DR73922 *John Snowdon*	Colas

Plasser & Theurer 08-4x4S - RT – Switch/Crossing Tamper – ZWA

DR73923	*Mercury*	Colas

Plasser & Theurer 08-16/4x4 C100 - RT – Tamper – ZWA

DR73924		Colas	DR73927		Balfour Beatty
DR73925	*Europa*	Colas	DR73928		Balfour Beatty
DR73926	*Stephen Keith Blanchard*	Balfour Beatty			

Plasser & Theurer 08-4x4S - RT – Switch/Crossing Tamper – ZWA

DR73929	Colas	DR73930	Colas

Plasser & Theurer 08-16/4x4C100 - RT – Tamper – ZWA

DR73931	Colas

Plasser & Theurer 08-4x4/4S - RT – Switch/Crossing Tamper

DR73932	SB Rail

Plasser & Theurer 08-16/4x4C100 - RT – Tamper – ZWA

DR73933	SB Rail	DR73934	SB Rail

Plasser & Theurer 08-4x4/4S - RT – Switch/Crossing Tamper – ZWA

DR73935	Colas	DR73936	Colas

Infrastructure Companies - Network Rail

Network Rail

Plasser & Theurer 08-16/4x4 C100 - RT – Tamper – ZWA

DR73937		Balfour Beatty	
DR73938		Balfour Beatty	
DR73939	*Pat Best*	Balfour Beatty	

Left: *Another of the major players in the ownership and operation of track machines is Balfour Beatty. Painted in company blue and white livery, Plasser & Theurer 08-16/4x4 C100 RT No. DR73937 is illustrated at East Croydon.* **Antony Christie**

Plasser & Theurer 08-4x4/4S - RT – Switch/Crossing Tamper – ZWA

DR73940	SB Rail	DR73941	SB Rail	DR73942	Colas

Plasser & Theurer 08-16/4x4C100 - RT – Tamper – ZWA

DR73943	Balfour Beatty	DR73944	Balfour Beatty	DR73945	Balfour Beatty

Plasser & Theurer Euromat 08-4x4/4S – ZWA

DR73946	VolkerRail

Plasser & Theurer 08-4x4/4S - RT – Switch/Crossing Tamper ZWA

DR73947	Colas	DR73948	Colas

Plasser & Theurer 08-16/90 275 – Switch/Crossing Tamper – ZWA

DR75201 (S)	Balfour Beatty	DR75202 (S)	Balfour Beatty

Plasser & Theurer 08-16/90 SP-T – Switch/Crossing Tamper – ZWA

DR75203	MLP Maintenance

Plasser & Theurer 08-275ZW – Switch/Crossing Tamper – ZWY

DR75204	Trackwork

Matisa B45 Tamper – ZWA

DR75301	VolkerRail	DR75302	VolkerRail	DR75303	VolkerRail
		Gary Wright			

Left: *Although the vast majority of track machines in the UK are built by Plasser & Theurer, a number of Matisa-built machines are in use. In this illustration is B41UE tamping machine No. DR75407, a machine owned and operated by Colas Rail.* **Antony Christie**

Matisa B41UE Tamper – ZWA

DR75401	VolkerRail	DR75405	VolkerRail	DR75408	Balfour Beatty
DR75402	VolkerRail	DR75406	Colas	DR75409	Balfour Beatty
DR75403(S)	VolkerRail		*Eric Machell*	DR75410	Balfour Beatty
DR75404	VolkerRail	DR75407	Colas	DR75411	Balfour Beatty

Matisa B66UC Tamper – ZWA

DR75501	Balfour Beatty	DR75502	Balfour Beatty

Plasser & Theurer RM95RT – Ballast Cleaner – ZWA

DR76323	Network Rail	DR76324	Network Rail

Plasser & Theurer RM900RT Ballast Cleaner – ZWA / ZWQ

DR76501	(HOBC-1)	Network Rail	DR76503	(HOBC-3)	Network Rail
DR76502	(HOBC-2)	Network Rail	DR76504	(HOBC-4)	Network Rail

Plasser & Theurer VM80 NR – ZWA

DR76701	(HOBC-3)	Network Rail	DR76710(S)	(HOTRT-2)	Network Rail
DR76702	(HOBC-2)	Network Rail	DR76711(S)	(HOTRT-1)	Network Rail
DR76703	(HOBC-1)	Network Rail			

Matisa D75 Undercutter – ZWA

DR76750	(HRTRT-2)	Network Rail	DR76751	(HRTRT-1)	Network Rail

Plasser & Theurer 09-16 CM NR – ZWA

DR76801	(HOBC-3)	Network Rail	DR76802	(HOBC-4)	Network Rail

Plasser & Theurer AFM 2000 RT – Rail Finishing Machine – ZWA

DR77001	SB Rail	DR77002	SB Rail

Plasser & Theurer USP 6000 – Ballast Regulator – ZWA

DR77010	Network Rail

Plasser & Theurer USP 5000C – Ballast Regulator – ZWA

DR77315(S)	Balfour Beatty	DR77322	Balfour Beatty	DR77336 (S)	Balfour Beatty
DR77316(S)	Balfour Beatty	DR77327	Colas		

Right: Plasser & Theurer USP 5000C ballast regulator machine No. DR77327 is seen at Newton Abbot, Devon. This is a machine owned and operated by Colas Rail.
Antony Christie

Matisa R24S – Ballast Regulator – ZWA

DR77801	VolkerRail	DR77802	VolkerRail

Plasser & Theurer USP 5000RT – Ballast Regulator – ZWA

DR77901		DR77906	Network Rail
DR77903	Colas	DR77907	Network Rail
DR77904	Network Rail	DR77908 (* Previously DR77902)	SB Rail
DR77905	Network Rail	DR77909	Network Rail

Network Rail

Plasser & Theurer Self-Propelled Heavy Duty Twin Jib Crane – YJB

DR78213	VolkerRail	DR78218	Balfour Beatty	DR78223	Balfour Beatty
DR78215	SB Rail	DR78219	SB Rail	DR78224	Balfour Beatty
DR78216	Balfour Beatty	DR78221	Balfour Beatty		
DR78217	SB Rail	DR78222	Balfour Beatty		

Cowans Sheldon Self-Propelled Heavy Duty Twin Jib Crane – YJB

DR78226	Colas	DR78231	Network Rail	DR78235	Colas
DR78229	Network Rail	DR78234	Network Rail	DR78237	Network Rail

Left: *Crane-builder Cowans Sheldon was responsible for the construction of a number of twin-jib heavy-duty track cranes. These twin jib units were designed to lift a complete section of 60ft track with sleepers and rails in position and stack them on either the ground or on rail wagons. No. 78226 is a vehicle owned and operated by Colas Rail.* **Antony Christie**

Donelli PD350 Single Line Track Relayer

DR78416	Balfour Beatty	DR78417	Balfour Beatty	DR78490	VolkerRail

Harsco Track Technologies NTC Power Wagon – YJA

DR78701	Balfour Beatty	DR78702	Balfour Beatty

Matisa P95 Track Renewal Train – YJA

DR78801	Network Rail	DR78811	Network Rail	DR78821	Network Rail	DR78831	Network Rail
DR78802	Network Rail	DR78812	Network Rail	DR78822	Network Rail	DR78832	Network Rail

Schweebau SPML15 – Rail Grinder – ZWA

DR79200	Loram

Loram/Barclay SPML17 – Rail Grinder – ZWA

DR79201	Loram

Speno RPS 32-2 – Rail Grinder – ZWA

DR79221	Speno	DR79223	Speno	DR79225	Speno
DR79222	Speno	DR79224	Speno	DR79226	Speno

Loram C21 – Rail Grinder – ZWA

Set 01		Set 02		Set 03	
DR79231	Loram	DR79241	Loram	DR79251	Loram
DR79232	Loram	DR79242	Loram	DR79252	Loram
DR79233	Loram	DR79243	Loram	DR79253	Loram
DR79234	Loram	DR79244	Loram	DR79254	Loram
DR79235	Loram	DR79245	Loram	DR79255	Loram
DR79236	Loram	DR79246	Loram	DR79256	Loram
DR79237	Loram	DR79247 *Roger Smith*	Loram	DR79257 *Martin Elwood*	Loram

642005	Network Rail	642021	Network Rail	642037	Network Rail
642006	Network Rail	642022	Network Rail	642038	Network Rail
642007	Network Rail	642023	Network Rail	642039	Network Rail
642008	Network Rail	642024	Network Rail	642040	Network Rail
642009	Network Rail	642025	Network Rail	642041	Network Rail
642010	Network Rail	642026	Network Rail	642042	Network Rail
642011	Network Rail	642027	Network Rail	642043	Network Rail
642012	Network Rail	642028	Network Rail	642044	Network Rail
642013	Network Rail	642029	Network Rail	642045	Network Rail
642014	Network Rail	642030	Network Rail	642046	Network Rail
642015	Network Rail	642031	Network Rail	642047	Network Rail
642016	Network Rail	642032	Network Rail	642048	Network Rail
642017	Network Rail	642033	Network Rail	642049	Network Rail
642018	Network Rail	642034	Network Rail	642050	Network Rail
642019	Network Rail	642035	Network Rail		
642020	Network Rail	642036	Network Rail		

Right: *The annual Rail Head Treatment Train (RHTT) operation run by Network Rail operates from around the second week of October until early December. The dates are flexible due to the level of leaf fall. The RHTT wagons, which are based at York when not in use, operate 'toped and tailed' by main-line locomotives, usually hired in from DB-Cargo, DRS, Colas Rail Freight or the private sector. By the nature of their work, the RHTT wagons and indeed the powering locos get very dirty after just the first trip. In this view we see a rather grubby RHTT wagon at Westbury.* **CJM**

Right: *EWS-liveried Class 66s Nos. 66119 and 66053 are seen arriving at Westbury on 5 December 2015 with the 08.55 Bristol Barton Hill to Westbury RHTT service. As soon as the annual service is complete the locos have to be hand-washed to remove the brown grime from their bodywork.* **CJM**

Windhoff Multi Purpose Vehicle (MPV) – YXA

DR98901 + DR98951	Network Rail	DR98912 + DR98962	Network Rail	DR98923 + DR98973	Network Rail
DR98902 + DR98952	Network Rail	DR98913 + DR98963	Network Rail	DR98924 + DR98974	Network Rail
DR98903 + DR98953	Network Rail	DR98914 + DR98964	Network Rail	DR98925 + DR98975	Network Rail
DR98904 + DR98954	Network Rail	DR98915 + DR98965	Network Rail	DR98926 + DR98976	Network Rail
DR98905 + DR98955	Network Rail	DR98916 + DR98966	Network Rail	DR98927 + DR98977	Network Rail
DR98906 + DR98956	Network Rail	DR98917 + DR98967	Network Rail	DR98928 + DR98978	Network Rail
DR98907 + DR98957	Network Rail	DR98918 + DR98968	Network Rail	DR98929 + DR98979	Network Rail
DR98908 + DR98958	Network Rail	DR98919 + DR98969	Network Rail	DR98930 + DR98980	Network Rail
DR98909 + DR98959	Network Rail	DR98920 + DR98970	Network Rail	DR98931 + DR98981	Network Rail
DR98910 + DR98960	Network Rail	DR98921 + DR98971	Network Rail	DR98932 + DR98982	Network Rail
DR98911 + DR98961	Network Rail	DR98922 + DR98972	Network Rail		

Infrastructure Companies

Network Rail

Names applied:
DR98926+DR98976 *John Denyer*
DR98914+DR98964 *Dick Preston*
DR98915+DR98965 *Nigel Cummins*
DR98923+DR98973 *Chris Lemon*

Left: *A fleet of 32 twin-vehicle Multi Purpose Vehicles (MPVs) is operated by Network Rail and can be used for a wide variety of work, including carrying out rail cleaning, de-icing and weed control operations. Twin set Nos. DR98929 and DR98979 are seen passing Horley on the London to Brighton line.*
Antony Christie

Rail Wagon – YEA 'Perch'

DR979001	N Rail	DR979028	N Rail	DR979055	N Rail	DR979082	N Rail	DR979109	N Rail
DR979002	N Rail	DR979029	N Rail	DR979056	N Rail	DR979083	N Rail	DR979110	N Rail
DR979003	N Rail	DR979030	N Rail	DR979057	N Rail	DR979084	N Rail	DR979111	N Rail
DR979004	N Rail	DR979031	N Rail	DR979058	N Rail	DR979085	N Rail	DR979112	N Rail
DR979005	N Rail	DR979032	N Rail	DR979059	N Rail	DR979086	N Rail	DR979113	N Rail
DR979006	N Rail	DR979033	N Rail	DR979060	N Rail	DR979087	N Rail	DR979114	N Rail
DR979007	N Rail	DR979034	N Rail	DR979061	N Rail	DR979088	N Rail	DR979115	N Rail
DR979008	N Rail	DR979035	N Rail	DR979062	N Rail	DR979089	N Rail	DR979116	N Rail
DR979009	N Rail	DR979036	N Rail	DR979063	N Rail	DR979090	N Rail	DR979117	N Rail
DR979010	N Rail	DR979037	N Rail	DR979064	N Rail	DR979091	N Rail	DR979118	N Rail
DR979011	N Rail	DR979038	N Rail	DR979065	N Rail	DR979092	N Rail	DR979119	N Rail
DR979012	N Rail	DR979039	N Rail	DR979066	N Rail	DR979093	N Rail	DR979120	N Rail
DR979013	N Rail	DR979040	N Rail	DR979067	N Rail	DR979094	N Rail	DR979121	N Rail
DR979014	N Rail	DR979041	N Rail	DR979068	N Rail	DR979095	N Rail	DR979122	N Rail
DR979015	N Rail	DR979042	N Rail	DR979069	N Rail	DR979096	N Rail	DR979123	N Rail
DR979016	N Rail	DR979043	N Rail	DR979070	N Rail	DR979097	N Rail	DR979124	N Rail
DR979017	N Rail	DR979044	N Rail	DR979071	N Rail	DR979098	N Rail	DR979125	N Rail
DR979018	N Rail	DR979045	N Rail	DR979072	N Rail	DR979099	N Rail	DR979126	N Rail
DR979019	N Rail	DR979046	N Rail	DR979073	N Rail	DR979100	N Rail	DR979127	N Rail
DR979020	N Rail	DR979047	N Rail	DR979074	N Rail	DR979101	N Rail	DR979128	N Rail
DR979021	N Rail	DR979048	N Rail	DR979075	N Rail	DR979102	N Rail	DR979129	N Rail
DR979022	N Rail	DR979049	N Rail	DR979076	N Rail	DR979103	N Rail	DR979130	N Rail
DR979023	N Rail	DR979050	N Rail	DR979077	N Rail	DR979104	N Rail	DR979131	N Rail
DR979024	N Rail	DR979051	N Rail	DR979078	N Rail	DR979105	N Rail	DR979132	N Rail
DR979025	N Rail	DR979052	N Rail	DR979079	N Rail	DR979106	N Rail	DR979133	N Rail
DR979026	N Rail	DR979053	N Rail	DR979080	N Rail	DR979107	N Rail	DR979134	N Rail
DR979027	N Rail	DR979054	N Rail	DR979081	N Rail	DR979108	N Rail		

Continuous Welded Rail Clamping Wagon – YEA 'Perch'

DR979409	Network Rail	DR979412	Network Rail	DR979415	Network Rail

Continuous Welded Rail End of Train Wagon – YEA 'Porpoise'

DR979505	Network Rail	DR979509	Network Rail	DR979513	Network Rail	DR979515	Network Rail
DR979506	Network Rail	DR979511	Network Rail	DR979514	Network Rail		

Continuous Welded Rail 'Chute' Wagon – YEA 'Porpoise'

DR979500	Network Rail	DR979502	Network Rail	DR979507	Network Rail	DR979510	Network Rail
DR979501	Network Rail	DR979503	Network Rail	DR979508	Network Rail	DR979512	Network Rail

Continuous Welded Rail Gantry Wagon – YEA 'Perch'

DR979604	Network Rail	DR979611	Network Rail	DR979614	Network Rail
DR979607	Network Rail	DR979612	Network Rail		
DR979609	Network Rail	DR979613	Network Rail		

Plasser & Theurer EM-SAT RT900 Survey Vehicle

DR999800(S) *Richard Spoors*   Network Rail   DR999801(S)   Network Rail

RailVac Machine - Swedish Rail Vacuum KFA

99 70 9515 001-4 (99709)	Railcare, Sweden*	* Operated in the UK - based at Totton
99 70 9515 002-2	Railcare, Sweden*	* Operated in the UK - based at Bletchley
99 70 9515 003-0	Railcare, Sweden*	* Operated in the UK - based at Westbury
99 70 9515 004-8	Railcare, Sweden*	* Operated in the UK - based at Westbury

Right: *At the start of 2017, four RailVac vehicles were in operation with Network Rail. These Swedish vehicles are hauled to worksites and then operate under their own power sucking ballast and debris from the track and placing it in on-board containers. Viewed from its cab end, No. 99 70 9515 004-8 is seen at Taunton.*
Antony Christie

Windhoff MPV - High Output Plant System (GW electrification train)

DR96901 (99 70 9131 001)	Network Rail		DR96914 (99 70 9131 014)	Network Rail
DR96903 (99 70 9131 003)	Network Rail		DR96915 (99 70 9131 015)	Network Rail
DR96905 (99 70 9131 005)	Network Rail		DR96916 (99 70 9131 018)	Network Rail
DR96906 (99 70 9131 006)	Network Rail		DR96920 (99 70 9131 020)	Network Rail
DR96910 (99 70 9131 010)	Network Rail		DR96921 (99 70 9131 021)	Network Rail
DR96911 (99 70 9131 011)	Network Rail		DR96922 (99 70 9131 022)	Network Rail
DR96913 (99 70 9131 013)	Network Rail		DR96923 (99 70 9131 023)	Network Rail

Names applied
DR96901 *Brunel*   DR96923   *Gavin Roberts*

Plasser & Theurer Unimat 09-4x4/4S

DR74001 (928001) (99 70 9128 001-3)   SB Rail
DR74002 (99 70 9128 002-1)   Network Rail

Winter Snow Patrol Train 'Perch'

99709594014-1 IS   977986 IS

Recent Additions

SVI RT250 Crane/platform vehicle	DR 99 70 9231 001-7	Network Rail
SVI PT500 Wire/platform	DR 99 70 9231 004-1	Network Rail
SVI RSM9 Platform	DR 99 70 9231 005-8	Network Rail
SVI APV250 Platform	DR 99 70 9231 007-4	Network Rail
Plasser & Theurer PW	99 70 9310- 477-3 (DR92477)	Network Rail
Plasser & Theurer NPW	99 70 9310- 478-1 (DR92478)	Network Rail
Kirow KRC 250S 25T Crane	DRK81626 (DR 99 70 9319 012-9)	Network Rail
Kirow KRC 1200U 125T Crane	DR 99 70 9319 013-7	Network Rail

Alstom Transport

Address: ✉ PO Box 70, Newbold Road, Rugby, Warwickshire, CV21 2WR
🖰 info@transport.alstom.com ✆ 01788 577111 ⓘ www.transport.alstom.com
Managing Director: Paul Robinson
Facilities: Following the assembly of the Virgin Trains Class 390 'Pendolino' stock, Alstom closed down its UK production facility at Washwood Heath, Birmingham. However, the company still operates from many specialist sites in mainland Europe and if it wins further new-build contracts in the UK these will be assembled in Europe.
Depots: Chester (CH), Liverpool - Edge Hill (LL), Manchester - Longsight (MA), Wolverhampton - Oxley (OY), Wembley (WB)

Class 08

Vehicle Length: 29ft 3in (8.91m)
Height: 12ft 8⅝in (3.87m)
Width: 8ft 6in (2.59m)

Engine: English Electric 6K
Horsepower: 400hp (298kW)
Electrical Equipment: English Electric

Number	Depot	Pool	Livery	Owner	Operator
08451	PO	ATLO	BLK	ALS	ALS
08454	EH	ATLO	BLU	ALS	ALS
08611	WB	ATLO	BLU	ALS	ALS
08617	EH	ATLO	BLU	ALS	ALS
08696	WB	ATLO	BLU	ALS	ALS
08721	AT	ATLO	BLU	ALS	ALS
08790	OX	ATLO	BLU	ALS	ALS
08887	EH	ATZZ	BLK	ALS	ALS

Names applied
08617 *Steve Purser*
08721 *Longsight TMD*

Bombardier Transportation

Address: ✉ Litchurch Lane, Derby, DE24 8AD
🖰 info@bombardier.com ✆ 01332 344666 ⓘ www.bombardier.com
Chief Country Representative: Paul Roberts **Works:** Derby (ZD), Crewe (ZC)
Facilities: Bombardier Transportation is one of the largest transport companies in the world, with offices and facilities in many countries. Its product range extends well beyond rail vehicles and includes aircraft, boats and leisure equipment. In terms of the UK, two main sites are located in Derby (Litchurch Lane) and Crewe. New-build work is undertaken at the Derby site.

Class 08

Vehicle Length: 29ft 3in (8.91m)
Height: 12ft 8⅝in (3.87m)
Width: 8ft 6in (2.59m)

Engine: English Electric 6K
Horsepower: 400hp (298kW)
Electrical Equipment: English Electric

Number	Depot	Pool	Livery	Owner	Operator	Name
08511	ZD	-	RSS	RSS	BOM	
08602 (004)	ZD	KDSD	BLU	BOM	BOM	*Lionheart*
08682 (D3849)	ZD	KDSD	SPL	BOM	BOM	

Left: *Bombardier Transportation at Derby Litchurch Lane, one of the major train construction sites in the UK, has a need for shunting power to move part and complete vehicles and trains around the large works complex. Two ex-BR Class 08s are owned by Bombardier and in 2016 Railway Support Services (RSS) had their spot hire loco No. 08511 working at the Litchurch Lane site.* **Antony Christie**

Progress Rail International Inc

Address: ✉ Progress Rail International Inc, 9301 West 55th Street, LaGrange, Illinois, USA, 60525

Progress Rail International Inc, Muncie, Indiana, USA

✆ info@progressrail.com ✆ +1 (800) 255 5355, ⓘ www.progressrail.com

Facilities: Formerly part of General Motors, Progress Rail is one of the two largest loco builders in the world. Its main production facility is in Muncie, Indiana, USA. In terms of the UK, the JT42CWRM or Class 66 locomotives were all built at the Canadian facility; however, the latest and final order placed in 2013 by GBRf saw production move to Muncie, Indiana. Progress Rail is part of the Caterpillar Group. In the UK Progress Rail International operates from premises at Longport, near Stoke-on-Trent, where the bodyshell of withdrawn Class 66 No. 66048 is stored.

General Electric (GE)

Address: ✉ GE Transportation Rail, 2901 East Lake Road, Erie, Pennsylvania, USA, 16531

UK office: Inspira House, Martinfield, Welwyn Garden City, Herts, AL7 1GW

✆ info@getransportation.com ✆ 01707 383700 ⓘ www.getransportation.com

Chief Executive Officer: Lorenzo Simonelli

Facilities: General Electric entered the UK loco arena in recent years, and built Class 70s for Freightliner and Colas Rail Freight. GE operates a construction facility in Erie, Pennsylvania, USA.

Hitachi Europe Ltd

Address: ✉ 16 Upper Woburn Place, London, WC1H 0AF

✆ hirofumi.ojima@hitachi-eu.com ✆ 0207 970 2700, ⓘ www.hitachi-rail.com

Facilities: Hitachi's first UK contract was to design, build and introduce the Class 395 EMUs for domestic services on HS1. In 2009 it formed the construction arm of Agility Trains, awarded the IEP project to design, build and introduce new passenger trains in the UK. In 2015 the company opened construction facilities at Newton Aycliffe, County Durham.

At present the company is building the next generation of high-speed trains – Class 800 and 801 for the East Coast and Great Western routes. Hitachi is also fulfilling an order for electric multiple units for use in Scotland and a high-speed train order for further bi-mode sets to operate in the West of England.

Arlington Fleet Group

Address: ✉ Eastleigh Rail Works, Campbell Road, Eastleigh, Hampshire, SO50 5AD

✆ info@Arlington-fleet.co.uk ✆ 02380 698789 ⓘ www.arlington-fleet.com

Managing Director: Barry Stephens

Facilities: Arlington Fleet Group offers high-quality rail engineering services to all vehicle owners. The company is based in the former loco/carriage works at Eastleigh.

Depots: Eastleigh (ZG), Shoeburyness (SN)

Class 07

Vehicle Length: 26ft 9½in (8.16m)
Height: 12ft 10in (3.91m)
Width: 8ft 6in (2.59m)

Engine: Paxman 6RPHL MkIII
Horsepower: 275hp (205kW)
Electrical Equipment: AEI

Number	Depot	Pool	Livery	Owner	Operator
07007 (D2991)	ZG	MBDL	BLU	AFG	AFG

Class 08

Vehicle Length: 29ft 3in (8.91m)
Height: 12ft 8⅝in (3.87m)
Width: 8ft 6in (2.59m)

Engine: English Electric 6K
Horsepower: 400hp (298kW)
Electrical Equipment: English Electric

Number	Depot	Pool	Livery	Owner	Operator
08567	ZG	MBDL	EWS	AFG	AFG

Class 47

Vehicle Length: 63ft 6in (19.35m)
Height: 12ft 10⅜in (3.91m)
Width: 9ft 2in (2.79m)
Electric Train Heat fitted

Engine: Sulzer 12LDA28C
Horsepower: 2,580hp (1,922kW)
Electrical Equipment: Brush

Number		Depot	Pool	Livery	Owner	Operator
47810(S)	(47247/655)	ZG	MBDL	BLU	AFG	-
47818(S)	(47240/663)	ZG	MBDL	BLU	AFG	-

Ex-DB (Germany) Class 323

Number	Depot	Pool	Livery	Owner	Operator
323-539-7	ZG	-	GRN	NHR	AFG
323-674-2	ZG	-	GRN	NHR	AFG

Former German shunting locos, built by Gmeinder and now owned by Northumbria Rail and used at Eastleigh Works by Arlington Fleet Group for pilotage.

Left: *In addition to ex-BR and German locos, Arlington Fleet Group, based at Eastleigh has this ex-Ministry of Defence Ruston & Hornsby 0-6-0, works No. 466617, which was MoD No. 428 and now sports Class 01 No. 01508. The loco is very similar to a Ruston Class 07. It is seen here from its small cab end.* **Richard Tuplin**

Ex-Class 508 Barrier Vehicles

Former Class 508 driving cars now used as EMU barrier/translator vehicles, based at Eastleigh.

Number	Depot	Pool	Livery	Owner	Operator	Name
64664	ZG	-	GRN	ANG	AFG	*'Livet' Angel of Inventions*
64707	ZG	-	GRN	ANG	AFG	*'Labezerin' Angel of Success*

Left: *Two very useful vehicles on the books of AFG, Eastleigh, are two ex-Class 508 driving cars which have been modified as EMU translator coaches. Conventional drawgear is maintained at the inner end and auto couplers are provided at the former cab ends. All windows have been plated over but the bi-parting doors remain. The two vehicles, painted in AFG's green, are seen at Eastleigh.* **Antony Christie**

CAF (Construcciones y Auxiliar de Ferrocarriles)

Address: C/ José Miguel Iturrioz, 26 20200 Beasain (Guipúzcoa), Spain
    ✆ +34 943 88 01 00   ✍ caf@caf.net   ⓘ www.caf.net

Chairman: Andres Arizkorreta Garcia

Facilities: CAF currently operate a major construction plant in Spain. In the future a major facility will be opened in the UK. The company currently has orders for Arriva Northern, FTPE and Caledonian Sleepers amounting to almost 500 vehicles.

Arriva Train Care

Address: ✉ Arriva Train Care, PO Box 111, Crewe, Cheshire, CW1 2FB
✆ allservicedeliverymanagers@lnwr.com ✆ 01270 508000 ⓘ www.lnwr.com
Managing Director: Mark Knowles
Facilities: ATC is owned by Arriva and based at Crewe, with outbased facilities at Bristol, Eastleigh, Cambridge and Tyne.
Depots: Crewe (CO), Bristol Barton Hill (BK), Eastleigh (EH), Cambridge (CA), Tyne (TY)

Class 08, 09

Vehicle Length: 29ft 3in (8.91m)	Engine: English Electric 6K	
Height: 12ft 8⅝in (3.87m)	Horsepower: 400hp (298kW)	
Width: 8ft 6in (2.59m)	Electrical Equipment: English Electric	

Number	Depot	Pool	Livery	Owner	Operator	Name
08442	EH	MBDL	BRT	LNW	ATC	*Richard J Wenham Eastleigh Depot December 1989 - July 1999*
08516	BK	MBDL	LNW	LNW	ATC	*Rory*
08810	EH	MBDL	GRY	LNW	ATC	
08830	CO	MBDL	BLU	LNW	ATC	
09204	CC	MBDL	ATC	LNW	ATC	

Right: *The Arriva Train Care depot at Crewe operates ex-BR Class 09/2 No. 09204 for depot and yard pilot operations. The loco has been repainted in parent company Arriva Train Care colours. Complete with a solid yellow warning end, No. 09204 is seen at Crewe in June 2016.*
Jack Boskett

Pullman Group (Colas Rail Freight)

Address: ✉ Train Maintenance Depot, Leckwith Road, Cardiff, CF11 8HP
✆ sales@pullmans.net ✆ 029 2036 8850 ⓘ www.pullmans.net
Managing Director: Colin Robinson
Facilities: Pullman Group operates from part of the former Canton depot in Cardiff and provides a quality engineering service to all types of rail vehicles.
Depot: Cardiff Canton (CF)

Class 08

Vehicle Length: 29ft 3in (8.91m)	Engine: English Electric 6K	
Height: 12ft 8⅝in (3.87m)	Horsepower: 400hp (298kW)	
Width: 8ft 6in (2.59m)	Electrical Equipment: English Electric	

Number	Depot	Pool	Livery	Owner	Operator	Name
08499	CF	WSXX	BLU	DBS	PUL	*Redlight*

Knorr Bremse Rail Services

Address: ✉ Wolverton Works, Stratford Road, Wolverton, Milton Keynes, MK12 5NT
✆ info@railcare.co.uk ✆ 08000 741122 ⓘ www.railcare.co.uk
Managing Director: Colin Love **Depots:** Glasgow (ZH), Wolverton (ZN)
Owner: Knorr Bremse

Class 08

	Vehicle Length: 29ft 3in (8.91m)	Engine: English Electric 6K
	Height: 12ft 8⅝in (3.87m)	Horsepower: 400hp (298kW)
	Width: 8ft 6in (2.59m)	Electrical Equipment: English Electric

Number	Depot	Pool	Livery	Owner	Operator	Name
08568	ZH	RCZH	KBR	KBR	KBR	St Rollox
08629	ZN	RCZN	KBR	KBR	KBR	Wolverton
08649	ZN	RCZN	KBR	KBR	KBR	Bradwell
08730	ZH	RCZH	KBR	KBR	KBR	The Caley

Loram UK

Address: ✉ Vehicles Workshop, RTC Business Park, London Road, Derby, DE24 8UP
✆ enquiries@rvel.co.uk ✆ 01332 331210 ⓘ www.rvel.co.uk

Managing Director: Andy Lynch
Depot: Derby (DF)
Parent Company: Loram

Class 08

	Vehicle Length: 29ft 3in (8.91m)	Engine: English Electric 6K
	Height: 12ft 8⅝in (3.87m)	Horsepower: 400hp (298kW)
	Width: 8ft 6in (2.59m)	Electrical Equipment: English Electric

Number	Depot	Pool	Livery	Owner	Operator
08536	DF	RVLS	-	LOR	LOR

Class 31/1 & 31/4

	Vehicle Length: 56ft 9in (17.29m)	Engine: English Electric 12SVT
	Height: 12ft 7in (3.91m)	Horsepower: 1,470hp (1,097kW)
	Width: 8ft 9in (2.65m)	Electrical Equipment: Brush
	Class 31/4 - Electric Train Heat fitted	

Number		Depot	Pool	Livery	Owner	Operator
31106		DF	RVLO	BLU	HJA	LOR
31468(S)	(31568, 31321)	DF	RVLS	BLK	LOR	LOR

Siemens Transportation

Address: ✉ Kings Heath Facility, Heathfield Way, Kings Heath, Northampton, NN5 7QP
✆ enquiries@siemenstransportation.co.uk ✆ 01604 594500
ⓘ www.siemenstransportation.co.uk
✉ Ashby Park, Ashby de la Zouch, Leicestershire, LE65 1JD
✆ uk.mobility@siemens.com ✆ 01530 258000 ⓘ www.siemens.co.uk/mobility

Managing Director UK: Vernon Baker
Depots: Ardwick, Manchester (AK), Kings Heath, Northampton (NN), Three Bridges, Hornsey (HE), Northam (NT)

Facilities: Siemens is a provider of UK EMU and DMU rolling stock with various derivatives of its 'Desiro' and 'Desiro City' product line. While having maintenance facilities in the UK, Siemens performs all new-build undertakings in mainland Europe at its Krefeld/Uerdingen factory in Germany. Testing of vehicles is also performed in Germany at the world-famous test track at Wildenrath before delivery to customers.

Siemens operates lifetime maintenance contracts for its Class 185 stock at Ardwick, Manchester, Class 350 stock at Ardwick and Kings Heath, Northampton, Class 380 stock at Shields (Glasgow), Class 444 and 450 stock at Northam near Southampton, Three Bridges and Hornsey for the Thameslink Class 700 stock, and at Wimbledon for the new Class 707 five-car sets for South West Trains.

Class 01.5

Number	Depot	Pool	Livery	Owner	Operator	Name
01551 (H016)	AK	MBDL	WAB	WAB	SIE	Lancelot

Vivarail

Address: ✉ Quinton Rail Technology Centre, Station Road, Long Marston, Stratford-upon-Avon, Warwickshire. CV37 8PL

✆ info@vivarail.co.uk ✆ 07815 010373 ⓘ www.vivarail.co.uk

Chairman: Adrian Shooter

Vivarail, based at Long Marston, is masterminding the re-use of redundant ex-London Transport 'D' stock, rebuilding it to main-line standards as either two- or three-car DEMUs, using two 3.2lit Ford underfloor engines below each power car. Vivarail has purchased 150 motor cars and 300 trailer vehicles from LUL. A three-car test formation was built in 2015 and will be tested on the main line and branch lines in 2017. At the end of December 2016 the project was set back by a fire and main line testing has been placed on hold.

230001

DM(A) 300001 - ex-LUL car 7058, TS 300201 - ex-LUL car 17128, DM(B) 300101- ex-LUL car 7511

Above: *The brainchild of Quinton Rail Technology is the adaptation of ex-London Transport 'D' stock into main-line diesel trains for secondary and branch line use. One prototype three-car set has been converted and was scheduled for active trials in 2017, but due to a fire this was postponed. The DM(A) driving car is seen outside the workshop at Long Marston.* **Jack Boskett**

Wabtec
Brush Traction, Loughborough

Address: ✉ PO Box 17, Loughborough, Leicestershire, LE11 1HS

✆ sales@brushtraction.com ✆ 01509 617000 ⓘ www.brushtraction.com

Managing Director: John Bidewell

Facilities: The world-famous name of Brush Traction, based in Loughborough, is now part of the Wabtec Group. In recent years the site has been responsible for the majority of UK loco building. The company has been synonymous with loco building for the UK and overseas markets for many years. Although recent main-line loco builds have been awarded overseas, the facilities at the Loughborough plant from which the Class 31, 47, 57, 60 and Eurotunnel Shuttle locos emerged are still available for new-build work. Recently the site has concentrated on rebuild operations including the highly successful re-engining of the HST fleet with MTU power units for First Group, East Coast, Grand Central and Network Rail. In 2016 the site was completing work on the re-engining of a Class 73 with an MTU power unit. The site is fully rail-connected. In late 2012, Wabtec purchased L H Group Services.

Doncaster

Address: ✉ PO Box 400, Doncaster Works, Hexthorpe Road, Doncaster, DN1 1SL
✆ wabtecrail@wabtec.com ✆ 01302 340700 ⓘ www.wabtecrail.co.uk

Managing Director: John Meehan **Depot:** Doncaster (ZB)

Class 08

Vehicle Length: 29ft 3in (8.91m)
Height: 12ft 8⅝in (3.87m)
Width: 8ft 6in (2.59m)

Engine: English Electric 6K
Horsepower: 400hp (298kW)
Electrical Equipment: English Electric

Number	Depot	Pool	Livery	Owner	Operator	Name
08472	EC	HBSH	BLK	WAB	VEC	
08571	ZB	HBSH	WAB	WAB	VEC	
08596	EC	HBSH	WAB	WAB	VEC	
08615	LH	HBSH	WAB	WAB	-	
08669	ZB	HBSH	WAB	WAB	WAB	*Bob Machin*
08724	ZB	HBSH	WAB	WAB	WAB	
08764	PO	MBDL	BLU	WAB	ALS	*Old Tom*
08853	ZB	HBSH	BLU	WAB	WAB	
08871	ZB	MBDL	GRN	WAB	Tata Steel	

Left: *Wabtec, with main sites at Doncaster, Loughborough and Kilmarnock is one of the leading rail vehicle engineering operations in the UK and has a need for shunting power. Locos are frequently to be found shunting at the Doncaster operation. In addition the company provide spot hire locos to other operators and engineering functions. Painted in Wabtec black livery, No. 08724 is seen in the yard at Doncaster in summer 2016.* **CJM**

Left: *The original five Eurostar Passenger Services (EPS) 'Nightstar' generator coaches, rebuilt from Mk3 sleeper stock but never turned a wheel in passenger service which have been dumped around the railway for many years. One vehicle, No. 96374 (the original 10585), has for a long time been stored at Wabtec, where at one time it was used as a generator to test electric systems of refurbished stock. The coach is seen dumped in the yard in mid-2016.* **CJM**

Scotland (previously Brush Barclay)

Address: ✉ Caledonia Works, West Langlands Street, Kilmarnock, Ayrshire, KA1 2QD
✆ sales@brushtraction.com ✆ 01563 523573 ⓘ www.brushtraction.com

Managing Director: John Bidewell
Facilities: The Wabtec site in Scotland concentrates on vehicle overhaul and refurbishment, including EMU, DMU and loco-hauled vehicles as well as HST stock.

Rail Operations Group (ROG)

Address: ✉ ROG, Wyvern House, Railway Terrace, Derby. DE1 2RU
✆ enquiries@railopsgroup.co.uk   ① www.railopsgroup.co.uk
Managing Director: K Watts

Rail Operations Group is a Train Operating Company authorised by the ORR. It was formed in 2015 to facilitate the movement of rolling stock between depots and workshops for overhaul, repair and refurbishment. The company also provides drivers and staff on a spot hire basis and is authorised to instruct drivers. The company started off by operating two hired-in Class 37s, Nos. 37800 and 37884, but in 2016, when a number of Class 47s became available from Riviera, these were purchased. The company, now with a much expanded portfolio, operates the Class 37s and 47s, as well as operating self-powered EMU and DMU trains.

Class 47

Vehicle Length: 63ft 6in (19.35m)		*Engine: Sulzer 12LDA28C*	
Height: 12ft 10³⁄₈in (3.91m)		*Horsepower: 2,580hp (1,922kW)*	
Width: 9ft 2in (2.79m)		*Electrical Equipment: Brush*	
Electric Train Heat fitted			

Number	Depot	Pool	Livery	Owner	Operator
47769 (47491)	CP	RTLO	VIR	RIV	ROG
47812 D1916 (47657)	LR	GROG	ROG	RIV	ROG
47815 D1748 (47660)	LR	GROG	ROG	RIV	ROG
47843 (47623)	LR	GROG	ROG	RIV	ROG
47847 (47577)	LR	GROG	ROG	RIV	ROG
47848 (47632)	LR	GROG	ROG	RIV	ROG

Above: *With Rail Operations Group bodyside branding, former Riviera Class 47 No. 47812 is seen passing Basingstoke hauling an off-lease Class 442 to Arlington Fleet Group at Eastleigh. The '47s' are likely to remain in a version of blue livery.* **Mark V. Pike**

Left: *The two Class 37s operated by Rail Operations Group, on hire from Europhoenix Ltd, Nos. 37800 and 37884, are both fitted with drophead auto couplers, allowing the connection to Dellner-fitted rolling stock. The locos also sport a jumper cable socket on the front end and this can be coupled to most modern EMU sets and allows the electric stock's brakes to be operated by the Class 37. For this an additional control panel has been installed in the Class 37 cab. The drophead coupling as fitted to No. 37800 is illustrated.* **CJM**

■ Class 86 No. 86259 is also operated by ROG

Train Engineering Companies – Rail Operations Group

Europhoenix Ltd

Address: ✉ 58A High Street, Stony Stratford, Milton Keynes, MK11 1AX
✍ info@europhoenix.eu ✆ 01467 624366 ⓘ www.europhoenix.eu

Facilities: Europhoenix has purchased redundant Class 56, 86 and 87 locos; these are offered to Continental European operators fully refurbished and modified to suit customer needs.

Class 37

Vehicle Length: 61ft 6in (18.74m)				Engine: Ruston		
Height: 13ft 0¼in (3.96m)				Horsepower: 1,750hp (1,304kW)		
Width: 8ft 11⅝in (2.73m)				Electrical Equipment: English Electric		

Number	Owner	Pool	Location	Livery	Owner	Operator/Notes
37503 (37021)	EPX	EPUK	LR	EWS	EPX	Spares loco
37510 (37112)	EPX	EPUK	LR	DRC	EPX	Spot hire
37608 (37512)	EPX	EPUK	LR	EPX	EPX	Hirr to Colas Rail Freight
37611 (37690)	EPX	EPUK	LR	DRC	EPX	Spot hire, for Colas Rail Freight
37670 (37182)	EPX	EPUK	LR	EWS	EPX	Spares loco
37800 (37143)	EPX	GROG	LR	EPR	EPX	Spot hire - with ROG drophead Dellner fitted
37884 (37183)	EPX	GROG	LR	EPR	EPX	Spot hire - with ROG drophead Dellner fitted

Name applied
37608 *Andromeda*

Left: *Europhoenix Ltd is the provider of two Class 37/8s to Rail operations Group and provides other spot hire cover. Its two Class 37/8s sport green and grey Phoenix livery and are fitted with drophead Dellner couplers allowing connection to modern like-coupling-fitted EMU stock (detailed on previous page). No. 37800 complete with Rail Operations Group branding is seen passing Wandsworth Town with a refurbished Class 375 bound for Ramsgate.* **Antony Christie**

Coaching Stock

Mk 3	Height: 12ft 9in (3.88m)	
Vehicle Length: 75ft 0in (22.86m)	Width: 8ft 11in (2.71m)	

NX5G - NGV (Ex 'Nightstar' generator van)

Number	Depot	Livery	Owner
96371(S) (10545)	LR	EPS	EPX

Left: *Europhoenix purchased withdrawn European Passenger Services Mk3 generator van No. 96371 at the start of 2016 with a plan to adapt it as a state-of-the-art generator van for charter and other services. After purchase the vehicle was taken to Leicester depot where this illustration was taken. A lot of work will be needed to return this vehicle to front-line use.* **CJM**

Right: *In January 2016, UKRL No. 56098 was named* Lost Boys 68-88 *in recognition of the secondmen who joined the railway between those years and have now formed an association.* **CJM**

Although officially owned by the Class 58 Loco Group, Class 58 No. 58016 is currently stored at UKRL's Leicester depot and will eventually be restored to main-line operational condition. **CJM**

Electric Traction Limited

Address: ✉ Woodlands, Manse Road, Inverurie, Aberdeenshire, Scotland, AB51 3UJ

Depot: Long Marston (LM)

Electric Traction Ltd provides spot hire of Class 86 and 87 traction, as well as providing engineering and graphic design services to the rail industry.

Class 86

Vehicle Length: 58ft 6in (17.83m) Power Collection: 25kV ac overhead
Height: 13ft 0⅝in (3.97m) Horsepower: 5,900hp (4,400kW)
Width: 8ft 8¼in (2.64m) Electrical Equipment: GEC

Number	Depot	Pool	Livery	Owner	Operator	Name
86101	WA	GBCH	SCS	ETL	GBR	*Sir William Stanier FRS*
86401	WA	GBCH	SCS	ETL	GBR	*Mons Meg*

Class 87

Vehicle Length: 58ft 6in (17.83m) Power Collection: 25kV ac overhead
Height: 13ft 1¼in (3.99m) Horsepower: 7,860hp (5,680kW)
Width: 8ft 8¼in (2.64m) Electrical Equipment: GEC

Number	Depot	Pool	Livery	Owner	Operator	Name
87002	WN	GBCH	SCS	ETL	GBR	*Royal Sovereign*

Eversholt Rail Group (Previously HSBC Rail)

Address: ✉ PO Box 29499, 1 Eversholt Street, London, NW1 2ZF

　✉ info@eversholtrail.co.uk ✆ 0207 380 5040 ⓘ www.eversholtrail.co.uk

Chief Operating Officer: Mary Kenny

Owned by C K Investments

Harry Needle Railroad Company

Address: ✉ Harry Needle Railway Shed, Barrow Hill Roundhouse, Campbell Drive,
Chesterfield, Derbyshire, S43 2PR
Managing Director: Harry Needle
Depot: Barrow Hill (BH)
Harry Needle Railroad Company also operates as a scrap dealer in dismantling locomotives and rolling stock.

Class 01.5

Number	Depot	Pool	Livery	Owner	Operator	Note
01552 (TH167V)	BH	HNRL	IND	HNR	IND	
01564 (12088)	-	HNRL	BLK	HNR	IND	Preserved at Aln Valley Railway

Class 08 and 09

Vehicle Length: 29ft 3in (8.91m)
Height: 12ft 8⅝in (3.87m)
Width: 8ft 6in (2.59m)
Engine: English Electric 6K
Horsepower: 400hp (298kW)
Electrical Equipment: English Electric

Number	Depot	Pool	Livery	Owner	Operator		Number	Depot	Pool	Livery	Owner	Operator
08389◊	BH	HNRL	EWS	HNR	HNR		08834	AN	HNRL	HNR	HNR	NOR
08500	BU	HNRL	EWS	HNR	-		08865	BH	HNRL	EWS	HNR	-
08527	BH	HNRL	JAR	HNR	-		08868	CP	HNRL	ATC	HNR	LNW
08578	BH	HNRL	EWS	HNR	QRT		08877	BH	HNRL	BRD	HNR	-
08630	BH	HNRL	BLK	HNR	Celsa		08892	HE	HNRL	DRS	HNR	HNR
08653	BH	HNRL	EWS	HNR	QRT		08904	BH	HNRL	EWS	HNR	-
08676	-	HNRL	EWS	HNR	EKR		08905	BH	HNRL	EWS	HNR	IND
08685	BH	HNRL	EWS	HNR	EKR		08918	BH	HNRL	EWS	HNR	BUR
08700	BH	HNRL	BLU	HNR	BOM		08924	BH	HNRL	GBR	HNR	GBR
08701	BH	HNRL	-	HNR	QRT		08929(S)	LM	HNRS	BLK	HNR	-
08714	BH	HNRL	DBS	HNR	Hope		08943	CZ	MBDL	HNR	HNR	NRM
08765	BH	HNRL	ORG	HNR	HNR		08954	LL	HNRS	BLU	HNR	ALS
08786	BH	HNRL	BRD	HNR	HNR		09006	BH	HNRL	EWS	HNR	NEM
08802	BH	HNRL	-	HNR	-		09014	BU	HNRS	ORG	HNR	-
08818	BH	HNRL	HNR	HNR	GBR		09018	BU	HNRS	HNR	HNR	LAF
08824	BH	HNRL	BLK	HNR	-		09201	BH	HNRL	BRD	HNR	LAF

◊ Remote control fitted

Name applied	
08630	*Celsa Endeavour*

Left: *One of the largest suppliers of spot hire standard 0-6-0 diesel-electric shunting locos is HNRC, which has a sizeable collection of well-restored and maintained examples. Painted in Arriva Train Care livery, No. 08868 is seen at Crewe.* **Jack Boskett**

Class 20

Vehicle Length: 46ft 9¼in (14.26m)
Height: 12ft 7⅝in (3.84m)
Width: 8ft 9in (2.66m)
Engine: English Electric 8SVT Mk2
Horsepower: 1,000hp (745kW)
Electrical Equipment: English Electric

Number	Depot	Pool	Livery	Owner	Operator		Number	Depot	Pool	Livery	Owner	Operator
20016(S) ø	BH	HNRS	BLU	HNR	-		20088(S) ø	LM	HNRS	RFG	HNR	-
20056	BH	HNRL	COR	HNR	TAT		20096	BH	GBEE	BLU	HNR	HNR
20066	BH	HNRL	TAT	HNR	HCM*		20107‡	BH	GBEE	ORG	HNR	HNR
20081(S) ø	LM	HNRS	BLU	HNR	-		20110	BH	HNRL	GRN	HNR	ELR
							20118	BH	GBEE	RFG	HNR	HNR

20121(S)	WEN	HNRS	ORG	HNR	HNR		20168	BH	HNRL	WHT	HNR	Hope
20132‡	BH	GBEE	RFG	HNR	HNR		‡ Main line certified		ø Reported for sale			
20138(S)	LM	HNRS	RFT	HNR	-		* HCM Hope Construction Materials					
20166	WEN	HNRS	ORG	HNR	HNR							

Number		Depot	Pool	Livery	Owner	Operator	Note
20311	(20102)	BH	GBEE	ORG	HNR	HNR	
20314	(20117)	BH	GBEE	ORG	HNR	HNR	Allocated number 92 70 0020314-5
20901	(20101)	BH	GBEE	GBN	HNR	HNR	
20903(S)	(20083)	LM	HNRS	DRS	HNR	-	
20904(S)	(20041)	LM	HNRS	DRS	HNR	-	
20905	(20225)	BH	GBEE	GBN	HNR	HNR	
20906	(20219)	LAF	HNRL	WHT	HNR	LAF	

20056 carries Tata Steel No. 81.
20066 carries Tata Steel No. 82.

Names applied

20118	*Saltburn-by-the-Sea*
20132	*Barrow Hill Depot*
20168	*Sir George Earle*

Right: *The HNRC Class 20 fleet is frequently in demand for hire contracts to haul TOC and London Transport stock. Looking resplendent in Railfreight large logo livery, Nos. 20132 and 20118 are seen at Derby.* **Antony Christie**

Class 31

Vehicle Length: 56ft 9in (17.29m)	Engine: English Electric 12SVT
Height: 12ft 7in (3.91m)	Horsepower: 1,470hp (1,097kW)
Width: 8ft 9in (2.65m)	Electrical Equipment: Brush

Number	Depot	Pool	Livery	Owner	Operator
31235	BH	-	-	HNR	-
31285	BU	-	NRL	HNR	-
31459	BH	-	BLK	HNR	-
31465	BH	-	NRL	HNR	Weardale

Class 37/0

Vehicle Length: 61ft 6in (18.74m)	Engine: English Electric 12CSVT
Height: 13ft 0¼in (3.96m)	Horsepower: 1,750hp (1,304kW)
Width: 8ft 11⅝in (2.73m)	Electrical Equipment: English Electric

Number	Depot	Pool	Livery	Owner	Operator/Note
37029	BH	HNRS	GRN	HNR	HNR (at Epping & Ongar Railway)
37165(S) (37374)	CS	HNRS	CIV	HNR	-

Right: *With its body rubbed down for pre-paint attention, HNRC Class 47/7 No. 47703 has been parked up at Wabtec Doncaster for several years. The loco has seen use as a power supply for coach refurbishment and it is understood that it will soon be repainted and made fully operational.* **CJM**

HNRC

Class 47

	Vehicle Length: 63ft 6in (19.35m)	Engine: Sulzer 12LDA28C
	Height: 12ft 10½in (3.91m)	Horsepower: 2,580hp (1,922kW)
	Width: 9ft 2in (2.79m)	Electrical Equipment: Brush
	Electric Train Heat fitted	

Number	Depot	Pool	Livery	Owner	Operator	Notes/Name
47703 (47514)	BH	HNRL	-	HNR	Wabtec	
47714 (47511)	OD	HNRL	ANG	HNR	SEC	At RIDC (Old Dalby test track)
47715 (47502)	BH	HNRL	NSE	HNR	HNR	*Haymarket*
47761 (47038/564)	BH	HNRL	RES	HNR	(Stored)	
47853 (47614)	BH	GBHN	BLU	HNR	GBRf	Banking loco Liverpool Dock Branch

RIDC - Rail Innovation and Development Centre, Old Dalby

Beacon Rail

Address: ✉ Beacon Rail Leasing, 111 Buckingham Palace Road, London, SW1W 0SR
✆ rail@beaconrail.com.com ✆ 0207 015 00001 ⓘ www.beaconrail.com
UK and international loco, multiple unit and wagon hire company.

Managing Director (UK): Neil Bennett **Parent Company:** Pamplona Capital Management

Left: One of the leading names in UK and European locomotive, multiple unit and wagon leasing is Beacon Rail. In the UK its prime assets are the Class 68 and 88 fleets operating for Direct Rail Services. Two of the company's portfolio, Nos. 68020 and 68004 pass Teignmouth Docks in summer 2016 with a Network Rail test train. **CJM**

Nemesis Rail

Address: ✉ Nemesis Rail Ltd, Burton Depot, Burton-on-Trent, DE14 1RS
✆ enquiries@ nemesisrail.com ✆ 01246 472331 ⓘ www.nemesisrail.com
Formed from the demise of FM Rail

Depot: Burton (BU)

Class 31/1

	Vehicle Length: 56ft 9in (17.29m)	Engine: English Electric 12SVT
	Height: 12ft 7in (3.91m)	Horsepower: 1,470hp (1,097kW)
	Width: 8ft 9in (2.65m)	Electrical Equipment: Brush

Number	Depot	Pool	Livery	Owner	Operator	Name
31128	BU	NRLO	BLU	NEM	NYM	*Charybdis*

Class 33/1

	Vehicle Length: 50ft 9in (15.47m)	Engine: Sulzer 8LDA28A
	Height: 12ft 8in (3.86m)	Horsepower: 1,550hp (1,156kW)
	Width: 9ft 3in (2.81m)	Electrical Equipment: Crompton Parkinson

Number	Depot	Pool	Livery	Owner	Operator	Name
33103	BU	MBDL	BLU	NEM	-	*Swordfish*

Class 37/5

	Vehicle Length: 61ft 6in (18.74m)	Engine: English Electric 12CSVT
	Height: 13ft 0¼in (3.96m)	Horsepower: 1,750hp (1,304kW)
	Width: 8ft 11⅝in (2.73m)	Electrical Equipment: English Electric

Number	Depot	Pool	Livery	Owner	Operator
37679(S) (37123)	BU	MBDL	TGG	NEM	-

Class 45/1

			Vehicle Length: 67ft 11in (20.70m)		Engine: Sulzer 12LDA28B	
			Height: 12ft 10½in (3.91m)		Horsepower: 2,500hp (1,862kW)	
			Width: 9ft 1½in (2.78m)		Electrical Equipment: Crompton Parkinson	

Number	Depot	Pool	Livery	Owner	Operator	Name
45112	BH	MBDL	BLU	NEM	NEM	*Royal Army Ordnance Corps*

Class 47

			Vehicle Length: 63ft 6in (19.35m)		Engine: Sulzer 12LDA28C	
			Height: 12ft 10⅜in (3.91m)		Horsepower: 2,580hp (1,922kW)	
			Width: 9ft 2in (2.79m)		Electrical Equipment: Brush	
			Class 47/4 and 47/7 - Electric Train Heat fitted			

Number	Depot	Pool	Livery	Owner	Operator
47375	BU	MBDL	MAR	CRS	CRS
47488	BU	MBDL	MAR	CRS	NEM
47701	BU	MBDL	BLK	NEM	NEM

Number	Depot	Pool	Livery	Owner	Operator
47744	BU	MBDL	EWS	NEM	NEM

Nos. 47488/701/744 also destined for export to Hungary for Continental Railway Solutions

Right: *A company entitled Continental Railway Solutions is currently providing refurbished Class 47s to an operator in Hungary. In 2016 No. 47375, renumbered to 92 70 0047 375-5, was shipped to Budapest and is now in operation. This will be followed by No. 47488, which is allocated the international number 92 70 0047 488-1. The locos are being restored by Nemesis Rail at Burton-on-Trent. No. 47375 is seen being roaded to the docks for export through the streets of Burton-on-Trent. The loco has been named* Falcon *in Hungary.* **John Tuffs**

Porterbrook

Address: ✉ Ivatt House, The Point, Pinnacle Way, Pride Park, Derby, DE24 8ZS
🖰 enquiries@porterbrook.co.uk ✆ 01332 285050 ⓘ www.porterbrook.co.uk

Managing Director: Paul Francis
Owned by: ACP, AIMCo, EDF, Hastings Management

Transmart Trains

Address: ✉ Green Farm House, Falfield, Wootton-under-Edge, Gloucestershire, GL12 8DL
Managing Director: Oliver Buxton
Depots: Selhurst (SU), Stewarts Lane (SL). Part of Cambrian Transport

Class 73

‡ *At Barry Railway*
• *Not main-line certified*

			Vehicle Length: 53ft 8in (16.35m)		Power: 750V dc third rail or English Electric 6K	
			Height: 12ft 5⅛in (3.79m)		Horsepower: electric - 1,600hp (1,193kW)	
			Width: 8ft 8in (2.64m)		diesel - 600hp (447kW)	
					Electrical Equipment: English Electric	

Number	Depot	Pool	Livery	Owner	Operator
73118 ‡		-	GRY	TTS	TTS
73133 •	BM	-	GRN	TTS	SWT

■ Former 'Gatwick Express' Class 488 vehicles Nos. 72505, 72620, 72621, 72629, 72710 from sets 488206 and 488311 are also owned by Transmart Trains.

Class 20 Loco Ltd

Class 20

			Vehicle Length: 46ft 9¼in (14.26m)		Engine: English Electric 8SVT Mk2
			Height: 12ft 7⅞in (3.84m)		Horsepower: 1,000hp (745kW)
			Width: 8ft 9in (2.66m)		Electrical Equipment: English Electric

Number	Depot	Pool	Livery	Owner	Operator
20205	SK	MOLO	BLU	C2L	Spot hire
20227	SK	MOLO	LUL	C2L	Victor Railfreight

Listings provide details of locomotives and stock authorised for operation on the UK National Rail network and that can be seen operating special and charter services.
Preserved locomotives authorised for main-line operation are found in the preserved section.

Bo'ness & Kinneil Railway

Number	Type	Depot	Livery	Operator	Use
464	AO3/BCK	BT	CAL	BOK	Charter train use
1375 (99803)	AO2/TK	BT	CAL	BOK	Charter train use
3096 (99827)	AD11/FO	BT	MAR	BOK	Charter train use
3115	AD11/FO	BT	MAR	BOK	Charter train use
3150	AD11/FO	BT	MAR	BOK	Charter train use
4831 (99824)	AC21/TSO	BT	MAR	BOK	Charter train use
4832 (99823)	AC21/TSO	BT	MAR	BOK	Charter train use
4836 (99831)	AC21/TSO	BT	MAR	BOK	Charter train use
4856 (99829)	AC21/TSO	BT	MAR	BOK	Charter train use
5028 (99830)	AC21/TSO	BT	MAR	BOK	Charter train use
13229 (99826)	AA11/FK	BT	MAR	BOK	Charter train use
13230 (99828)	AA11/FK	BT	MAR	BOK	Charter train use

Flying Scotsman Railway Ltd

Number	Type	Depot	Livery	Operator	Notes/Name
316 (S) (975608)	AO11/PFK	CS	PUL	FSL	Pullman *Magpie*
321 (S)	AO11/PFK	CS	PUL	FSL	Pullman *Swift*
337 (S)	AO11/PSK	CS	PUL	FSL	Pullman Car No. 337

Great Scottish & Western Railway Co

Number	Type	Depot	Livery	Operator	Notes
313 (S) (99964)	AO11/PFK	CS	MAR	GSW	Royal Scotsman
317 (99967)	AO11/PFK	CS	MAR	GSW	Royal Scotsman
319 (99965)	AO11/PFK	CS	MAR	GSW	Royal Scotsman
324 (99961)	AO11/PFP	CS	MAR	GSW	Royal Scotsman
329 (99962)	AO11/PFP	CS	MAR	GSW	Royal Scotsman - *StateCar No. 1*
331 (99963)	AO11/PFP	CS	MAR	GSW	Royal Scotsman
1999 (99131)	AO10/SAL	CS	MAR	WCR	Royal Scotsman

Hastings Diesels Limited

The following vehicles are owned by Hastings Diesels Ltd and kept at St Leonards. Usually a six-car train is formed, which is fitted with central door locking and is main-line certified (original class numbers shown in brackets).
60000 (201), 60019 (202), 60116 (202), 60118 (202), 60501 (201), 60528 (202), 60529 (202), 69337 (422 EMU), 70262 (411 EMU).
In autumn 2014, the set **1001** was formed of **60116+60529+70262+69337+60501+60118**

Left: *Hastings Diesels Ltd, based at St Leonards depot, Hastings, has a stunning collection of preserved former Southern Region DEMU stock, now supplemented by a handful of ex-EMU intermediate vehicles. The six-car 'Hastings' set is used for charters on the main line several times each year. It is restored to 1950s SR green with full yellow warning ends. Running as set No. 1001, the train is seen at Gloucester.* **Jack Boskett**

5237		AD2Z/SO	CS	MAR	WCR	
5239	The Red Knight	AD2Z/SO	CS	MAR	WTN	
5249		AD2Z/SO	CS	MAR	WCR	
5278	Melisande	AC2A/TSO	CS	CHC	WTN	
5419		AC2A/TSO	CS	WCR	WTN	
5487		AC2C/TSO	CS	WCR	WCR	
5756 (S)		AC2E/TSO	CS	WCR	WCR	
6000		AC2F/TSO	CS	WCR	WCR	
6012		AC2F/TSO	CS	WCR	WCR	
6014 (S)		AC2F/TSO	CS	ICS	WCR	
6021		AC3F/TSO	CS	WCR	WCR	
6022		AC2F/TSO	CS	WCR	WCR	
6103		AC2F/TSO	CS	WCR	WCR	
6115 (S)		AC2F/TSO	CS	WCR	WCR	
6135 (S)		AC2F/TSO	CS	ICS	WCR	
6312 (92925)		AX51/GEN	CS	WCR	WCR	
6528 (5592)		AG2C/TSOT	CS	WCR	WCR	
6723		AN1D/RMBF	CS	WCR	WCR	
6724		AN1D/RMBF	CS	WCR	WCR	
9104 (S) (9401)		AH2Z/BSOT	CS	WCR	WCR	
9391	Pendragon	AE2Z/BSO	CS	PUL	WTN	
9392		AE2Z/BSO	CS	WCR	WCR	
9448 (S)		AE2C/BSO	CS	WCR	WCR	
9493		AE2D/BSO	CS	WCR	CWR	
13227		AA11/FK	CD	WCR	WCR	
13306 (S)		AA11/FK	CS	WCR	WCR	
13320	Anna	AA11/FO	CS	WCR	WCR	
13321 (99316)		AA11/FK/RBR	CS	WCR	WCR	
13440 (S)		AA1A/FK	CS	GRN	WCR	
17102 (99680)		AB1A/BFK	CS	MAB	WCR	
17168 (S) (99319)		AB1D/BFK	CS	WCR	WCR	
18756 (25756)		AA21/SK	SH	MAR	WCR	
18806 (99722)		AA21/SK	CS	WCR	WCR	
18893 (99712)		Kitchen	CS	WCR	WCR	
19208 (99884)	Car No. 84	AA21/SK	CS	WCR	WCR	
21256 (99304)		AB31/BCK	CS	WCR	WCR	
21266		AB31/BCK	CS	WCR	WCR	
34525 (S) (99966)		AR51/GEN	CS	WCR	WCR	
35407 (99886)		AB21/BSK	CS	MAR	WCR	LNWR livery ('Q of Scots')
45018 (99052)		AO10/SAL	CS	QOS	WCR	
45026 (S)		SAL	CS	MAR	WCR	LMS Inspection Saloon
96175		GUV	CS	MAR	WCR	Water carrier
99723 (35459)		AB21/BSK	CS	WCR	WCR	

WCR* - Owned by Scottish Highland Railway Co

Below: *West Coast Railway Co owns a large number of Mk1 and Mk2 passenger vehicles which are used by the charter market for steam and modern traction powered specials. Most are restored to lined maroon livery. Mk2 SO No. 5249 is shown.*
Antony Christie

Loco Support Coaches

Most preserved locomotives authorised for main-line operation, either steam or diesel, operate with a support coach conveying owners' representatives, engineering staff and light maintenance equipment. Support coaches can be allocated to a specific locomotive or operate with a pool of locos.

Number	Type	Depot	Livery	Support Coach for
14007 (99782) *Mercator*	AB11/BSK	NY	MAR	61264 or 60163
17015 (14015)	AB11/BFK	TM	CHC	Tyseley
17019 (14019)	AB11/BFK	CS	MAR	61994
17025 (14025)	AB11/BFK	CS	MAR	45690
17096	AB1B/BFK	SL	CHC	35028
21096 (99080)	AB31/BCK	NY	MAR	60007
21232 (99040)	AB31/BCK	SK	MAR	46201
21236 (99120)	AB31/BCK	ZG	GRN	30828
21249	AB21/BCK	SL	CCM	60163
35317	AD21/BSK	BQ	GRN	46100
35322 (99035)	AB21/BSK	CS	MAR	70000 and WCRC traction
35329	AB21/BSK	RL	GRN	Mid-Hants fleet
35449 (99241)	AB21/BSK	CS	MAR	45231
35451	AB21/BSK	MI	GRN	34046
35461 (99720)	AB21/BSK	CL	CHC	5029
35463 (99312)	AB21/BSK	CS	WCR	WCR fleet
35464	AB21/BSK	PR	MAR	Swanage Railway
35465 (99991)	AB21/BSK	BQ	CCM	Jeremy Hosking / 70000
35468 (99953)	AB21/BSK	YK	MAR	National Railway Museum, 60103
35470	AB21/BSK	TM	CHC	Vintage Trains fleet
35476 (99041)	AB21/BSK	SK	MAR	46233
35479	AB21/BSK	SH	MAR	61306
35486 (99405)	AB21/BSK	--	MAR	60009 or 61994
35508	AB1C/BSK	BQ	MAR	East Lancs fleet
35517 (17088)	ABIK/BSK	BQ	MAR	East Lancs fleet
35518 (17097)	AB11/BFK	SH	GRN	34067
80204 (35297)	NNX	TN	MAR	61994
80217 (35299)	NNX	CS	MAR	WCRC fleet
80220 (35276)	NNX	NY	MAR	62005

Below: *Main-line-certified preserved steam and diesel locomotives usually operate with a support coach, in which the loco owner's support team can travel together with a limited supply of spare parts, stored in the former luggage brake of the vehicles. Operated by the National Railway Museum, York, coach No. 99953 (35468) usually operates with steam loco No. 60103* Flying Scotsman. **Antony Christie**

Above: *Most of the preserved railways in the UK have a diesel shunting locomotive on their roster to provide power as required for shunting, works trains and even passenger services. On the Paignton and Dartmouth Railway between Paignton and Kingswear, Class 08 No. D3014* Samson *is available.* **CJM**

Diesel Units

Number	Base
Unclassified	
APT-E	NRS
LEV1	NNR
RB004	TEL
79018	MRC
79612	MRC
79900	ECC
79960	NNR
79962	KWV
79963	NNR
79964	KWV
79976	GCR
79978	COL
Class 100	
51118	MRC
56097	MRC
56301	MNR
Class 101	
50222	BIR
50256	EKR
50338	BIR
51187	CRT
51188	ECC
51189	KWV
51192	ELR
51205	CRT
51210	WEN
51226	MNR

Number	Base
51228	NNR
51247	WEN
51427	GCR
51432	SWN
51434	MNR
51498	SWN
51499	MNR
51503	MNR
51505	EAR
51511	NYM
51512	CRT
51513	EAR
51803	KWV
53160	MRC
53164	CHS
53170	ECC
53193	GCR
53203	GCR
53204	NYM
53253	MRC
53266	GCR
53321	GCR
53746	WEN
54055	CRT
54062	NNR
54365	EAR
54408	SPV
56343	EKR
56352	ELR
56358	EAR
59117	MNR
59539	NYM

Number	Base
Class 104	
50447	LAN
50454	LAN
50455	TEL
50479	TEL
50494	CVR
50517	CVR
50528	LAN
50531	TEL
50547	CVR
50556	TEL
56182	CVR
59137	CVR
59228	TEL
Class 105	
51485	ELR
56121	ELR
56456	LAN
Class 107	
51990	STR
52005	NVR
52006	AVR
52008	STR
52025	AVR
52030	STR
59791	NVR
Class 108	
50599	EAR
50619	DFR

Number	Base
50632	PBR
50929	KWV
50980	BWR
51562	ELR
51565	KWV
51566	DFR
51567	MRC
51568	KEI
51571	KES
51572	WEN
51907	LAN
51909	MSR
51914	DFR
51919	BVR
51922	ELR
51933	DFR
51941	SVR
51942	PBR
51947	BWR
51950	GWR
51973	MRC
52044	PBR
52048	BVR
52053	KEI
52054	BWR
52062	GWR
52064	SVR
53628	KEI
53645	GCR
53926	GCR
53971	KES
54223	EAR

Preserved Motive Power

54270	PBR	59740	SDR	59510	GWR	51622	GCR
54279	LDL	59761	BRC	59513	PDR	55966	MRC
54490	LAN			59514	SWI	55976	MRC
54504	SWN	**Class 116**		59515	YEO	59609	MRC
56208	SVR	51131	BAT	59516	SWN		
56224	ECC	51138	GCR	59517	PDR		
56271	MSR	51151	GCR	59520	PBR	**Class 140**	
56484	MRC	59003	PDR	59521	MRC	140001 - 55500/01	KEI
56491	KEI	59004	PDR	59522	CHS		
56492	DFR	59444	CHS	59603	CHS	**Class 141**	
56495	KLR					141103	WED
59245	APF	**Class 117**		**Class 118**		141108	COL
59250	SVR	51339	GWR	51321	BAT	141110	WED
59387	DFR	51342	EPO			141113	MRC
59389	GCR	51346	SWN				
		51347	GWI	**Class 119**		**Class 201, 202 and 203**	
Class 109		51351	PBR	51073	ECC	60116	HAD
50416	LAN	51353	MRC	51074	SWI	60118	HAD
56171	LAN	51356	SWN	51104	SWI	60501	HAD
		51359	NLR			60529	HAD
Class 110		51360	ECC	**Class 120**		60750	WPH
51813	WEN	51363	GWR	59276	GCR	201001	HAD
51842	WEN	51365	GWR				
52071	LHR	51367	STR	**Class 121**		**Class 205**	
52077	LHR	51371	TLW	55019	BRM	60117	PBR
59701	CVR	51372	TIT	55023	CPR	60822	SWI
		51375	CPR	55024	BRM	60828	PBR
Class 111		51381	MFM	55028	SWN	60154 X 1101	EKR
59575	MRC	51382	GWR	55029	RST	60669	SWI
		51384	EPO	55032	WEN	60800 X 1101	EKR
Class 114		51388	SWN	55033	COL	70549	ELR
50015	MRC	51392	SWN	54289	ECC	Set 205009	EDR
50019	MRC	51395	MRC	56287	COL	Set 1118	LAV
54057	STR	51397	PBR			Set 205025	MHR
56006	MRC	51398	MRC	**Class 122**		Set 205028	DAR
56015	MRC	51400	WEN	55000	SDR	Set 1132	DAR
		51401	GWI	55001	ELR	Set 205033	LDL
Class 115		51402	STR	55003	GWR	Set 205205	EPO
51655	(BIR)	51405	GWR	55005	BAT		
51663	WSR (frame)	51407	GWR	55006	ECC	**Class 207**	
51669	SPV	51413	TLW	55009	MNR	60127	SWI
51677	(BIR)	59486	SWN	55012	SHI	60130 X 207202	ELR
51859	WSR	59488	PDR			60138	WPH
51880	WSR	59492	SWN	**Class 126**		60142	SPV
51886	BRC	59494	PDR	51017	BKR	60145	SEL
51887	WSR	59500	WEN	51043	BKR	60149	SEL
51899	BRC	59503	PDR	59404	BKR	60616	SPV
59659	MRC	59506	WSR	79443	BKR	60904 X 207202	ELR
59664	(BIR)	59507	PDR			60916	SPV
59678	WSR	59508	GWI	**Class 127**			
59719	PDR	59509	WEN	51616	GCR	901001	CVR
				51618	LAN		

Left: *Heritage or first-generation DMMU sets are very popular with light railways to provide passenger services when steam or main-line diesel traction is not viable as well as preserving part of our railway heritage. This three-car Class 118 set formed of vehicles 51880, 59678 and 51859 is based on the West Somerset Railway and is seen at Blue Anchor.* **CJM**

Preserved Motive Power

Electric Units

Unclassified		**Class 373 (Eurostar)**		77558 (5759)	EKR	76277 (405)	DAR
28249	NRM	3308 (DM)	NRM	14573 (6307)	COV	70589 (412)	PRI
29666	MRC			16117 (6307)	COV	413	MRC
29670	MRC	**Class 405 (SUB)**		65321 (5791)	COV	417	DAR
79998	DEE	S8143S	NRM	77112 (5793)	COV	428	LUL
79999	DEE	4732	COV				
				Class 419 (MLV)		**Class 457**	
BEL		**Class 411/412 (CEP)**		68001	EKR	67300	COV
85	SOU	61742	DAR	68002	EKR		
87	KEI	61743	DAR	68003	EVR	**Class 488**	
91	RAM	61798	EVR	68004	MNR	72501	ECC
		61799	EVR	68005	EVR	72617	ECC
BIL		61804	EVR	68008	EKR		
10656 (2090)	NRS	61805	EVR	68009	EKR	**Class 489**	
12123 (2090)	NRS	70229	EVR			68500	ECC
		70257	GCR	**Class 421 (CIG)**		68506	ECC
COR		70273	DFR	62364	DFR		
10096	RYE	70284	NIR	62378	DFR	**Class 501**	
11161	EKR	70292	SMP	69339	GCR	61183	COV
11179	NRM	70296	NIR	76726	DFR	75186	COV
11201	BLU	70354	EVR	76740	DFR		
11825	RYE	70527	WRN	76747	DAR	**Class 502**	
		70531	SMP	76797	DFR	28361	TEB
DD		70539	EVR	76811	DFR	29896	TEB
13004	NIR	70576	SNI	76812	DAR		
		70607	EVR	Set 1496	DAR	**Class 503**	
Class 302		Set 1198	PBR	Set 1497	MNR	28690	COV
75033	MFM	Set 7105	EKR	Set 1498	Ireland	29298	COV
75250	MFM			Ser 1753	FIN	29720	COV
		Class 414 (HAP)					
Class 303		61275	NRM	**Class 422 (BEP)**		**Class 504**	
303023/032	BKR	61287 (4311)	COV	69304	NIR	65451	ELR
		75395	NRM	69310	DAR	77172	ELR
Class 306		75407 (4311)	COV	69318	COL		
306017	EAR			69332	DAR		
		Class 415 (EPB)		69333	LDL		
Class 307		14351 (5176)	NIR	69337	HAD		
75023	ERM	14352 (5176)	NIR				
		15345	COV	**Class 423 (VEP)**			
Class 308		15396 (5176)	NIR	(42)3417	SHL		
75881	ERM			76398 (3905)	DAR		
		Class 416 (EPB)		76875	NRM		
Class 309		65302	FIN				
309616	COV	65304	FIN	**Class 438 (TC)**			
309624	COV	65373 (5759)	EKR	76275 (404)	PRI		

Right: *Although unable to operate in their intended form of traction, a sizeable number of electric multiple units of both ac and dc power types are preserved. Many are cosmetically restored. Class 423 4-VEP No. 3905 showing faded Connex-livery is stored un-preserved on the Dartmoor Railway at Meldon.* **Antony Christie**

Preserved Motive Power

Over the years a number of former BR locomotives have, after withdrawal from normal duties, been taken up for use by industrial operators. The list below represents those that are understood to be still in existence in late 2016. Some locos operated at preservation sites are deemed to be 'industrial' but these are grouped in the preserved section.

Class 08/09

08220	Traditional Traction, working at EMD Longport
08375	Hanson Cement, Ketton
08411	Rye Farm, Sutton Coldfield
08441	Virgin East Coast, Bounds Green
08445	Daventry International Railfreight Terminal (DIRFT) – at LH Group, Burton
08447	John G. Russell Transit, Hillington, Glasgow
08460	Railway Support Services, at Marcroft
08484	Rye Farm, Wishaw
08502	Garston Car Terminal, Liverpool
08503	Barry Island Railway
08535	Corus, Shotton Works
08580	Colne Valley Railway
08593	Rye Farm, Wishaw
08598	Chasewater Light Railway
08600	LH Group Services, Barton-under-Needwood
08613	Hanson Traction, Washwood Heath
08622 (H028) (7)	Weardale Railway
08631	LNWR Heritage, Crewe
08643	Aggregate Industries, Whatley
08648	P D Ports, Teesport No. 20
08652	Hanson Aggregates, Whatley
08670	Virgin East Coast, Bounds Green
08683	RSS Sutton Coldfield, Hire to Bombardier Derby
08699	Weardale Railway
08709	Traditional Traction, Colne Valley Railway
08728	St Modwen Storage, Long Marston
08731	Aggregate Industries, Merehead
08738	Colne Valley Railway
08743 *Bryan Turner*	LH Group Services, Barton-under-Needwood
08774 *Arthur Vernon Dawson*	AV Dawson, Middlesbrough
08787	Hanson Aggregates, Machen
08788	Tata Steel, Shotton
08807	AV Dawson, Middlesbrough
08809	Corus, Shotton (at Washwood Heath 12/10)
08818 *Molly*	Faber Prest Ports, Flixborough Wharf
08823 (D3991)	Daventry International Railfreight Terminal (DIRFT)
08846	RSS, Wishaw, Sutton Coldfield
08847	Norwich Crown Point
08865	Rye Farm, Wishaw
08870 (H024)	Weardale Railway
08872	European Metal Reprocessing, Attercliffe
08873	LH Group Services, at Freightliner, Southampton
08903 *John W. Antill*	SembCorp Utilities Teesside, Wilton
08912	AV Dawson, Middlesbrough
08913	LH Group Services, Barton-under-Needwood
08915	Stephenson Railway Museum
08933	Aggregate Industries, Merehead
08936	Weardale Railway
08939	Colne Valley Railway
08947	Aggregate Industries, Whatley Quarry
09022	Boston Docks Co
09023	European Metal Reprocessing, Attercliffe

Class 11

12088	Butterwell

Class 14

D9529 (14029)	Aggregate Industries, Bardon Quarry

Right: *A fleet of 23 un-powered trailer cars is on the MER roster; not all are in service and several are under long-term restoration. Car No. 46 is illustrated, a cross-bench saloon built in 1899 by G F Milnes. The vehicle is seen in the siding at Laxey.* **CJM**

Locomotive

Number/Name	Type	Builder	Year
LM344 *Pig*	60SL 4-wheel	Simplex	1980

Works No. 60SL751, ex-Bord na Mona Peat Railway No. LM344. Currently working on Isle of Man Steam Railway at Santon

Right: *The Manx Electric Railway and the Isle of Man Steam Railway have the use on one industrial four-wheel Simplex loco, which can be found on either railway, being roaded between the two systems as needed. In summer 2016 the loco, known as* Pig, *is seen stabled with engineering wagons at Santon on the Isle of Man Steam Railway system.* **CJM**

Freight and Service Vehicles

Number	Type	Builder	Year
1	Tower wagon	G F Milnes	1894
3	Van	G F Milnes	1894
4	Travelling Post Office van	G F Milnes	1894
8	Open wagon	G F Milnes	1897
10	Open wagon	G F Milnes	1897
11	Van 6-ton	G F Milnes	1898
12	Van 6-ton	G F Milnes	1899
13	Van 5-ton	G F Milnes	1903
14	Van 5-ton	G F Milnes	1904
16	Mail van	MER	1908
21	Flat wagon	MER	1926
26	Freight trailer	G F Milnes	1918*
45	Flat wagon	G F Milnes	1899§
52	Flat wagon with work lift	G F Milnes	1893±
RF308	Tipper wagon	Hudson	1993■
13/24-4	Tipper wagon	W G Allan	1997
13/24-5	Tipper wagon	W G Allan	1997
13/24-6	Tipper wagon	W G Allan	1997
7442/2	Trailer	Wickham	2014

* Rebuilt from frame of power car 10
§ Rebuilt from trailer passenger car 45 in 2004
± Rebuilt from passenger trailer 52 in 1947, lift fitted 2008
■ Former Channel Tunnel vehicle

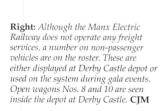

Right: *Although the Manx Electric Railway does not operate any freight services, a number on non-passenger vehicles are on the roster. These are either displayed at Derby Castle depot or used on the system during gala events. Open wagons Nos. 8 and 10 are seen inside the depot at Derby Castle.* **CJM**

Snaefell Mountain Railway

The Snaefell Mountain Railway is a 3ft 6in (1067mm)-gauge twin-track line which operates from Laxey to Snaefell Summit, a distance of 5 miles (8km). It is energised at 550V dc using the overhead power collection system. The line climbs the Snaefell Mountain and reaches 2,034ft (620m) above sea level. The depot is located at Laxey, where there is a passenger interchange with the Manx Electric Railway. Trains operate only between April and September.

Power Cars

Number	Type	Builder	Year
1	Vestibuled saloon	G F Milnes	1895
2	Vestibuled saloon	G F Milnes	1895
4	Vestibuled saloon	G F Milnes	1895
5	Vestibuled saloon	H D Kinnin	1971
6	Vestibuled saloon	G F Milnes	1895

Above: *Sadly during 2016 one of these historic vehicles was destroyed in a run-away accident and now only five vehicles remain. Displaying Snaefell Mountain Railway wood and red livery, car No. 5, a 1971-rebuild, is seen at Bungalow.* **CJM**

Left: *1895-built Vestibule saloon No. 1 is currently painted in Snaefell Mountain Tramway blue and white livery and in July 2016 is seen departing from Bungalow heading for Snaefell Summit.* **CJM**

Freight and Service Vehicles

Number	Type	Builder	Year
-	Flat wagon	MER	1981
-	Flat wagon	P Keefe	?
-	Flat / tipper	Alena	1940
-	Tower wagon	MER	1998
4	Wickham (11730)	Wickham	1991

Douglas Horse Tramway

One of the only remaining commercial horse-drawn tramways in the world, the Douglas Horse Tramway operates during the summer months between Douglas Sea Terminal and Derby Castle. The 1.6-mile (2.6km) 3ft (914mm)-gauge line is twin track and operates between 09.00 and 18.00. The horses are stabled near to Derby Castle and the welfare of the animals is uppermost in the operation, with each horse working only two or three return trips before returning to 'depot'.

Horses (2016-season)

Ian	Steve	Robert	Robin	Torrin
Mark	Philip	Una	Andrew	Teddy
Douglas	Charles	Fletcher	Kevin	
Keith	Amby	Alec	William	
Rocky	John	Bobby	Harry	

■ Most of the above horses are scheduled to continue service in the 2017 season

Right: *Douglas Horse Tramway saloon No. 36 arrives at Derby Castle powered by* Steve. *All the tram cars are double-ended with the horse 'running round' at either end of the journey. In the background of the picture is the tramway vehicle depot.* **CJM**

Passenger Trailer Cars

Number	Type	Builder	Year
1	Single-ended saloon	Milnes Voss	1913
11	Toastrack saloon	Starbuck	1886
12	Toastrack saloon	G F Milnes	1888
14	Double-deck car	Metro C&W	1883
18	Double-deck car	Metro C&W	1883
21	Toastrack saloon	G F Milnes	1890
22	Toastrack saloon	G F Milnes	1890
27	Single-deck saloon	G F Milnes	1892
28	Single-deck saloon	G F Milnes	1892
29	Single-deck saloon	G F Milnes	1892
32	Toastrack saloon	G F Milnes	1896
33	Toastrack saloon	G F Milnes	1896
34	Toastrack saloon	G F Milnes	1896
35	Toastrack saloon	G F Milnes	1896
36	Toastrack saloon	G F Milnes	1896
37	Toastrack saloon	G F Milnes	1896
38	Toastrack saloon	G F Milnes	1902
39	Toastrack saloon	G F Milnes	1902
40	Toastrack saloon	G F Milnes	1902
42	Toastrack saloon	G F Milnes	1905
43	Toastrack saloon	United Elec	1907
44	Toastrack saloon	United Elec	1907*
45	Toastrack saloon	Milnes Voss	1908
47	Toastrack saloon	Milnes Voss	1911
49	Saloon/Toastrack	Vulcan Motor	1935

* Royal saloon

Right: *The Horse Tramway has a fleet of some 25 vehicles, but not all are available for service, with many under restoration. The vehicles were built between 1883 and 1935. Illustrated is No. 45, built in 1908 by Milnes Voss as a standard Toastrack saloon.* **CJM**

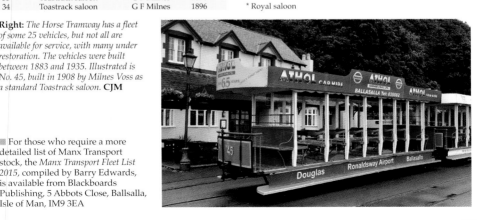

■ For those who require a more detailed list of Manx Transport stock, the *Manx Transport Fleet List 2015*, compiled by Barry Edwards, is available from Blackboards Publishing, 5 Abbots Close, Ballsalla, Isle of Man, IM9 3EA

Isle of Man Railways

Isle of Man Steam Railway

The Isle of Man Steam Railway is a 3ft (914mm)-gauge line operating from Douglas to Port Erin, a distance of 15.3 miles (24.6km). The main depot and workshop is located at Douglas and much of the railway is single line with passing places at most stations. The railway usually opertates four round trips each day. The line is mainly operated by steam traction, but a diesel is available and sometimes operates the line's popular dining train.

Locomotives

Number	Name	Builder	Wheel Arrangement	Year built	Notes
1	Sutherland	Beyer Peacock	2-4-0T	1873	
4	Loch	Beyer Peacock	2-4-0T	1874	
5	Mona	Beyer Peacock	2-4-0T	1874	
6	Peveril	Beyer Peacock	2-4-0T	1875	In Museum at Port Erin
8	Fenella	Beyer Peacock	2-4-0T	1894	
9	Douglas	Beyer Peacock	2-4-0T	1896	
10	G. H. Wood	Beyer Peacock	2-4-0T	1905	
11	Maitland	Beyer Peacock	2-4-0T	1905	
12	Hutchinson	Beyer Peacock	2-4-0T	1908	
13	Kissack	Beyer Peacock	2-4-0T	1910	
14	Thornhill	Beyer Peacock	2-4-0T	1880	
15	Caledonia	Dubs & Co	0-6-0T	1885	
16	Mannin	Beyer Peacock	2-4-0T	1926	In Museum at Port Erin
17(S)	Viking	Schoema	0-4-0	1958	Diesel-hydraulic - out of use
18	Ailsa	Hunslet	0-4-0	1994	Diesel pilot loco
21(S)	-	Motive Power	Bo-Bo	2013	MP550-B1 diesel-electric - out of use

Left: *One of the highlights for any visitor to the Isle of Man is a visit to the steam railway to watch operations at Douglas station. Shunting from the depot and onto the train, loco No. 13 Kissack is seen adjacent to Douglas station.* **CJM**

Right: *Built for use on Channel Tunnel construction trains, the Isle of Man steam railway operates Hunslet 0-4-0 diesel pilot loco No. 18 Ailsa. Usually kept at Douglas depot, the loco is used for depot pilot operations and moving passenger stock from the depot to the station. Currently the loco is in white livery.* **CJM**

Railcars

Number	Name	Builder	Year built	Notes
19	-	Walker	1949	Ex-County Donegal Railway
20	-	Walker	1950	Ex-County Donegal Railway

Passenger Coaches

Number	Builder	Style	Year built
C1	Brown Marshalls	4-wheel	1873
F9	Brown Marshalls	Bogie	1881
F10	Brown Marshalls	Bogie	1881
F11	Brown Marshalls	Bogie	1881
F15	Brown Marshalls	Bogie	1894
F18	Brown Marshalls	Bogie	1894
F21	Metropolitan C&W	Bogie	1896
F25	Metropolitan C&W	Bogie	1896
F26	Metropolitan C&W	Bogie	1896
F27	Metropolitan C&W	Bogie	1897 *
F28	Metropolitan C&W	Bogie	1897 *
F29	Metropolitan C&W	Bogie	1905
F30	Metropolitan C&W	Bogie	1905
F31	Metropolitan C&W	Bogie	1905
F32	Metropolitan C&W	Bogie	1905
F35	Metropolitan C&W	Bogie	1905
F36	Metropolitan C&W	Bogie	1905
F39	Bristol & South Wales	Bogie	1887
F43	Metropolitan C&W	Bogie	1908
F45	Metropolitan C&W	Bogie	1913
F46	Metropolitan C&W	Bogie	1913
F47	Metropolitan C&W	Bogie	1923
F48	Metropolitan C&W	Bogie	1923
F49	Metropolitan C&W	Bogie	1926
F54	Metropolitan C&W	Bogie	1923
F63	Metropolitan C&W	Bogie	1920
F66	Metropolitan C&W	Bogie	1920
F67	Metropolitan C&W	Bogie	1920
F74	Metropolitan C&W	Bogie	1921

* Luggage/Kitchen

Right: *Usually two or three passenger rakes of stock are formed up to operate the daily timetable. Stock is mainly kept at Douglas, but a carriage shed is also located at Port Erin where the train starting from that end of the line is kept overnight. Car F54, a composite brake coach, is seen from its first class seating end. Trains on the Isle of Man Railway today operate as all one class.* **CJM**

Freight & Service Vehicles

Number	Type	Builder	Year
G1	Van 6-ton	Metropolitan C&W	1873
W2	Well	IOMR	1998
WW111	Well	IOMR	2014
2	Crane 8-ton	Richard Gibbins	1893
Gr12	Van 6-ton	Swansea Wagon	1879
G19	Van 6-ton	IOMR	1921
F23	Flat	Metropolitan C&W	1896
F33	Flat	Metropolitan C&W	1905-25
F40	Flat	Metropolitan C&W	1905-25
F41	Flat	Metropolitan C&W	1905-25
F44	Flat	Metropolitan C&W	1905-25
F50	Flat	Metropolitan C&W	1911-25
F57	Flat	Metropolitan C&W	1911-25
F71	Flat	Metropolitan C&W	1911-25
F65	Hopper	Metropolitan C&W	1910 *
F70	Hopper	Metropolitan C&W	1922 *
F73	Flat	Metropolitan C&W	1920
M69	2-plank wagon	Metropolitan C&W	1926
M78	2-plank wagon	Metropolitan C&W	1926
F430	Flat	Hudson	1980?
RF274	Flat	Hudson	1980?

* Coach chassis

Right: *While the Isle of Man Steam Railway does not operate any freight trains these days, a number of freight vehicles are on the active roster. These are either used for demonstration purposes or for engineering trains, moving mechanical plant, supplies or ballast to worksites which are often otherwise difficult to reach. Hopper car F70 is seen at Douglas. This former passenger car chassis has its ballast hoppers supporting water tanks.* **CJM**

Northern Ireland Railways (NIR)

Class 3000

Three-car suburban sets for use in the Belfast area. Built by CAF, with seating for 200 standard class passengers. Each vehicle powered by one MAN D2876 LUH03 of 453hp (338kW). Max speed 90mph (145km/h). Introduced in 2004-05.

3001	3009	3017
3002	3010	3018
3003	3011	3019
3004	3012	3020
3005	3013	3021
3006	3014	3022
3007	3015	3023
3008	3016	

Sets 3001-3006 are fitted with CAWS and Irish Rail safety equipment to allow cross-border operation if needed.

These sets do not operate in multiple with 40xx sets in passenger traffic.

Left: *CAF-built Northern Ireland Class 3000 set No. 3011 is seen at Coleraine with a service to Portrush.* **CJM**

Class 4000

Three-car suburban sets for use in the Belfast area. Built by CAF, with seating for 212 standard class passengers. Each vehicle powered by one MTU 6H1800 R84 of 520hp (390kW). Max speed 90mph (145km/h). Introduced in 2010-12.

4001	4009	4017
4002	4010	4018
4003	4011	4019
4004	4012	4020
4005	4013	
4006	4014	
4007	4015	
4008	4016	

These sets do not operate in multiple with 30xx sets in passenger traffic.

Left: *Introduced in 2010-2012, the 20 members of Class 4000, also built by CAF, have a slightly different front end design. Set No. 4016 is seen at Belfast Great Victoria Street.* **CJM**

Class 111

These three locomotives are the same as the Irish Rail Class 071s and were built by General Motors in the late 1970s. The 57ft (17.37m)-long double-cab design is mounted on a Co-Co wheel configuration and carries an EMD 12-645-E3C prime mover. They have a top speed of 90mph (145km/h). Today the NIR fleet operates in departmental service.

8111	*Great Northern*	8112	*Northern Counties*	8113	*Belfast & County Down*

Class 201

Two locomotives of the 34-strong Class 201 fleet are owned by NIR for use on the Belfast-Dublin 'Enterprise' services. Built by General Motors EMD in Canada in 1994-95, these 3200hp (2400kW) locos are classified as JT42HCW, and have a top speed of 102mph (164km/h). They are fitted with retractable buffers, auto couplers, event recorders and NIR cab controls.

| 8208 | *River Lagan* | 8209 | *(River Foyle)* |

Service Stock

Five former Class 80 DMU vehicles and one Class 450 DMU set are retained by NIR for autumn sandite and rail cleaning, and are usually to be found at Yorkgate depot, Belfast. These vehicles are likely to be replaced by on-track plant in the near future.

Class 80

| 8069 (DMBSO) | 8097 (DMBSO) | 8752 (DTSO) |
| 8094 (DMBSO) | 8749 (DTSO) | |

Class 450

Set 5 8455+8795+8785 *Galgorm Castle*
Stored at Ballymena

Irish Railways (IR)

Class 071

A fleet of 18 Irish Rail Class 071s was built by General Motors, Canada, in the late 1970s. The 57ft (17.37m)-long double-cab design is mounted on a Co-Co wheel configuration and have a EMD 12-645-E3C prime mover. They have a top speed of 90mph (145km/h). These locos are currently going through an overhaul project.

071	078	083
072	079	084
073	080	085
074	081	086
075	082 *Cumann Na nInnealtoiri /*	087
076	*The Institution Of*	088
077	*Engineers Of Ireland*	

Right: *The 18 members of Class 071 are all still in service sporting a variety of different liveries. The locos can be found throughout the IR network. No. 087, complete with its international number 92 60 0117087-3, is seen outside Dublin Connolly depot.* **CJM**

Class 201

IR has a fleet of 32 Class 201 main-line diesel-electric locos. Built by General Motors EMD in Canada in 1994-95, these 3200hp (2400kW) locos are classified as JT42HCW and have a top speed of 102mph (164km/h). Several different variants exist within the current fleet. Locos Nos. 201-205/210-214 have fixed buffers and use shackle couplings. Nos. 215-226/229/232/234 have push-pull control, retractable buffers, electronic fuel systems and both knuckle and shackle couplings. Nos. 206-209/228/230/231/233 are similar to the 215 batch but have event recorders and cab equipment to allow operation on the NIR network.
* Loco No. 216 dedicated to Belmond Pullman Train and painted in Belmond blue livery.

201(S)	*Abhainn na Sionnainne*	*River Shannon*	214(S)	*Abhainn na Broshai*	*River Brosna*
202(S)	*Abhainn na Laoi*	*River Lee*	215	*An Abhainn Mhor*	*River Avonmore*
203(S)	*Abhainn na Coiribe*	*River Corrib*	216*	*Abhainn na Dothra*	*River Dodder*
204(S)	*Abhainn na Bearu*	*River Barrow*	217	*Abhainn na Fleisce*	*River Flesk*
205(S)	*Abhainn na Feoire*	*River Nore*	218	*Abhainn na Garbhoige*	*River Garavogue*
206	*(Abhainn na Life)*	*River Liffey*	219	*(Abhainn na Tulchann)*	*River Tolka*
207	*Abhainn na Bóinne*	*River Boyne*	220	*An Abhainn Dhubh*	*River Blackwater*
210(S)	*Abhainn na hEirne*	*River Erne*	221	*Abhainn na Feilge*	*River Fealge*
211(S)	*Abhainn na Suca*	*River Suck*	222	*(Abhainn na Dargaile)*	*River Dargle*
212(S)	*Abhainn na Slaine*	*River Slaney*	223	*Abhainn na hAinnire*	*River Anner*
213(S)	*Abhainn na Muaidhe*	*River Moy*	224	*Abhainn na Féile*	*(River Feale)*

Irish Railways

225(S)	Abhainn na Daoile	River Deel	230	Abhainn na Bandan	(River Bandon)
226	Abhainn na Siuire	(River Suir)	231	Abhainn na Maighe	(River Maigue)
227	(Abhainn na Leamhna)	River Laune	232	(Abhainn na Chaomaraigh)	River Cummeragh
228	An Abhainn Bhui	(River Owenboy)	233	Abhainn na Chlair	River Clare
229	Abhainn na Mainge	River Maine	234	(Abhainn na hEatharlai)	River Aherlow

Left: *The 1994-1995-built General Motors Class 201 Co-Co diesel-electric locos are the mainstay of loco operations, powering the 'Enterprise' service between Belfast and Dublin, the InterCity service between Dublin and Cork and the luxury 'Grand Hibernian' train. Painted in InterCity colours No. 221 is seen at Mallow on the rear of the 12.20 Cork to Dublin on 20 April 2016.* **CJM**

Class 2600

A fleet of 17 Class 2601 vehicles was introduced in 1993-94, built by Tokyu Car in Japan. Each two-car set seats 130 standard class passengers. The top speed is 70mph (110km/h). Today the remaining 16 vehicles operate in eight pairs allocated to Cork, usually working on the Mallow, Midleton and Cobh routes, occasionally being seen in the Limerick area.

| 2601 + 2602 | 2605 + 2616 | 2607 + 2608 | 2611 + 2612 |
| 2603 + 2604 | 2606 + 2615 | 2610 + 2613 | 2614 + 2617 |

Left: *Built by Tokyu Car, a two-car Class 2600 set, with car No. 2615 nearest the camera, is seen at Cork.* **CJM**

Class 2800

A fleet of 10 Class 2801 vehicles was introduced in 2000, built by Tokyu Car in Japan. Each two-car set seats 85 standard class passengers. The top speed is 75mph (120km/h). Today the sets are allocated to Limerick, working local services.

| 2801 + 2802 | 2805 + 2806 | 2809 + 2810 | 2813 + 2814 | 2817 + 2818 |
| 2803 + 2804 | 2807 + 2808 | 2811 + 2812 | 2815 + 2816 | 2819 + 2820 |

Left: *Class 2800 vehicles Nos. 2817 and 2818 stand under the overall roof at Galway. These vehicles were originally built with a front end gangway but these have now been removed.* **CJM**

Dublin 'Luas' Trams

Trams returned to the streets of Dublin in 2004, and currently two lines operate with three batches of Alstom Citadis trams. Overhead power is provided at 750V dc. The maximum loading capacity for each tram is 358 passengers.

Alstom Citadis TGA301 five-section vehicles introduced 2002-03

3001	3005	3009	3013	3017	3021	3025
3002	3006	3010	3014	3018	3022	3026
3003	3007	3011	3015	3019	3023	
3004	3008	3012	3016	3020	3024	

Right: *An expanding tram network operates through and around the city of Dublin. Three breeds of Alstom Citadis trams are in operation. The 26 members of the 30xx series, which are five-section sets, operate on the Red line, alongside the 40xx units. Set No. 3015 is seen on a street-running section in the city centre.* **CJM**

Alstom Citadis TGA401 five-section vehicles introduced 2002-03

4001	4003	4005	4007	4009	4011	4013
4002	4004	4006	4008	4010	4012	4014

Right: *Originally used on the Green Line, the 14 40xx series five-section trams now share duties with the 30xx series on the Red Line. No. 4005 is illustrated on a street-running section.* **CJM**

Alstom Citadis TGA402 seven-section vehicles introduced 2008-2010

5001	5005	5009	5013	5017	5021	5025
5002	5006	5010	5014	5018	5022	5026
5003	5007	5011	5015	5019	5023	
5004	5008	5012	5016	5020	5024	

Right: *The 26 seven-section trams numbered in the 50xx series are used on the Green Line. Surprisingly these seven-section trams seat less than the five-section sets with just 70 seats, but with huge amounts of room for standing passengers. Set No. 5022 is seen at Sandyford, the location of the Green Line depot.* **CJM**

Coupling Codes & Couplings

With the introduction of modern traction from the 1950s a number of different methods of multiple operation were introduced, covering the different control principles of locomotives, for example those using electro-pneumatic or electro-magnetic systems.

Six main systems are in operation today:

Blue Star ★ using the electro-pneumatic system and fitted to Classes 20, 25, 31, 33, 37, 40 and 73.

Green Spot ● a unique system installed on some Class 47s operated by the freight sector.

Orange Square ■ an English Electric system used only on the Class 50s.

Red Diamond ◆ a 1970s system developed for the modern freight locos of Classes 56 and 58.

In addition to the above coded systems, the American-developed main-line locos of Classes 59, 66, 67 and 70 use the US standard AAR (Association of American Railroads) system. Direct Rail Services (DRS) has also developed a unique system, which is installed on some of the company's Class 20, 37, 47 and 57 locos.

A number of locomotives have either been built with or modified to incorporate Time Division Multiplex (TDM) remote operation equipment, which uses coach lighting-type Railway Clearing House (RCH) nose-end jumper cables.

Some of the surviving first generation DMMU sets carry a **Blue Square** ■ multiple operation system.

Details of the main coupling systems in operation in the UK are included in the accompanying illustrations.

Standard Coupling

Above: *Class 59 and 66 front-end layout (non-DB-S operated). 1-Coupling hook, 2-Coupling shackle, 3-Air brake pipe (red), 4-Main reservoir pipe (yellow), 5-Buffer, 6-Association of American Railroads (AAR) jumper socket. No. 66726 is illustrated.* **CJM**

Standard Coupling

Above: *Standard coupling arrangement to be found on many classes of UK loco. 1-Electric Train Supply (ETS) jumper socket, 2-Main reservoir air pipe (yellow), 3-Vacuum brake pipe, 4-Coupling hook and shackle, 5-Air brake pipe (red), 6-Electric Train Supply (ETS) jumper cable. No. 47580 is illustrated.* **CJM**

Drophead Buckeye with TDM Coupling

Above: *The unique front-end layout of the Royal Mail Class 325. 1-Brake pipe (red), 2-Main reservoir pipe (yellow), 3-Electric Train Supply (ETS) socket, 4-Time Division Multiplex (TDM) jumper socket, 5-Drophead buckeye coupling, 6-Electric Train Supply (ETS) cable.* **CJM**

Couplings

Drophead Dellner Coupling

Above: *Following the introduction of Virgin Trains 'Voyager' and 'Pendolino' stock, a fleet of 16 Class 57/3s was introduced with drophead Dellner couplers and cabling to provide 'hotel power'. The coupling is seen in this illustration in the raised position. 1-Electric Train Supply (ETS) jumper socket, 2-Main reservoir pipe (yellow), 3-Air brake pipe (red), 4-Coupling hook, 5-Dellner coupling face, 6-Electric Train Supply (ETS) jumper cable.* **CJM**

BSI Coupling

Above: *With the birth of modern multiple unit trains came the Bergische Stahl Industrie (BSI) automatic coupling, first seen in the UK on the Tyne & Wear Metro vehicles in 1978. The modern generation of UK DMUs now concentrates on the Compact BSI coupler with a CK2 coupling interface. The couplers are engaged by the compression of the two coupling faces, which completes a physical connection and also opens a watertight cover to an electrical connection box. The full train air connection is made during the coupling compression process. The coupling is completed by the driver pressing a 'couple' button in the driving cab. 1-Emergency air connection, 2-Coupling face, 3-Electric connection (behind plate), 4-Air connection. The coupling shown is on a Class 166.* **CJM**

Tightlock with Drum Connection

Above: *The Tightlock coupler is a derivative of the Association of American Railroads (AAR) Type H coupler, later under the control of the American Public Transportation Association (APTA). A modified Type H coupler was introduced in the UK from the early 1970s and has become a standard fitting on many of the later BR and several post-privatisation EMUs. The UK Tightlock design can be supplied with or without an electrical connection box and with or without a pneumatic connection. This view shows a fully automated version as fitted to the 'Networker' fleet. Attachment is achieved by driving the two vehicles together, which physically connects them, while a 'roll-cover' box opens to connect electric and pneumatic services. 1-Emergency air connector, 2-Manual release handle, 3-Semi-rotary electric/pneumatic cover, 4-Physical coupler.* **CJM**

Tightlock with Nose End Connections

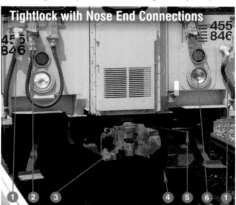

Above: *The BR Southern Region-designed Class 455 and 456 units have a semi-automatic Tightlock used for physical connections, while air and electrical connections are made by waist-height flexible pipes. 1-Main reservoir pipe (yellow), 2-Control jumper, 3-Tightlock coupler, 4-Couple/Uncouple drum switch, 5-Manual release handle, 6-Control jumper receptacle.* **CJM**

Dellner Coupling with Drum Connector

Above: *Dellner couplers have become the standard in the UK and much of Europe; these are fully automatic and come in various forms. 1-Emergency air supply, 2-Dellner coupling plate, 3-Pneumatic connection, 4-Roll-cover to electrical connections, 5-Air supply. Coupling of a Class 360 is illustrated.* **CJM**

Couplings

Dellner Coupling

Above: *A large number of different designs of Dellner couplers exist on UK rolling stock. Some feature full automatic operation including pneumatic and electrical connections, while others only provide physical coupling. This view shows a pair of 'Voyager' units coupled together with Dellner couplers. The electrical connection box is above the physical coupler. After trains are 'pushed' together the driver operates a 'couple' button in the cab to complete the attachment. Uncoupling is achieved by the driver pressing an 'uncouple' button and driving the trains apart.* **CJM**

Dellner Coupling

Left: *The Virgin Trains 'Pendolino' stock uses Dellner couplers with a rotary covered electrical connector plate above. These couplers are supplemented by electric train supply connections on either side to provide 'hotel power' to Class 390 sets from attached Class 57 locos. 1-Electric Train Supply (ETS) socket, 2-Emergency air connector, 3-Electrical connector plate under semi-rotary cover, 4-Dellner physical coupler, 5-Pneumatic connections. In normal use the Dellner coupler on 'Pendolino' stock is covered by a front fairing.* **CJM**

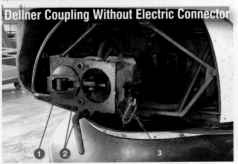

Dellner Coupling Without Electric Connector

Above: *Under the front-end fairing of the Eurostar Class 373 stock a standard Scharfenberg coupler is located for assistance purposes and shunting. No electrical provision is made and the couplers are seldom used. 1-Scharfenberg coupling face, 2-Pneumatic connections, 3-Manual uncoupling handle.* **CJM**

Dellner Coupling With Electric Connector

Above: *In as-installed condition and having never been coupled to another set, a Class 380 Scharfenberg coupler is viewed, showing the auto opening electrical connection box above. 1-Electrical connection box, 2-Coupling face plate, 3-Pneumatic connection.* **CJM**

Couplings

Right: *If High Speed Trains are required to be coupled to conventional hook couplings an adaptor coupling is carried on the HST for this purpose. It has to be first attached to the front of the HST by opening the front panel and attaching the aluminium bar to a coupling lug. The other end is then at the right level and length to attach to a standard loco hook coupling without the loco's buffers touching the HST's bodywork. Standard air connection is provided. Locos fitted with swing-head or combination couplers cannot be used to assist HST stock. A Class 59/1 is seen attached to HST power car No. 43150 in this view at Westbury.* **Greg Welsh**

Emergency HST Bar Coupling

Right: *With the introduction of combination couplings on Class 66s and 67s and the deployment of Class 66s as East Coast 'Thunderbirds' came the need to develop a revised HST bar coupling, which could attach to the extended jaw of the auto coupler. To use this coupling method, a pair of short extension air hoses are required to bridge the increased space between the HST and Class 67 hoses. The Class 67 to HST coupling using the auto coupler and extension hoses is shown with the attachment of No. 67030 and Virgin East Coast power car No. 43315.* **Antony Christie**

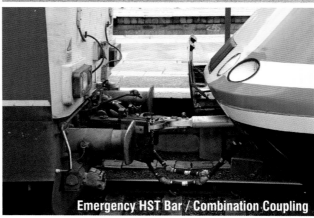

Emergency HST Bar / Combination Coupling

Right Below: *All DBS Class 66s (except Nos. 66001/002) and all Class 67s are fitted with swing-head combination couplers allowing attachment to other like-fitted locos or rolling stock using a knuckle coupling. Two Class 66s are seen here attached using the swing-head coupler. Note that the buffers do not touch and that all traction and braking forces are transmitted through the coupler. Standard buffer-beam air connections are provided on one main reservoir and one brake pipe. The auto coupler can be disconnected by using the white uncoupling handle seen on the left.* **Antony Christie**

DBS Combination Coupler

Couplings

Transport for London
London Underground

Address: ✉ Floor 11, Windsor House, 50 Victoria Street, London, SW1H 0TL
✆ pressoffice@tfl.gov.uk
✆ 0845 604 4141
ⓘ www.tfl.gov.uk

Managing Director: Peter Austin

Operations: The London Underground system, now operated by Transport for London (TfL), operates services on 10 lines in and around the capital and uses a mix of surface and tunnel stock.

Bakerloo Line
Tube Line. Operates services between Elephant & Castle and Harrow & Wealdstone.
Rolling Stock: 1972 Mk2, livery - red, white and blue, allocated to Stonebridge Park. Scheduled for replacement in 2018-19.

Central Line
Tube Line. Operates services between West Ruislip/Ealing and Epping.
Rolling Stock: 1992, livery - red, white and blue, allocated to Hainault.

Circle Line
Sub-Surface Line. Operates circle network in Central London and the branch from Edgware Road to Hammersmith.
Rolling Stock: 'S' stock, introduced 2013-14, livery - red, white and blue, allocated to Hammersmith.

District Line
Sub-Surface Line. Operates services between Wimbledon, Richmond, Ealing, Edgware Road, Kensington Olympia and Upminster.
Rolling Stock: 'S' stock, livery - red, white and blue, allocated to Ealing Common and Upminster.

Jubilee Line
Tube Line. Operates services between Stanmore and Stratford.
Rolling Stock: 1996, livery - red, white and blue, allocated to Wembley Park.

Metropolitan Line
Sub-Surface Line. Operates services from Amersham, Chesham, Watford and Uxbridge to Aldgate.
Rolling Stock: 'S' stock, livery - red, white and blue, allocated to Wembley Park.

Northern Line
Tube Line. Operates services between Morden and Edgware, Mill Hill East and High Barnet.
Rolling Stock: 1995 stock, livery - red, white and blue, allocated to Morden.

Piccadilly Line
Tube Line. Operates services between Heathrow Airport/Uxbridge and Cockfosters.
Rolling Stock: 1973 stock, livery - red, white and blue, allocated to Northfields and Cockfosters.

Victoria Line
Tube Line. Operates services between Brixton and Walthamstow Central.
Rolling Stock: 2009 stock, livery - red, white and blue, allocated to Northumberland Park.

Waterloo & City Line
Tube Line. Operates services between Waterloo and Bank.
Rolling Stock: 1992 stock, livery - red, white and blue, allocated to Waterloo.

Right: *Over the last few years 191 new 'S' type London Underground train sets have entered service on the Metropolitan, Circle and Hammersmith & City lines. The fleet consists of 133 S7 and 58 S8 sets. An S7 set led by car 21307 approaches Wimbledon Park with a District Line service to Wimbledon.* **CJM**

For space reasons, we are unable in this publication to provide vehicle numbers for London Underground stock. These are available in our sister publication *London Underground Rolling Stock Guide.*

Transport for London Croydon Tramlink

Contact details as London Underground.

Bombardier *Flexity Swift* CR4000

Train Length: 98ft 9in (30.1m)	Seating: 70	
Width: 8ft 7in (2.65m)	Horsepower: 643hp (480kW)	
Power Supply: 750V dc overhead	Eleetrical Equipment: Bombardier	

2530	2533	2536	2539	2542	2545	2548	2551§	§ Stored
2531	2534	2537	2540	2543	2546	2549	2552	
2532	2535	2538	2541	2544	2547	2550	2553	

Stadler *Variobahn*

Train Length: 106ft 2½in (32.37m)	Seating: 70	
Width: 8ft 7in (2.65m)	Horsepower: 650hp (483kW)	
Power Supply: 750V dc overhead	Electrical Equipment: Stadler	

2554	2556	2558	2560	2562	2564
2555	2557	2559	2561	2563	2565

Name applied
2535	**Stephen Parascandolo** 1980-2007

Right: *One of the big success stories for Transport for London is the Croydon Tramlink, which uses a mix of Bombardier 'Flexity Swift' and Stadler 'Variobahn' vehicles. In this view at East Croydon, one of the earlier Bombardier vehicles, No. 2532, is illustrated.* **CJM**

Light Rail

Above: *In 2017, a fleet of 12 Stadler 'Variobahn' five-section trams was in operation. All Croydon trams are dual-ended. Set No. 2558 is seen at East Croydon.* **CJM**

Transport for London
Docklands Light Railway

Operated by KeolisAmey Docklands for Transport for London under contract until 2021.

Class B90 (twin)

Train Length: 94ft 5in (28.80m)
Width: 8ft 7in (2.65m)
Power Supply: 750V dc third rail

Seating: 52 + 4 tip-up
Horsepower: 375hp (280kW)
Electrical Equipment: Brush

22	25	28	31	34	37	40	43
23	26	29	32	35	38	41	44
24	27	30	33	36	39	42	

Class B92 (twin)

Train Length: 94ft 5in (28.80m)
Width: 8ft 7in (2.65m)
Power Supply: 750V dc third rail

Seating: 54 + 4 tip-up
Horsepower: 375hp (280kW)
Electrical Equipment: Brush

45	51	57	63	69	75	81	87
46	52	58	64	70	76	82	88
47	53	59	65	71	77	83	89
48	54	60	66	72	78	84	90
49	55	61	67	73	79	85	91
50	56	62	68	74	80	86	

Class B2K (twin)

Train Length: 94ft 5in (28.80m)
Width: 8ft 7in (2.65m)
Power Supply: 750V dc third rail

Seating: 52 + 4 tip-up
Horsepower: 375hp (280kW)
Electrical Equipment: Brush

01	03	05	07	09	11	13	15	92	94	96	98
02	04	06	08	10	12	14	16	93	95	97	99

Owner Codes

201	20189 Ltd (Michael Owen)
AEA	AEA Rail Technology
ALS	Alstom
ANG	Angel Trains
ATW	Arriva Trains Wales
AUT	Arriva UK Trains
BAA	British Airports Authority
BCC	Bridgend County Council
BEA	Beacon Rail
BOM	Bombardier
BOT	Bank of Tokyo (Mitsubishi)
BRO	Brodie Engineering
BTM	BTMU Capital Corporation
C20	Class 20 Locomotive Ltd
CBR	CB Rail
CCC	Cardiff County Council
COL	Colas Rail
CRW	Chiltern Railways
CWR	Cotswold Rail
DBR	DB Regio
DBS	DB-Schenker West
DBS/T	DB-Schenker/Transfesa
DRS	Direct Rail Services
ECR	Euro Cargo Rail (DBS)
ECT	ECT Main Line Rail
EMT	East Midlands Trains
ETL	Electric Traction Ltd
EU2	Eurotunnel Europorte2
EUR	Eurotunnel
EUS	Eurostar
EVL	Eversholt Leasing
FGP	First Group
FLF	Fastline Freight
FLR	Freightliner
FOS	Foster Yeoman
GBR	GB Railfreight
GTL	Grand Central Railway Ltd

HAN	Hanson Traction
HEC	Hunslet Engine Co
HBS	Halifax-Bank of Scotland
HJA	Howard Johnson Associates
HNR	Harry Needle Railroad
IRY	Ian Riley
JAR	Jarvis
KBR	Knorr Bremse Rail
KRS	Knights Rail Services
LOR	Loram UK
MAG	Macquarie Group
NRL	Network Rail
NYM	North Yorkshire Moors Railway
PTR	Porterbrook
QWR	QW Rail Leasing
RCL	Railcare Limited
RIV	Riviera Trains
RML	Royal Mail
RMS	RMS Locotech
RTR	RT Rail
S4G	Stratford Class 47 Group
SCS	Serco Caledonian Sleepers
SEC	Serco
SIE	Siemens
SNB	Société Nationale des Chemins de fer Belges
SNF	Société Nationale des Chemins de fer Français
SOU	Southern (Govia)
SWT	South West Trains (Stagecoach)
TTS	Transmart Trains
URL	UK Rail Leasing
VTN	Vintage Trains
WAB	Wabtec
WCR	West Coast Railway Co
WYP	West Yorkshire PTE

DMU and EMU Vehicle Codes

BDMSO	Battery Driving Motor Standard Open
DM	Driving Motor
DMBO	Driving Motor Brake Open
DMBS	Driving Motor Brake Standard
DMCL	Driving Motor Composite Lavatory
DMCO	Driving Motor Composite Open
DMF	Driving Motor First
DMFLO	Driving Motor First Luggage Open
DMRFO	Driving Motor Restaurant First Open
DMS	Driving Motor Standard
DMSL	Driving Motor Standard Lavatory
DMSO	Driving Motor Standard Open
DTCO	Driving Trailer Composite Open
DTPMV	Driving Trailer Parcels Mail Van
DTSO	Driving Trailer Standard Open
MBC	Motor Brake Composite
MBSO	Motor Brake Standard Open
MC	Motor Composite

MFL	Motor First Lavatory
MPMV	Motor Parcels Mail Van
MS	Motor Standard
MSL	Motor Standard Lavatory
MSLRB	Motor Standard Lavatory Restaurant Buffet
MSO	Motor Standard Open
MSRMB	Motor Standard Restaurant Micro Buffet
PTSO	Pantograph Trailer Standard Open
RB	Restaurant Buffet
TBFO	Trailer Brake First Open
TCO	Trailer Composite Open
TFO	Trailer First Open
TPMV	Trailer Parcels Mail Van
TSO	Trailer Standard Open
TSRMB	Trailer Standard Restaurant Micro Buffet
(A) - A Car	
(B) - B Car	

Data Tables

This cross number checklist indicates in which section of the *abc Rail Guide 2016* full details of rolling stock can be found.

Number Cross-Link Codes

3MP	3M Productions	FLR	Freightliner	RAF	Railfilms
AFG	Arlington Fleet Group	FSL	Flying Scotsman Railway Ltd	RCL	Railcare
ALS	Alstom	FTP	First TransPennine	RIV	Riviera Trains
ASR	Abellio ScotRail	GAR	Abellio Greater Anglia	RRS	Ridings Railtours
ATC	Arriva Train Care	GBR	GB Railfreight	RVE	Rail Vehicle Engineering
ATW	Arriva Trains Wales	GSW	Great Scottish & Western Rly	S4L	Stratford Class 47 Group
AXC	Arriva CrossCountry	GTL	Grand Central Railway	SEC	Serco Railtest
BAR	British American Railway	GWR	Great Western Railway	SET	South Eastern Trains
BOK	Bo'ness & Kinneil Railway	HAN	Hanson Traction	SCS	Serco Caledonian Sleepers
BOM	Bombardier Transportation	HEC	Heathrow Connect	SIE	Siemens
C2C	c2c Railway	HEX	Heathrow Express	SIL	Stagecoach Island Line
COL	Colas	HNR	Harry Needle Railroad Co	SNF	SNCF (French Railways)
CRW	Chiltern Railways	IND	Industrial	SRP	Scottish Railway Preservation Soc
DBC	DB Cargo	JHS	Jeremy Hosking	SUP	Support Coaches
DBR	DB Regio	LMI	London Midland	SWT	South West Trains
DRS	Direct Rail Services	LOG	London Overground	TSG	Thameslink, Southern and
ECR	Euro Cargo Rail	MER	Merseyrail		Great Northern
EMT	East Midlands Trains	MHR	Mid-Hants Railway	TTS	Transmart Trains
EPX	Europhoenix Ltd	MRL	Mendip Rail Ltd	URL	UK Rail Leasing
ETL	Electric Traction Ltd	NEM	Nemesis Rail	VEC	Virgin East Coast
EUR	Eurotunnel / Europorte 2	NOR	Northern Railways	VSO	Venice Simplon Orient Express
EUS	Eurostar UK	NRL	Network Rail Limited	VTN	Vintage Trains
EXP	Exported	NYM	North Yorkshire Moors Railway	VWC	Virgin West Coast
FHT	First Hull Trains	OLS	Off Lease	WAB	Wabtec
		PRE	Preserved	WCR	West Coast Railway
		PUL	Pullman Rail		

Locomotives – Diesel & Electric

D0226	PRE	D2139	PRE	D2767	PRE	D7076	PRE	LMS7051	PRE
		D2148	PRE	D2774	PRE			LMS7069	PRE
D4	PRE	D2178	PRE	D2854	PRE	D8000	PRE		
		D2182	PRE	D2858	PRE			E5001	PRE
12	PRE	D2184	PRE	D2860	PRE	D8233	PRE	E26020	PRE
		D2192	PRE	D2866	PRE			E27000	PRE
44	MRL	D2199	PRE	D2867	PRE	D8568	PRE	E27001	PRE
120	MRL			D2868	PRE				
		D2203	PRE			D9500	PRE	9005	EUR
D200	PRE	D2205	PRE	D2953	PRE	D9502	PRE	9007	EUR
		D2207	PRE	D2956	PRE	D9504	PRE	9011	EUR
D821	PRE	D2229	PRE			D9513	PRE	9013	EUR
D832	PRE	D2245	PRE	D3000	PRE	D9516	PRE	9015	EUR
		D2246	PRE	D3002	PRE	D9518	PRE	9018	EUR
D1010	PRE	D2271	PRE	D3014	PRE	D9520	PRE	9022	EUR
D1013	PRE	D2272	PRE	D3101	PRE	D9521	PRE	9024	EUR
D1015	PRE	D2279	PRE	D3255	PRE	D9523	PRE	9026	EUR
D1023	PRE	D2280	PRE	D3261	PRE	D9524	PRE	9029	EUR
D1041	PRE	D2284	PRE	D3452	PRE	D9525	PRE	9033	EUR
D1048	PRE	D2298	PRE	D3489	PRE	D9526	PRE	9036	EUR
D1062	PRE			D4067	PRE	D9529	PRE	9037	EUR
		D2302	PRE	D4092	PRE	D9531	PRE		
		D2310	PRE	D4095	PRE	D9537	PRE	9701	EUR
D2023	PRE	D2324	PRE			D9539	PRE	9702	EUR
D2024	PRE	D2325	PRE	D5500	PRE	D9551	PRE	9703	EUR
D2041	PRE	D2334	PRE			D9553	PRE	9704	EUR
D2046	PRE	D2337	PRE	D5705	PRE	D9555	PRE	9705	EUR
D2051	PRE	D2371	PRE					9706	EUR
D2117	PRE			D6700	PRE	DELTIC	PRE	9707	EUR
D2118	PRE	D2511	PRE					9711	EUR
D2133	PRE	D2578	PRE	D7017	PRE	DS75	PRE	9712	EUR
D2138	PRE	D2587	PRE	D7018	PRE			9713	EUR
		D2595	PRE	D7029	PRE	LMS7050	PRE	9714	EUR

Data Tables

No.	Code	No.	Code	No.	Code	No.	Code	No.	Code
9715	EUR	03119	PRE	08410	GWR	08617	ALS	08795	GWR
9716	EUR	03120	PRE	08411	IND	08622	BAR	08799	DBC
9717	EUR	03128	PRE	08417	NRL	08623	DBC	08802	HNR
9718	EUR	03134	PRE	08418	WCR	08624	FLR	08804	DBC
9719	EUR	03141	PRE	08423	BAR	08629	KBR	08805	LMI
9720	EUR	03144	PRE	08436	PRE	08630	HNR	08807	IND
9721	EUR	03145	PRE	08441	IND	08631	PRE	08809	IND
9722	EUR	03152	PRE	08442	ATC	08632	DBC	08810	ATC
9723	EUR	03158	PRE	08443	PRE	08635	PRE	08818	HNR
		03162	PRE	08444	PRE	08641	GWR	08822	GWR
9801	EUR	03170	PRE	08445	IND	08643	MRL	08823	IND
9802	EUR	03179	PRE	08447	IND	08644	GWR	08824	HNR
9803	EUR	03180	PRE	08451	ALS	08645	GWR	08825	PRE
9804	EUR	03189	PRE	08454	ALS	08648	BAR	08830	ATC
9806	EUR	03196	WCR	08460	IND	08649	KBR	08834	HNR
9808	EUR	03197	PRE	08471	PRE	08650	MRL	08836	GWR
9809	EUR	03381	WCR	08472	WAB	08652	MRL	08846	IND
9810	EUR	03399	PRE	08473	PRE	08653	HNR	08847	IND
9812	EUR			08476	PRE	08663	GWR	08850	NYM
9814	EUR	05001	PRE	08479	PRE	08669	WAB	08853	WAB
9816	EUR			08480	DBC	08670	IND	08865	HNR
9817	EUR	06003	PRE	08483	GWR	08676	HNR	08868	HNR
9819	EUR			08484	IND	08678	WCR	08870	BAR
9820	EUR	07001	PRE	08485	WCR	08682	BOM	08871	WAB
9821	EUR	07005	PRE	08490	PRE	08683	IND	08872	IND
9823	EUR	07007	AFG	08495	DBC	08685	HNR	08873	FLR
9825	EUR	07010	PRE	08499	PUL	08690	EMT	08874	BAR
9827	EUR	07011	PRE	08500	HNR	08691	FLR	08877	HNR
9828	EUR	07012	PRE	08502	HNR	08694	PRE	08879	DBC
9831	EUR	07013	PRE	08503	IND	08696	ALS	08881	PRE
9832	EUR			08507	RIV	08699	IND	08885	BAR
9834	EUR	08011	PRE	08511	BOM	08700	HNR	08887	ALS
9835	EUR	08012	PRE	08516	ATC	08701	HNR	08891	FLR
9838	EUR	08015	PRE	08523	BAR	08704	RIV	08892	HNR
9840	EUR	08016	PRE	08525	EMT	08706	DBC	08896	PRE
		08021	PRE	08527	HNR	08709	DBC	08899	EMT
01509	CRW	08022	PRE	08528	PRE	08714	HNR	08903	IND
01551	SIE	08032	PRE	08530	FLR	08721	ALS	08904	HNR
01552	HNR	08046	PRE	08531	FLR	08724	WAB	08905	HNR
01564	HNR	08054	PRE	08535	IND	08728	IND	08908	EMT
		08060	PRE	08536	LOR	08730	KBR	08911	PRE
03018	PRE	08064	PRE	08556	PRE	08731	MRL	08912	IND
03020	PRE	08102	PRE	08567	AFG	08735	DBC	08913	IND
03022	PRE	08108	PRE	08568	KBR	08737	LSC	08915	IND
03027	PRE	08114	PRE	08571	WAB	08743	IND	08918	HNR
03037	PRE	08123	PRE	08573	BAR	08750	BAR	08922	DBC
03059	PRE	08133	PRE	08575	FLR	08754	BAR	08924	HNR
03062	PRE	08164	PRE	08578	HNR	08756	BAR	08925	GBR
03063	PRE	08168	PRE	08580	DBC	08757	DBC	08927	PRE
03066	PRE	08195	PRE	08585	FLR	08762	BAR	08929	HNR
03069	PRE	08202	PRE	08588	BAR	08764	WAB	08933	IND
03072	PRE	08220	IND	08590	PRE	08765	HNR	08934	GBR
03073	PRE	08238	PRE	08593	DBC	08767	PRE	08936	BAR
03078	PRE	08266	PRE	08596	WAB	08769	PRE	08937	PRE
03079	PRE	08288	PRE	08598	PRE	08772	PRE	08943	HNR
03081	PRE	08308	BAR	08600	IND	08773	PRE	08944	PRE
03084	PRE	08331	PRE	08602	BOM	08774	IND	08947	MRL
03089	PRE	08359	PRE	08604	PRE	08780	PRE	08948	EUS
03090	PRE	08375	IND	08605	DBC	08784	DBC	08950	EMT
03094	PRE	08377	PRE	08611	ALS	08785	FLR	08954	HNR
03099	PRE	08388	PRE	08613	BAR	08786	HNR	08956	NRL
03112	PRE	08389	HNR	08615	WAB	08787	IND	08994	DBC
03113	PRE	08401	GBR	08616	LMI	08790	ALS	08995	DBC

Data Tables

09001	PRE	20169	PRE	25283	PRE	31530	PRE	37216	PRE
09002	GBR	20177	PRE	25309	PRE	31601	BAR	37218	DRS
09004	PRE	20188	PRE	25313	PRE	31602	BAR	37219	COL
09006	HNR	20189	GBR	25321	PRE			37227	PRE
09007	LOG	20205	C2L	25322	PRE	33002	PRE	37240	PRE
09009	GBR	20214	PRE	26001	PRE	33008	PRE	37248	PRE
09010	PRE	20227	C2L	26002	PRE	33012	PRE	37250	PRE
09012	PRE	20228	PRE	26004	PRE	33018	PRE	37254	COL
09014	HNR	20301	DRS	26007	PRE	33019	PRE	37255	PRE
09015	PRE	20302	DRS	26010	PRE	33021	PRE	37259	DRS
09017	PRE	20303	DRS	26011	PRE	33025	WCR	37261	PRE
09018	HNR	20304	DRS	26014	PRE	33029	WCR	37263	PRE
09019	PRE	20305	DRS	26024	PRE	33030	PRE	37264	PRE
09022	IND	20308	DRS	26025	PRE	33035	PRE	37275	PRE
09023	IND	20309	DRS	26035	PRE	33046	PRE	37294	PRE
09024	PRE	20311	HNR	26038	PRE	33048	PRE	37308	PRE
09025	PRE	20312	DRS	26040	PRE	33052	PRE	37314	PRE
09026	PRE	20314	HNR	26043	PRE	33053	PRE	37372	PRE
09106	DBC	20901	GBR			33057	PRE	37401	DRS
09201	HNR	20903	HNR	27001	PRE	33063	PRE	37402	DRS
09204	ATC	20904	HNR	27005	PRE	33065	PRE	37403	PRE
		20905	GBR	27007	PRE	33102	PRE	37405	DRS
12052	PRE	20906	HNR	27024	PRE	33103	NEM	37407	DRS
12077	PRE			27050	PRE	33108	PRE	37409	DRS
12082	PRE	21544	ECR	27056	PRE	33109	PRE	37413	DRS
12088	IND	21545	ECR	27059	PRE	33110	PRE	37418	PRE
12093	PRE	21546	ECR	27066	PRE	33111	PRE	37419	DRS
12099	PRE	21547	ECR			33116	PRE	37421	COL
12131	PRE			31101	PRE	33117	PRE	37422	DRS
		21610	ECR	31105	NRL	33201	PRE	37423	DRS
15224	PRE	21611	ECR	31106	LOR	33202	PRE	37424	DRS
				31108	PRE	33207	WCR	37425	DRS
18000	PRE	21901	EUR	31119	PRE	33208	PRE	37503	EPX
		21902	EUR	31128	NEM			37510	EPX
20001	PRE	21903	EUR	31130	PRE	37003	PRE	37516	WCR
20007	PRE	21904	EUR	31162	PRE	37009	PRE	37517	WCR
20016	HNR	21905	EUR	31163	PRE	37023	PRE	37518	WCR
20020	PRE	21906	EUR	31190	BAR	37025	COL	37601	DRS
20031	PRE	21907	EUR	31203	PRE	37029	HNR	37602	DRS
20035	PRE	21908	EUR	31206	PRE	37032	PRE	37603	DRS
20048	PRE	21909	EUR	31207	PRE	37037	PRE	37604	DRS
20056	HNR	21910	EUR	31210	PRE	37038	DRS	37605	DRS
20057	PRE			31233	NRL	37042	PRE	37606	DRS
20059	PRE	24032	PRE	31235	HNR	37057	COL	37607	DRS
20063	PRE	24054	PRE	31255	PRE	37059	DRS	37608	EPX
20066	HNR	24061	PRE	31270	PRE	37069	DRS	37609	DRS
20069	PRE	24081	PRE	31271	PRE	37075	PRE	37610	DRS
20081	HNR			31285	HNR	37097	PRE	37611	EPX
20087	PRE	25035	PRE	31289	PRE	37108	PRE	37612	DRS
20088	HNR	25057	PRE	31327	PRE	37109	PRE	37667	DRS
20096	HNR	25059	PRE	31414	PRE	37116	COL	37668	WCR
20098	PRE	25067	PRE	31415	PRE	37142	PRE	37669	WCR
20107	HNR	25072	PRE	31418	PRE	37146	COL	37670	EPX
20110	HNR	25083	PRE	31435	PRE	37152	PRE	37674	PRE
20118	HNR	25173	PRE	31438	PRE	37165	HNR	37676	WCR
20121	HNR	25185	PRE	31452	BAR	37175	COL	37679	NEM
20132	HNR	25191	PRE	31454	BAR	37188	COL	37685	WCR
20137	PRE	25235	PRE	31459	HNR	37194	DRS	37688	DRS
20138	HNR	25244	PRE	31461	PRE	37198	NRL	37703	DRS
20142	GBR	25262	PRE	31463	PRE	37199	COL	37706	WCR
20154	PRE	25265	PRE	31465	HNR	37207	COL	37710	WCR
20166	HNR	25278	NYM	31466	PRE	37214	WCR	37712	WCR
20168	HNR	25279	PRE	31468	LOR	37215	PRE	37714	PRE

Number	Code	Number	Code	Number	Code	Number	Code	Number	Code
345044	CRO	350239	LMI	357012	C2C	357327	C2C	365534	GTR
345045	CRO	350240	LMI	357013	C2C	357328	C2C	365535	GTR
345046	CRO	350241	LMI	357014	C2C			365536	GTR
345047	CRO	350242	LMI	357015	C2C	360101	GAR	365537	GTR
345048	CRO	350243	LMI	357016	C2C	360102	GAR	365538	GTR
345049	CRO	350244	LMI	357017	C2C	360103	GAR	365539	GTR
345050	CRO	350245	LMI	357018	C2C	360104	GAR	365540	GTR
345051	CRO	350246	LMI	357019	C2C	360105	GAR	365541	GTR
345052	CRO	350247	LMI	357020	C2C	360106	GAR		
345053	CRO	350248	LMI	357021	C2C	360107	GAR	373001	EUS
345054	CRO	350249	LMI	357022	C2C	360108	GAR	373002	EUS
345055	CRO	350250	LMI	357023	C2C	360109	GAR	373003	EUS
345056	CRO	350251	LMI	357024	C2C	360110	GAR	373004	EUS
345057	CRO	350252	LMI	357025	C2C	360111	GAR	373007	EUS
345058	CRO	350253	LMI	357026	C2C	360112	GAR	373008	EUS
345059	CRO	350254	LMI	357027	C2C	360113	GAR	373009	EUS
345060	CRO	350255	LMI	357028	C2C	360114	GAR	373010	EUS
345061	CRO	350256	LMI	357029	C2C	360115	GAR	373011	EUS
345062	CRO	350257	LMI	357030	C2C	360116	GAR	373012	EUS
345063	CRO	350258	LMI	357031	C2C	360117	GAR	373013	EUS
345064	CRO	350259	LMI	357032	C2C	360118	GAR	373014	EUS
345065	CRO	350260	LMI	357033	C2C	360119	GAR	373015	EUS
345065	CRO	350261	LMI	357034	C2C	360120	GAR	373016	EUS
		350262	LMI	357035	C2C	360121	GAR	373017	EUS
350101	LMI	350263	LMI	357036	C2C			373018	EUS
350102	LMI	350264	LMI	357037	C2C	360201	HEC	373019	EUS
350103	LMI	350265	LMI	357038	C2C	360202	HEC	373020	EUS
350104	LMI	350266	LMI	357039	C2C	360203	HEC	373021	EUS
350105	LMI	350267	LMI	357040	C2C	360204	HEC	373022	EUS
350106	LMI			357041	C2C	360205	HEC		
350107	LMI	350368	LMI	357042	C2C			373101	EUS
350108	LMI	350369	LMI	357043	C2C	365501	GTR	373102	EUS
350109	LMI	350370	LMI	357044	C2C	365502	GTR	373103	EUS
350110	LMI	350371	LMI	357045	C2C	365503	GTR	373104	EUS
350111	LMI	350372	LMI	357046	C2C	365504	GTR	373105	EUS
350112	LMI	350373	LMI			365505	GTR	373106	EUS
350113	LMI	350374	LMI	357201	C2C	365506	GTR	373107	EUS
350114	LMI	350375	LMI	357202	C2C	365507	GTR	373108	EUS
350115	LMI	350376	LMI	357203	C2C	365508	GTR		
350116	LMI	350377	LMI	357204	C2C	365509	GTR	373201	EUS
350117	LMI			357205	C2C	365510	GTR	373202	EUS
350118	LMI	350401	FTP	357206	C2C	365511	GTR	373203	EUS
350119	LMI	350402	FTP	357207	C2C	365512	GTR	373204	EUS
350120	LMI	350403	FTP	357208	C2C	365513	GTR	373205	EUS
350121	LMI	350404	FTP	357209	C2C	365514	GTR	373206	EUS
350122	LMI	350405	FTP	357210	C2C	365515	GTR	373207	EUS
350123	LMI	350406	FTP	357211	C2C	365516	GTR	373208	EUS
350124	LMI	350407	FTP			365517	GTR	373209	EUS
350125	LMI	350408	FTP	357312	C2C	365518	GTR	373210	EUS
350126	LMI	350409	FTP	357313	C2C	365519	GTR	373211	EUS
350127	LMI	350410	FTP	357314	C2C	365520	GTR	373212	EUS
350128	LMI			357315	C2C	365521	GTR	373213	EUS
350129	LMI	357001	C2C	357316	C2C	365522	GTR	373214	EUS
350130	LMI	357002	C2C	357317	C2C	365523	GTR	373215	EUS
		357003	C2C	357318	C2C	365524	GTR	373216	EUS
350231	LMI	357004	C2C	357319	C2C	365525	GTR	373217	EUS
350232	LMI	357005	C2C	357320	C2C	365527	GTR	373218	EUS
350233	LMI	357006	C2C	357321	C2C	365528	GTR	373219	EUS
350234	LMI	357007	C2C	357322	C2C	365529	GTR	373220	EUS
350235	LMI	357008	C2C	357323	C2C	365530	GTR	373221	EUS
350236	LMI	357009	C2C	357324	C2C	365531	GTR	373222	EUS
350237	LMI	357010	C2C	357325	C2C	365532	GTR	373223	EUS
350238	LMI	357011	C2C	357326	C2C	365533	GTR	373224	EUS

Data Tables

373229	EUS	375613	SET	375829	SET	376033	SET	377159	GTR
373230	EUS	375614	SET	375830	SET	376034	SET	377160	GTR
373231	EUS	375615	SET			376035	SET	377161	GTR
373232	EUS	375616	SET	375901	SET	376036	SET	377162	GTR
		375617	SET	375902	SET			377163	GTR
374001	EUS	375618	SET	375903	SET	377101	GTR	377164	GTR
374002	EUS	375619	SET	375904	SET	377102	GTR		
374003	EUS	375620	SET	375905	SET	377103	GTR	377201	GTR
374004	EUS	375621	SET	375906	SET	377104	GTR	377202	GTR
374005	EUS	375622	SET	375907	SET	377105	GTR	377203	GTR
374006	EUS	375623	SET	375908	SET	377106	GTR	377204	GTR
374007	EUS	375624	SET	375909	SET	377107	GTR	377205	GTR
374008	EUS	375625	SET	375910	SET	377108	GTR	377206	GTR
374009	EUS	375626	SET	375911	SET	377109	GTR	377207	GTR
374010	EUS	375627	SET	375912	SET	377110	GTR	377208	GTR
374011	EUS	375628	SET	375913	SET	377111	GTR	377209	GTR
374012	EUS	375629	SET	375914	SET	377112	GTR	377210	GTR
374013	EUS	375630	SET	375915	SET	377113	GTR	377211	GTR
374014	EUS			375916	SET	377114	GTR	377212	GTR
374015	EUS	375701	SET	375917	SET	377115	GTR	377213	GTR
374016	EUS	375702	SET	375918	SET	377116	GTR	377214	GTR
374017	EUS	375703	SET	375919	SET	377117	GTR	377215	GTR
374018	EUS	375704	SET	375920	SET	377118	GTR		
374019	EUS	375705	SET	375921	SET	377119	GTR	377301	GTR
374020	EUS	375706	SET	375922	SET	377120	GTR	377302	GTR
374021	EUS	375707	SET	375923	SET	377121	GTR	377303	GTR
374022	EUS	375708	SET	375924	SET	377122	GTR	377304	GTR
374023	EUS	375709	SET	375925	SET	377123	GTR	377305	GTR
374024	EUS	375710	SET	375926	SET	377124	GTR	377306	GTR
374025	EUS	375711	SET	375927	SET	377125	GTR	377307	GTR
374026	EUS	375712	SET			377126	GTR	377308	GTR
374027	EUS	375713	SET	376001	SET	377127	GTR	377309	GTR
374028	EUS	375714	SET	376002	SET	377128	GTR	377310	GTR
374029	EUS	375715	SET	376003	SET	377129	GTR	377311	GTR
374030	EUS			376004	SET	377130	GTR	377312	GTR
374031	EUS	375801	SET	376005	SET	377131	GTR	377313	GTR
374032	EUS	375802	SET	376006	SET	377132	GTR	377314	GTR
374033	EUS	375803	SET	376007	SET	377133	GTR	377315	GTR
374034	EUS	375804	SET	376008	SET	377134	GTR	377316	GTR
		375805	SET	376009	SET	377135	GTR	377317	GTR
375301	SET	375806	SET	376010	SET	377136	GTR	377318	GTR
375302	SET	375807	SET	376011	SET	377137	GTR	377319	GTR
375303	SET	375808	SET	376012	SET	377138	GTR	377320	GTR
375304	SET	375809	SET	376013	SET	377139	GTR	377321	GTR
375305	SET	375810	SET	376014	SET	377140	GTR	377322	GTR
375306	SET	375811	SET	376015	SET	377141	GTR	377323	GTR
375307	SET	375812	SET	376016	SET	377142	GTR	377324	GTR
375308	SET	375813	SET	376017	SET	377143	GTR	377325	GTR
375309	SET	375814	SET	376018	SET	377144	GTR	377326	GTR
375310	SET	375815	SET	376019	SET	377145	GTR	377327	GTR
		375816	SET	376020	SET	377146	GTR	377328	GTR
375601	SET	375817	SET	376021	SET	377147	GTR		
375602	SET	375818	SET	376022	SET	377148	GTR	377401	GTR
375603	SET	375819	SET	376023	SET	377149	GTR	377402	GTR
375604	SET	375820	SET	376024	SET	377150	GTR	377403	GTR
375605	SET	375821	SET	376025	SET	377151	GTR	377404	GTR
375606	SET	375822	SET	376026	SET	377152	GTR	377405	GTR
375607	SET	375823	SET	376027	SET	377153	GTR	377406	GTR
375608	SET	375824	SET	376028	SET	377154	GTR	377407	GTR
375609	SET	375825	SET	376029	SET	377155	GTR	377408	GTR
375610	SET	375826	SET	376030	SET	377156	GTR	377409	GTR
375611	SET	375827	SET	376031	SET	377157	GTR	377410	GTR
375612	SET	375828	SET	376032	SET	377158	GTR	377411	GTR

377412	GTR	377475	GTR	378136	LOG	379006	GAR	380115	ASR
377413	GTR			378137	LOG	379007	GAR	380116	ASR
377414	GTR	377501	GTR	378138	LOG	379008	GAR		
377415	GTR	377502	GTR	378139	LOG	379009	GAR	385001	ASR
377416	GTR	377503	GTR	378140	LOG	379010	GAR	385002	ASR
377417	GTR	377504	GTR	378141	LOG	379011	GAR	385003	ASR
377418	GTR	377505	GTR	378142	LOG	379012	GAR	385004	ASR
377419	GTR	377506	GTR	378143	LOG	379013	GAR	385005	ASR
377420	GTR	377507	GTR	378144	LOG	379014	GAR	385006	ASR
377421	GTR	377508	GTR	378145	LOG	379015	GAR	385007	ASR
377422	GTR	377509	GTR	378146	LOG	379016	GAR	385008	ASR
377423	GTR	377510	GTR	378147	LOG	379017	GAR	385009	ASR
377424	GTR	377511	GTR	378148	LOG	379018	GAR	385010	ASR
377425	GTR	377512	GTR	378149	LOG	379019	GAR	385011	ASR
377426	GTR	377513	GTR	378150	LOG	379020	GAR	385012	ASR
377427	GTR	377514	GTR	378151	LOG	379021	GAR	385013	ASR
377428	GTR	377515	GTR	378152	LOG	379022	GAR	385014	ASR
377429	GTR	377516	GTR	378153	LOG	379023	GAR	385015	ASR
377430	GTR	377517	GTR	378154	LOG	379024	GAR	385016	ASR
377431	GTR	377518	GTR			379025	GAR	385017	ASR
377432	GTR	377519	GTR	378201	LOG	379026	GAR	385018	ASR
377433	GTR	377520	GTR	378202	LOG	379027	GAR	385019	ASR
377434	GTR	377521	GTR	378203	LOG	379028	GAR	385020	ASR
377435	GTR	377522	GTR	378204	LOG	379029	GAR	385021	ASR
377436	GTR	377523	GTR	378205	LOG	379030	GAR	385022	ASR
377437	GTR			378206	LOG			385023	ASR
377438	GTR	377601	GTR	378207	LOG	380001	ASR	385024	ASR
377439	GTR	377602	GTR	378208	LOG	380002	ASR	385025	ASR
377440	GTR	377603	GTR	378209	LOG	380003	ASR	385026	ASR
377441	GTR	377604	GTR	378210	LOG	380004	ASR	385027	ASR
377442	GTR	377605	GTR	378211	LOG	380005	ASR	385028	ASR
377443	GTR	377606	GTR	378212	LOG	380006	ASR	385029	ASR
377444	GTR	377607	GTR	378213	LOG	380007	ASR	385030	ASR
377445	GTR	377608	GTR	378214	LOG	380008	ASR	385031	ASR
377446	GTR	377609	GTR	378215	LOG	380009	ASR	385032	ASR
377447	GTR	377610	GTR	378216	LOG	380010	ASR	385033	ASR
377448	GTR	377611	GTR	378217	LOG	380011	ASR	385034	ASR
377449	GTR	377612	GTR	378218	LOG	380012	ASR	385035	ASR
377450	GTR	377613	GTR	378219	LOG	380013	ASR	385036	ASR
377451	GTR	377614	GTR	378220	LOG	380014	ASR	385037	ASR
377452	GTR	377615	GTR	378221	LOG	380015	ASR	385038	ASR
377453	GTR	377616	GTR	378222	LOG	380016	ASR	385039	ASR
377454	GTR	377617	GTR	378223	LOG	380017	ASR	385040	ASR
377455	GTR	377618	GTR	378224	LOG	380018	ASR	385041	ASR
377456	GTR	377619	GTR	378225	LOG	380019	ASR	385042	ASR
377457	GTR	377620	GTR	378226	LOG	380020	ASR	385043	ASR
377458	GTR	377621	GTR	378227	LOG	380021	ASR	385044	ASR
377459	GTR	377622	GTR	378228	LOG	380022	ASR	385045	ASR
377460	GTR	377623	GTR	378229	LOG			385046	ASR
377461	GTR	377624	GTR	378230	LOG	380101	ASR		
377462	GTR	377625	GTR	378231	LOG	380102	ASR	385101	ASR
377463	GTR	377626	GTR	378232	LOG	380103	ASR	385102	ASR
377464	GTR			378233	LOG	380104	ASR	385103	ASR
377465	GTR	377701	GTR	378234	LOG	380105	ASR	385104	ASR
377466	GTR	377702	GTR	378255	LOG	380106	ASR	385105	ASR
377467	GTR	377703	GTR	378256	LOG	380107	ASR	385106	ASR
377468	GTR	377704	GTR	378257	LOG	380108	ASR	385107	ASR
377469	GTR	377705	GTR			380109	ASR	385108	ASR
377470	GTR	377706	GTR	379001	GAR	380110	ASR	385109	ASR
377471	GTR	377707	GTR	379002	GAR	380111	ASR	385110	ASR
377472	GTR	377708	GTR	379003	GAR	380112	ASR	385111	ASR
377473	GTR			379004	GAR	380113	ASR	385112	ASR
377474	GTR	378135	LOG	379005	GAR	380114	ASR	385113	ASR

Data Tables

❏ 385114	ASR	❏ 387152	GWR	❏ 390005	VWC	❏ 395011	SET	❏ 444002	SWT
❏ 385115	ASR	❏ 387153	GWR	❏ 390006	VWC	❏ 395012	SET	❏ 444003	SWT
❏ 385116	ASR	❏ 387154	GWR	❏ 390107	VWC	❏ 395013	SET	❏ 444004	SWT
❏ 385117	ASR	❏ 387155	GWR	❏ 390008	VWC	❏ 395014	SET	❏ 444005	SWT
❏ 385118	ASR	❏ 387156	GWR	❏ 390009	VWC	❏ 395015	SET	❏ 444006	SWT
❏ 385119	ASR	❏ 387157	GWR	❏ 390010	VWC	❏ 395016	SET	❏ 444007	SWT
❏ 385120	ASR	❏ 387158	GWR	❏ 390011	VWC	❏ 395017	SET	❏ 444008	SWT
❏ 385121	ASR	❏ 387159	GWR	❏ 390112	VWC	❏ 395018	SET	❏ 444009	SWT
❏ 385122	ASR	❏ 387160	GWR	❏ 390013	VWC	❏ 395019	SET	❏ 444010	SWT
❏ 385123	ASR	❏ 387161	GWR	❏ 390114	VWC	❏ 395020	SET	❏ 444011	SWT
❏ 385124	ASR	❏ 387162	GWR	❏ 390115	VWC	❏ 395021	SET	❏ 444012	SWT
		❏ 387163	GWR	❏ 390016	VWC	❏ 395022	SET	❏ 444013	SWT
❏ 387101	GTR	❏ 387164	GWR	❏ 390117	VWC	❏ 395023	SET	❏ 444014	SWT
❏ 387102	GTR	❏ 387165	GWR	❏ 390118	VWC	❏ 395024	SET	❏ 444015	SWT
❏ 387103	GTR	❏ 387166	GWR	❏ 390119	VWC	❏ 395025	SET	❏ 444016	SWT
❏ 387104	GTR	❏ 387167	GWR	❏ 390020	VWC	❏ 395026	SET	❏ 444017	SWT
❏ 387105	GTR	❏ 387168	GWR	❏ 390121	VWC	❏ 395027	SET	❏ 444018	SWT
❏ 387106	GTR	❏ 387169	GWR	❏ 390122	VWC	❏ 395028	SET	❏ 444019	SWT
❏ 387107	GTR	❏ 387170	GWR	❏ 390123	VWC	❏ 395029	SET	❏ 444020	SWT
❏ 387108	GTR	❏ 387171	GWR	❏ 390124	VWC			❏ 444021	SWT
❏ 387109	GTR	❏ 387172	GWR	❏ 390125	VWC	❏ 399201	NOR	❏ 444022	SWT
❏ 387110	GTR	❏ 387173	GWR	❏ 390126	VWC	❏ 399202	NOR	❏ 444023	SWT
❏ 387111	GTR	❏ 387174	GWR	❏ 390127	VWC	❏ 399203	NOR	❏ 444024	SWT
❏ 387112	GTR			❏ 390128	VWC	❏ 399204	NOR	❏ 444025	SWT
❏ 387113	GTR	❏ 387201	GTR	❏ 390129	VWC	❏ 399205	NOR	❏ 444026	SWT
❏ 387114	GTR	❏ 387202	GTR	❏ 390130	VWC	❏ 399206	NOR	❏ 444027	SWT
❏ 387115	GTR	❏ 387203	GTR	❏ 390131	VWC	❏ 399207	NOR	❏ 444028	SWT
❏ 387116	GTR	❏ 387204	GTR	❏ 390132	VWC			❏ 444029	SWT
❏ 387117	GTR	❏ 387205	GTR	❏ 390134	VWC	❏ 411198	PRE	❏ 444030	SWT
❏ 387118	GTR	❏ 387206	GTR	❏ 390135	VWC			❏ 444031	SWT
❏ 387119	GTR	❏ 387207	GTR	❏ 390136	VWC	❏ 421399	PRE	❏ 444032	SWT
❏ 387120	GTR	❏ 387208	GTR	❏ 390137	VWC	❏ 421496	PRE	❏ 444033	SWT
❏ 387121	GTR	❏ 387209	GTR	❏ 390138	VWC	❏ 421497	PRE	❏ 444034	SWT
❏ 387122	GTR	❏ 387210	GTR	❏ 390039	VWC	❏ 421498	PRE	❏ 444035	SWT
❏ 387123	GTR	❏ 387211	GTR	❏ 390040	VWC			❏ 444036	SWT
❏ 387124	GTR	❏ 387212	GTR	❏ 390141	VWC	❏ 432417	PRE	❏ 444037	SWT
❏ 387125	GTR	❏ 387213	GTR	❏ 390042	VWC			❏ 444038	SWT
❏ 387126	GTR	❏ 387214	GTR	❏ 390043	VWC	❏ 442401	OLS	❏ 444039	SWT
❏ 387127	GTR	❏ 387215	GTR	❏ 390044	VWC	❏ 442402	OLS	❏ 444040	SWT
❏ 387128	GTR	❏ 387216	GTR	❏ 390045	VWC	❏ 442403	OLS	❏ 444041	SWT
❏ 387129	GTR	❏ 387217	GTR	❏ 390046	VWC	❏ 442404	OLS	❏ 444042	SWT
❏ 387130	GWR	❏ 387218	GTR	❏ 390047	VWC	❏ 442405	OLS	❏ 444043	SWT
❏ 387131	GWR	❏ 387219	GTR	❏ 390148	VWC	❏ 442406	OLS	❏ 444044	SWT
❏ 387132	GWR	❏ 387220	GTR	❏ 390049	VWC	❏ 442407	OLS	❏ 444045	SWT
❏ 387133	GWR	❏ 387221	GTR	❏ 390050	VWC	❏ 442408	OLS		
❏ 387134	GWR	❏ 387222	GTR	❏ 390151	VWC	❏ 442409	OLS	❏ 450001	SWT
❏ 387135	GWR	❏ 387223	GTR	❏ 390152	VWC	❏ 442410	OLS	❏ 450002	SWT
❏ 387136	GWR	❏ 387224	GTR	❏ 390153	VWC	❏ 442411	OLS	❏ 450003	SWT
❏ 387137	GWR	❏ 387225	GTR	❏ 390154	VWC	❏ 442412	OLS	❏ 450004	SWT
❏ 387138	GWR	❏ 387226	GTR	❏ 390155	VWC	❏ 442413	OLS	❏ 450005	SWT
❏ 387139	GWR	❏ 387227	GTR	❏ 390156	VWC	❏ 442414	OLS	❏ 450006	SWT
❏ 387140	GWR			❏ 390157	VWC	❏ 442415	OLS	❏ 450007	SWT
❏ 387141	GWR	❏ 387301	C2C			❏ 442416	OLS	❏ 450008	SWT
❏ 387142	GWR	❏ 387302	C2C	❏ 395001	SET	❏ 442417	OLS	❏ 450009	SWT
❏ 387143	GWR	❏ 387303	C2C	❏ 395002	SET	❏ 442418	OLS	❏ 450010	SWT
❏ 387144	GWR	❏ 387304	C2C	❏ 395003	SET	❏ 442419	OLS	❏ 450011	SWT
❏ 387145	GWR	❏ 387305	C2C	❏ 395004	SET	❏ 442420	OLS	❏ 450012	SWT
❏ 387146	GWR	❏ 387306	C2C	❏ 395005	SET	❏ 442421	OLS	❏ 450013	SWT
❏ 387147	GWR			❏ 395006	SET	❏ 442422	OLS	❏ 450014	SWT
❏ 387148	GWR	❏ 390001	VWC	❏ 395007	SET	❏ 442423	OLS	❏ 450015	SWT
❏ 387149	GWR	❏ 390002	VWC	❏ 395008	SET	❏ 442424	OLS	❏ 450016	SWT
❏ 387150	GWR	❏ 390103	VWC	❏ 395009	SET			❏ 450017	SWT
❏ 387151	GWR	❏ 390104	VWC	❏ 395010	SET	❏ 444001	SWT	❏ 450018	SWT

Data Tables

Also by Colin J Marsden

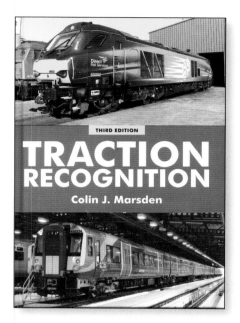

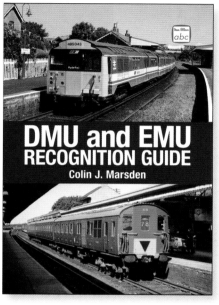

abc Traction Recognition
3rd edition

Hardback
210mm x 150mm
288 pages
ISBN 978 07110 37922
£20

abc DMU and EMU Recognition Guide

Hardback
210mm x 150mm
392 pages
ISBN 978 07110 37403
£25

Available from all good bookshops

Crécy Publishing Ltd
www.crecy.co.uk